S0-ARL-258

QUALITATIVE METHODS
A Handbook of
Social Science Methods
Volume II

QUALITATIVE METHODS

Volume II of
Handbook of
Social Science Methods

by
ROBERT B. SMITH and
PETER K. MANNING
Editors

BALLINGER PUBLISHING COMPANY
Cambridge, Massachusetts
A Subsidiary of Harper & Row, Publishers, Inc.

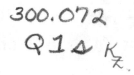

300.072
Q1△ K_Z.

21 6246

Copyright © 1982 by Ballinger Publishing Company. All rights reserved. No part of this publication may be reproduced, stored in a retrieval system, or transmitted in any form or by any means, electronic, mechanical, photocopy, recording or otherwise, without the prior written consent of the publisher.

International Standard Book Number: 0–88410–909–7
(previously ISBN 0–8290–0086–0)

Library of Congress Catalog Card Number: 79–18148

Printed in the United States of America

Library of Congress Cataloging in Publication Data (Revised)
   Main entry under title:

   Handbook of social science methods.

   Includes bibliographical references.
   CONTENTS: v. 1. Qualitative methods.
   1. Social sciences—Research—Collected works.
2. Social sciences—Methodology—Collected works.
I. Smith, Robert Benjamin, 1936-   . II. Manning,
Peter K.
H62.H2457   300'.72   79–18148
ISBN 0–88410–909–7   AACR1
(previously ISBN 0–8290–0086–0) (v.1)

This Book is dedicated to a resolution of the debate between Herbert Blumer and Paul F. Lazarsfeld concerning the efficacy of qualitative and quantitative methods for social research.

Contents

List of figures

List of tables

Foreword

The interrelated volumes of *A Handbook of Social Science Methods* are designed to help both professionals and students to study important problems in a rigorous manner. A problem is considered important if it is pertinent to a developing theoretical paradigm or to a pressing social need. A research methodology is considered rigorous if it is suited to the problem under analysis, is implemented with objectivity, allows replication by other social scientists, and contributes to the qualitative, quantitative, and theory development process of cumulative social science.

Cumulative or *normal* social science is firmly based upon one or more past social scientific achievements, achievements that some particular group of social scientists acknowledge for a time as supplying the foundation for further research (Kuhn, 1970: 10). This process of cumulative social science, which is diagrammed in Figure 1, coordinates the volumes of *A Handbook of Social Science Methods*. If this process is followed more widely, then the social sciences will become highly cumulative and more successful in their aim, which is the steady extension of the scope and precision of social scientific theories. Such theories will make possible a more creative or revolutionary social science that is, a social science in which anomalies between formal theories and empirical findings create a crisis and a transition to a new theory that is more adequate to the subject matter being studied. In Figure 1 the arrow feeding back from "Formal Theorizing" to "Theoretical Paradigms" portrays this aspect of revolutionary social science.

A Handbook of Social Science Methods is directed toward the synthesis of the diverse directions and styles of social science research methodology by defining and elaborating this process of cumulative social science. Its generic theme helps the student and practitioner of social research first to become sensitized to the moral and political problems of social research and to pertinent theoretical paradigms (see the volume *An Introduction to Social Research*), and then to link relevant, paradigm-guided qualitative research (the *Qualitative Methods* volume), quantitative research (the *Quantitative Methods* volumes), and formal theory development and verification (the *Formal Theorizing* volumes).

This process unfolds as follows. Briefly, theoretical paradigms are intellectual frameworks that more or less fit some aspect of the empirical social world. Paradigms point out significant problems, provide conceptual models and concepts for analysis, and specify criteria for the evaluation of the quality of scientific work. Paradigms guide exploratory, focused, and theoretical research.

Exploratory research is the firsthand observation of the empirical social world. It is often based on qualitative data such as field notes, diaries, and field interviews. It has two objectives (Blumer, 1969: 40–42): (1) to

Figure 1. The Process of Cumulative Social Science.

Paradigms	Social Research		Formal Theorizing
Paradigms, Types of Research, Ethical and Political Problems	Qualitative Research: Exploration, Inspection and Patterning	Quantitative, Research: Focused Survey Research and Statistical Analysis	Languages for Consolidating Evidence, Social Structural Theories

familiarize researchers with a sphere of social life that is unfamiliar and unknown to them; and (2) to enable researchers to develop and sharpen theoretical paradigms so that the research problem, concepts, interpretations, and conjectures will be empirically grounded and adequate to the reality of those aspects of the empirical social world under scrutiny.

Focused research strives for rigorous empirical analysis and corroboration of findings. It is best based on the insights and findings from prior, paradigm-guided exploratory studies. It requires the specification and development of clear, discriminating concepts and indices, along with the controlled assessment of casual relationships between these elements (Blumer, 1969: 43). An elaboration procedure (Lazarsfeld & Rosenberg, 1955: 109–99; Schachter, 1959) is often utilized to control for possible spurious relationships. When elaborating variables, the analyst ascertains whether a relationship between two variables still exists when possible spurious factors are controlled. Spurious factors cause the relationship observed between two variables. The effect of spurious factors can be assessed readily if the variables are gauged quantitatively and if statistical or experimental controls are introduced. Focused research may involve the close inspection of qualitative data (Blumer, 1969: 43–47); but more often quantitative data from social surveys, experiments, and archives are analyzed in this way. The end products of focused research are a more adequate theoretical paradigm and a consolidated, organized system of empirically sound relationships between the variables under analysis—a "middle-range" empirical theory.

Findings from social research provide a base for the development of formal theories. The process of theoretical social science involves at least four interdependent operations: (1) the consolidation of findings from previous theoretical and empirical studies pertinent to the theory-building task; (2) the reconceptualization of these variables and their synthesis into a "middle-range" causal system or formal theory written in a verbal, logical, or mathematical language; (3) confirmatory research—the derivation and testing of logically deduced implications from the formal theory; and (4) the modification and trimming of the theory and the underlying theoretical paradigm to account for anomolous empirical facts. The format of this *Handbook* allows these volumes to be used to explain the process of theoretical social science. Here the volumes on *Formal Theorizing* are used in conjunction with *Quantitative Methods* to present the fundamentals of theory development and verificational research, and the *Qualitative Methods* volume is used to encourage the generation of grounded theory.

These volumes of *A Handbook of Social Science Methods* answer the need to explicate the process of cumulative social research and formal theorizing. They make available to professionals and students new techniques and emphases without ignoring established methods. Each volume is self-contained, introducing the reader to a different aspect of social science research methods. The volumes can be used to emphasize either empirical social research (*Qualitative Methods and Quantitative Methods*), theoretical social science (*Formal Theorizing and Quantitative Methods*), or the process of cumulative social science (*Qualitative Methods, Quantitative Methods, and then Formal Theorizing*).

The intelligent use of these volumes will:

1. sensitize the reader to ethical and political problems in social research;
2. explicate the role of theoretical and research paradigms in motivating social science research;
3. present strategies for critically evaluating evidence and discerning the empirical social world; and
4. illustrate the competent practice of cumulative, paradigm-guided social science research, teaching methods for qualitative and quantitative analysis, and formal theorizing.

Robert B. Smith

References

Blumer, Herbert *Symbolic interactionism: Perspective and method.* Englewood Cliffs, N.J.: Prentice-Hall, 1969.

Kuhn, Thomas. S. *The structure of scientific revolutions* (2nd ed., enl.). Chicago: University of Chicago Press, 1970.

Lazarsfeld, Paul F., & Rosenberg, Morris *The language of social research.* New York: Free Press, 1955.

Merton, Robert K. *On theoretical sociology:* Free Press, 1967.

Schachter, Stanley *The psychology of affiliation.* Stanford, Calif.; Stanford University Press, 1959.

Preface

This volume presents examples of research utilizing as one principal component qualitative methods. It seeks to reduce the specious distinction between qualitative and quantitative methods. We desire that researchers will be led by this book and other volumes of the Handbook to introduce quantification into their descriptive studies and thus to cross-check their rich firsthand observations. Researchers should also strive for continuity in their research programs by continuing to elaborate their studies by using the more focused methodologies of experimentation and survey research. Conversely, we hope that others will be led by this book to base their abstract quantitative analyses on firsthand observations of the empirical social world. Perhaps the low percentage of explained variances that characterize much quantitative and evaluative research is a consequence in inappropriate impositions of research designs and accounting schemes and measures on the empirical social world. These often do not adequately capture the reality being studied. Instead of simply doing artificial scientistic social research, it is important to develop quantitative studies based on intimate knowledge of the empirical social world.

Scholars as diverse as Herbert Blumer and Samuel Stouffer have made statements similar to these. Stouffer's dissertation, *An Experimental Comparison of Statistical and Case History Methods of Attitude Research* (University of Chicago, 1930), although often thought to advocate the use of quantitative measures over qualitative case studies, actually supports the use of both. His experiment gauged the extent of agreement between attitude ratings gauged by statistical and by case-study techniques. Stouffer first administered an attitude scale to students that measured their attitudes about Prohibition. The students also were asked to write essays about Prohibition and to express their views about alcoholic beverages. These essays were then assessed by judges who rated the content as indicative of pro- or anti-Prohibition attitudes. These judges did not have knowledge of the students' scores on the attitude scale. Stouffer reported a very high correlation of $+.86$ between the two measures and drew several conclusions. The first suggested that the two indices could be used interchangeably (p. 49):

. . . as far as the present investigation shows, the test scores or the case history ratings could be used as indices of what they both purport to measure, without any important differences in results, if either set of indices was to be studied in its relationship to other variables.

His second conclusion highlighted some of the potential benefits of quantification (pp. 50–51):

The fact that a simple test, which can be taken in 10 or 15 minutes and scored rapidly and objectively, is a fairly valid measure of attitudes would make it possible to study cheaply in a single investigation the relationship between the attitudes of several thousand subjects and a number of background characteristics. Take prohibition, for example. To what extent is this attitude associated with factors in the childhood environment? By dividing and successively sub-dividing our several thousand subjects according to various background factors which presumably could be determined with rough but sufficient accuracy from a direct questionnaire, one could evaluate the relative association between each of these factors and the present attitude score. The use of a large number of subjects permits the introduction of experimental controls which may be superior to the mathematical controls of partial and multiple correlation and which, indeed, may be the only possible controls if the background categories are broad and qualitative. Moreover, by giving a retest with a parallel form of the test one could measure the relationship between the various factors and the shift over a period of time, thus getting clues, of importance to the theory of attitudes, as to the conditions under which an attitude changes.

Stouffer's third conclusion extolled some of the virtues of qualitative studies (pp. 51–52):

The fact that, contrary to the expectation of some students of attitudes, the present study has shown that it is possible to get fairly high agreement, even among laymen with extremely diverse viewpoints, in interpretation of attitudes from case history materials should lend encouragement to those who see in the case history a useful tool of attitude measurement. The case history provides a sequence of events in their cultural setting. A classification of these sequences into types, even if the research is based on a smaller number of cases than would be possible through statistical inquiry, should be a fruitful approach to the interpretation of process of attitude formation. In particular, it should give clues to connecting links which escape the statistical worker who is limited to the consideration of the relationships expressed in abstract mathematical symbols. The present investigation shows that a fairly high agreement was reached by judges, even though the case histories were shorter and scantier of detail than they might be if obtained for a special study of the sequence of events in attitude formation. One particular caution should be added, besides those advanced in the section on reliability of the case histories. The present investigation measured the agreement of judges in making a single inference from a case history. As high an agreement might not be expected if the inference involved more elaborate conceptualization, such as lifting from the data a schematic picture of causal process.

A fourth conclusion is immediately apparent to the contemporary reader of Stouffer's almost-50-year-old dissertation. The students' case-study essays, which comprise an appendix to the dissertation, provide vivid insight about the meaning of attitudes toward Prohibition. Without these qualitative documents the contemporary reader would gain little knowledge about the students' attitudes. Stouffer's study comes alive when the reader juxtaposes these rich descriptions with the quanitative attitude ratings.

The chapters in *Qualitative Methods* will help the reader gather and analyze vivid qualitative data. Whenever possible, we have tried to interweave general discussions with specific examples and applications of general principles. The book begins with an introductory essay written by Peter Manning. The subsequent chapters are organized in four main sections: Exploration: Perspective and Method; Interviews; Documents; Inspection and Patterning. These divisions were suggested by Herbert Blumer's (1969) essay on the perspective and method of symbolic interactionism. The first three sections discuss the symbolic-interactionist perspective and methods of data gathering: the last section, styles of qualitative data analysis.

The chapters on data gathering discuss participant observation, undisclosed participant observation, interviewing and the use of informants, and documents and unobtrusive observations. These topics are organized by the typology described in Figure 1 (Gold, 1958), based on two dimensions of the investigator; whether or not the investigator's identity is known by the subjects of the study, and whether or not the investigator participates in the setting being studied. The names of the chapter authors are in parentheses.

The chapters on Inspection and Patterning—qualitative data analysis— are designed to help the reader to abstract basic social processes. They discuss the social process perspective (Bigus, Hadden, & Glaser) and

Figure 1.   Dimensions of the Investigator.

	Investigator's Identity	
	Known by Subjects	Not known by subjects
Participates in setting	Participant observation (Rock) (Arnold) (Davis)	Undisclosed participant observation (Arnold) (Zimmerman & Wieder)
Investigator		
Does not participate in setting	Interviewing and use of informants (Blauner & Wellman) (Zimmerman & Wieder) (Somers et al)	Documents and unobtrusive observations (Reitzel & Lindemann) (Ogilvie, Stone, & Kelly (Danzger)

analytic induction (Manning). The concluding chapter discusses enumerative induction, quantification in symbolic interactionisn (Smith).

This book has been a joint development over the last year or so, but was originally conceived of, organized, and assembled by Smith. We are grateful to the contributors for their efforts to maintain the high quality of the individual chapters. We would both like to thank Michael Connolly for his sustaining belief in this project and his efforts to make it a reality. We each are grateful to a number of people who have contributed to the book's realization. John Van Maanen of the Massachusetts Institute of Technology critiqued Manning's introductory essay. At the University of California, Santa Barbara, Don Zimmerman and Sal Salerno offered helpful comments. Manning thanks his family: Victoria, Kerry, Sean, Peter, and Merry Kathleen for their tolerance. Smith thanks Ms. Alice H. Smyth and Ms. Annelise Katz, librarians of the Social Relations Library, Harvard University, for library privileges that greatly facilitated this project. Smith thanks Abigail Smith and our children, Sarah and Noah and Zephyr our cat for their affection and encouragement. He also thanks Lawrence McCormick for his legal advice that facilitated publication.

> Robert B. Smith
> Cambridge, Massachusetts
>
> Peter K. Manning
> East Lansing, Michigan

REFERENCES

Blumer, Herbert. *Symbolic interactionism: Perspective and method.* Englewood Cliffs, N.J.: Prentice-Hall, 1969.

Gold, Raymond L. Roles in sociological field observations. *Social Forces*, 1958, *36* (March): 217–23.

Stouffer, Samuel. *An experimental comparison of statistical and case history methods of attitude research.* Unpublished Ph.D. dissertation, University of Chicago, 1930. (Now published by the Arno Press, New York, 1980.)

QUALITATIVE METHODS
A Handbook of
Social Science Methods
Volume II

Qualitative Methods

PETER K. MANNING

Prefatory Note

There is a certain romantic aspect to social life that all sociologists, to a greater or lesser degree, indulge in: We entangle ourselves in the outward appearances of events and wonder about their "inward," "hidden" or "invisible" features. I recall one morning when a graduate school professor of mine was readying himself on short notice to drive to a distant city to investigate a mysterious attack of fainting among textile workers. It was said that there was gas leaking into the factory from somewhere, or that there were small bugs in the raw cotton that were biting the women and causing them to fall, weakened and exhausted, to the floor. It sounded intriguing, a naturally occurring puzzle, and all within driving distance! Later, after the data were gathered from interviews, some brief observation, and health records, my office-mate at the time was paid to "make sense" of the situation. He pondered the elaborate diagrams, matrices, and tables, but they just didn't make sense. The expected flow of contagion was not clearly there; the links among groups were attenuated; the pattern was weak. He despaired. Fortunately, the professors in question (another had joined the team after the early-morning dash) did not lose hope. They sought the inner mysteries and made them apparent, then published not only a frequently reprinted article, but a book as well.

Another story may also serve to illustrate my point. I have always wanted to do a study of "cowboys," especially rodeo cowboys, in large part because they represent certain beguiling themes—freedom, "toughness," risk-taking, chaotic careers, entrepreneurial styles—some of which seemed to contrast with other occupations I have studied, namely physicians. Given an interest in *how* people make sense of situations and carve out lives from the shreds of evidence we are given of order, a study of cowboy work was challenging. I began to talk with my family about it. Unfortunately, I am allergic to horses. I break into paroxysms of sneezing, wheezing, and coughing whenever I come within six feet of the beasts; I also fear horses for their size and "unpredictability." I don't like to camp, hunt, or fish, nor do I love "the great out-of-doors." Cowboys are nomadic during rodeo season, traveling from city to city, and a study of their careers would involve traveling all summer and the early fall for several years. With or without my family it would be difficult and demanding. It would mean hanging out in small Western towns, drinking beer, hearing a lot of stories, enduring the usual excesses of masculine culture, and probably overcoming a number of adolescent phobias as well as enduring allergic reactions. So I never did the study. In fact I may never do it, as I find I now have less tolerance for inchoate, "free" life-styles. Outer mystery, inner banality. We are always so situated.

One young sociologist, Don Ball, considered sociology the job of taking the fun out of social life and experience. He was and is correct. However, it need not be. There is fun left inside social life; not all mysteries are destroyed by investigation because some new ones *always* appear. The dash to investigate fainting in the factory, the thought-about run for the rodeo, each contained its enthralling mysteries and its potential and actual discoveries. I hope you find the puzzles and the mysteries, and I hope they grow from the placement of yourself in a social situation—that unlike the dissuaded cowboy who spends the summer at a typewriter in East Lansing, Michigan, you follow your mysteries, track them down, and find new ones. If they become scientific projects, what follows should help.

SCIENCE AND COMMON SENSE

We are always situated in a particular time, place, social situation, and meaning-world. Such cognitive matters as the self-concept, sense of change, or stability in the internal and external environment, and the meanings imputed to those environments, are complemented by the feelings that we associate with experiencing being. From this sense of being, sometimes modified and altered—e.g., we may feel our consciousness being "raised" or "lowered" at a given moment, or we may think in highly abstract ways such as computer languages or in codes—comes our sense of being social and human. It is precisely this *sense* of social structure, or of being located socially, psychologically, and physically, as it is shared with others, mobilized, and communicated to and with them, that is the basis for collective action: society.

This statement is a statement of a *perspective* on the social world; it is an interpretation of social action or an "interpretation of interpretations" as Rock has called it (see page 34.) Such perspectives not only organize the way people live and make sense of their lives, they also order the ways in which social scientists attempt to make methodical sense of other people's lives, feelings, plans, dreams, and behaviors. Behind any such approach to the social world, as Smith notes in the Foreword to this work, lies a theoretical scientific paradigm (a perspective that has been relatively formalized, written down, tested by research, and proven to have a scientific utility). A paradigm is a basis for a science. All social science aims for systematic knowledge of the social world that is reproducible, valid, systematic, and methodically gathered and presented.

Scientific knowledge differs in one important sense from "personal" or

"private" experience: It is public knowledge. It must meet public requirements of systematic knowledge.[1] On the other hand one must not forget that
fundamentally all knowledge is based upon, rooted in, and inextricably
bound to experience, common-sense experience such as is described above.
Thus, all scientific methods depart to some degree from common-sense
knowledge: This range is from the most unconscious knowledge, of which
we are rarely aware, to the most abstracted and nonempirical knowledge,
such as that produced by mathematical logicians (see Douglas, 1976: 15ff).
That is, when we do science, or study social life scientifically, we always
draw to some degree upon our own knowledge of situations or persons "like
that"—events and episodes that seem to resemble the reported ones—our
knowledge *about* rather than personal knowledge *of*. (See Douglas, 1976,
Preface and Introduction.)

However, the degree to which knowledge is gathered for scientific
purposes and the manner in which it is gathered are variably based on direct,
personal detailed observation of face-to-face human conduct in a specific
place within a specified time frame. If the data are gathered by individuals
participating (directly or indirectly) in social life for the purpose of reporting
it scientifically, it is called *field research* or *participant observation*. Field
research can be more than observation, as it may include records-gathering,
interviewing, photographic records, or tape recordings of conversations. It
can hardly be less than observation. On the other hand participation is not a
requisite for a field study, insofar as data may be gathered less directly by
observation or other means. Further, as Denzin (1970) has pointed out, all
scientific work involves interaction between the scientific observer, the data,
the situation, and the theory, and in this sense all scientific work involves
sense-making, symbolic interpretation and analysis of data in terms of some
social construction—e.g., a theory, hypothesis, or perspective.

A primary distinction within all the social sciences is between *qualititative* methods—those in which the person reports data in terms of verbal
descriptions, pictures, recorded voices, and the like—and *quantitative*
methods, where the data are reported in discrete quantities, usually using
statistical techniques to quantify effect and to infer the generality of the
findings from the sample to a population. On the one hand, as this volume
shows, this is a useful distinction, for most of the papers do not present
quantitative data in tables and charts. On the other hand there are papers
that do, and some of the classics of fieldwork (e.g., Becker et al., *Boys in
White*, 1961; Hughes, *French Canada in Transition*, 1943, Suttles, *The
Social Order of the Slum*, 1968, and Skolnick, *Justice Without Trial*, 1966
present and in places rely heavily on quantitative data to support their
arguments and inferences. Keep in mind that the term *qualitative research*
is a general indicator, not an exclusive label, and that most of the finest
social research involves systematic field observation in association with other

techniques. In addition, in a way we are always "gathering data," "participating" and making sense of the phenomena we are studying as members of
the society in which they (and we) are located.

This volume is focused upon qualitative research, and presents
systematic overviews or approaches as well as examples of that modality in
research reports and case studies. Note that the table of contents includes
chapters on *exploration,* which deals primarily with fieldwork and participant observational studies, *interviews* and *documents* as additional modes of
doing qualitative research, and a final section on *inspection* and *patterning.*
Running through these reports are several themes that are found, either
explicitly or implicitly, in all types of qualitative research.

Qualitative methods are varied, their subjects are diverse, and their
aims differ. The closer one is to the ongoing, face-to-face empirical world of
everyday life, the more the facts and concrete data at hand will force one to
wrestle with the enormous complexity of that experience. Studies of the
detail of everyday life can sometimes be overwhelming. There have been
entire studies of driving to work (Wallace, 1965), the first experience of
having intercourse with a prostitute (Stewart, 1972), how to read (Heap,
1976), how janitors manage their customers (Gold, 1952), and of the social
world of the dwarf (Truzzi, 1968). These studies of microworlds are done, it
would appear, out of interest in such worlds. They represent *substantive*
studies rather than *theoretical* studies that attempt to develop, explicate,
formulate, or in some fashion refine social knowledge (cf. Johnson, 1975:
22).

The work reported here, in whatever qualitative mode, is directed to
theoretical issues. Some of the papers are meant to present advice on *how* to
carry out a type of qualitative research (Arnold, Davis, Blauner & Wellman,
Zimmerman & Weider, Reitzel & Lindemann, Danzger, and Ogilvie et al),
while some undertake to synthesize an approach as well. All the authors
draw extensively upon their own research or report it in the context of
making more generic points. All are directed to sharpening our knowledge,
to refining the paradigm in which they are cast (primarily, but not
exclusively, the symbolic-interactionist paradigm), and to presenting empirical data.

I would like to suggest in this introduction some of the problems and
issues that are more likely than others to be encountered by qualitative
methodologists and researchers. The aim of this book is to show, by example
and by systematic argument, *how, when, what,* and *why:* In this case, how
to do qualitative research; when to do it (under what conditions it is the best
approach to a theoretically defined problem); what sort of qualitative
research to do; with what considerations in mind (involvement, costs, and
efficacy); and why to do it. The primary theme of this essay is that all social
science research begins with our experience in the world and then becomes

progressively more formalized and systematic as additional knowledge, insight, and precision of definition and concept accrue. As the prefatory note illustrates, the initial basis for undertaking research may be transformed into a scientific question, but the complex feelings, understandings, and rich initial intuitions, hunches, and nuanced insights remain.

I wish to begin with a dilemma and then to describe some of the ways social scientists have attempted in their research to overcome it. Attempts to deal with and systematically explicate our experience in qualitative terms create ongoing dilemmas that qualitative researchers have tried to "solve" or minimize by clarifying publicly the *when, what,* and *how* of their often craftlike approaches to social research methods and to social research itself. Their approaches will be instructive for others because they deal with the relationship among everyday life, the experience of everyday life, and the social construction of knowledge: How it is presented, formalized, conceptualized, and made available to a wider audience of readers. Following this section, which attempts to highlight issues by supplying examples, arguments, and issues from the chapters of this volume, there is a discussion of politics and ethics. The final section outlines the ordering of the selections in this volume.

THE DILEMMA OF QUALITATIVE RESEARCH

To greater or lesser degrees all social research involves the understanding of social meanings, or the subjective states experienced by individuals and imputed to events, relations, and other entities. The further one moves toward the common-sense world of meanings, and the further from the experimental world, the more obvious is the place of the self in the research process. The study of social meanings intrinsically involves the self as that which reflects upon and takes itself as an object. It is through the self that the meanings of social life are filtered. When social researchers embark on studies, they place themselves in the social world as an *object*: Thus, in qualitative work the *self* is the tool by which one gathers data. This situation, the situation of research, of asking questions of social life, of trying to understand, capture, and evoke its nuances, raises and makes problematic the self. As Dewey (1938) wrote, the problematic situation is the beginning point of thought. Once the self becomes the prime tool, a dilemma arises: The reflexive or mutually determinant relationships between the self and the data gathered make a clear identification of what is "data" and what is "self." Data are gathered as the self is maintained—through interaction. Many facets of experience must be synthesized by social researchers, and self and data must be articulated, separated, and maintained both for oneself and others in different ways.

What I mean by "different ways" is the form of explanation and *justification* that social researchers utilize. Within the quantitative mode of work a rather well-developed format, style, rhetoric of presentation has evolved. (Look at a quantitatively oriented article in one of the major journals such as the *American Sociological Review, The American Journal of Sociology, Social Forces, Social Psychology, etc.*) In the qualitative mode, on the other hand, no such facile formulaic style is used or available. Descriptions of the method, of the theory employed and the analysis tend to be more widely variable. (Look, for contrast, at the *American Anthropologist, Urban Life,* or *Theory and Society.*) Insofar as writers have attempted to wrestle with the dilemma described above, they have been most successful in describing their work as a less systematic version of quantitative work. The argument of this essay is that because there is no consensus within the group of persons who judge, do, write, and publish qualitative work concerning adequate canons of proof, credible data, and appropriate technique, there is both diversity within the field of qualitative studies and greater variation in the kinds of studies that are regarded as adequate (Becker, 1970: chap. 4). As a result, perhaps, there is a more abundant literature on the subject of the justification and rationalization than there is on other related topics in the literature on qualitative methods. In order to discuss the papers in the volume, it is necessary to organize them around some general themes that are of concern to social researchers, whether qualitatively or quantitatively oriented. These are the issues with which the essay began: the *why* of qualitative methods, *when* to use them as opposed to other available methods, *what* to do once one has decided to use qualitative methods, and more precisely, *how* to carry out such a study. Each of these provides a heading for the next segment of this essay.

Why

The *whys* of any method are captured in the literature of the philosophy of science. This literature is abundant and growing. Smith's discussion of paradigms and of logical deductive versus inductive theory captures and articulates many of the questions surrounding why one might choose a particular theoretical paradigm, approach, and modality associated with that paradigm. Most of the recent work on qualitative analysis has focused as well on the whys—providing rationales for doing qualitative work (see Bruyn, 1966; Glaser & Strauss, 1967; Becker, 1970; and Schatzman & Strauss, 1973).

When

There is considerably less literature on the issue of *when* to do qualitative as against quantitative research. If one is working within a theoretical tradition, then the theory should suggest ideas worthy of exploring, testing, or elaborating. On the other hand one of the principal assertions of qualitative workers is that not only should the method fit the problem that is chosen for study, but that there should exist a ". . . basic interconnection between the nature of the social world one wants to study and the methods one should use" (Douglas, 1976: xii). Thus, problem choice and theoretical predisposition will both interact in determining one's initial stance toward a researchable problem. Manning's essay on analytic induction suggests how such an interplay acted in the study of abortion-seeking. The Lindesmith study of opiate addiction is used as another case in point. Davis's work on abortion, which followed upon some of the ideas expressed in the analytic-induction essay, shows further how method can be played out in terms of the changing strategies or approaches to data-gathering that were employed. Insights into this process are also found in the papers by Zimmerman and Weider, Blauner and Wellman, and most dramatically in the Bigus, Hadden, and Glaser paper.

It should be noted that this devotion to some sense of fit between the defined social world and the research approach, method, strategies, and tactics is peculiarly associated with qualitative work. This is so for three abiding reasons having to do with the underlying assumptions of the approach.

The first is the commitment to *close detailed observation* that permits the observer to, as it were, "let the facts speak for themselves." This is an overstatement, of course, since one's perspective will give shape to the relevant facts, how they relate to key concepts, and the relationships between these findings or facts and a theory. The point is that this commitment, as Filstead writes, is an important one to qualitative researchers:

It is no simple task to acquire this wealth of knowledge; whether it can ever be completely acquired is problematic; but, the more intersubjective personal knowledge sociologists have at their disposal, the more accurate will be their interpretations and predictions of human behavior. The researcher has "to get to know well the persons involved and to see and hear what they do and say" if he hopes to come close to understanding human behavior. The tendency in sociology to dehumanize the subject matter by reducing everything to an inventory-like describability has to be re-thought. The knowledge needed to understand human behavior is embedded in the complex network of social interaction. To assume what it is without attempting to tap it; to refuse to tap it on the grounds of scientific objectivity; or to define this knowledge with constricting operational definitions, is to do a grave injustice to the character and nature of the empirical social world that sociologists seek to know and understand. (Filstead, 1970:7)

The second reason is a commitment to a *microsociological focus* on symbolic worlds that are in flux and process. Rock writes, "A microsociological focus transforms society into a mosaic of unique configurations of events and meanings. When it is observed in detail any social scene contains structures and contours that can never be wholly reproduced elsewhere" (see p. 39). The uniqueness of social scenes carefully observed can be a trap or a logical paradox: If one focuses on particular features of social scenes rather than the generic, then one is reduced, as Rock suggests, to describing unique things and events. One is reduced to cataloging the bizarre, the weird, the strange. And if this occurs, the themes of work become stylistic matters rather than theoretical ones. It may be that there develops an impetus to use bizarre examples precisely to contrast with the reader's assumptions about everyday life (see Manning, 1946b).

A third commitment of many, if not most, qualitative researchers is to *low-level abstraction* and persistent resistence to building models, totalistic logics, or theories that are all-encompassing. Even the model of the social world adopted by qualitative researchers is tenderly grasped, and assertions are made with reservations. The Bigus, Hadden, and Glaser paper as well as the Manning, and Arnold chapters in this book provide examples of this resistance to excessive abstraction, especially if adopted, as in the case of deductive theory, a priori, or before the research begins.

Perhaps one way to resolve this question of *when* to use qualitative methods is to begin with the most generic questions and issues and then work from there to select the particular research approach that is both theoretically sound and practically possible. Jack Douglas, in his fine book on fieldwork, has provided a useful list that should be used to orient oneself to the *when* question. I recommend it highly to those undertaking any sort of research project:

The researcher must always begin his research with an idea of what kind of data he wants (his research goals), what the situation allows, and what his practical constraints are. The goal of one's research is the first crucial question. Its answer has fundamental implications for all his research and its results. The goals chosen largely determine the general methods used and thus the kinds of data produced—their truthfullness and usefulness. Most researchers begin their research and end it without ever clearly formulating and answering the basic questions:
    1. What are the goals of this research?
    2. What, in view of these goals, is the kind of data I want this research to produce?
    3. What research will allow me to achieve these goals and get this kind of data?
    4. Given these goals and this research setting, what research methods should be used *ideally*?
    5. What research methods are practical in this research setting?
    6. Given this estimate of the practical methods, is it possible to approximate sufficiently the goals and kinds of data we want to make this research desirable? (Douglas, 1976:8) [2]

Given this list, one should still be aware that *goals*, in spite of this clear statement, are never altogether clear, mutually supportive, unilaterally determined, and so on.[3] Social research, as often as not, is a response to a sudden opportunity. Several projects with which I have been associated began with chance encounters, phone calls, an ad in a journal. One of the principal reasons I embarked on a study of the police in London was that my wife and I had decided as undergraduates when we talked of marriage·that we would like to go to England. The only other country I yearned to see was Japan, and neither of us spoke the language. So it was that on my first sabbatical, we went to England to do police research. Once there, my problem shifted as I talked to people, as opportunities arose, as many of my assumptions about police work were altered by my experience as a member of the middle-class suburban world in which we lived, and as I became "less American" and more a marginal, or what Douglas (1976) has called, a "limbo" member of English society. The goal statements that are formalized in research proposals (as mine was) usually are transformed as one goes along, as one actually tries to do the study. As Van Maanen somewhat cynically wrote (personal communication, July, 1977):

I'm not sure what an up-front research goal means other than a sort of focusing device and, more importantly, an entree ploy marshalled out to give other reasons to believe that we know what we're doing. My goal [in a study of socialization to police work done with fieldwork and questionnaires; cf. Van Maanen, "Epilogue" in Manning and Van Maanen (eds.) (1978) was cast as to discover how people came to learn how to do police work[1] . . . In the early stages of the study, this seemed more of a rhetorical or almost ideological remark, devoid of substance.

I cannot echo this more strongly, because it fits so closely with my own experience (cf. Manning, 1976b) of beginning with a shockingly broad and ill-defined goal, shaping it in conversations with the persons I wanted to study, and trying it out in more detail as I got closer to the "on the ground" experience of policing the streets of London. Perhaps two examples from police research will add an ironic twist to the problem of definitions of one's research goals.

1. A friend of mine was initiating some research on detectives. He had begun the study because the brief study he had just finished was a success, and the federal agency that had supported it had some additional money to fund further studies by individual scholars. He was encouraged to study detectives for a year supported by an extended grant. As he and his wife had developed a very pleasant life-style in a houseboat on a nearby river, and liked the area, they agreed to work on "the way detectives solve cases." [My paraphrase—P.K.M.] In a way, he had jumped at a research opportunity and funding for a year, and was in addition "handicapped" because there is so little literature written by sociologists on detectives. In an interview with a detective, he laid out his research plans and ideas and had the officer tell him, "that sounds a lot like the book written by Jerry Skolnick, *Justice Without Trial.*" The sociologist later revealed to me that he had only a few leads and that he was in fact relying heavily on Skolnick's study of vice detectives.

2. I was working with narcotics detectives in a Far Western city. We had been talking about how in general academics rarely spend time with police officers and that police and professors often view each other in stereotypic fashion. Professors, they thought, were unaware of the realities of the job, were quick to criticize, and would in fact be shocked at just how bad it was on the streets. I said that I thought many professors wrote about policing within a narrow administrative perspective. Coming up to the office, riding in the elevator, I said something about how the police generally dealt with perceived threats to society (or some such jargon-like generalization). One of the officers, who was completing his M.A. at the local university, replied, "Well, yes . . . a number of us have taken sociology courses and we often ask ourselves, "How would Durkheim view this?" He laughed, and I burst out laughing. The joke was on me in several senses.

These two stories illustrate several of the above points; you should be aware of these kinds of dynamics when you develop or are considering your own research goals and objectives. First, much research is done expediently and on short notice, and the details are fleshed out quickly in the first few weeks in the field. Second, much research is shaped by the responses that people we meet and negotiate with make to our ideas. The process of goal setting, obviously, is an *interactional process* involving both researchers and hosts, or "subjects." Insofar as the groups studied participate in the same symbolic works—e.g., police officers who have been educated under LEEP and other federal funds in the criminal justice programs and professors who both teach them and do research on policing—they will be aware of the front work that research requires and be able to penetrate and probe it. Third, the factual knowledge of the average person about social science is rapidly accelerating. No longer can one do social research in a school, in a police department, or in a large government agency and not expect employees there to have read many of the same things you have. In view of these points and Van Maanen's candid remarks it is perhaps most realistic to view the steps outlined by Douglas as recursive: When you reach 6, you go back to 1, etc., over the course of your research. This procedure may not be close to the ideal of science as presented in high school texts, but it fits well with the pattern of most social science research projects.

What

Once one decides to undertake a piece of social research utilizing qualitative methods, one must ask, "What?" That is, one must consider the basic technical questions associated with any social research: What will it cost in terms of personal effort, time, money, and emotional drain? What will be the consequences of my undertaking such a study—how and in what way will I be *involved*? Finally, one must ask the central questions of *efficacy*: How can I ascertain the *validity* and *reliability* of my findings?

What biases, if any, can be found in qualitative data, given certain aims, settings, and techniques? The essays in this volume that deal with specific qualitative techniques—the chapters by Arnold, Davis, Zimmerman & Weider, Reitzel & Lindemann, Danzger and Ogilvie et al—and those that present general modes of analysis—such as the papers by Manning, and Bigus, Hadden & Glaser—bear on these central issues of method and technique. However, some more specific considerations might be of use to the student undertaking a project. These *what* issues are more difficult to resolve for the qualitative worker precisely because there is less consensus in the field concerning what is acceptable or credible data, (see Becker, 1970: chap. 4). These issues, and the ways they are resolved, are of course related to the central dilemma of qualitative work outlined above. Let us discuss these issues of cost, involvement, and efficacy.

Qualitative methods typically do not *cost* as much in dollars as do other types of research. Particularly in this computer age analysis—including the coding, punching, and running of data—can account for as much as 60-75 percent of the total cost of the research. On the other hand qualitative research tends to be time-consuming and requires a great deal of physical energy (many fieldworkers engaged in projects spend 12-16 hours a day "in the field" and then attempt to dictate or type notes on the experience). Note Arnold's point that six times as much time out of the field must be undertaken for every hour in the field (this is probably a variable, but it's close to a working estimate). The appeal of the small project, the documents research, library study, observation of a local school or of a fraternity party may be deceptive. The costs may be figured in terms other than dollars or even time. There are exceptions to the general rule that qualitative research does not rely heavily on computer machinations (an exception is the work done on the General Inquirer, included here in the chapter by Ogilvie, Stone, and Kelly). Taping data is also time-consuming and expensive if one intends to have transcriptions made. Further, the time entailed by a qualitative project may be inexactly understood at the beginning of a project. A contrast is provided in an experiment that terminates when the number of trials needed have been acquired, or in a sample survey study that ends when a predetermined sample size (the N) has been gathered. Because qualitative work gives over control more to the process of observation itself, it is far more difficult to predict the time required. Often, arbitrary cut-off points are employed, as mentioned in Davis's chapter in this volume. Although one can decide to do work for a set period of time, it is often true that qualitative work extends itself almost interminably. Many scientists have difficulty in firmly establishing an end point to their research unless other, external, events intervene: Money runs out, or a job waits, or the term is over, or time must be left to write to meet a deadline set by someone else.

An additional problem of qualitative research is that of *involvement*. The Arnold, the Davis, and Blauner & Wellman papers poignantly describe the ways in which the involvements of researchers with the people they research can pattern and affect the course of that research. Some of the political and moral issues, as well as the personal ones attendant on all social research, are outlined by Somers et al and Blauner & Wellman (see below). In the several field researches in which I have been involved, both within and outside of the United States, I have always felt a sense of loneliness, disattachment, and deracination upon leaving the field, even when the field was just a few miles from my home. The other side of over-rapport in the scene itself is feelings of loss upon withdrawing. Be prepared, when doing fieldwork, to experience emotional changes—anxiety, fear, apprehension, camaraderie, anger, respect, dislike, hate. Not all qualitative research portends this sort of involvement, but fieldwork certainly does (see Wolff, in Vidich, Bensman, & Stein, eds., 1964; Johnson, 1975: chap. 6). If one gets close enough to describe in detail a social situation or social world, then one may well become immersed in that world, and begin to feel as "they" do about things. Police researchers often begin to "think like a cop," to watch for "suspicious people," interpret crime stories in the newspapers, note people who look "odd" or out of place or time, and become more cynical (cf. Buckner, 1967; Manning, 1972). Davis reports growing sympathy with the politically oriented crusaders for change in abortion laws, and Van Maanen's ethical commitment and involvement could have led to a heavy fine or a jail sentence for contempt of court. When one tries to penetrate behind appearances, to understand problematic meanings, and to uncover the self-deceptive practices of others, one both becomes a part of that intersubjective world *and* stands outside of it. Role-alternation (Berger, 1963) is required. The finest discussion of these issues is found in Douglas' *Investigative Social Research* (1976: 108-23). But this involvement need not be direct experience; it can be the obsessional involvement of any qualitative social researcher, as the historian of Victoriana who wakes up in a motel in Monterey, California, in Brian Moore's story, *The Great Victorian Collection* (1975), to see out his window the very museum he has dreamed of. He creates it, and then walks into it as a palpable reality. Less dramatic and totalistic involvements, called "going native," occur to greater or lesser degree in all social research.

The *efficacy* of one's tactics cannot be handled as easily in qualitative research as by the tests of validity and reliability used in quantitative research. To understand this statement one has to appreciate the *natural history* of a piece of qualitative research, especially of fieldwork. The aim of social research is to uncover the realities that lie behind the appearances of social life, to explicate the hidden rules that guide our behavior. Many of the issues that we conceive of as problematic—such as abortion, drug use, prostitution, the subjects of the chapters in this volume—are covered by participants with elaborate justications, rationalizations, and self-deceiving fronts and "lines." People engaged in illegal behavior are often unwilling to openly discuss the details of their involvements: Women who fear a potential stigma may be careful to conceal their pregnancy or abortion search; drug users and especially drug dealers are cautious about whom they talk with about their work (see Becker, 1970a; Polsky, 1967). If one probes into areas where self-deception is likely to be high and people "cover up" what they are unwilling to reveal—areas like sex, money, death, and success—then traditional canons of research validity are more difficult to apply (Douglas, 1976: chaps. 4 and 5). If one is working in areas where there is no conflict between the group studied and other groups and where cooperation is easily obtained, then fieldwork will be easier to accomplish and can be evaluated by rules of evidence that more closely appproximate those applied to quantitative data. It is best not to assume that people are being truthful and to make every effort to double and triple check what is said. The model of the society that one employs, as Douglas (1976) emphasizes, is critical in evaluating one's data. If one assumes a cooperative model, then conventional measures of reliability and validity may be applied; if one uses a conflict model, and attempts to probe into problematic issues, then more complicated and specialized techniques of ascertaining validity and reliability must be employed (Manning & Fabrega, 1976).

When one works with quantitative data, the notion of a sampling frame is critical. A sample means a proportion of the total number of eligible units. Quantitative social research asserts that prior to research a delineation of the universe of units from which a sample will be drawn must be undertaken— e.g., the total number of students in a given university. A variety of kinds of samples can be drawn—e.g., random, stratified random, cluster, accidental, expedient or situational, snowball, or combinations of these patterns (see Selltiz, Jahoda, Deutsch, & Cook, 1959, appendix B, for a full discussion of these modes of sampling). The sample provides the basis for establishing the generality of the findings, especially when used in conjunction with statistical inference. The sample one chooses, controlling for the variables of interest to be sure that they are either random or specifically controlled, gives one the basis for making statistical measures of distribution of the variables as revealed in the data. Comparisons can be made against probability tables to determine whether the results could have been obtained by chance alone. Denzin argues that samples should always be drawn with a theoretical rationale in mind and with "confidence in the observations so that generalizations to other groups and situations not explicitly examined can be made" (1970: 81). The quality controls one places on the data are intended to assure that the data accurately measure what they are said to measure, given a theoretical frame of reference, specific expectations, and concepts (validity), and that they repeatedly measure what they are said to measure (reliability). Generally, samples are noninteractive in kind—they fail to capture relations between natural social units.

Denzin's attempt to integrate two modes of sampling, interactive—(i.e., samples of *natural* groups, encounters, relations—and noninteractive—e.g., the Gallup Poll, where individuals are selected for certain attributes and are not part of a social group sharing interaction and group feelings or norms— is unusual, for qualitative research has rarely used samples of any kind. Even the relevant units, such as encounters, relationships, settings, or behavioral sequences, may be ill-defined, especially at the initiation of the research process. Qualitative research may involve observations of a group of persons over an extended period of time; it may involve a universe of events—all the riots in a particular year; it may be a search of "relevant literature" on a given topic such as the impact of disability upon social interaction. On the other hand, as the Danzger paper shows, rigid criteria can be employed to guide interpretations. Further, qualitative research can hinge on the validity of particular *key* observations, such as the events leading to or producing a riot or a successful abortion search (Manning, this volume), and this focus produces concern for the validity of *particular* observations and interactions.

In our research on narcotics policing,[4] for example, we found that the raids made on alleged drug users or dealers were the focal concern of several of the units studied, and that close observation of them was more significant in understanding narcotics policing than the hours spent "hanging around" in the office, or in surveillance activities, or even in court. This was true because the raids were a source of arrests (which were looked at by senior officers as signs of "productivity"), and arrests meant court appearances (which in turn meant overtime pay), and because they allowed officers to participate in dramatic "crime-work" involving arrests, the use of guns and violence, and encounters with the elusive villians that they attempt to control. Thus, a few raids were symbolically imperative to observe, but no sample could be used, nor could the number of raids observed be meaning- fully compared to hours spent observing other types of activities (such as surveillance, for example). When qualitative research focuses on meanings and symbolic worlds, it will tend to define events of interest that cannot be understood by their distribution—their existence and consequences are more significant than the numbers of times they appear in the world. Obvious examples are disasters, riots, and other "unique" events such as political assassinations. However, unless one is trying to establish the routine bases of some practice within an organization—e.g., how many arrests or raids are executed within the unit so that comparisons with other units can be made— distributions are not likely to be gathered. They may be, and they may be very useful, as Arnold suggests in his chapter.

As a result of the focus of much qualitative work, questions of *validity* are usually of more concern than those of *reliability*. Actor's meanings, or the shared assumptions that they have about the world, as well as the specific meanings that are part of their own life-worlds, become the baseline against which research data is assessed. Several criteria of this sort have been advanced, among them the competence criteria suggested by the anthropologist Ward Goodenough (1964). If the researcher can act competently within a culture on the basis of his knowledge, then the data have face validty. If one relies on this model, then ways to deal with the ignorance, the evasiveness, the lying, and deceit of informants must be developed as well as elicitation for information or the observation of behavior patterns. In this regard recent works by Johnson (1975) and Douglas (1976), as well as the paper in this volume by Davis, are suggestive. Any valid field data are gounded in trust. One must attempt to establish trusting relationships and to maintain them over time with one's informants. Trust is never established once and for all: It must constantly be negotiated and renegotiated (for examples see Manning, 1972; and Johnson, 1975).

Once trust is established, which is itself a major hurdle in most work where overt observation or participation occurs, one can try other modes of data-gathering, such as interviewing key informants (those close to the scenes one most wants to observe). Interviews can be checked against observations and against one's own direct and indirect experience. Data gathered can be cross-checked against other sorts of data, especially with independent sources (other informants, other materials such as other research reports, conversations with other researchers on the same project, previous fieldnotes, etc.). All of these techniques are ways to establish the validity of one's data. However, if we consider validity as a question of the generalizability of findings, or alternatively a question of whether the identified causal variables are acting, then qualitative research is likely to be faulted.

Ways in which one establishes the *reliability* of qualitative research have been extensively discussed by McCall and Simmons (1969) and by Becker (1970). Denzin suggests that if one wants to establish the degree of stability in response under conditions of repeated observation (one useful definition of reliability), then one should consider the various sources of *change*—in the observer, in the data-gathering process, in the subjects observed, in the situations observed, or in the interpretations one is making of one's data. Most attention has been given to changes in situations or subjects and in the data-gathering process itself in conventional discussions of reliability and validity. However, some evidence for changes in the observer has been presented in Davis's paper and in important papers by Geer (1964), Wax (1952), Gusfield (1955), S.M. Miller (1953), and others (Dalton, 1959; Van Maanen, 1978). Ways to develop and improve validity and reliability have not been well addressed in the literature of qualitative analysis, and they are not valued by many qualitative researchers in many cases. The work of Bigus, Hadden, and Glaser is an important advance in bringing such issues to the attention of researchers. They urge them to try to formulate theoretical propositions that are generic and are based upon theoretical sampling. Reliability can be addressed in qualitative work in a variety of ways, but most attention has been paid to the changes in the observer and ways to standardize observations. Black and Reiss (1968) and

Sykes and Clark (1974) have tried through the use of standardized forms and multiple observers to reduce the error in field observations. The use of standardized forms is highly recommended to all qualitative workers.

Finally, one of the most slippery of issues of this kind is the question of "bias" in qualitative research. Defleur argues (1975) that two sources of error can be identified—random error, which is attributable to uncontrolled variables, and systematic error. Researchers dealing with time-series data may assume that unknown systematic errors cancel themselves, or that biases remain constant over time. Defleur's argument, using a sample of official statistics (arrests made by the Chicago Police Department, narcotics division, 1942-1970) and her fieldwork, was that there were systematic biases in the arrests by race and census tract over time due to the discretionary and policy-based actions of narcotics officers. The trends identified, she argues, are not due to changes in the use or dealing of drugs, but instead reflect the differential interest of the officers in given perceived political and social problems within the city—e.g., hippies who clustered in given areas of the city. It is her view then that the "systematic biases" of official records can be traced to the ways in which the police perceive and act upon the demands of the political structure, community needs and expectations, and the police view(s) of the drug problem. Police policies, not written but tacit and gathered through field observation and interviewing by Defleur, affect arrest activity. She argues further that "systematic errors themselves changed over time, making trend analysis meaningless (1975: 102)." She concludes by discussing several ways in which these biases might be overcome: self-report studies, victimization surveys, and direct observational studies such as those done by Black and Reiss (1968).

There are a number of points of criticism of this formulation of the concept of "bias" that are of central importance for qualitative methods in general. If we understand the conceptual problems lying behind the definitions of "bias," then we are better able to avoid biases in the data we gather. The first problem is in the definition of bias itself, which implies (Defleur never states a definition) that in this instance there is an accurate and valid measure of drug use that stands apart from the data she has on the activities of the narcotics division. The term "bias" requires that one have a statistical or logical model that represents an unbiased data pattern. In this case the requirements would be a logical model of the relationships between dealing and using and the enforcement system itself (which must in turn be a cybernetic model that takes into account the impacts of enforcement and deterrence on the activities of the user), explicating the expected relationships between use and rates of arrest, for example. This has not been done. In addition, data would be required on the *actual use patterns* (or dealing patterns, since persons are arrested for drug possession, for conspiracy, for possession of the implements of crime, and for other drug-related charges). In the absence of these data, Defleur is speculating about the impact of enforcement practices and policies upon arrests, and is doing this through reconstruction of situations occurring up to 25 years previously. What she does show is changes in the locale, race, sex, and age of those arrested. But do these changes reflect changes in the use patterns of these groups, in their visibility, or in their behavior quite apart from the activities of the narcotics division? Second, there is a serious conceptual and measurement problem in the research which obviates the effort to identify bias in drug arrests. Most drug arrests are not made by specialized units: They are made by patrol units (see Johnson and Bogomolny, 1973; DEA Newsletter, April, 1977; Manning, forthcoming). Somewhere between 75 and 95 percent of all arrests for drugs are made by regular patrol officers. Johnson and Bogomolny (518-24; tables 84 and 89) show that only 5 percent of all drug arrests in 1971 were made by investigative units in the Chicago Department. Thus, on the basis of this data Defleur can at best expect to uncover not bias in drug arrests, but bias in drug arrests by this specialized unit. The trends and patterns in the city at large as measured by the activities and pattern of arrests for the patrol division might show entirely different patterns. They might, for example, run counter to the trends in the reported data.

There is a second conceptual problem in this research. "Arrests" are in many ways a misleading measure of police activity or of the "deviance" that they are mandated to control. Arrests do not indicate what *numbers* of persons are arrested in a given episode: Persons in a house where drugs are found can be arrested for being on the premises; people can be arrested in order to force them to testify where evidence of their involvement is weak or unproven; cases are routinely dropped for lack of evidence, as a result of deals between the prosecutors and police. In general, then, the "deviance" indicated by arrests is a very diffuse clustering of behaviors and meanings. More important, perhaps, is the fact that charges and arrests are not equivalent. The charges brought against persons for given drug activities are a far more precise legal indicator of the interests of the prosecutor's office and the police, and thus of some general notion of community concern, than are arrests. For example, the fact that possession of small quantities of marijuana (one ounce or so) is *not* resulting in prosecutions in large cities in this country (some by policy, some by law, some by tacit agreement among prosecuting attorneys), indicates community concern. Charges, rather than arrests, would be a better means of assessing the negotiated concern of the criminal justice system; on the other hand they would be a less sensitive indicator of the activities of individuals.

Because of these flaws in the research the claim of "bias" cannot be easily assessed. In short, if claims about bias are made, they are always drawn against the background of some implicit or explicit model of what "reality" is like such that one could ascertain deviations from reality and identify sources other than the independent or causal variables that might be acting. In this case the inference is that there is some "real" constant level while the attention and interest of the police shift over time. Each may be true, although this article reveals more about the shifting interest of the police than about use patterns. However, it is not possible from this article to clearly establish what is claimed.[5]

In qualitative research in general there is a similar problem: What would the situation have been like if some biasing effect (observer, data change, etc.) had *not* been introduced? Since the commitment of qualitative methods is often to exploration of a problem, to theory-building rather than to theory-testing, researchers often find it difficult to address the question of "bias." Defleur's attempt to combine qualitative field research with her quantitative data is to be congratulated, but it is rare that a clear model of relations is established such that questions of bias can be dealt with. Qualitative methodologists should develop more refined methods of specifying the world they hope to study if they intend to test theories or to do theoretically oriented qualitative work. Methods such as analytic induction are among the more promising (see Manning's chapter, this volume), since they allow for the constant readjustment of theory and data in order to specify causal relations. However, as Manning points out, there continues to be a great deal of disagreement about the claims that have been made for analytic induction.

A theme that runs through the dilemma of qualitative work is that of the *reflexivity* of the research process itself: By participation in the setting, or by observing it, one may change the process being studied. Obviously, this principle is an issue in all sciences. Elaborate critiques of experimental work by Orne (1962), Rosenthal (1976), Friedman (1967), and Cicourel (1973) and of survey research (Hyman et al, 1954) reveal that investigators, by nonverbal cues such as smiling or frowning when giving instructions, can affect the outcomes of experiments in the same fashion that interviewers can elicit different patterns of answers depending on their personal attributes or style (Manning, 1967). One significant form of qualitative research, fieldwork, is less subject to these sources of bias for three reasons.[6] First, fieldworkers are participating in ongoing social systems where things *other than* the experiment or the observation tend to dominate the attention of participants. Police officers are more oriented to their supervisors, and to those they control, than to observers, so that observers' impact is less profound than it might be in a contrived experimental situation governed entirely by the rules and procedures of the experiment. Second, given time in the setting, fieldworkers can observe variations in behavior and gather detailed descriptions of *key* situations of interest. It is difficult to dissemble or misrepresent a situation to persons who are present over long periods of time. Becker (1970: 52) summarizes this principle in a fundamental statement about the nature of fieldwork evidence:

But the fieldworker typically gathers his data over an extended period of time, in a variety of situations, using several ways of getting at the questions he is interested in, all of these reducing the danger of bias. Because he observes over a long time, he finds it hard to ignore the mass of information supporting an appropriate hypothesis he may neither have expected nor desired, just as the people he studies would find it hard, if they wanted to deceive him, to manipulate such a mass of impressions in order to affect his assessment of the situation. Because he does not constrain himself with inflexible and detailed procedural rules, he can use a variety of devices to elicit talk and action from his subjects.

In short, the very large number of observations and kinds of data an observer can collect, and the resulting possibility of experimenting with a variety of procedures for collecting them, means that his final conclusions can be tested more often and in more ways than is common in other forms of research. We therefore act correctly when we place great reliance on fieldwork evidence.

Finally, he notes that flexibility in methods permits greater likelihood of overcoming the observer's effect on the setting studied.

HOW

How one does fieldwork has been well discussed by Arnold, and other qualitative approaches are described in chapters by Davis, Zimmerman & Weider, and the chapters in the section on interviews. In addition, there are a number of short books that cover this topic (Lofland, 1971, 1976; Johnson, 1975; Douglas, 1976). The idea that one learns a *how*, or a set of techniques, and then proceeds easily to carry out a study, is a misrepresentation of the complexity of any research project. However, part of the tradition of qualitative work, whether it be literary criticism, historical analysis, or participant observation, is the claim that "Some people can do it, others can't." This claim is often leveled by quantitative social researchers against qualitative researchers as a way of discrediting the work, making it appear to be idiosyncratic. For instance, "Goffman can do it, or Howard Becker, but no one else can write like they do. . . ." The problem with this statement is self-evident—no one has contributed as much to theoretical physics as Einstein, but his standard is not applied evenly to all contributions in that field. Lesser works are viewed as valid and significant for the science.

In some sense it is true that not all researchers have the ability to convey the detailed and rich depictions of social life found in such classics as Goffman's *Asylums* (1961) and *The Presentation of Self* (1959) or Becker *et al.*, *Boys in White* (1961). But there is a more profound set of issues lurking in this oft-heard remark. If a researcher is insensitive to the field situation, not only will the fieldnotes incompletely capture basic ideas but the notes will be incomplete; they will omit aspects of the relationships of the observer to the scene itself and thus contribute to an inability to detect the problems of bias discussed above. Because the personal relations experienced in the setting will also affect such basic patterns of work as recording (writing down), recalling, and intelligently organizing fieldnotes, it is evident that omissions, distortions, changes in memory, and other cognitive changes can often result. John Johnson (1975: 187), in a very candid statement, recalls how his perception and recall of events was intertwined with personal experience, and the consequences of these states of feeling for his (and by implication others') research:

An investigator's observational records are highly variable. This fact is supported by many writings in the traditional field-research literature. As a field researcher develops a better understanding of activities in a given setting, the observational records will change to reflect the observer's changing understanding. My field experiences in the social welfare agencies readily support this field-research truth. But there are also other sources of variability. The quantity and quality of the observational records vary with the fieldworker's feelings of restedness or exhaustion, reactions to particular events, relations with others, consumption of alcoholic beverages, the number of discrete observations, and so forth. Added to these are a wide range of unanticipated technical problems with tape recorders, transcription, and typing and typists; all these seem to continually subvert rational intentions and the best-laid plans.

Thus, all reports in qualitative style should contain a discussion of the impact of the researcher on the subject of the research, whether it be a person, a situation, an organization or several organizations, or a profession. Such a section should include data on the natural history of the project—access, role development in the setting, ethical problems, development of key informants and information sources, exit, and epilogue (any effects of the research after one has left the scene).[7] In the section on role development, in particular, one should be sensitive to issues of *trust* and how these might relate to the validity and reliability of the data.

There are no absolute guidelines for doing social research. Any good study will be concerned with the issues raised in this section, but will also have a number of options to employ in case the planned approach, strategy, and tactics fail: A researcher may be refused entree, may be unable to interview the planned target group or sample, may discover a new problem in the middle of an ongoing project, may redefine major concepts and measures. The possibilities are endless. To avoid failure, one should always employ several strategies, have several modes of implementing them, and have optional problems and sites in mind before undertaking a study. Recall, too, that even "failed" studies are data and can illustrate social processes and group structure. They are in fact learning experiences that, if published, can contribute to the body of knowledge in the social sciences. At very least, they are significant personal experiences for investigators. This point makes a useful transition to the following section on the ethical and political aspects of social research. In it I attempt, with special reference to the paper by Useem and Marx in Volume 1, *An Introduction to Social Research*, to emphasize that all social research has moral and political meanings, and that a personal awareness of these aspects is as important in scientific research as is commitment to scientific procedures.

SOCIAL RESEARCH, ETHICS, AND POLITICS

The essays in Volume 1 by Etzioni, Useem and Marx, and Van Maanen are especially pertinent to qualitative research. They confront the contemporary concern with the political consequences of different types of research and with professional ethics. These chapters highlight the possible ethical and political problems associated with basic, applied, and policy research and, more practically, to help researchers consider these problems when designing and implementing their own research studies.

In "On Policy Research" Amitai Etzioni points out differences among policy, applied and basic research and discusses certain problems of policy research. Policy research is aimed at mapping alternative approaches and specifying practical differences in the intention, effect, and cost of proposed programs. Since the policy researcher usually advocates one alternative over others, policy research is inherently critical and partisan, never "value-neutral." Thus, there are three aspects to policy research: (1) formulation of alternative goals and strategies; (2) specification of the consequences of alternative programs; and (3) advocacy of specific policy recommendations. The policy researcher adopts a critical stance and long-term perspective. Etzioni discusses this perspective in-depth, giving special attention to the problems policy researchers face in communicating their results to policy-makers.

Doing any kind of social research—policy, applied, or basic—always involves ethics, or standards of conduct, with respect to gathering, interpreting, and publishing data. Among other reasons this is because knowledge can be used by others, because published work can offend those studied (often with unanticipated consequences), and because researchers can be caught between conflicting obligations to themselves, to sponsors, to the persons they study, and to those who gave them permission to do the study. Political questions also arise in choice of what to study, how one studies it, what one does with the data, and the uses of the data to the extent—that one can control such matters. Researchers should never reduce their projects solely to a series of technical or methodological questions. They must bear in mind the ethical and political dimensions of their research. The day when "science" could rationalize any intrusion into another person's privacy or public conduct are gone.[8]

Michael Useem and Gary T. Marx, in their chapter, explicate some of the "ethical dilemmas and political considerations in social research." Their generic theme urges social scientists to carefully assess potential ethical and political consequences *before* the implementation of social research studies, as well as after the fact. This assessment should affect the eventual research design and utilization of findings by helping to reduce anticipated adverse ethical and political consequences.

Useem and Marx examine the roles and related audiences of the social researcher, focusing on the ethical and political aspects of five roles. They examine the relationship between the researcher and: (1) the subjects of the research, (2) the consumers of the research report, (3) the sponsor of the research, (4) professional colleagues, and (5) lawyers and other functionaries in the legal system.

In discussing the direct relationship between the researcher and research *subjects* the necessity of protecting the rights of the latter is stressed. This implies that the researcher must obtain the informed prior consent of the subject without resorting to manipulative means, that subjects are not to be harmed either physically or psychologically by their participation in the research, and that their anonymity is to be protected.

Useem and Marx stress that social researchers are responsible for the misuse of their findings by *consumers* or clients who utilize research findings. For example, studies of socially determined differences in scores on intelligence tests have been used by segregationists to buttress arguments for individual and institutional racism. Sympathetic studies of student activists that describe characteristics of protest-prone types of students can be used by concerned college administrators to limit the enrollment of such types. Careful studies of the combat motivation of groups of soldiers can be used by militarists to strengthen the armies of antidemocratic regimes. There are various strategies for minimizing misuse of research findings. These involve not studying problems where misuse is likely; limiting the availability of research reports that might be misused; alternatively, publishing the findings in as many journals as possible, thereby reaching a vast audience and minimizing the possibility of distortion by propagandists; assiduously pointing out the limitations of one's data; and actively combating misuse by after-hours activism and debate. These should be carefully considered and used whenever possible. As noted above, however, science is public knowledge, and it is exceedingly difficult to "control" the uses others make of one's published results. Many social scientists, perhaps cynically, believe that the norm of science concerning publication and shared information makes it impossible to *do* science *and* control the uses of one's data (cf. Berger, 1963). Useem and Marx have suggested ethical or personal guidelines that might change the present abuses of social science knowledge by greater concern for the role of the consumer in social research. For example, researchers often make tacit and/or explicit bargains concerning access to their data, publication approval, or other restrictions on information in exchange for access to an organization. Prior awareness of the constraints this may generate should reduce investigators' willingness to undertake such research.

Useem and Marx note that social scientists are increasingly involved in expensive, large-scale research projects that require outside funding. Typical sponsoring agencies might be the National Science Foundation (NSF), the National Institutes of Health (NIH), the Ford Foundation, private business firms, interest groups, etc. The outside funding of social science research leads to at least two kinds of problems. Because the sponsoring agency has contributed the money, it may stipulate conditions, attempt to change the direction of the research once it has begun, or may alter the investigator's published conclusions. Contrariwise, because of vital substantive interests and commitments to the scientific norm of freedom of inquiry, the researcher may utilize the money for purposes other than (or in addition to) those initially promised. With respect to the first problem, the authors urge researchers not to accept funding from sponsors whose goals and interests are divergent from their own; once a grant is accepted, resist any pressure to distort the findings and conclusions. With respect to the second, we stress the need for equity—the researcher should fulfill the obligations of the agreement and negotiate with the sponsor any proposed changes in the goals of the research before implementing studies tangential to the agreed-upon plan. As Becker ("Whose Side Are We On?" 1970) has pointed out, the most compromising aspects of research are those of which we are unaware—our tacit biases, political persuasions, and perspectives. Most difficult of all to detect and control are the subtle compromises made in the course of the research—how far to push for certain information, how critical to be of an organization or group, what informants to quote, how much to reveal of the seamy or unattractive side of persons or groups, etc. Furthermore, the relative value of some research in an area may in the long run outweigh short-run considerations.

Norms governing the relationship between a researcher and his professional colleagues are specified in the codes of ethics of several social science associations. These codes specify ethical guidelines in research, but Useem and Marx stress an often-overlooked norm. They urge social scientists to minimize or reduce any potentially damaging consequences their study may have on the research opportunities of others.

Useem and Marx explicate two salient aspects of the relationship between social scientists and the legal system. The first involves privacy rights; the second, participation in illegal activities. A social researcher may uncover information of interest to the police and other investigatory agencies. The researcher may be in conflict with these authorities by trying to protect the privacy of his respondents by restricting access to subpoenaed information. Van Maanen's essay is an excellent case in point. One practical means of combatting this problem is to make it impossible for individuals, including the researchers, to identify the subjects or respondents in studies on sensitive topics where individual interviews or questionnaires are used. This is done by designing "fail-safe" systems for masking the subject's identity. However, as Van Maanen's paper points out so well, when one is dealing with data that are gathered about specific incidents that come to the attention of others or that are evidence needed in court, one cannot conceal so well the identities of those involved, or control access by making individual names nonretrievable. The investigator is still a witness, and may be called to testify, as was Van Maanen. In our narcotics research we observed a case involving multiple assaults (shooting) with a deadly weapon in the course of a raid on a dealing operation. One of the team was required to testify as to the validity of the officers' description and also had been asked to provide a deposition (which was published in the local newspaper along with a brief characterization of our research). Such events cannot be anticipated in detail, nor can the limits of one's obligations to those studied be easily specified a priori. One of the most common problems surrounding the relationships between the host group and the researchers has to do with the limits of moral obligations that are built up in the course of the study. In some sense they cannot be anticipated, nor are they easily covered by general ethical or political statements. For example, do you answer the phone in a narcotics unit if you disapprove of narcotics policing (even though you are actively engaged in research on the subject)? Do you assist in raids by searching, assembling evidence, watching prisoners, etc.? Do you constrain prisoners, use, hold, or shoot guns where legally permissable? Do you loan subjects money? How much? These sorts of nuanced and morally charged relationships typically grow more complex over time, and should be at least considered by any researcher beginning work in a morally or politically charged subject area.

The investigator may also be vulnerable to charges from individuals who believe that an investigation has invaded their privacy. A practical procedure for avoiding this problem (which is now required in most universities) is to obtain the written consent of subjects prior to their participation in the research study.

In the course of an investigation, particularly one requiring participant observation of people violating laws—studies of drug subcultures, underground political movements, delinquents, organized crime, etc.—involvement might require the researcher to participate in or to observe illegal acts. The investigator is afforded no special protection against participation in illegal acts. As noted by Yablonsky (1968), Polsky (1967), and Manning (1972), observing the law sometimes involves not observing it. There are a number of stories concerning the compromised situation that many observers of the police (all those I have spoken with at length concerning their research) inevitably encounter: Serious violations of departmental regulations and the law are observed frequently. I have participated in numerous such scenes myself, ranging from avoidance of duty, excessive breaks, voyeurism, drinking on duty both in and out of uniform and during legal hours in clubs and after hours, assault, lying, violation of traffic laws, searching without a warrant, and so on. I have reported these events in publications but have never been asked to testify against an officer or to compromise my tacit approval of the events I observed. As Van Maanen demonstrates so convincingly, one's moral and personal relationships become so complex and invisible that one is swept away by events before any clear rational position has been developed. One observer of police, Kirkham, claims he would have lied to cover for an officer who brutally assaulted a man for verbal abuse (1976). Kirkham generally justifies all police misconduct on the basis of the ingratitude of the citizenry and the need to protect society from criminals. His view is shared by few sociologists, but it is a considered ethical position. One should recall, however, that the lack of legal protection makes fieldwork of some kinds personally, professionally, and legally risky. You are on your own when you research dangerous, illegal, or immoral activities; remember, too, that you will begin to identify with those you study more than the authorities, and will thus face many ethical and political quandaries in such research.

THE ORGANIZATION OF THE VOLUME

Thematic papers underscore certain basic aims of this volume. The main headings of the book—exploration, interviews, documents, and inspection and patterning—derive from Blumer's outline of the stages of social research, but they also reflect the theory-building or generating emphases found in each of the major paradigms (to varying degrees, of course). In each section a general paper sets a number of major queries and issues and initiates the section. Following each of the general papers there are exemplary research papers and critical assessments of techniques and methods of qualitative research. In addition, each section contains at least one detailed case example of research practice and analysis. There is a model of movement from the more generic to the more specific within each of the sections. In this way the book should be a model for *doing* research, rather than simply a set of "lectures" about research. There is something about the social sciences that makes them craftlike, learned by doing and by apprenticeship, and not easily reducible to abstract instructions, predetermined rules of procedures, caveats, and lists of techniques. Qualitative researchers may work more like carpenters, plumbers, and meatcutters than like mathematicians, experimentalists, and philosophers, but there are examples of quantification in symbolic interaction. See Smith's concluding chapter on enumerative induction.

NOTES

[1] In this sense distinctions between types of scientific methods within sociology are perhaps less significant than distinctions within sociology between scientific and

nonscientific approaches and metaphors. For example, Nisbet has argued that sociology is an art form, and others reject the notion that sociology is or can be "scientific"—e.g., Blum et al, *Theorizing* (1974).

[2] In addition more abstract statements about the interconnections of problem, theory, and method are found in Polyani (1958), C. Wright Mills (1959), Merton (1961), and Denzin (1970). The essays of Freud are among the most stimulating in this respect, for Freud uniquely transferred attention from his clinical material or cases to his attempts to develop a more abstract theory of human behavior.

[3] The following section draws heavily upon suggestions made by John Van Maanen.

[4] "Police and Illicit Substance Control," NILECJ Grant# 76-NI-99-0109, Jay R. Williams, Peter K. Manning, and Lawrence John Redlinger.

[5] It is interesting to note that a criticism of Defleur's research claimed that she had not partialed out the effects of other independent or causal variables, such as the conditions of living in the city (Austin, 1976). However, this claim was addressed with Defleur's data in a response which showed that these variables did not act as predicted and that "other factors," such as the police interest, were more powerful predictors of arrest rates in Chicago over the period studied.

[6] Summarized from Becker (1970: 51-62).

[7] Van Maanen's forthcoming monograph on his field experiences studying the police, *Watching the Watchers*, promises to be perhaps the most detailed and careful treatment of these issues in the literature.

[8] Those who wish to investigate some of the ethical and political aspects of qualitative social research in particular should read, along with the excellent overviews provided in this volume by Useem and Marx, works by Becker (1970)—especially his essays, "Which Side are We On?" and "Problems in the Publications of Field Studies"—Vidich, Bensman, & Stein, Eds., 1964; Manning, in Douglas, Ed., 1972; Sjoberg & Nett, 1968; and Douglas, 1976.

REFERENCES

Austin, R. Comment on Defleur. *American Sociological Review*, 1976, 41 (October): 893-96.

Becker, H. S. *Sociological work*. Chicago: Aldine, 1970. (a)

Becker, H. S. Practitioners of vice and crime. In R. W. Habenstein (Ed.), *Pathways to data*. Chicago: Aldine, 1970. (b)

Becker, H. S., Geer, B., & Hughes, E. C. *Boys in white*. Chicago: University of Chicago Press, 1961.

Berger, P. *Invitation to sociology*. Garden City, N.Y.: Doubleday, 1963.

Black, D. J., & Reiss, A. J. A series of studies sponsored by OLEA, Department of Justice, 1968.

Blum, A. *Theorizing*. London: Heinemann, 1974.

Bruyn, S. *The humanistic perspective in sociology*. Englewood Cliffs, N.J.: Prentice-Hall, 1966.

Buckner, H. T. *The Police: The culture of a social control agency*. Unpublished Ph.D. dissertation, University of California, Berkeley, 1967.

Cicourel, A. *Cognitive sociology*. New York: Free Press, 1973.

Dalton, M. *Men who manage*. New York: John Wiley, 1959.

DEA Newsletter. April, 1977.

Defleur, L. Biasing influences on drug arrest records: Implications for deviance research. *American Sociological Review*, 1975, *40* (February): 88-103.

Denzin, Norman K. *The research act*. Chicago: Aldine, 1970.

Dewey, J. *Logic: The theory of inquiry*. New York: Irvington, 1978.

Douglas, Jack D. *Investigative social research*. Beverly Hills, Calif.: Sage, 1976.

Filstead, W. (Ed.). *Qualitative methodology*. Chicago: Markham, 1970.

Friedman, N. *The social nature of psychological research*. New York: Basic Books, 1967.

Geer, B. First Days in the Field. In P. Hammond (Ed.), *Sociologists at work*. New York: Basic Books, 1964.

Glaser, B. G., & Strauss, A. The discovery of grounded theory. Chicago: Aldine, 1967.

Goodenough, W. Cultural anthropology and linguistics. In Dell Hymes (Ed.), *Language in culture and society*. New York: Harper & Row, 1964.

Goffman, E. *The presentation of self in everyday life*. Garden City, N.Y.: Doubleday Anchor Books, 1959.

Goffman, Erving *Asylums*, Chicago: Aldine, 1961.

Gusfield, J. R. Fieldwork reciprocities in studying a social movement. *Human Organization*, 1955, *14:* 29-34.

Heap, J. Cognitive style in reading. Unpublished ASA paper, 1976.

Hughes, E. C. *French Canada in transition*. Chicago: University of Chicago Press, 1973.

Hyman, H., et al. *Interviewing in social research*. Chicago: University of Chicago Press, 1954.

Johnson, John *Doing fieldwork*. New York: Free Press, 1975.

Johnson, W., & Bogomolny, R. Selective Justice: Drug law enforcement in six American cities. In *Drug use in America: Problem in perspective*. Appendix Volume III. *Technical papers of the second report of the National Commission on Marijiana and Drug Abuse*. Washington, D.C. U.S. Gov. Printing Office, 1973.

Kirkham, G. *Signal zero*. Philadelphia: J.B. Lippincott, 1976.

Lofland, J. *Analyzing social settings*. Belmont, Calif.: Wadsworth, 1971.

Lofland, J. *Qualitative methods*. New York: John Wiley, 1976.

Mc Call, G., and Simmons, J. L. (Eds.). *Issues in participant observation*. Reading, Mass.: Addison-Wesley, 1969.

Manning, P. K. Problems in interpreting interview data. *Sociology and Social Research*, 1967, *51* (April): 302-16.

Manning, P.K. Observing the police...In J.D. Douglas (Ed.), *Observance of deviance* New York: Random House, 1972.

Manning, P.K. Fieldwork and the new ethnography. *Man*, 1976, (a), n.s. II (March): 39–52.

Manning, P.K. The researcher—An alien in the police field. In A. Neiderhoffer & A. Blumberg (Eds.), *The ambivalent force* (2nd ed.). New York: Dryden, 1976, (b).

Manning, P.K. Organizational problematics. *Cuaderni di Criminologia Clinica* (Italian). Forthcoming.

Merton, R. K. *Social theory and social structure* (Rev. ed.). New York: Free Press, 1961.

Miller, S. M. The participant observer and "Over-Rapport." *American Sociological Review*, 1953, *18*: 97-99.

Mills, C. Wright. *The sociological imagination*. New York: Grove, 1959.

Moore, B. *The great Victorian collection*. New York: Ballantine, 1975.

Orne, M. On the social psychology of the psychological experiment. *American Psychologist*, 1962, *17*: 776-83.

Polsky, N. *Hustlers, beats and others*. Chicago: Aldine, 1962.

Polyani, K. *Personal knowledge*. Chicago: University of Chicago press, 1958.

Rosenthal, R. *Experimenter effects in behavioral research*. New York: Irvington, 1976.

Schatzman, & Strauss, A. *Field Research: Strategies for a natural sociology*. Englewood Cliffs, N.J.: Prentice-Hall, 1973.

Selltiz, C., Jahoda, M., Deutsch, S. & Cook, S. *Research methods in social relations*. Chicago: Dryden, 1959.

Sjoberg, G. & Nett, R. *A methodology for social research*. New York: Harper & Row, 1968.

Skolnick, J. *Justice without trial*. New York: John Wiley, 1966.

Stewart, G. L. On first being a john. *Urban Life and Culture*, 1972, *1* (October): 255-74.

Suttles, G. *Social order of the slum*. Chicago: University of Chicago Press, 1968.

Sykes, R., & Clark, J. P., Deference exchange in police-civilian encounters. *American Journal of Sociology*, 1975, *81* (November): 584-600.

Truzzi, M. Lilliputians in Gulliver's land: The social role of the dwarf. In M. Truzzi (Ed.), *Sociology and everyday life*. Englewood Cliffs, N.J.: Prentice Hall, 1968.

Van Maanen, J. Epilogue. In P. K. Manning & John Van Maanen (Eds.), *Policing*. Santa Monica, Calif. Goodyear, 1978.

Wallace, A. F. C. Driving to work. In M. E. Spiro (Ed.), *Context and meaning in cultural anthropology*. New York: Free Press, 1965.

Wax, R. Reciprocity as a field technique. *Human Organization*, 1952, *11*: 34-37.

Wolff, K. Surrender and community studies. In A. Vidich, J. Bensman, & M. Stein (Eds.), *Reflections on community studies*. New York: John Wiley, 1964.

Yablonsky, L. On crime, violence, LSD and legal immunity for social scientists. *American Sociologist*, 1968, *3* (May): 148-49.

PART ONE
EXPLORATION:
PERSPECTIVE
AND METHOD

There is a particular demand associated with fieldwork. It stems from two sources: The first is that nothing in the structure of the gathered data will speak for itself; generic presuppositions, guiding principles, and rules of thumb must be applied in the field as well as at the typewriter. The second source of constraint is parallel to the first, for there is nothing more boring, banal, and brutal than a poorly done piece of fieldwork. On the whole it is difficult to have fieldwork research published, and this problem must in part stem from these well-known constraints. The tradition of fieldwork is not without reference to important theoretical works—those of Simmel, Mead, the Chicago school including Park and Burgess and later Hughes and Becker, and more recently the work of Glaser and Strauss on grounded theory (see the paper by Glaser and others in this volume). However, as Rock so clearly points out, the tradition is equivocal at key points—the resistance to conceptualizing macro-structures; the difficulty involved in studying process and change with linguistic concepts that are cast in a subject-object logic; the tender grasping of collective action viewed from the perspective of the individual; and the unwillingness to formulate rules of correspondence and identity and thus to enable the rejection of empirical claims bearing on (or not bearing on) the implicit theoretical structure of symbolic interactionism.

Reports of fieldwork tend to take the form of individualistic "confessionals," entirely descriptive narratives, tales told out of school; only rarely does one read a theoretically grounded piece of scholarship or craft. Fieldworkers often reject preconceived theories and hypotheses, and so must often develop, make sense of, identify, and conceptualize their problem as they go along. Much social research is informal, "seat-of-the-pants" work, lacking clarity and precision even as it unfolds; this is most true of exploratory field work.

In this section, however, we are concerned with *how* the fundamentals of qualitative research so well stated by David Arnold in his chapter are worked out in the field by participant observers and by undisclosed observers—researchers who are "passing."

We use the words *strategy* and *tactics* to capture a rough analogy with the military—the notion that one has an overall plan of attack points to the

29

fact that one articulates key domains of concern, such as types of data to gather, persons and groups one is concerned with, and basic categories of data. One might delineate two broad data-gathering and analytic strategies—the synchronic and the focused. Figure 1 diagrams their logic.

In synchronic strategy the explorer first gathers data and then closely scrutinizes them to assess their substantive worth. On the basis of this assessment the researcher decides either to continue in this direction or to adopt a different tack. Next the researcher gathers new data, scrutinizes them, and perhaps starts to develop analytic categories and relationships (grounded theory) to organize the data. Then a new decision is formulated about what to observe next. This strategy provides maximum feedback between the data, concepts, relationships and the subsequent emergence of new data, concepts, relationships, etc. The preliminary results determine the subsequent focus of the research; the latter affects the next set of results and their conceptualization, these in turn affect the next direction of the research, and so on. As a consequence the research process unfolds like a logic tree, with many branches and nodes. This strategy maximizes the potential benefits of qualitative research—namely, freedom to explore interesting byways and paths, to shift analytic foci, and to discover analytic categories and relationships that are adequate to the reality being studied. However, the application of this strategy may be inefficient and time consuming because of the lack of problem structure.

The focused-fieldwork strategy is more direct and structured, but at the risk of inflexibility. The researcher following this strategy focuses on a restricted set of topics, gathers data, and then analyzes it. As the diagram suggests, there is little feedback between the gathered data, conceptualization, and analysis and the gathering and analysis of new data. The main advantage of this approach is its efficiency. The main disadvantage is the possibility that interesting patterns discovered in the subsequent data analysis may be insufficiently documented. Also, there may be an overabundance of data bearing on a trivial topic—the wrong questions may have been asked.

Nanette Davis's research, which she describes in "Researching an Abortion Market," combines aspects of both strategies. Her research strikes a good balance between the structure provided by the focused strategy and the responsiveness of the synchronic. She also discusses the tactics of her research.

The guiding stategy for data gathering and analysis must be complemented with a specific plan of attack, the *tactics*. These are the face-to-face modes of carrying out a study—whether to interview first and then to observe the behavior of a group, or vice versa; whether to carry a tape recorder or a notebook or both; whether to make requests for organizational data immediately or from time to time as the occasion arises. It is often impossible to foresee all the contingencies of a piece of research, and thus

Figure 1. Two Strategies for Gathering and Analyzing Qualitative Data.

Synchronic data gathering and analysis

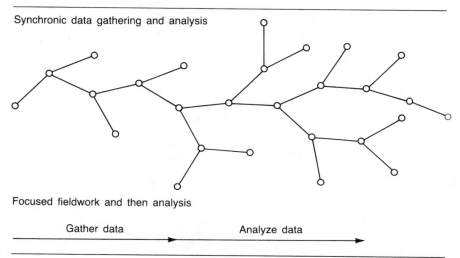

Focused fieldwork and then analysis

Gather data   Analyze data

one's strategies and tactics are constantly shifting to adjust to the developing or emerging problem. This kind of flexibility is found in all types of social research. It does not end with the fieldwork or data-gathering phase, but continues as one attempts to explain a social process or structure. The degree to which one emphasizes sensitizing concepts, exploration, and metaphorical language differs from paradigmatic group to paradigmatic group within sociology. Thus, more or less formalization may occur prior to the entering of the field—the strategic period. As we see in subsequent sections, a degree of a priori theorizing is required by any competent piece of social research; it is the degree that is at issue.

Chapter One
Symbolic interaction[1]

PAUL ROCK

Interactionism is microsociological: It organizes its imagery and methodology so that they can effectively reproduce the perspectives that order social process.

It has not been listed in the great debates about the master schemes of sociological explanation. Marxism, functionalism, and structuralism have been translated into comprehensive systems whose parts are carefully elucidated and welded together. The logic of their properties has received extended abstract exposition. Indeed, that exposition has often been identified as the prime intellectual task. It has been held that the social world cannot be explored until the basic grammar of its possibilities is first formulated. It has also been held that the workings of such systems have some adequate (but unexplicated) correspondence with those of the world itself.

By contrast, even in its major writings symbolic interactionism has undergone no such translation. Its very christening was performed apologetically, and its name was called a "somewhat barbarous neologism" by its author (Blumer, 1969a: 1fn; also see Shibutani, 1970). It is ordered by certain generic themes that challenge the possibility of furnishing a rationally organized, competent, and definitive account of human activity. Those themes, which focus on the nature of being and of knowledge, conspire to prevent interactionism from becoming one of the grand sociological edifices. Attempts have been made to explicate the perspective (Mannis & Meltzer, 1978), but they typically revolve around the assertion that it is mischievous to engage in abstract and ungrounded analysis (see Glaser & Strauss, 1967). Interactionism is distinguished by an antirationalist strain that prohibits its own systematic presentation. My very effort (Rock, 1979) to impose order on the position runs counter to the fundamental principles upon which it rests.

Any sympathetic search for the components of this perspective must thus proceed to the substantive writings of its adherents. It can rarely be found in a pure form. Since little attention has been paid to the construction of a consistent and contained paradigm, interactionism is fused at the margins with ethology (a term that has come to mean the study of basic organizational similarities between animal and human groups); ethnomethodology (the analysis of the procedures that men routinely employ to create social items); conflict theory; phenomenology (in its American sense an adaptation of the work of Alfred Schutz on the structures of social appearance); and formalism (a sociological emphasis upon the analytic importance

---

[1]I am indebted to Peter Manning for his help in the preparation of this chapter.

33

of the forms of social life). Yet a unity of convention, style, rhetoric, and vision can be teased from the corpus of interactionist studies. That unity is marked by a concern with what is conceived to be *real* in social affairs. Interactionism is informed by the effort to fashion an analysis that does not violate its understanding of social reality. It is currently phrased in the language of "faithfulness," "naturalism," and "humaneness." While that language has not always been used, even the earliest interactionist writings reveal a highly developed sensibility.

THE INTERACTIONIST MODEL OF THE SOCIAL WORLD

All reality is infinitely reducible, and social reality is peculiarly susceptible to endless reduction. The "individual" is no more real than "society" and no less real than the atom (Simmel, 1950: 6-7.) Any discipline's resolution of what constitutes its real subject matter is therefore characterized by some arbitrariness. In part that resolution may be determined by pragmatic criteria. Certain problems must be solved and their solution demands the evolution of a particular vocabulary and a particular definition of what comprises viable knowledge. In part, it may be determined by a sense of what is plausible and fitting. The aesthetic component of any perspective conveys a sense of appropriateness and rightness which can never be entirely defended against hostile outsiders.

Although interactionism has centered on many seemingly pragmatic issues (see Hughes, 1971; Becker, 1971; and Huber, 1973), its chief concerns have been scholastic. They have been devoted to the construction of a model of man that meets aesthetic canons (McCall & Simmons, 1978). Humans are conceived to possess distinctive attributes that cannot be properly neglected. Their lives, their projects, and their world are symbolically ordered. They do not confront a universe of "raw data" or of mechanical forces and reactions, but one compounded out of processes and phenomena upon which they bestow meaning. In a sense, class, the family, deviancy, and the church have no autonomous existence apart from their enactment and recognition in the daily lives of people. However constraining they may be, they are not parts of some independent order of events.

All sociology must thus be a sociology of knowledge, because it is an interpretation of interpretations. Sociologists cannot pretend to have dealings with a reality that is entirely of their own making. The methodological implications of this position are clear. The basic objects of sociological inquiry are brought into being through the organized workings of people's symbolic capacity. No adequate analysis of those objects can take place without some reconstruction of the sense people make of their world. They do not cope with situations but with their definitions of those situations. These are basic generic themes of the perspective.

Reflecting its model of humanity, interactionism specifies three fundamental features of the collective life. First, people can make reflexive use of
the symbols they employ. They can interpret and unravel the meanings of
events without merely reacting to them. Second, people are symbolic objects
to themselves. They construct, judge, and modify themselves as social
entities. It is to these selves that indications are made about the significance
of the settings in which they are anchored. Third, perspectives and plans
emerge out of the interplay between a socially constituted self and a socially
constituted environment. In turn they flow back into the social world and
change it. Selves and settings are lent an additional structure by their
location in time. They are awarded biographies, and their emergent properties are traced to define a range of possible futures. The unfolding present
continually recasts the meaning of the past and continually transforms
anticipations of the future.

Symbolism encapsulates, recapitulates, and rehearses. It permits people
to experiment with the world in their imagination. It also has the paradoxical
quality of being collaboratively sustained and of allowing sustained collaboration. The social world is always in the making. People collectively
negotiate, affirm, and challenge the meanings of themselves and their
activities: common purposes can be realized or obstructed in an orderly
fashion; identities can be offered for recognition; and accounts of behavior
can be supported or rejected. Selves and performances (as concerted displays
of those selves) are constantly being reflected and refracted in the responses
of others. In this negotiation of what passes for real in society, social structure
and the outlines of the possible are built up and maintained. Such practices
translate a potentially meaningless world into an entity that appears patterned and intelligible. The social facts generated by what Durkheim called
the "collective representations" endow social life with a concreteness and
organization, but it is an organization that is created, sustained, and
destroyed in everyday interaction.

Dwelling almost entirely on America, interactionism has not yet acknowledged the existence of any one symbolic canopy that embraces the
whole of social life. Territorial diversity, structural heterogeneity, and the
spatial ordering of intimacy and social distance combine to produce a
multiplicity of social worlds (see Lemert, 1967, chap. 1). Society is composed
of innumerable symbolic universes that are variously in conflict, coexistence,
symbiosis, or harmony with one another. The worlds of the pimp, real estate
agent, farmer, boxer, and schoolteacher have their unique contours and
patterns of articulation with other worlds. People are rarely members of
single groups alone. Their lives consist of many crossings of boundaries,
attempts to reconcile disparate stances, and efforts to conceal or reveal
significant affiliations (see Goffman, 1968). They oscillate between experiencing themselves as insiders and outsiders, participants and observers,
alienated and attached. Such oscillations enhance reflexivity by periodically

forcing them to manage the unfamiliar. In their resolution of these problems of symbolic manipulation, social reality is opened up to further possibilities of reformulation.

The complexity and openness of social performances have been considered compelling reasons for the adoption of its distinctive method—participant observation—which the interactionists employ to capture information (Ritzer, 1975: 125-126). In participant observation sociologists use themselves as instruments to cut into the variety and nuances of meaning that organize any activity. It is only by locating themselves in the flow of social process that sociologists can manage to witness and experience the matters that generate action. Other research techniques are thought to be excessively insensitive and clumsy in their response to the social world, especially in the initial stages of research (Blumer, 1969a: 24-27).

The transformations and permanence of symbolism are taken to be the appropriate subject matter of sociology. Yet there are influential spheres outside the symbolic life that are also granted an uneasy recognition. There are processes and phenomena that are apprehended through symbolism but do not exist in symbolism alone. The biological changes undergone during the life cycle (Hughes, 1971, chap. 13); the effects of organic disorder (Scheff, 1966; Manning & Fabrega, 1972); and the impact of the seasons (Hughes, 1971, chap. 13) cannot be experienced without imagery, but they are not merely imagery. There are the relations between them and the development of social life that can be only uncertainly understood. Made manifest in symbols, they shape perspectives through which they are perceived with a changed understanding. Illness may be a socially constructed status, but interactionism does not treat it solely as symbolic artifice.

Not all is equally open to negotiation within the social world itself. Enduring and central structures may increasingly resemble parts of some natural order (Simmel, 1950: 10-11). Recurrent transactions can generate perspectives that come to be taken for granted. What everyone else assumes can appear as objectively rooted, that is detached from any particular authorship (Scheff, 1967). Symbols themselves have different capacities to mobilize sentiments of respect, fear, or admiration. Symbolism may thus become resistant to individual or collective efforts at redefinition. Any individual confronts an array of social realities: some of them seem fluid and responsive; others are recalcitrant; others are so silently presupposed that they cannot even be identified (Shibutani 1961). Much social action revolves around the reconciliation or management of these realities: small social worlds must present strategies for handling competing definitions of the situation (Denzin, 1970).

Social behavior is explained by the interactionists in terms of intertwined dialectical processes and stages. Change occurs not in simple chains of actions and reactions or of disorders and adjustments. Change is a complex series of fluid transformations. Old elements are continually being worked into new forms and combinations. Their novelty is an accomplishment of symbolism. The capacity of people to interpret the world enables them to synthesize contrasting or conflicting facets into new configurations, which in turn feed back into the world and present new possibilities of action, response, and understanding. It is in this sense that interactionism defines the social world as emergent, in a state of becoming. It denies the possibility of explanation by reference to a limited set of initial conditions, because those conditions do not exercise an unchanging influence of social process (Davis, 1963: 10). They undergo progressive translation over time. The causal effect of a condition may indeed be reversed at a later stage of development. Prediction cannot be built on a knowledge of original causes, because the causes themselves are transmuted in often unforeseeable ways. The past is endlessly reconstituted as the social world itself changes.

It is intellectually convenient to grasp such dialectical process as a sequence of stages, each emerging from its predecessor and each setting the possibilities of its successor (Park, 1937). Each stage is an unstable equilibrium that articulates a world of events in a new manner; what may affect the process at one point may not do so at another. Very few social phenomena are instantaneously produced out of the convergence of social forces. Rather, their "established" forms receive definition over time, and in their growth they are shaped by processes that are often neglected by sociologists working in other traditions (see Schur, 1963). Juvenile delinquency or marijuana use are not to be analyzed simply as the outcome of social disorganization, status frustration, functional adaptation, or conflict (see Cohen, 1965). Unlike the men spawned by Cadmus's teeth, they do not arise full grown. Conditions such as disorganization must be translated back into forms that have an identifiable bearing on the world of everyday meaning and experience. People live in that world, and with the materials provided by those forms they order, plan, and change their lives. Without that translation there must always be unexplicated leaps from the explanation to the thing that is being explained. The invocation of the dialectic animates what is otherwise a mechanical account of social action. Analyses resting on concepts of disorganization or functional adaptation cannot take meanings for granted, because the interplay between meanings generates structures that can never be predicted by those concepts alone.

SOME ANALYTIC FOCI

Interactionism addresses itself to four levels of dialectical process. It is concerned with (1) the ways in which the self renders its environment socially significant, is transformed by such a rendition, and construes the environment anew; (2) the way in which social worlds are built up by negotiated perspectives that continually redefine reality; (3) the manner in which social worlds influence one another and engender new constellations of meaning; and (4) the relationship between such worlds and the larger, overarching symbolism that lends some coherence to society. It is clear that these four levels are interdependent; that they represent no more than different analytic incisions into the one process.

A social world that is described as fluid and emergent cannot be neatly divided into discrete parts that are united by invariant relations. The symbolic interactionists define as tantamount to myth-making any attempt to generate theory that rests on an exhaustive catalog of nice distinctions among social phenomena. No sociological explanation at all can be possible unless affairs are momentarily frozen for inspection, but flux defies precise definition. In their effort to produce accounts that are faithful to what is considered importantly human, interactionists reject the construction of abstract, detailed descriptions such as those offered by computer simulations or mathematical models.

Social life has a vital, temporal organization that would be lost by a sociology focusing on social statics. While interactionism does not wholly discard the concept of social structure, its stress upon activity and process relegates ideas of structure to a most minor place (see Blumer, 1969b). It works instead upon descriptions of limited segments of social life whose evolution can be rendered intelligible. The career of a high school teacher (Becker, 1971), the organization of a ward for tuberculosis patients (Roth, 1963), the moral history of a taxi dancer (Cressey, 1932), and transactions between the police and juvenile delinquents (Werthman & Piliavin, 1967) present materials for the analysis of important facets of human behavior. They are explored to illuminate an elementary grammar of sociation, a grammar whose rules give order to the allocation of territorial rights, the programming of patients' futures, and the meeting of immigrant and native American. As I shall argue below, the specification of those rules not only makes a limited theorizing possible, it also represents the interactionist solution to the problems posed by examining constellations of meaning.

The selection of a low level of analytic magnification is another major consequence of treating symbolic matters as central to sociology. Symbolic interactionism attempts to relate the procedures that are routinely employed to build up social scenes. Any practice that invokes causes, forces, or principles that are too abstract from the actor's perspective or too removed from visible settings is held to lack persuasiveness. Persuasiveness would be restored only by a meticulous documentation of the stages that intervene between the unobservable and the observable. Class conflict, social integration, or international relations can never be adequately comprehended at this, the phenomenal level. Although people may incorporate symbolic conceptions of these abstract states into their lives, it is only as symbolism that they can receive legitimate attention (see Edelman, 1971).

It is a further consequence of adopting such a level of magnification that interactionism commends a reluctance to generalize features of social worlds. A microsociological focus transforms society into a mosaic of unique configurations of events and meanings. Observed in detail, any social scene reveals structures and contours that can never be wholly reproduced elsewhere.

Perspectives, meanings, and identities are inextricably anchored in their contexts. A man praying, fighting, or drinking receives social significance from the setting of his behavior. Perspectives form and are formed by the social reality of other perspectives. Over time the progressive synthesis and elaboration of meanings that distinguish any enduring relationship will create an organization of beliefs that is largely unique. The prostitute does not only play a different role from that of the fishmonger, she is the inhabitant of a different world. Some of people's behavior may be explained by alluding to a community of economic experience, common problems in dealing with customers, and difficulties of handling competition. Yet competition, customers, and economic exchange are situationally defined and have no exact symbolic equivalence in the worlds of the fishmongers and prostitutes. Sociological analysis must defer to this lack of equivalence, but it must also recognize some correspondence between the constitutions of different worlds, however unmeasurable and problematic that correspondence might be. The only alternative is the virtual abandonment of attempts to understand social activity; a slumping back into a torpor of relativism; and the building of a Tower of Babel in which each social world is awarded its own untranslatable language. The very use of terms such as *prostitute*, *fishmonger*, *exchange*, and *competition* affirms the belief that some social properties *are* generalizable.

The interactionists respond to this central dilemma of the sociology of knowledge by resorting to a disciplined use of "sensitizing concepts" (Blumer, 1969c). Such concepts represent the loosest of ideal-types which receive modification and refinement as soon as they are applied in substantive analysis. Thus, *prostitute* and *fishmonger* are given a rudimentary definition that is increasingly amplified as the details of their social worlds are made known. When the prostitute is again extricated from her context and treated as an instance of a general type, the amplified detail surrounding her must be discarded until it can be established that it necessarily and invariably accompanies prostitution. Sensitizing concepts can never be the components of a grand theory until our ignorance of the social world is largely dispelled.

As a consequence of its emphasis upon the emergent and the unique, interactionism recognizes two distinct spheres of knowledge. A knowledge *of* events flows from a specific refocusing of attention that renders them problematic. They become studied with a diligence and a curiosity that cannot be extended to all everyday affairs. A knowledge *about* events enables us to accommodate them in our lives, but it is neither detailed nor based upon rigorous examination (James, 1910). Knowledge about social life serves most of our practical purposes well enough. However, it cannot act as a sure foundation upon which to erect a viable sociology. What men take for granted or what some authority ratifies cannot stand without scientific support. Hence, Becker remarks that his work with Everett Hughes taught him to be "skeptical of conventional wisdom; just because everyone thinks something is so does not make it so. At the same time, one must not dismiss conventional wisdom altogether, but rather see it as one of the elements people use in interpreting their experience and organizing their own actions." (Becker, 1968: 272). Common sense suppositions become a resource as well as a problematic entity to be explained, but they cannot be taken as a definitive account of the nature of the social world.

Abundant ideas structure our common sense thinking. Social class, nationality, imperialism, and the state are structures that shape our understanding. They occupy a legitimate place in any analysis that allots them a role in ordering the symbolic contours of society (Rock, 1973). There are, however, no immediate grounds for accepting them as sociologically plausible. They are not always scientifically accredited, and when they *are* subjected to a critical examination, many are demonstrably inadequate by interactionist criteria. Whatever their forcefulness may be at the level of rhetoric or practical utility, our knowledge of the phenomena they describe is generally so meagre that they must occupy, at best, a tentative and suspect status in explanation. Moreover, they are often so abstract that they cannot be readily anchored in identifiable and observable phenomena. The procedures used to infer them from the familiar and the visible are frequently undiscussed and unexplained.

Common sense knowledge provides a serviceable guide to the conduct of our lives. Nevertheless, it typically defies explication and systematization. We make reasonable inferences about social organization, but we cannot precisely describe their origins and nature. In consequence, knowledge about phenomena can do no more than generate the sensitizing concepts that become most uncommon-sensical in use. Analysts mediate the contradictions between their concepts and the social reality they seek to elucidate.

Rather than proceed to discuss massive social processes, interactionism serially attends to fragments of social life in the attempts to enlarge scientific knowledge. It enjoins its adherents to adopt a posture of humility before a world that is defined as more mysterious and more recalcitrant than is commonly supposed. Irony, subtlety, and uniqueness so abound that the mere logical extrapolation of models is not a reliable style of discovery. Indeed, Hughes asserts that knowledge of an institution simply produces knowledge about institutions as a sociological class (Hughes, 1942). Detailed understanding cannot be generalized without warrant. Interactionism thus proposes a Cartesian exploration of social life. Grand schemes must be surrendered to the gradual delineation of areas of relatively certain knowledge. However pressing social or intellectual problems may be, they cannot be discussed unless they are amenable to scientific inquiry.

Symbolic interactionism does not explain everyday social process by locating it in a system of enveloping structures. It does not treat the master abstractions of sociological theory as a reservoir from which hypotheses can be deduced. Rather, it builds its conceptions of society up from modest analyses of a host of minor occurrences.

This strategy of limited induction is an integral part of the interactionist conception as to what constitutes the nature of adequate knowledge. By practicing a systematic distrust of what passes for authoritative understanding, interactionism cannot take for granted the accounts that are offered by common sense knowledge. A rejection of most a priori classifications and explanations forces interactionists to become strangers to even the most familiar scenes. They must regard as anthropologically bizarre and problematic what others take to be commonplace. The interpretations of others become ethnographic data rather than competing sociologies. The assumption of this intellectual position makes only the most tentative categorizations possible. Each social event must be viewed as if it were utterly novel; as if its connections with other events were as yet undemonstrated; and as if its developments were as yet uncharted.

This strategy becomes even more compelling in a sociology that cannot invoke deep structures to further analysis. Such a sociology is thrown back on a detailing of the myriad ways in which social phenomena present themselves. The diversity and richness of the world of appearances do not readily lend themselves to classification. The uniqueness of each event must be somehow accommodated in a scheme that necessarily depends on the tracing of formal similarities among phenomena (Blumer, 1969). It is only by inferring unobservable uniformities that elaborate typologies can be constructed.

There is a final bar to the development of a systematic interactionist sociology. Any extended account of behavior is given vitality by a set of stylistic conventions that rest on persuasive metaphor. The thematic core of all sociological models is structured around imagery that conjures up tangible and familiar processes. Explanation must apparently portray social life as if it were a mathematical system, an organism, a human being, a conflict between warring individuals, a cybernetic process, or a dispute between scholars. It is this last model, the analogy of a ritual confrontation between schoolmen, that furnishes interactionism with its own dialectical imagery.

Each dominant model is governed by a logic that is peculiar to itself. Mathematical transformations are not akin to the equilibrating mechanisms of an organism. A logic may be simply inappropriate when it is applied to processes for which it was never designed. The internal consistency and plausibility of a model are no indication of the scope of its generalizability. When a phenomenon is observed through the perspectives provided by the model, features that are incongruent are typically thrown out of focus or given some logically coherent explanation. As Kenneth Burke has observed, a way of seeing is always a way of not seeing. Thus, when society is likened to a person, a series of mechanical interactions, or a mathematical system, there is always a risk that what is taken to be true of the model will also be taken as true of society itself.

The greater the level of analytic abstraction, the more central must animating imagery become. All imagery is capable of providing illumination, but it must be checked by a set of operations that can assess how well it fits what it portrays. Since society is not fundamentally regulated by a mathematical, cybernetic, or organic logic, the models upon which those logics are based must be employed most gingerly.

Sociology is not yet buttressed by a viable set of tests of correspondence. It is bedeviled by the tendency to mistake logical coherence for rigorous demonstration. The interactionists maintain that the abstract workings of metaphorical models have so problematic a relationship to those of the social world that they should be rejected as a guide. Unless it can be shown that in all relevant respects there is a close relationship, highly abstract expositions should be discarded (Brittan, 1973). Clearly, symbolic interactionism is constrained to employ its own metaphor, but it does so with circumspection.

Much of what I have described as the basics of interactionism remains a series of latent preoccupations. The perspective constantly veers toward proclaiming the impossibility of the sociological enterprise. It is indeed conceivable that explicit attention is not given to these themes because, paradoxically, analysis can flow only when they are neglected.

Interactionism confronts the difficulties of explaining a fluid, uncertain world of meanings by resorting to a number of intellectual devices. Those devices include the sensitizing concept, a rejection of grand theory, an emphasis upon restrained induction, and the use of a logic that is peculiarly suitable to symbolic transactions. Nevertheless, there must be some systematization and analysis that violates what is thought to be socially "real." Sociology cannot work solely with meanings and understandings that enjoy a currency in everyday life. Processes and connections that are not apprehended by common sense knowledge must be distinguished. Were they not, there would be no legitimate place for the sociologist, and any person undergoing an experience would be capable of explaining it more fully than an observer.

Interactionism manages the issues presented by the uniqueness of events and the socially situated nature of meanings by asserting the supremacy of form over content. It employs a modified version of Simmel's formal sociology (Simmel, 1950). The intellectual lineage back to Simmel is reasonably clear: Robert Park, one of the progenitors of interactionism, studied under him, and there are references to the utility of studying social forms throughout interactionist writings (Levine, 1971).

The social world may be viewed as an agglomerate of unique phenomena that are under the sway of their own discrete laws of development. At an extreme the appropriate response to such a conception is the abandonment of sociology. There can be no generalization, prediction, or comparison. The English, French, Cuban, and American revolutions would thus be constituted by their own peculiar properties which were entirely idiosyncratic. Any explanation that attempts to embrace them all must molest them. Indeed, it would be improper to refer to them as instances of a category called revolution at all.

However, the world may also be viewed as an arena in which a few social forms combine and interact to create an infinite number of visible social scenes. Underlying a seeming distinctiveness may be found formal similarity. One form of sociation—conflict—can manifest itself in warfare, a rivalry between university departments, and in the breakdown of friendship. Another form—intimacy—can occur within a family, a battle unit, or a delinquent gang. Despite the fact that no single war will ever be exactly repeated or that no academic strife will ever take precisely the same course, there are sufficient regularities to permit viable generalization. Ironically, a sociology that is wedded to the appreciation of meaning must relegate meaning to a secondary place.

Interactionism can be read as the attempt to construct a dictionary of social forms. It provides a set of categories rather than a systematic theory. Unlike Simmel's own mathematical and geometrical imagery, the metaphors generating these interactionist forms have been ethological, (Goffman, 1971), ecological (Park, 1936), and theatrical (Messinger et al., 1962). The forms of symbiosis (Park, 1939), the career (Hughes, 1971), commitment (Becker, 1971), and role (Goffman, 1961) litter analysis. They are collated and related to manufacture descriptions of an elementary social order that is held to structure all the apparent flux of society. It is in the display of these forms that social life is realized. Goffman's discussion of the etiquette that enables people to meet, interact, and part; Becker's analysis of the commitments that bind people to the routine and the orderly; Hughes' and Glaser and Strauss' conception of the career as a basic form of organized process, are all parts of a depiction of society as relatively stable and patterned. For the interactionist such forms represent the simple particles of sociation. A listing of their properties can only contribute to an understanding of what makes social life fundamentally possible.

Forms can be interpreted as enjoying a life that is relatively independent of the specific circumstances of their appearance. The situated detail of a war is analytically separate from the manner in which the form of conflict typically develops. There is a discernible logic to the unfolding of a conflict or a career; this logic can be detected among the innumerable and diverse instances in which it is displayed. Sociology is, at its most basic, devoted to the deciphering of that logic of the pure principles of sociation.

There is obviously a constant tension between this formalism and the other themes of interactionism (Rock, 1973). Formalism is relatively inattentive to the symbolic content of activity. But it is an inevitable mode of analysis which partially reconciles the difficulties posed by studying what is both unique and general. Interactionists handle the tension largely by grounding their discussion in a series of detailed ethnographies. They minutely describe the features of the world they are observing, report the language and symbols that the world's inhabitants themselves employ, and give little space to abstract reasoning of their own. These conventions of style can create an ambience that conveys something of the subjective life of that world. The formalist analysis is then unobtrusively woven into the larger reporting so that it may retain some semblance of intimate connectedness to that subjective life. Much interactionist writing is thus governed by a stylistic delicacy that suggests a faithfulness actually lacking. The rhetoric and phrasing practiced by the members of the school is as important as the more obviously cerebral features of their work.

It is in this sense that a successful piece of symbolic interactionism is prestigious art, blending artifice and illusion with the trappings of simplicity and naturalism. As an artistic accomplishment, it defies analytic dismemberment. Its basic appeal is to the sensibilities of its readers, being capable of enlightening them without appearing to radically disfigure the social life it describes.

RESERVATIONS

In this chapter I have attempted to trace what I understand to be the principal outlines of the interactionist perspective. Although it is evident that many symbolic interactionist assertions can be challenged, I have not chosen to do this. Yet I have four reservations that touch upon some themes in the central argument of the school. They concern the seeming purposelessness of much interactionist work; the somewhat pontifical statements of what represents social reality; the strictures concerning the impossibility of prediction; and the systematic reticence to explore what is the core of interactionism, the nature of symbols and symbolization.

Without a reasonably clear set of criteria to delineate what constitutes a satisfactory answer to a sociological problem, analysis can proceed indefinitely and without direction. An aesthetic solution can be endlessly elaborated and endlessly found wanting by aesthetic tests. Description can become ever more refined with no effective check on its growth. The absence of a pragmatic canon is actually the absence of any canon. The scholastic pursuit of understanding is not subject to any disciplining at all. The basic contradiction of interactionism is that any analysis will molest its objects, and further, ameliorating analysis works even more damage. Much of the formlessness of the school's activity can be attributed to the lack of any of the organizing principles that guide research. The corpus of interactionist works contains much redundancy and little purposeful exploration. In one sense symbolic interactionism suffers from a critical absence of problems.

Second, as Simmel has argued, all phenomena are the products of the synthesizing and creative work of their observer. While it is proper to acknowledge the necessity of treating actors' interpretations as central, those interpretations do not enjoy a monopoly over the definition of sociological reality. The special province of sociology is the examination of unintended consequences. Such consequences do not necessarily receive full recognition by those whom they affect. Rather, it is the business of the sociologist to attend to the effects of action that are unanticipated and perhaps not understood by the actor. In so doing the sociologist maps out an order of processes that are inevitably foreign to everyday understanding. This order has a reality that is in important respects as valid as that conjured by common sense. Any assessment of the level of abstraction at which this order is constructed must be governed by largely pragmatic criteria. The aesthetic test is again uninformative, because it cannot prescribe either the appropriate extent or the magnification of the perspective that is adopted. Once it is conceded that there is an infinite number of alternative realities rather than one master reality, more substantial reason must be advanced for the shunning of abstraction.

The interactionist antipathy to theoretical formalization also flows from its assertion that initial conditions can never provide the kind of knowledge necessary for prediction. Qualitative transformations are held to alter the development of social process so that only retrospective understanding is possible. It may nevertheless be argued that the assembling of a sufficient number of cases should permit the substitution of inductive for deductive reasoning. If social life is orderly and patterned, the same initial conditions will therefore give rise to the same developments. The mere recognition of those conditions would then warrant reasonable anticipations about their future states.

It may be further argued that the elaborate apparatus of interpretative inquiry could play a more restricted role in interactionist analysis. The minute dynamics of every process do not require listing if the generic forms of processes can be identified. The interior life of a deviant career need not be carefully specified if the career can be sensibly expected to undergo a number of predictable evolutions. Interactionism's resort to formalism prepared the possibility of phenomenologically external accounts of action. The fond chronicling of subjective worlds may be prompted more by the aesthetic satisfaction that is achieved than by any rigorously intellectual demands.

Finally, interactionism is marred by its failure to embark upon a comprehensive examination of what is meant by meaning, symbolism, definition of the situation, and the like. The school's central concepts are introduced as if they were self-evident in their implications. Far from being translucent, they mirror little of the analytic elusiveness and subtlety of the events and phenomena they purport to describe. The structure of interpretative activity is inordinately complex. They depend upon the simultaneous operation of a number of semantic processes that grasp and create the significance of gestures, speech, body displays, physical props, the juxtaposition of phenomena with particular contexts, the temporal ordering of communication, and so on. This whole array cannot be usefully subsumed under the concept of symbolic activity and then dismissed. Although some work has been devoted to the exploration of these matters, the interactionists have not undertaken systematic, concerted analysis to illuminate what is pivotal to their whole conception of social behavior.

Further, the models of symbolic worlds that enjoy currency in the school rarely reflect the densely textured and multitiered nature of social reality. That style of analysis is surrendered in favor of the prizing out of simple social forms from the more recalcitrant whole. Parsimony makes such work attractive, but it would be misleading to assume that simplicity adequately characterizes forms or that the fabric of social life is not correspondingly misrepresented. Elegance and simplicity are aesthetic considerations in research, but they are qualities that conflict with the injunction to faithfully replicate social reality.

REFERENCES

Becker, H. Preface to History, culture, and subjective experience. In H. Becker et al (Eds.), *Institutions and the person*. Chicago: Aldine, 1968.

Becker, H. *Sociological work*. London: Allen Lane, 1971.

Blumer, H. The methodological position of symbolic interactionism. In *Symbolic interactionism*. Englewood Cliffs, N.J.: Prentice-Hall, 1969. (a)

Blumer, H. Sociological implications of the thought of George Herbert Mead. In *Symbolic interactionism. Ibid.* (b)

Blumer, H. What is wrong with social theory? In *Symbolic interactionism. Ibid.*(c)

Brittan, A. *Meanings and situations*. London: Routledge and Kegan Paul, 1973.

Cohen, A. The sociology of the deviant act. *American Sociological Review*, 1965, *30*.

Cressey, P. *The taxi-dance hall*. Chicago: University of Chicago Press, 1932.

Davis, F. *Passage through crisis*. Indianapolis: Bobbs-Merrill, 1963.

Denzin, N. Rules of conduct and the study of deviant behavior. In J. Douglas (Ed.), *Deviance and respectability*. New York: Basic Books, 1970.

Edelman, M. *Politics as symbolic action*. Chicago: Markham, 1971.

Glaser, B. & Strauss, A. *The discovery of grounded theory*. Chicago: Aldine, 1967.

Goffman, E. Role-distance. In *Encounters*. Indianapolis: Bobbs-Merrill, 1961.

Goffman, E. *Stigma*. Harmondsworth: Penguin Books, 1968.

Goffman, E. *Relations in public*. London: Allen Lane, 1971.

Huber, J. Symbolic interaction as a pragmatic perspective: The bias of emergent theory. *Americay Sociological Review,* 1973, 38 (April).

Hughes, E. The study of institutions. *Social Forces,* 1942, 20.

Hughes, E. *The sociological eye.* Chicago: Aldine-Atherton, 1971.

James, W. *Psychology.* New York: Holt, 1910.

Lemert, E. *Human deviance, social problems, and social control.* Englewood Cliffs, N.J.: Prentice-Hall, 1967.

Levine, D. Introduction to Georg Simmel, *On Individuality and social forms.* Chicago: University of Chicago Press, 1971.

Manning, P., & Fabrega, H. Disease, illness, and deviant careers." In R. Scott and J. Douglas (Eds.), *Theoretical perspectives on deviance.* New York: Basic Books, 1972.

Mannis, J. G., & Meltzer, B. N. *Symbolic interaction:* A reader in social psychology (3rd ed.). Boston: Allyn & Bacon, 1978.

McCall, G. J., & Simmons, J. L. *Identities and interactions* (2nd ed.) New York: Free Press, 1978.

Messinger, S., et al. Life as theater. *Sociometry,* 1962. 25.

Park, R. Human ecology. *American Journal of Sociology,* 1936, *42.*

Park, R. Introduction to R. Adams, *Interracial marriage in Hawaii.* New York: Macmillan, 1937.

Park, R. Symbiosis and socialization. *American Journal of Sociology,* 1939, *45.*

Ritzer, G. *Sociology: A multiple paradigm science.* Boston: Allyn & Bacon, 1975.

Rock, P. Phenomenalism and essentialism in the sociology of deviancy. *Sociology,* 1973, 7.

Rock, P. *The making of symbolic interactionism.* London: Macmillan, 1979.

Roth, J. *Timetables.* Indianapolis: Bobbs-Merrill, 1963.

Scheff, T. *Being mentally ill.* Chicago: Aldine, 1966.

Scheff, T. Toward a sociological model of consensus. *American Sociological Review,* 1964, 32.

Schur, E. *Narcotic addiction in Britain and America.* London: Tavistock, 1963.

Shibutani, T. *Society and personality.* Englewood Cliffs, N.J.: Prentice-Hall, 1961.

Shibutani, T. *Human nature and collective behavior.* Englewood Cliffs, N.J.: Prentice-Hall, 1970.

Simmel, G. The field of sociology. In K. Wolff (Ed.), *The Sociology of Georg Simmel,* New York: Free Press, 1950.

Werthman, C., & Piliavin, I. Gang members and the police. In D. Bordua (Ed.), *The police.* New York: John Wiley, 1967.

Chapter Two
Qualitative field methods[1]

DAVID O. ARNOLD

Once upon a time, on a dark and chilly night, a man was searching for something under a streetlight. A policeman noticed him and asked what the trouble was. "I lost my keys," replied the man. So for the next half-hour the officer helped him search under the streetlight for the lost keys. Finally the policeman asked the man, "Are you sure you lost them here?" "Oh, no, I didn't lose them here, I lost them in the alley around the corner." "Then why in hell haven't you been looking over there?" demanded the cop. "Because there isn't any light over there," was the man's reply.

The social sciences have a number of powerful streetlights. However, much of what we are looking for is located in dark alleys. If social research is to fulfill its potential, we will have to search for the keys to social phenomena wherever they may be. If there is no streetlight there, we'll just have to use a flashlight or even matches; it won't do us any more good to limit our investigations to the few brightly lit areas than it did the gentlemen in the above story.

Our lights are the various methods of social research. Some of them are quite bright; others cast flickering shadows at best. But our problem lies not so much in the varying strength of our lights as in how we select those with which we conduct our searches. Because there is such a great variation in the strength of the various techniques available to social scientists, it has been very tempting to select the most powerful ones and to use them for all of our research. Thus, we have many social scientists who do only such research as can be carried out in a small-group laboratory using strict methods of matching, randomization, control groups, one-way mirrors, videotapes, quantitative measures of interaction, etc. Even more researchers never consider studying something if it can't be done by conducting a survey. They develop precise definitions of the population of interest, draw a careful random sample, send out trained interviewers with interview schedules containing standardized attitude scales and other items, and then analyze the data using multivariate statistical techniques, aided by the latest computer facilities and programs. I am not suggesting that these techniques are not as good as their proponents claim.[2] What I am suggesting is that techniques such as these are like carbon arc streetlights: when they are good, they are very, very good, but when they are not, they are horrid. Experimental designs, for example, require researchers to limit their investigations to one or just a very few causal variables in a given study. But social reality is much more complex than that, and at times we must also look at the world in its multivariabled confusion. The fact that we'll have to investigate it with less powerful lights, such as historical analysis, unstructured interviewing, participant observation, or the like, should not deter us.

The choice of a research method should be based on a rational evaluation of ends and means, not on a personal commitment to a particular technique. A technician might properly have a commitment to a particular research technique; the commitment of social researchers must be to theoretical and substantive concerns. Unfortunately, however, many researchers have failed to follow up a concern because they were one-method people, and that method did not suit that concern. Others have continued to utilize their one method in situations where another method would be better and where sticking to a less appropriate method forced a distortion of the concern itself.

Related to this situation we find social researchers taking moral stands for or against certain techniques. Some, for instance, see certain high-powered techniques being used to carry out trivial research,[3] and because they want to do nontrivial research, believe they can't utilize those techniques. Our research methods are tools, and should be viewed the same way carpenters view their tools. They do not get hung up on a single tool and proceed to build only what can be built with that tool. Carpentry has no "bench saw-ists" or "claw hammer-ers" to correspond with our participant observers and survey researchers. Carpenters determine what they intend to construct and then use whatever tools are most suited to the job. The alternative position is analogous to a carpenter noticing that some people using bench saws are turning out poor quality cabinets, and concluding that since s/he wants to construct first-rate cabinets s/he will not even learn how to use a bench saw, but instead will work solely with a pocket knife and a keyhole saw. This sort of cart-before-the-horse carpentry is ridiculous, but no more so than our "methods-before-the-problem" social research.

To avoid this error, it is best not to plunge into instructions on how to conduct qualitative field research. Before you do any field work—or any other kind of research, for that matter—it is essential that you consider the advantages and disadvantages of any method under consideration for the questions at hand, and be able to determine the suitability of each technique that might be employed. Even if you are not planning to carry out a research project, but intend merely to read a report of someone else's research, examination of these methodological considerations is crucial if you are to adequately evaluate what you read. Thus, I will start by defining qualitative field methods, setting this definition in the context of other methods and of social research goals, and then examining the advantages and drawbacks of fieldwork, considering when the approach is appropriate. After examination of these considerations, I will discuss the everyday practicalities of fieldwork, such as note-taking, data analysis, and the like.

TYPES OF RESEARCH METHODS

The most basic distinction between types of research methods is not that between qualitative and quantitative research, but that between using available data and collecting new data. Research that utilizes new data is typically more time-consuming, more complex, and more expensive. On the other hand it allows greater flexibility, since such researchers aren't limited to analyzing such data as happens to be available, nor are they limited to someone else's conceptualization of the problem or of specific components of the problem. Thus, again we have not a case of better and worse but of strength and limitation which must be evaluated with respect to the particular research problem at hand.

Riley (1963: 21) points out that available data includes both "raw materials not originally intended for research purposes at all," and "systematically organized data which may be analyzed for your new objective." The range of sources of available data is limited only by the researcher's imagination. Available data can be used to carry out cross-cultural research, which compares total societies (for example, the Human Relations Area Files, which classified the anthropological research of hundreds of different cultures by numerous substantive topics). They can also be used to compare subunits of total societies, such as regions, communities, etc.—U.S. Census materials are especially useful in this regard—and to make comparisons between individuals—secondary analysis of survey data is a popular method here. For some research questions examination of current documents or analysis of historical materials is useful. For recorded forms of communication, including speeches, newspaper articles, song lyrics, etc., content analysis is suitable. However, while all of these available data techniques can be helpful in dealing with certain questions, they tend to be quite limited. Occasionally, an entire study can be built around one of them, but their greatest effectiveness usually is as an adjunct to a study whose primary data source is original for the specific purpose at hand. Since most available data techniques are by comparison so easy and inexpensive to use, they can be drawn upon as a carpenter draws upon plastic wood and corner braces to fill in small gaps and add additional support to the construction.

This leaves us with the collection of new data as our main source of information for answering social research questions. The three main sources of new data are interviewing, observation, and experimentation, although there are a number of more specialized techniques. Experimentation involves manipulating some aspect of what is being studied to determine its impact on other aspects. While experiments in social research are usually conducted in a laboratory setting, they can also be carried out in a "natural" setting, where, except for the experimental manipulation, things are as they would be were no research being conducted.[4]

In contrast to experimentation, interviewing and observation (except when an adjunct to experimental research) attempt to study the social world "as it really is," uninfluenced by the researcher. When interviewing, we intrude only to ask questions. When observing, we don't even intrude that much. But in either case we go out into the field in an attempt to find out what is going on. Trained field researchers can see things the participants themselves may not perceive. They can also see things that the participants do perceive, but which, for one reason or another, the researcher chooses to learn directly. By interviewing researchers can find out things that aren't amenable to observation (internal states such as attitudes, information about past events), as well as things that could be observed but which are easier to learn about by asking. Thus, the choice among types of new data is dependent upon what the researcher wants to find out. If the concern is with the effects of changes in one of two variables, an experiment is called for. A study of attitudes necessitates interviewing. A delineation of the patterning of norms and social behavior of an organization, community, or other group of people calls for an observational study.

But this is not the whole picture, and here is where the qualitative-quantitative distinction becomes relevant—or more correctly, the unstructured-structured distinction, since the qualitative-quantitative dichotomy actually flows from this. Without even thinking of social research, what do "structured" and "unstructured" bring to mind? Structured is organized, neat, clean, everything in its place, easy to cope with. Therefore, structured is good and unstructured is bad—right? Wrong. Although they have often been evaluated in this way, it is not the best way to approach the issue. Before we can appropriately utilize highly structured research methods, two conditions must be met: (1) the phenomenon we wish to study must be highly structured, and (2) we must have a clear picture of what that structure is. The more we study human social life, the more we find that the first condition holds in a surprising range of instances. But the state of such fields as sociology, anthropology, political science, social psychology, is such that the second condition is truly met but rarely. True, we can often impose structure, forcing a set of categories on our objects of study, but then what we "learn" is shaped as much by the way we study it as by what it is really like.

This is not to say that the conditions are never met: For many topics of investigation they are at least met sufficiently so that any distortion resulting from structured techniques is minimal. The most obvious instance is preelection polling. The categories are clearly established and are known equally to those being studied and those studying them. There are also a number of other areas for which attitudes, and in some cases behavior, can be ascertained by asking structured questions. There are also a few areas of behavior for which highly structured methods of observing and recording are possible, as Robert Bales' pioneering work with categories of group interaction (1950) has demonstrated.

In these instances clearly delineated variables are studied, with data being accumulated in clearly demarcated categories. As a consequence precise numerical measurement and analysis is often possible, and even when it isn't, quantitative tabulation can be carried out, giving us results that are neat, clean, organized, and obtained with relative ease. Furthermore, because of the high degree of structure that runs through such a study and the precision afforded by statistics and other quantitative modes of data processing, the research consumer can double-check the producer. As a result, we don't have to take conclusions on faith; we can systematically evaluate the validity and reliability of research from a thorough reading of the report.

But what happens when either what we wish to study is not itself highly structured or, as occurs more frequently, when we don't yet know how structured it is or the precise manner in which its structure is manifested? Then, clearly, the methods we use to study it cannot be as structured. If we can structure our questions but do not know the form the answers will take, we might use a structured interview schedule with open-ended questions, which we can then code and, up to a point, subject to quantitative analysis. If we know only the general areas we wish to investigate but not the precise questions, we cannot introduce even this much structure into our methods.

This is where qualitative field methods enter the picture. True, they may be disorganized, messy, confused, and hard to cope with. But, like the pocket knife and keyhole saw of the carpenter, in some situations they provide the only viable way to build the finished product we seek. Furthermore, qualitative field methods provide a closeness and intimacy between researcher and subject matter that generates an excitement and satisfaction often missed by the social scientist who only views the world through the holes in IBM cards. And though things appear disorganized and confused along the way, the results, while most often not quantitative in format, can often be quite organized and structured. There is probably nothing as rewarding in social research as going into an apparently unordered and complex setting and, through hard work and perseverance, demonstrating in your research report that you were able to make sense out of it, that underneath the seeming disorder is a clear structure, a regular pattern of norms, behavior, etc.

Thus, in research involving interviewing or observation it doesn't really make sense to rank qualitative and quantitative methods. Each has its place, its advantages, and its rewards, and both are mutually complementary. Let's look more closely at the place of each. In the discussion above you might have gotten the impression from the example I used that there is some degree of affinity between interviewing and quantitative methods and between observation and qualitative methods. If I didn't give you this impression, let me give it to you now. But at the same time let me stress that it is only "some degree of affinity"; there is quantitative observation and there is qualitative interviewing, though they tend to occupy secondary roles.

The reason for these affinities is no accident. Language and categorization depend upon each other. Thus, when we think or speak, we customarily categorize. Indeed, we find it virtually impossible to speak, let alone think, without employing categories. Consequently, studies that involve interviewing deal with things that tend to be already structured categorically, whether they are asking about attitudes or about reportable (and thus perceived and thought about) behavior. Thus, interview studies tend to be in the form of quantitative surveys, with highly structured questions and answers, and to utilize high-speed, orderly tabulation and analysis of data. Where interviewing in social science research doesn't have these characteristics, it is usually because it is either supplementing a qualitative study, which is primarily observational, or it is directed at topics that lack one or both of the two conditions specified above: Either the topic is not highly enough structured or the investigator is not familiar enough with the structuring to structure data collection techniques to the same degree. In such cases the interviewee's responses are usually treated not so much as "answers" but as data to be subjected to the same sort of qualitative analysis undertaken on observational data.

Turning to the affinity between observation and qualitative methods, we find a mirror image of the interviewing-quantitative methods situation. While we can put behavior into categories with the aid of thought and language, the raw behavior itself is not manifested in categories. Categories used by researchers are imposed by them on the behavior at some stage of the investigation. For certain specialized purposes this can be done at the time the behavior is being observed, thereby permitting the entire endeavor to be conducted quantitatively.[5] But more often the behavior must first be observed and recorded in an uncategorized manner; only much later, after a great deal of such data have been collected and analyzed, can the investigator formulate categories that conform to the regularities that have been uncovered in the data.

It should be added that observation is not all visual—it is oral as well. Thus, observational studies involve studying verbal behavior too. But this verbal behavior differs from that encountered in interviewing in that it occurs naturally rather than in response to specific questions formulated by the researcher. This fact has two implications that are relevant to social research: (1) because it is formulated in response to concrete ongoing occurrences rather than in response to descriptive or explanatory questions, such "verbal behavior" (sociologese for "talk") is itself not as categorical as that collected by interviewing; (2) even where the talk is categorical (i.e., where it deals with classes of phenomena and thus is potentially amenable to quantitative treatment), investigators are unlikely to be fully aware of this fact until their research has proceeded further.

It should now be apparent that "qualitative field methods" refers to techniques for studying ongoing social life in its natural setting, that in doing this we study both verbal and nonverbal behavior, that the data are collected primarily by direct observation, although interviewing and written documents may also be utilized, and that the data are collected in relatively unstructured form, with any structure or order in the final report having emerged in the course of the analysis, rather than being present during the data-collection phase.

THE PLACE OF THEORY

Before we can get into the nuts-and-bolts, how-to-do-it of field research (or perhaps, in keeping with the carpentry analogy, the hammer-and-nails), we have to consider why the study is being conducted at all. This in turn requires that we consider why social research of any sort is done.

Sociologist Norman K. Denzin has argued that "the only justification for an empirical observation is the refinement, development, or refocussing of social theory" (1970: 2). The contrasting position, which is implicit in many of the ethnographies done by anthropologists, sociologists, and others, is that "everything that human beings do is important and is deserving of record, of entry into the legacy that we bequeath to unborn generations." This approach ignores the fact that we are physically incapable of recording everything and thus are necessarily selective, so that the only result of attempting to follow this dictum is that we give up the opportunity to exercise conscious, rational control over our decision-making activities. Denzin's approach is no more satisfactory, however, as it is predicated upon the erroneous assumptions that we are capable of perfect rationality, that serendipity cannot occur, and that nothing human beings do is interesting enough or important enough to justify recording for its own sake and for the possibility that at a future date it may turn out to have theoretical significance.

Why do we, in e. e. cummings' phrase, "commit social science"? The social sciences, in common with the physical and biological sciences, are motivated by four goals: description, explanation, prediction, and control. While there is a good deal of interplay among these (for example, an attempt at prediction that is partly successful and partly unsuccessful can lead to modifications and improvements in the description and explanation that led to the prediction), basically each successive goal is dependent upon the one before it. "Explanations" of law-breaking that accounted for crime on the basis of economic deprivation and deficient socialization among the poor collapsed when it was found that the "description" of crime as occurring overwhelmingly among the poor was a statistical artifact resulting from class biases in the institutions of social control. We need a reasonably accurate knowledge of anatomy before we can develop explanations of physiological functioning; we need physiological theories before we can engage in diagnosis; and we must be able to diagnose before we can cure.

The focus of research must be consistent with the state of knowledge in the field being investigated. If we already have a moderately valid social theory in some area, Denzin's suggestion that we not waste time building up more description, but rather design our research so as to refine, develop, or refocus that theory, appears reasonable. On the other hand, there are many areas of social life for which we still lack even the most rudimentary descriptive anatomies. In such instances it makes no sense to build upper stories on a nonexistent foundation; here we can follow the alternative view and do a more exploratory type of research, developing descriptions that will provide the basis for later explanations.

Since attempts at prediction and control of social phenomena, while properly based upon social research, are usually not actually built into the research, I won't pursue these further at this point.

A study is rarely pure description or pure explanation. A "what" study usually also makes some attempts to say "why," and a "why" study usually spells out "what" it is trying to explain. However, one of these goals usually predominates in any given study, and since which one it is will shape every stage of the research, the investigator must be clear about his goals from the start.

Qualitative field methods are well suited to describing organizations, groups, subcultures, and small communities. They are not well suited to describing total societies or cultures, far-flung or noninteracting categories of people, or particular delimited variables. Qualitative field methods are also quite useful for theory development in the same areas where they can provide descriptions. But once we move to the level of testing developed theories, they are of more limited usefulness. Once a theory has been developed, more structured techniques can usually be applied, and are typically more beneficial at this stage. However, qualitative field methods can still play a role here when used for the detailed analysis of deviant cases—that is, cases that don't fit the theory. This brings us to theory development again, since a frequent outcome of deviant case analysis is the modification or reformulation of the original theory.

In *Field Work: An Introduction to the Social Sciences* Buford Junker sets forth the following rule of thumb concerning the relative time typically required for the various phases of a field study. The actual observation occupies only one-sixth of the total time. (His estimates seem to be reasonably accurate; so if you estimate that a particular study will necessitate 100 hours in the field, you had better figure on close to four months of solid

40-hour weeks.) Recording one's observations tends to involve two hours at the typewriter for every hour in the field, or one-third; another third for analyzing all of this, and finally one-sixth for reporting or writing up the r, 1960: 12).

Other chapters in this book will familiarize you with the sequence of activities involved in other kinds of social research. In that context doesn't Junker's listing seem rather peculiar? A few years ago I completed an interview study ("survey") that, all told, took a little over three years (McGlothlin & Arnold, 1971). The first interviews were not conducted until the start of the study's second year. The entire first year had to be devoted to reviewing the literature, designing, pretesting, and revising the interview schedule, drawing the sample, and training the interviewers. But Junker seems to indicate that in contrast to the survey researcher, the field researcher starts right out collecting data. Why?

There are two reasons—one good, one not so good. In a survey, once you go out into the field with an interview schedule or questionnaire, you cannot change it. If halfway through the analysis stage you get an idea that requires the asking of an additional question, that's too bad. Since the question was not asked, all you can do is make a reasonable conjecture. In an experimental study, once you've started running your subjects, it's too late to modify the design to include another variable without either throwing asunder everything you've done up to that point or running another more elaborate experiment. One of the biggest advantages of qualitative field research is its flexibility in this respect. Early analysis is based on early observation, and later observation is based on this early analysis. This continual intertwining of data collection and analysis allows you to revise as the research progresses. Thus, there is no necessity for the long, pre-data-collection tasks required by other methods.

The second reason is that field researchers have traditionally tended to overdo this advantage. An examination of the methodological decisions in qualitative field research indicates that in many cases the researchers just fell into their studies with little if any forethought, except possibly concerning the practicalities of gaining access (e.g., Liebow, 1967: 233-42; Lofland, 1966: 269-72; Whyte, 1955: 283, 288-93). Unlike a survey researcher or experimentalist, a fieldworker can jump right into the field and still come up with something worthwhile. But the level of social research knowledge would be much higher today if slightly more time had gone into planning the studies that have been done before the observation was initiated, with respect to potential theoretical links to other studies, questions of sampling,[6] and the like (Douglas, 1976).

In other words, while I don't concur with Denzin's insistence that empirical observations be carried out only when they will make a direct contribution to social theory, I do feel that if we carry out each research project as an isolated, ad hoc, descriptive study, half our effort is for naught.

Empirical observations can only be cumulative when they are collected with an eye to the development of more general theory.

THE STARTING POINTS

Let us suppose you want to do a social science field study. You want to end up with a term paper, article, or book that tells what goes on and why in a readable and valid manner. How do you get there from here?

There are three points from which a study can start—theory, method, or substance. The researcher might start with some theoretical concern, with a decision to utilize a given research technique, or with some particular piece of the social world to examine. The first step in carrying out any study should be the integration of theoretical, methodological, and substantive concerns. If the starting point is "the refinement, development or refocusing of social theory" (Denzin, 1970: 2), this step is obvious. A piece of research has to look at *something*, and it has to use some method to do so. In this case the theoretical concern provides a standard for evaluating the efficacy of a given research technique or a given chunk of the social world.

The problem arises when theory is not part of the starting point. As I have indicated above, starting with a commitment to a particular research technique is like a carpenter deciding to build something with a radial saw and then looking around for something to build. But it does happen, and in at least one situation—a course devoted to developing skill in a particular method—it is probably justifiable. And in the context of a research agency having certain facilities and not others, it may prove the only practical way to proceed.

When it is settled that a field study is to be undertaken, alternative concrete areas can be evaluated in terms of relative practical advantages and disadvantages—problems of gaining access, legal or ethical problems, data collection, and the like. Another important but often overlooked consideration is the impact the subject will have on the investigator. In all types of research the presence of the investigator can affect the subject—this has been labeled "observer effect." But in fieldwork the converse also occurs. The investigator is in intimate and continued contact with the people and the situation under study and cannot expect to be unchanged by the experience.[7]

Let's assume you're starting a qualitative field study and have settled on a particular substantive topic—be it a community, organization, social movement, subculture, or whatever. How do you go about bringing in social theory? This requires intertwining two approaches: reading, and what might be described as sociological (or anthropological, etc.) daydreaming. While the library scholar may get by without looking directly at the world, the field researcher cannot get by without looking at the library. Getting overinvolved with obtuse debates on the philosophy of science may paralyze you for actually carrying out a project, reading as many examples of theoretically oriented research as possible can be a definite help, as can familiarity with various writings on theory construction.[8]

The second approach, the daydreaming side of bringing in theory, involves searching out analogies, no matter how farfetched they may at first appear. In what way might some aspect of the thing you are studying be "like" some aspect of something else, anything else? This requires imaginatively playing around with concepts and social categories. What might your topic, or some aspect of it, be an instance of? And what are other instances of that same category?

One of the most fruitful examples of this kind of "theory suggestion" can be found in Stanley Elkin's book *Slavery* (1959). Elkins wanted to understand how the consequences of being enslaved affected the personalities of those who were placed in this situation. He not only compared slavery in the United States with slavery in Latin America, but also with that in Nazi concentration camps! He was not suggesting that the situations as a whole were similar—physically or morally—but only that certain specified aspects of the two cases were sufficiently analogous so that a knowledge of how the aspects under study (truncated status sets and certain personality syndromes) were related in one instance might shed light on how they were related in the other. In another realm, if you are interested in how people behave in public libraries, you might get some hints from Cavan's study of how people behave in bars (1966). In fact, in a recent research project, one of my students found some evidence that people in library reading rooms use techniques to indicate willingness or lack of willingness to engage in interaction with other patrons that are strikingly similar to what Cavan found among bar patrons.

This sort of analogizing pays a double dividend. It can point the way toward uncovering better explanations of the particular phenomenon you are investigating, and it can lay the groundwork for the development of more general social theories. If you are studying adherents of a new and rapidly growing card game, for instance, you might discover a similarity between them and employees in a new and rapidly growing corporation studied by someone else. This could lead to formulation of a middle-range theory (Merton, 1957: Introduction) of social development that might also apply to emerging nations in Africa, communes in North America and the unionization of farm laborers.

There is no formal, mechanical procedure for locating the requisite analogies. That is why it requires a sort of daydreaming process. Creative social scientists must be as eclectic as possible. Everything is potential grist for their mill.[9]

The theory suggestion and theory construction aspects of your project will continue throughout the course of the study. Do whatever you can at the outset, then remain alert for additional possibilities as you proceed with your data collection and analysis.

IN THE FIELD

So much for the stages that can be carried out in the comfort of your home (or office or library). Now you're ready to move out into the field and start gathering data. The discussion of this work comes under three headings: (1) entering the field, (2) what you should observe, and (3) how to record and organize your observations. This will cover the data-collection problems, after which we can turn to data analysis, or how to make sense of all of this.

Entering the Field

In entering the field a little foresight goes a long way. McCall and Simmons warn the prospective field observer:

The role which he claims—or to which he is assigned by the subjects—is perhaps the single most important determinant of what he will be able to learn. Every role is an avenue to certain types of information but is also an automatic barrier to certain other types. The role assumed by the observer largely determines where he can go, what he can do, whom he can interact with, what he can inquire about, what he can see, and what he can be told. (1969: 29)

Since this role usually cannot be easily changed after work begins, fieldworkers should be careful to end up in the role best suited to their needs.

It is tempting to delay such questions and just barge ahead, trusting that things will take care of themselves in the field and that you and the best possible role for you to occupy will come together on the natural course of events. Don't bet on it! The "natural course of events" is just as likely to place you in a role that hampers your research endeavors.

It is also tempting at the start to hide the fact that you are doing research. Here again such a decision tends to be nonreversible, and the alternatives should be carefully evaluated at the outset. Rendering an account for some activity can be uncomfortable, and therefore people tend to utilize standard, socially acceptable accounts whenever they will fit, since they will usually be accepted without further questioning (Scott & Lyman, 1968). But if your account is later perceived as inaccurate, further questioning will occur, and the whole project could be jeopardized. People are often more perceptive than many social scientists give them credit for. While in some situations a discrepancy between role expectations and role performance will be ignored, in others it will raise immediate suspicions. Additionally, a role definition that is consistent with your research task will frequently permit observation or questioning beyond that allowed an ordinary member.

Raymond Gold has distinguished four basic stances that the field observer can assume (1958)—the complete participant, the participant-as-observer, the observer-as-participant, and the complete observer. Complete participants hide their research role from those they are studying. It is a difficult role to assume successfully, and being a basically dishonest role, it raises serious moral dilemmas as well. On the other hand, it is sometimes the only means by which certain data can be gathered. Certainly, if an alternative role is possible, the role of complete participant should not be considered. If an alternative role is not possible, careful consideration should be given before choosing between the complete participant role and dropping or modifying the envisioned research. Gold concludes that "while the complete participant role offers possibilities of learning about aspects of behavior that might otherwise escape a field observer, it places him in pretended roles which call for delicate balances between demands of role and self" (1958).

In the participant-as-observer role the researchers are again full participants in the setting they are studying, but here their research purposes are known to those they are studying. This avoids the pretense of the complete participant role, but it is not without problems of its own. As Gold points out, "When form of interaction is intimate, continuation of the relationship (which is no longer merely a field relationship) may become more important to one or both of the interactors than continuation of the roles through which they initiated the relationship" (1958). But while both of these full participant roles present problems to the fieldworker, they are the only possible roles for a really intensive study of a community, organization, social movement, subculture, or the like. The other two roles Gold discusses, while avoiding the difficulties of the first two, are more limited in applicability. Interaction for the observer-as-participant is briefer and more formal and useful mainly in interviewing situations. Complete observers attempt to avoid any interaction with those they are studying, and this is useful primarily in eavesdropping situations or for study of a community or other setting preliminary to initiating a more thorough study utilizing a different role. Gold points out that "of the four field work roles, this alone is almost never the dominant one. It is sometimes used as one of the subordinate roles employed to implement the dominant ones" (1958).

In addition to these four "master roles" there are additional role choices confronting the fieldworker. These are sorts of decisions confronting any newcomer to a social setting, though for fieldworkers the selection must be more self-conscious. They must decide what existing roles in the ongoing system they will occupy and how they will present themselves in these roles. These choices will affect how the "natives" define him and thus will influence his access to various sorts of data. There are only two general suggestions that can be made here. Before committing yourself to a specific role or style of presentation, think through the possible implications of this choice for future data gathering. The second suggestion is something that should be obvious, yet it is often violated: Don't attempt what you can't pull off. A role with less potential might be better if the ideal role can't be occupied successfully. There are exceptions to this, such as Eliott Liebow's study *Tally's Corner* or George Plimpton's participant observation studies of professional sports.[10] But these are exceptions, and normally a researcher should avoid roles in which he cannot be a normal occupant.

Observing

Once you have selected and begun to occupy your role (or roles), what do you do? Once you're in the field, how do you *do* field research? There are many answers to this, none of them absolute, none of them complete, but at least they help. They concern two questions, "What do you look at?" and "How do you recall it later?" Ideally, of course, you should look at everything and recall all of it later. That this cannot be done is due not just to human shortcomings: a videotape camera would also fall short of this ideal. It would faithfully record everything it saw, but it could only see where it was pointed. Human observers have the same problem. They can only be in one place at a time, and thus no matter how complete their data for a particular time and place, they will constitute a sample of all possible times and places—except for studies of extremely limited scope.

The problem is not how you observe everything, but rather how you see to it that what you do observe constitutes a representative sample of the phenomena that you wish to study. Of course, this in itself requires a thorough understanding of the phenomenon, and thus cannot be fully achieved from the start. Rather, you work toward it in a succession of ever-closer approximations. This is best done by a somewhat negative approach. As you learn new things about the social world you are studying, always ask yourself if there is any way in which what you think you are learning might be wrong, may be only a special and not a general occurrence. In what way might the time, place, people, etc., that you've been looking at differ from other times, places, people, etc.

For example, one of my central interests is subculture theory (Arnold, 1970b), and in line with this I have studied the subculture of sky-divers. After a short while I began to feel I had some picture of what sort of people were involved in this sport, how they viewed it, what some of the norms and elements of social organization were like, and so on. However, all my observations were conducted either at one particular drop zone, or, if away from that drop zone, with people who did all or most of their jumping there. I then took my parachute and notebook and went to a drop zone a few hundred miles away, where I found quite a different situation. I now have a more accurate picture of the sky-diving subculture that is a composite of the two settings in which I have done fieldwork. But asking the negative question again indicates that I still may not have a representative picture. The two drop zones I have studied thus far are commercial operations. A great deal of sport parachuting is carried out at drop zones of nonprofit clubs. Finally, since all my fieldwork to date has been in California, and since my research thus far indicates that sky-diving in other areas may differ in terms of social organization, etc., before I can consider my study completed I shall have to get further information about sky-diving outside of California. (For a preliminary report see Arnold, 1972).

Also try to make your observations representative as to such things as verbal versus nonverbal behavior (gestures, etc.), physical aspects of the setting (layout of the room, clothing, grooming, etc.), time variations in interaction (short versus long contacts, initiating, sustaining, and terminating contacts; etc.), different sorts of people (sex, age, ethnic, or status differences, newcomers vs. oldtimers, etc.), and other characteristics of the situation.

How can all of this be organized? Up to now, most of my answers have taken the form (a) you can't do it—not in general, anyhow—followed by (b) here are some suggestions, but don't take them as cure-alls. I'm afraid that as long as we're talking about qualitative field research, the rest of my answers will have to follow the same form.

Much of what you focus on will depend upon why you undertook the study in the first place, what theoretical questions led to initiating the research. But other questions will arise in the course of the project. You should be ready to shift the focus of your observations when necessary to gather data that will allow you to answer these questions; more important, in most instances you should already have this data. Since one of the greatest advantages of this form of research is its flexibility, you know from the start that you can't be certain what will end up being important and what won't. Therefore, it is important to start out with as broad a scope as possible, so that your data will be adequate to answer as wide a range of questions as possible.

Apprentice newspaper reporters learn that every story should answer "the five W's"—who, what, when, where, and why. If each of these are answered from a social research perspective, they can provide a handy framework for guiding field observation. "Who?" for us will mean not so much what particular individuals with what unique characteristics (though in some studies this might be pertinent), but rather what categories of people—age, sex, education, occupation, ethnic, and regional background, other involvements, or whatever, depending on the particular context. What do they do? When and where do they do it? How is it done (this is really an extension of the what)? Why do they do it—that is, how do *they* perceive and define what they are doing?

Another important source of guidance is found in the major concepts of your own field. Political scientists will probably want to look for power relationships, economists might look for exchange processes, social researchers for indicators of stratification, anthropologists for forms of kinship patterns, social psychologists for socialization, criminologists for social control, and so on.

Recording

So far I've been talking about what you look at. Let's now turn to the related problem of how you recall it later. The basic answer to this question is, Write it down. The essence of qualitative field research is not observation but field notes. Everyone observes to some degree. But memory is selective. Peter Berger has pointed out how people, as they reconstruct their past in their own minds, do so differently as their current situation changes. "At least within our own consciousness," he says, "the past is malleable and flexible, constantly changing as our recollection reinterprets and reexplains what has happened" (1963:57). Getting our observations down in unchanging paper and ink is our only protection against this. Even this isn't complete protection, since we might inadvertently interpret a statement in our notes differently than we had originally intended. This is a comparatively minor risk, however, and there isn't much we can do to eliminate it.

By "field notes" I don't mean brief summaries. Summaries constitute interpretation, not data. Your field notes should be as concrete, detailed, and complete as you can possibly make them. (Some examples of actual field notes are reprinted in the appendix to this chapter). This sounds like a lot of work because that's just what it is. As I mentioned, a rough rule of thumb is that writing up notes of a period of observation will require twice as much time as the original observation.

Since your field notes will constitute the main body of data that you will later be analyzing, they should be set up in a form that will facilitate that analysis. You will be reading them a number of times and hunting through them frequently in search of various sorts of material. To be easy to read, they must be typed. Abbreviations can save considerable time when writing up your notes, but too much esoteric abbreviation can make it difficult to read the notes later. Have some standard abbreviations that you use throughout your notes, but resist the temptation to create too many new ones as you go along. And create a dictionary of abbreviations as you devise them. You'll be surprised at how many abbreviations that seemed reasonable and obvious at the time will be undecipherable at a later date.

It is almost never possible to write complete notes on the spot. Even when it is, they will tend to be messy and hard to decipher, and thus must still be viewed as preliminary notes, subject to rewriting after each observation period. Sometimes it is impossible to take any notes on the spot, and memory must be relied on entirely. Even here, however, there might be a place for preliminary notes. If you will not be able to start typing your full field notes immediately, a few jottings, perhaps just a bare listing of events or a few quotes, might prove a great aid when you do reach your typewriter.

These are the two extremes. Most often you will be able to do some note-taking in the field, though only briefly and sporadically. How should this be handled? Unless your field situation is one that allows you to use a large notebook—and such a situation is hard to imagine—a pocket-sized, spiral-bound notepad is usually best. It can be carried inconspicuously, it always opens to the next blank page, and unlike separate cards or pieces of paper, assures that your notes are consecutive.

What goes into this notebook will ultimately depend upon how your own memory works, and that you can only learn with time. In general, however, it seems that most fieldworkers find that what is most difficult to recall later is not, as you might expect, what people said, but rather the order in which things occurred or were said. If you find that you also have this difficulty, get at your little notebook whenever you can and list the sequence in which things happened, using as few words as possible to refer to each event itself. Another alternative, incidentally, is to decide that for your particular study the sequence in which occurrences take place is unimportant, in which case you can sidestep this whole problem. But before making such a decision, make sure that ordering is *really* unimportant, and that this isn't just a cop-out.

The next most common memory problem seems to be forgetting who said or did what. Here again, if you run into this, and it seems important to be able to connect actor and action, get this down in the notebook, even if it means leaving out other things. If you get the bare bones down in your preliminary notes, especially bones that might otherwise be lost, the job of filling out the skeleton with flesh and blood for your final notes becomes much easier.

Tied in with this is the problem of labeling people. Assuming you wish to connect action to actor, you need some way of referring to each actor, so if the same person does or says a number of things at different times, they can all be attributed to him or her. When the total number of persons in the setting being observed is small and stable, the obvious solution is to refer to them by name. However, if the number of persons is too large or if turnover is too rapid for names to be learned, some other form of labeling will have to be employed. This will also be the case at first where names can be learned but as yet haven't been.

There are four types of labels that can be used in place of names:

1. In your notes you can simply assign numbers—#1 is the first person observed, etc. There are times when such a simple mode of labeling is

useful, but most often it is not. After you have observed half-a-dozen individuals and one of them engages in another action, you'll be hard-pressed to remember if he was #2 or #5.

2. When there is only one occupant of each role, the title of the role can be used as a label; if there are a small number of occupants, this can be combined with the first technique. Thus, your notes might refer to stock boy, clerk, first customer, second customer, delivery man.

3. When physical location of each actor remains constant, a map can be sketched and a code assigned each location and used to label the person who occupies it. But if the people move around, this method rapidly breaks down.

4. While each of these three techniques can be handy in some situations, the method of broadest applicability is a nickname that capitalizes on some observable characteristic of the actor. Labels I've used in my field notes include "White hair," "Hop step," "Freckles," and "Shorty." Anytime I learn the person's actual name I so indicate ("White hair = Mr. Martin") and use the name from there on. The only problem is to note characteristics that are more or less unique ("White hair" was at a parachute drop zone; at a rest home I might have labeled him "Beer belly") and that do not change ("Green shirt" could be used as a label only if the individual will not be observed on another occasion).

When typing your notes, the first time a new person is mentioned (whether by name, location, or whatever), set down whatever basic information you can about that individual (e.g., "White, early 20's, about 5'10", thin, crewcut, clean-shaven, slight accent [Scandinavian?], glasses, cowboy boots.") Alternatively, keep a file with such information apart from your regular notes.

How should you go about typing the notes? In the analysis stage you'll want a set of notes you can keep intact, plus one or more sets that can be sorted according to various analytic categories and perhaps cut into smaller pieces. The usual way to prepare for this is to type the notes in duplicate or triplicate. Lofland suggests making an original plus two carbon copies (1971). McCall suggests another method for those with access to a ditto machine: Type on ditto masters, and then you will be able to run off as many copies as you find you need (McCall & Simmons, 1969: 76). Either way, carbons or dittoes, leave enough room on one or both side margins to add additional comments, cross-references, or labels of analytic categories. On the other hand, double-spacing serves no purpose other than to speed up the reduction of forests.

I've assumed you'll be typing on 8½-X-11-inch sheets. This is the usual procedure, but once again feel free to deviate if there is some reason. For example, in a study where the difficulties of keeping notes in the normal narrative form seemed to outweigh the advantages, Cavan decided instead to treat "incidents" (describable events that took place in the course of the day) as basic bits-of-data; and to record these bits-of-data on 3 × 5 cards, and these in turn could be identified according to the day, the setting, and the social occasion at which they took place (1970: 5).

Another assumption in all I've been saying about field notes is that they will be written. Many researchers advocate using cassette tape recorders in the field and then having the tapes transcribed by a typist. This both saves time and permits more complete note-taking, and thus is advisable for the professional social researcher who has a grant to hire secretarial help. For students who have to do their own transcribing it is actually very time-consuming. Films and videotapes can provide useful supplements to regular field notes, but again are too costly for the average nonprofessional. A still camera, on the other hand, is more readily available, and film cost is moderate, so supplementing notes with still photos might be considered, provided using the camera doesn't hamper regular note-taking.[11]

ANALYSIS OF QUALITATIVE MATERIALS

Most published reports of qualitative field research include a discussion of research methods, usually in a methodological appendix. (Examples can be found in Festinger et al., 1956; Liebow, 1967; Lofland, 1966; Whyte, 1955; Wiseman, 1970.) Typically, these tell us, often in anecdotal form, how the investigators happened on their project and how they got established among the people they wished to study. Usually there is also some description of incidents that occurred in the field during the course of the investigation. These discussions make fascinating reading and are helpful in providing a sense of what was done in the field. But while they tell how the investigators got from their offices to the field and what they did while they were there, these descriptions almost never tell us how they got back from the field to their offices and what they did *there*. How they got from there (the field) to here (the published report) is a mystery.

One reason it is left a mystery is that it is a mystery to the social researchers themselves. The analysis of qualitative materials involves seemingly endless hours of work, much of it hit-or-miss and trial-and-error. If an investigator tells us what went on at this stage, it sometimes appears like the following:

On June 2 I tried to write up the variable events of late April and May. Yet I could not come to "sociological terms" with them. The result of two days' work was a 30 page epic saga. . . . As far as I could see I was not "doing sociology." (Cavan, 1970: 17)

A month later the situation hadn't improved:

During this time my general concerns were to find some direction for the continuing observations made thus far into a coherent report. . . etc. (Cavan, 1970: 19-20)

Yet shortly thereafter the same investigator is able to report:

I began to order the information I had accumulated so far for a preliminary field report. The days seemed productive; and I felt quite satisfied . . . (Cavan, 1970): 21

In other words, hang in there. At one point your observations appear so varied that there seems no way to bring about order. At another point everything seems so common-sensical that analysis and ordering seem not to be called for. These periods can be quite disheartening and even depressing. But continued rereading and rearranging of the notes eventually pays off, and out of the mixture of time, sweat, and field notes emerges an organized picture of what you've been observing in unorganized bits and pieces.

Although the analysis stage of each new study is itself a new and relatively unique experience, there are some tips and procedures that maximize the efficiency of your analytical efforts. First of all, "analysis" is not entirely a separate part of the study. As I indicated earlier, an important advantage of qualitative field research is that, unlike most other research designs in social research, it permits a continual intertwining of data collection and data analysis. Thus, the "analytic stage" actually commences as soon as the "observation stage" does; only the relative emphasis placed on each shifts. At first, most of your time is spent in the field or typing up field notes, with just short periods devoted to reading those notes, thinking about them, and perhaps typing analytical comments with the notes. Such comments, incidentally, should be clearly indicated as such, perhaps by a different color ribbon, different indentation, surrounding by brackets, or merely by labeling them as comments. Here, from my notes on the sky-diving subculture, is an example of such early stage, analytical comments:

P [i.e., sport parachuting] provides a high quantity of stories per unit of time actually expended in the sport itself. Also, jumping stories (esp. 1st person) are of interest to both jumpers and laymen. Seems to me "stories" (in whatever sport—or in nonsport activities) are of these types:

1. general (e.g. jokes); not concrete happenings.
2. 3rd person stories; may be true (or supposedly true—"this happened to a friend of mine . . .") or apocryphal.
3. 1st person stories; these might involve danger, excitement, etc.; might involve something else (not sure what; informational?).

One motivation for participation in certain activities might be to obtain stories, or license to tell stories.

Later on the time devoted to analytical tasks increases while that spent on observing and recording declines. In the later stages the only forays into the field might be to observe specific things to answer specific questions raised by the analysis for which you had not previously collected enough data to answer. But even at the early stages you are never just a recording machine that walks, but rather are continually digesting what you are learning, asking questions of yourself and your data, and attempting to find answers to those questions. The quotation above came after typing some notes following an evening of listening to some sky-divers and non-sky-divers shooting the bull over a pitcher of beer. It resulted in my paying more attention to such stories and seeing more in them during my later observation periods.

At first analysis is pretty much as I have described it: reading and thinking about your notes, adding analytical comments to the body of these notes, or perhaps just scratching remarks in the margins, and redirecting future observation accordingly. Eventually, however, you'll begin to have a sense that your notes are getting repetitious, that everything that constitutes the normal routine in the social world you have been observing is in your notes. When that happens, it is time to begin the main analysis. While most field workers have developed some systematic way of handling this work, rarely have they written it up. One social scientist, John Lofland, has, and so I will reprint his suggestions here (quoted, with permission, Lofland, 1971: 118-20.)

Perhaps foremost among concrete procedures is the establishment of some kind of *files*. Good filing devices include file folders, often having third-cut tabs, combined with "hanging files," which have overhanging metal "ears" that sit on metal rails in a file drawer. Using folders and hanging files, one can avoid the plague of "falling files" and can place numerous file folders into a single hanging file. Thus, one has maximum flexibility in grouping and regrouping data into categories of observations and ordering and reordering topics. Another possibility is to employ boxes, such as those in which more expensive bond paper is sold, and to establish shelves of these boxes containing material on various topics. Such boxes may be bought empty and in bulk from wholesale paper dealers. (See also C.W. Mills' discussion of filing in his "On Intellectual Craftsmanship," 1959: 195-226.)

Whatever the concrete details of the physical filing, the aim is to get the material out of the sheer chronological narrative of one's field or interview notes and into a *flexible storage, ordering* and *retrieval* format. It is here that the advice to have *multiple choices* of one's notes assumes supreme importance. The more copies of a particular observation, interview response or analytic idea one has, the more categories it can be filed under. The previously mentioned practice of putting one's notes on spirit masters seems a particularly good suggestion. Multiple carbons perform the same function, even though they produce fewer copies. And even if one lacks sufficient copies, cross-referencing notes can be made.

Mundane Files. Although I began by speaking of files as crucial stimulants to the analytic process, I want to emphasize that this is not their only function. Nor are analytic files the only kind one wants to keep, at least initially. Files must also be used to simply keep track of *people, places, organization, documents, and the like.*

Such mundane files are organized very much like those in any business enterprise, with information grouped under the most obvious categories, the better to locate it again. Thus, one will almost certainly want to have a folder on each person—or each leading person—under observation. The material that one accumulates through time on the most obvious of units can help—through review—to point up crucial things not considered about the unit. The bulk of such material may reveal patterns not previously contemplated.

A study of even a highly limited setting and number of people can produce a very complex set of facts, activities, etc., for which one needs aids in simply keeping the most mundane matters straight. Mundane files facilitate laying hands on a record of something that happened, let us say, several months in the past. One can easily spend hours trying to locate it in his chronological notes or analytic files, but a mundane file locates the material immediately.

Analytic Files Mundane files are likely to provide a stark contrast to the physically separate analytic files. Any given piece of information is easily imbued with multiple and diverse analytic significance. While a given piece of information has—by intent—only one or very few locations in one's mundane files, that same piece of information can—and should—have a variety of locations in one's analytic files. While one is tame in his mundane files, one can and should be wild in his analytic files. When a given episode, or whatever, suggests several kinds of notions or significances, write up the notions in a brief (or extended) fashion (along with the empirical material), label file folders, and enter those folders into one's fuller set of analytic files. Additional pieces of information may then be added to each of these file folders if they suggest the same kind of significance.

Early-on in this process of building analytic files, one need not be terribly concerned over whether or not a given category is indeed viable in the long run, ultimately makes any kind of sense, or whatever. The aim, rather, is to set up as many separate items (literally, file folders) as one is prompted to and feels reasonably excited about. The hard day of finally reckoning with one's analytic impulses comes later, during the period of concerted analysis.

Field Work File. In addition to mundane and analytic files, one ought to also have a folder in which one accumulates material on the process of doing the research itself. It is a relatively standard practice for the researcher to include in his report an account of how the research was done. A file already built on this topic will facilitate later writing of such account.

The heart of the analysis is the analytic files. The categories here will change as you proceed, but eventually they will stabilize, with some categories emerging as major concerns, others falling into place as secondary issues. Often these developments will send you back to the library to search out what other research or theoretical writings have to say about the topic. Eventually, when you're ready to write up your research, the file categories will provide the elements for the outline of the report. And if you have been writing notes to yourself as each bit of analysis falls into place, you'll find that a good part of your first draft is already written.

As an alternative to Lofland's file system, many fieldworkers, especially anthropologists, utilize key-sort punch cards. These come in various sizes, have an area for typing notes in the center, and have a series of holes around the edges. A short discussion of such cards, with an illustration, appears in Goode and Hatt (1952: 318-19). The most commonly used variety is manufactured by the McBee Keysort Company, Detroit, Michigan, and can be obtained through most stationery or office supply stores. When you are ready to begin analysis and start developing categories, each category can be assigned to one of the holes, all of which are numbered. If the notes on a particular card deal with the topic, a hand punch is used to remove the material between the hole and the edge of the card. After this has been done, you can insert a special needle (it looks something like a knitting needle) through the hole in the stack. When you lift the needle, all cards dealing with that topic will drop out, and you can readily analyze them. Thus, no matter what order the cards may be in, you can, within seconds and without any fancy computer equipment, pull out all notes dealing with a particular person, event, concept, or what-have-you. After examining these notes, you can toss the cards back into the pile and just as quickly retrieve all your notes on some other topic. If you also want to keep a set of notes in chronological order, you can either type a copy on regular paper the same size as the cards, with a sheet of carbon paper on regular paper the same size as the cards, with a sheet of carbon paper to make a copy on the cards, or type carbons on paper and tape one copy to the cards.

Finally, some researchers simply leave wide margins alongside their notes and later write in various topics and categories in the margins at the appropriate places. Analysis is then carried out simply by thumbing back and forth as needed. This sounds simple, and if the quantity of field notes is small, it is. As your notes grow, however, this method becomes more and more unwieldy, and thus is recommended only for very small-scale studies. Files or cards, while involving some extra work initially, will in the long run save time and assure a more thorough analysis of data for more complete studies.

CONCLUSION

This chapter boils down to the following: Qualitative field research is neither better nor worse, neither harder nor easier than other methods of social research; it is merely different. When other methods are more appropriate, they should be employed. When qualitative field research is more appropriate, it should be employed. I have tried to set forth some suggestions that will help you decide when to use it and how to go about doing so. They are just that—suggestions. They are not rules. The only rules are the ones you develop for yourself as you gain experience as a researcher. And reading them does not make you a researcher. That, too, comes only through experience. If all knowledge were in books, we wouldn't need any more research. My dictionary defines "research" as "diligent and systematic inquiry or investigation into a subject." The only addition I would make is to ignore the dictionary's classification of research as a noun and urge you to view it as a verb—and an active, not a passive one.

APPENDIX: STUDENT FIELD NOTES

Example 1

These notes are based on observation in a bar in Northern California and were taken by Noel T. Byrne while an undergraduate at Sonoma State University. The first excerpt is a good example of the degree of detail you should strive for in recording behavior; it also illustrates the handling of several different individuals and locations. In his original notes there is a map indicating the various areas referred to and a list of names to go along with those abbreviations not explained below. The second excerpt illustrates the intertwining of observations and analysis. In the original notes the discussions, reprinted here in italics, were typed with a red ribbon, while the rest of the notes were in black; "p" is pool.

At 7:27, a guy c. 30 enters (from the side entrance), approaches the south end of the bar (right next to the barmaid's station—BS), buys a draft, and goes to the pinball machine (PBM). After serving the draft, Sandy (the bartender, hereafter referred to as S) becomes engaged in a conversation with the guy sitting at the end of the bar (A).

Other than Jack (J) and myself, the only others sitting at a table are those at table #1.

Music has been playing on the jukebox since we entered. The two couples from table #1 dance as a new record begins. When the record ends, they return to the table; K appears to be looking for something, as does S. S: "Has anyone seen Kathy's purse"? After a few seconds K says, "Oh, here it is," and picks up a purse from under a chair near table #1. K then goes to area #1 where she buys 2 drinks. (I hear the word "tequilla" as she speaks to S). While K is at the bar, P and R go to the jukebox. K carries the 2 drinks back to the table and then joins P and R at the jukebox. (I don't see F anywhere; possibly he is in the restroom). F sits at table #1; the girls also return to the table while P goes to area #1 at the bar, where he remains standing, right foot on the footrail, weight on his forearms which are folded before him on the bar. S mixes a drink to P's right; P and S appear to be in conversation as S mixes the drink.

Population at 9:00—41; 19 girls. 39 people at 9:20, same sex ratio.

Pair of guys entered at 8:55, one tall and thin, other medium height with blonde hair, both c. 25-27. (Latter-Blondie; former-Spike) They get drafts, stand in girls' head alcove. At 9:20 I notice Spike standing by a girl, talking to her, he leaning on the wall, facing p-game, she on stool, facing game, both maintaining eye contact primarily on game but still conversing.

Using a p-game not as an involvement shield but as a cover for an interaction game? See Simmel on coquetry. Might further expand to cover other situations in which some activity exterior to the immediate face engagement functions as a covering dominant involvement; in the case of this type of attempted pick-up, the conversation is projected to one another and immediately present others as a subordinate side involvement, the p-game being the projected dominant main involvement of each.

Blondie comes to the bar directly on the east side of me and to my left. Spike leaves S-girl and follows him, saying something to Blondie as they walk. Blondie, as he walks, turned partly toward Spike, says "want a beer?" Spike says "no" (smiling) as he turned back in the direction from which he has come. His head is turned toward Blondie as he gives this answer although his body has begun the return trip. Meanwhile (he has been gone only about 20 seconds) another guy who had previously been standing in the area of the pinball machines had immediately moved into the position vacated by Spike and is now standing next to S-girl, back to wall, facing the p-tables and engaged in conversation with her. Spike sees them, stops, looks for a couple of seconds, no smile, and turns back toward Blondie who is now standing at the bar, back to p-tables, taps him on the arm saying "I'll have that beer after all." Blondie half-turns toward him. Spike has a (rueful) half-smile, repeats "Yeah, I'll have that beer" as he looks toward S-girl and the guy in conversation.

This episode indicates that mere conversation with a girl does not confer any particular pick-up rights of sociability prerogatives greater than those held by all others present. Spike does not attempt to claim the standing position he had vacated nor does he attempt to assert his role of specific interaction partner with relation to the girl now that the other guy had appropriated his position, although he had apparently not intended to relinquish either. This possibly indicates that territorial claims or possessionary rights, be they spatial or interpersonal, must be made manifest under some conditions; in this case of a specific location, it might, as Sherri Cavan suggest, take the form of surrogate paraphernalia which mark one's claim. Cross-sexed interpersonal rights might possibly require the ratification of the involved other, explicitly by a change in spatial location in the company of the initiator or implicitly by means of (consistent) rebuff to any overtures advanced by others.

Spike's smile might indicate not only ruefulness but also awareness of the "rules of the game" and that he had been outmaneuvered, that his departure was a slip that provided an opportunity quickly realized by the other.

Example 2

These notes are based on observation in a class at Sonoma State University, and were done by Linda Kuhlmann while an undergraduate sociology student at Sonoma State. They are an excellent example of handling of nonverbal behavior. (A) is the professor. Approx. 3/4 attendance, and the front row is empty.

A girl comes in late and (A) looks up at her. He is still standing with one leg in the chair with his arms resting on the bent leg. He asks, "Any questions left over from last time?" No answer; students look down.

(A) begins writing figures on the blackboard. Most students are writing them down and there is some side discussion. (A) looks at another late person but more quickly, then looks down. A question is asked about the figures and another late person. (A) does not use a great degree of eye contact. He glances at person while answering their question but looks away, up, down, sideways. He has rapid eye movement.

A question is asked and (A) listens, sipping his coffee. He answers the question, coffee mug in his hand and other hand in his pocket. He points to the figures with the hand with the coffee mug, not the hand in his pocket.

There is some side discussion with Jim and Lee. I can't hear but it appears humorous. Their bodies are shaking from controlled laughter. Now (A) is reading figures (instead of writing them on the board). Most students are taking notes. He looks again at a latecomer. The latecomer sits down as quickly as possible, glances around and then gazes down.

There is some side discussion with Jim and Lee. (A) writes more figures on the board, stops, and then puts his foot on the chair and leans against the board again. More side discussion between Jim and Lee.

(A) doesn't walk around except for a purpose—to write on board, etc. He uses some hand movement but from a stationary body position. He is showing a magazine to the class and for the first time walks around to the front of the table. He walks back to the far side of the table and returns to the position of foot on chair leaning against blackboard. He picks up another and follows the same procedure just described.

10:15 - Jim and another guy look up at the clock.

10:16 - Linda (not me) looks up at the clock. Lee and Jim are talking. (A) is still lecturing in the same foot on chair-leaning against blackboard position. He is doing some hand moving and finger pointing. His eye movement is horizontal.

Example 3

The following excerpts differ in several aspects from those above. The notes are from a study that employed several observers and had funds for secretarial help. The original notes were recorded on tape, then typed by standard forms having places for categorization and comments on each page. Each observation period is handled separately and has a cover sheet on which the following items are filled in: observation no.; participant observer (in this case Ken Stoddart, at the time of the study a graduate student in sociology at the University of California, Santa Barbara); no. of pages (21); city; date; time (9:00 p.m.-3:00 a.m.); duration; location(s); participants (along with their approximate ages); persons referred to; additional comments, and secretary's initials.

Field Notes	*Index-Category*
I asked Candy where she was from and she told me that she came to Vancouver from Long Beach, California.[1] She said, though, that she could never go back there because "the old man kicked me out." I asked Candy why her father had banished her from her home—and she told me that she was "drunk and raising hell all the time.[2]	1. *Background* residency 2. *Family* Relations

Field Notes

I asked *Candy* where she was staying, she told
me that she was living with a dozen people in "a
mansion" on East 18th Avenue.°1 *Candy* said that
it was a "really great" place to live and noted that
there was always lots of dope around. I asked her
what kind of dope they used in the house, and she
told me that there was "always acid and grass,
usually speed, and occasionally some smack."°4

Distribution
availability
(LSD)
(grass)
(speed)
(heroin)

Explanatory or interpretive comments:

°1 East 18th Avenue is not part of Vancouver
noted for "mansions."

Field Notes

Cory told us that four or five guys at the
Gastown Inn had called him a "pig." *Cory* said
that *Luigi* had cooled him off by telling him they
they were "only kidding" but *Cory*, "I'm still
fuckin' mad and I'm in a 'stomping' mood. I just
gotta stomp with someone—to get it out of my
system." *Cory* said that he wanted to stomp with
"us"—P.O.D. and I—because we were the only
two "men" he'd met since he arrived in Vancouver. He said that if the police came while he was
stomping with us, we wouldn't "turn him in" like
the rest of these punks would."

P.O.D. and I spent the next hour or so attempting to talk *Cory* out of "stomping." He kept
telling us that if we were his friends we'd be glad
to help him "get it out of his system." He told us
that he wanted to see blood and feel teeth breaking under his heels—and he added, it just had to
be over teeth and over blood. Occasionally, we
thought we had *Cory* talked out of the idea of a
"stomping party" involving us. Despite our efforts, though, the notion stayed with him. At one
point, he attempted to rile us by turning over—
and breaking our beer glasses. P.O.D. and I just
sat there.°2 He tried insulting us verbally: "You
drive a Honda; you drive a Ford; and you both

suck cock."°³ During *Cory's* various symbolic
assaults on us, P.O.D. and I either merely "sat
tight" or tried to talk him out of engaging us in
combat. No line of talk seemed to be able to
dissuade him. Finally, P.O.D. told *Cory* that we
were both "outlaws" and wanted to avoid any
possibility of contact with the police. P.O.D. gave
the impression that he was "on the run" from U.S.
officials. *Cory* accepted this as a valid excuse for
not "stomping" with him.°⁴

5. *Antisocial*
violence

Explanatory or interpretive comments:

°2 Somewhat terrified, I might add.
°3 The nature of these insults is related to Cory's
conception of us as "bikers."
°4 Quite obviously, we could have got up and left
the beer parlor. This, however, would have made
our return to "the field" somewhat difficult.

NOTES

¹ I am grateful to Norman K. Denzin, John Lofland, Jerry Mandel, and Roger
C. Owens for their detailed comments on an earlier draft of this chapter.

² Although this can be argued. Cf., inter alia, Cicourel (1964).

³ See C. Wright Mills' discussion of "abstracted empiricism" in *The Sociological
Imagination* (1959).

⁴ For an example of such a field experiment see Festinger, Schachter, & Back
(1963).

⁵ The Bales categories, mentioned earlier, provide the prime example of this
(Bales, 1950). Each element of interaction is coded upon its occurrence into one of
twelve categories. These elements are measured in terms of their frequency, duration,
or both, and then analyzed statistically. While this technique is useful for some
purposes, it does not permit study of any aspects of behavior not covered by the
twelve categories.

⁶ For a discussion of sampling in qualitative research see Arnold (1970a).

⁷ This is discussed at greater length in Glass & Frankiel (1968).

⁸ Cf., inter alia, Lofland (1977); Dubin (1978); Stinchcombe (1968); Glaser &
Strauss (1967); Zetterberg (1965).

⁹ For further discussion of this see Gordon (1968) and Koestler (1964).

¹⁰ Liebow is white; the men whose world he participated in are black (1967).
Plimpton's better-known works include *Out of My League* (1961) and *Paper Lion*
(1966). For a stimulating discussion of Plimpton's work in sociology see Stoll (1973).

¹¹ See Collier (1967), Gurry & Clarke (1977), Williams (1967: 34-37), and Royal
Anthropological Institute of Great Britain and Ireland (1951: 353-56) for discussion
of the use of photography in field research. The latter two references are also packed
with numerous hints and suggestions on other topics, and although they are aimed

primarily at anthropologists, they should be read by field researchers from all disciplines.

REFERENCES

Arnold, D. O. Dimensional sampling: An approach for studying a small number of cases. *The American Sociologist*, 1970, 5 (May): 147-50. (a)

Arnold, D.O. (Ed.). *The sociology of subcultures*. Berkeley: Glendessary Press, 1970. (b)

Arnold, D. O. The social organization of sky diving: A study in vertical mobility. Paper presented at the Pacific Sociological Association Meetings, Portland, Ore., April 13, 1972.

Bales, F. F. *Interaction process analysis: A method for the study of small groups*. Reading, Mass.: Addison-Wesley, 1950.

Berger, P. L. *Invitation to sociology: A humanistic perspective*. Garden City, N. Y.: Doubleday Anchor Books, 1963.

Cavan, S. *Liquor license: An ethnography of bar behavior*. Chicago: Aldine, 1966.

Cavan, S. Some notes on fieldwork. Dittoed paper.

Cicourel, A. V. *Method and measurement in sociology*. New York: Free Press, 1964.

Collier, J., Jr. *Visual anthropology: Photography as a research method*. New York: Holt, Rinehart and Winston, 1967.

Curry, T. J., & Clarke, A. C. *Introducing visual sociology*. Dubuque, Ia: Kendall/ Hunt, 1977.

Denzin, N. K. (Ed.). *Sociological methods: A sourcebook*. Chicago: Aldine, 1970.

Douglas, Jack. *Investigative social research*. Beverly Hills, Calif.: Sage, 1976.

Dubin, R. *Theory building*. New York: Free Press, 1978.

Elkins, S. M. *Slavery*. Chicago: University of Chicago Press, 1959.

Festinger, L., Rieken, H., & Schachter, S. *When prophecy fails*. Minneapolis: University of Minnesota Press, 1956.

Festinger, L., Schachter, S., & Back, K. *Social pressures in informal groups*. Stanford, Calif.: Stanford University Press, 1963.

Glaser, B. G., & Strauss, A. L. *The discovery of grounded theory*. Chicago: Aldine, 1967.

Glass, J. F., & Frankiel, H. H. The influence of subjects on the researcher: A problem in observing social interaction. *Pacific Sociological Review*, 1968, 11 (Fall): 75-80.

Gold, R. Roles in sociological field observations. *Social Forces*, 1958, 36 (March): 217-33.

Goode, W. J., & Hatt, P. K. *Methods in social research*. New York: McGraw-Hill, 1952.

Gordon, W. J. J. *Synectics*. New York: Harper & Row, 1961.

Johnson, John. *Doing field research*. New York: Free Press, 1976.

Junker, B. H. *Field work: An introduction to the social sciences*. Chicago: University of Chicago Press, 1960.

Koestler, A. *The act of creation*. New York: Macmillan, 1964.

Liebow, E. *Tally's corner*. Boston: Little, Brown, 1967.

Lofland, J. *Doomsday cult*. Englewood Cliffs, N. J.: Prentice-Hall, 1966.

Lofland, J. *Analyzing social settings*. Belmont, Calif.: Wadsworth, 1971.

Lofland, J. *Doing social life*. New York: Wiley Interscience, 1977.

McCall, G. J. & Simmons, J. L. (Eds). *Issues in participant observation*. Reading, Mass.: Addison-Wesley, 1969.

McGlothin, W. H. & Arnold, D. O. LSD revisited: A ten-year follow-up of medical LSD use. *Archives of General Psychiatry*, 1971, *24* (January): 35-49.

Merton, R. K. *Social theory and social structure* (rev. ed.). New York: Free Press, 1957.

Mills, C. W. *The sociological imagination*. New York: Oxford University Press, 1959.

Plimpton, G. *Out of my league*. New York: Harper & Row, 1961.

Plimpton, G. *Paper lion*. New York: Harper & Row, 1966.

Riley, M. W. *Sociological research II: Exercises and manual*. New York: Harcourt, Brace, 1963.

Royal Anthropological Institute of Great Britain and Ireland *Notes and queries on anthropology*. London: Routledge and Kegan Paul, 1951.

Scott, M. B. & Lyman, S. M. Accounts. *American Sociological Review*, 1968, 33, (February): 46-62.

Stinchcombe, A. L. *Constructing social theories*. New York: Harcourt, Brace, 1968.

Stoll, C. S. George Plimpton: The journalist as social observer." In M. Truzzi (Ed.), *The humanities as sociology*, Columbus, Ohio: Merrill, 1973.

Whyte, W. F. *Street corner society* (rev ed.). Chicago: University of Chicago Press, 1955.

Wiseman, J. P. *Stations of the lost*. Englewood Cliffs, N. J.: Prentice-Hall, 1970.

Williams, T. R. *Field methods in the study of culture*. New York: Holt, Rinehart and Winston, 1967.

Zetterberg, H. L. *On theory and verification in sociology* (3rd ed.). Totowa, N. J.: Bedminster Press, 1965.

Chapter Three
Researching an abortion market

NANETTE J. DAVIS

This fieldwork report documents how methodological flexibility and a critical approach were adopted for examining a complex abortion network (characterized by illegal activities and rapid change) over 28 months of field study.[1] The aim was to identify local referral networks in six Michigan communities—Detroit, Ann Arbor, Lansing, and Kalamazoo among urban centers, and Mount Pleasant and Alma among rural sites. I found that local community networks were connected to outstate abortion providers—legal clinics and hospitals in Washington, D.C., New York City, and Buffalo, and illegal office abortions in Chicago (Davis, 1973, 1974).

I utilized a cumulative research strategy that involved a *sequential* development of theory, methods, and data collection, adapted to changing situations and settings.[2] Discovering power relations and control among a network of organizations involved continuous redefining of the research problem, as new evidence developed or as tactics and methods had to be generated to fit changing field requirements.[3] The time line for the research and specific activities for each stage is outlined in Figures 1 and 2.

What should be emphasized is that these five stages with their various research activities were initially unplanned efforts to resolve problems of data gathering by employing different research approaches—methods, strategies, tactics, and techniques—in a flexible matter.

PHASE I: SEARCH FOR A MODEL (FIVE MONTHS)

The logic of discovery appears far more coherent in text or journal versions than real life. Throughout two years of fieldwork I set out to identify not only the apparently disconnected pieces of an intricate social puzzle, but also to construct the basic design for fitting such disparate parts together. On one level the model search was a sequential process, involving an interplay between theory, fieldwork experience, and data. On another level it should be emphasized that at the outset I was not clear about what I was studying. Thus, the model search required that I remain open to changes in the definition of those empirical unknowns.

I entered the field approximately at the same time as a vigorous social movement—comprised of clergy, Planned Parenthood, and feminist reformers—became involved in efforts to decriminalize abortion. Preliminary interviews with three local clergymen involved in abortion referral in East Lansing, Michigan, convinced me that abortion was still an underground subject. These clergymen remained evasive about their network involvements and contacts and instead dwelt on ethical-social problems of abortion.

Figure 1. A Sequential Development of the Research.

Phase I	Phase II	Phase III	Phase IV	Phase V
Search for a model	Formal & informal interviewing	Participant observation	Structured techniques	Reconstructing the model

1 2 3 4 5 6 7 8 9 10 11 12 13 14 15 16 17 18 19 20 21 22 23 24 25 26 27 28
Months

This entrée turned out to be a false start not merely because as an outsider, I lacked credibility, but more important, at this point I did not have a firm enough grasp of a descriptive model to generate appropriate questions and hypotheses. My enthusiasm for the fieldwork phase of the project had to be dampened in favor of a return to the drawing board.

Before entering the field, I had worked with some theoretical ideas drawn from Lemert's (1964) social control conception. Adapted to the abortion event, this approach provided a broad orientation for examining some fundamental institutional features such as legal control, professional ideologies and sanctions, and intergroup conflict. Lemert, Becker, and other labeling theorists hold that the power to enact norms is concentrated among certain established groups, often against the interests of less powerful social groups (e.g., blacks, women, young, etc.). The model predicts that under-dogs' reactions to control are to generate rule violations and alternative social organizations, implying that rule evasions are a normal part of social and economic arrangements. (See Lemert, 1951, 1967; Becker, 1963, 1964, 1971; Kitsuse, 1962: 247-57.)

A review of available literature and abortion reform documents seemed to confirm this view. On the one hand criminalizing abortion closed off access to legal organizations, which led women to seek services from marginal or underworld practitioners. The medical system tacitly supported the illegal system through referrals and noncompliance with the law (e.g., a physician's refusal to testify against an offending colleague). The control thesis appeared to fit the empirical case, but propositions generated from this model seemed too general, if not common-sensical. (See Davis, 1972, 1975; Manning, 1975.)

Redefining social control as a problem of political economy required a shift in perspectives. Rather than investigating rule violations, I turned to sources of power, types of resource control, and cost consequences for women and the public. The political economy approach, moreover, strongly

Figure 2. The Research Activities.

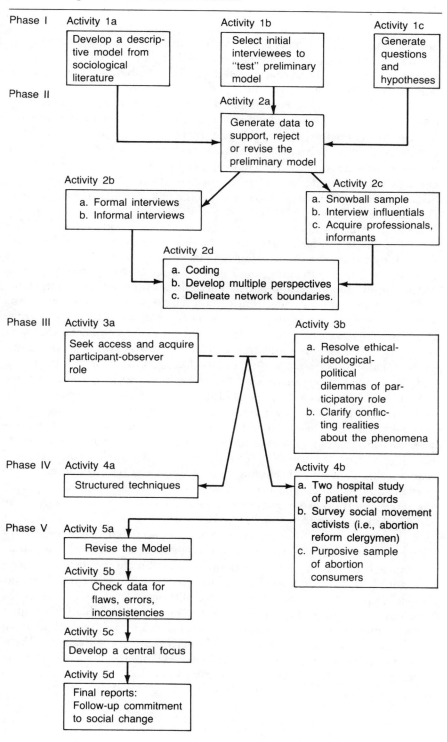

favored an exchange conception. This emphasized the interdependencies among established groups, especially transactions between controlling occupations and organizations that affected supply, distribution, use, and regulation of abortion as a social resource.

The next step was to operationalize "resource," not only in the familiar economic sense of buying and selling, prices and profits, supply and demand, but also to include the political processes by which organizations operated to distribute abortion services. The market concept permitted a more precise picture of the structure than the more general political economy model, and one that had a precedence in deviance studies (Schur, 1965; Packer; 1967). Social regulation, it became apparent, was the outcome of a twofold process. On the one hand abortion use and distribution occurred as transactions between providers and consumers as well as among providers. On the other hand legitimate producers attempted to contain a demand situation over which they had relatively little professional control. Various strategies (e.g., quotas, psychiatric screening, high costs) employed by control groups to restrict supply generated alternative market forms (gray or black markets).

The market model underwent certain modifications, including: (1) the social values of involved groups (e.g., medical, legal, social agencies) as these determine "gains" of "costs" or transactions; (2) the conditions that constrain organizations serving abortion clientele, such as law, economic costs, professional traditions, mandates, and the like; and (3) a risk notion of cost. This is clarified by comparing reform clergymen and physicians on these dimensions. Clergymen articulated strong social reasons for changing the abortion law, perceived legal constraints as arbitrary social arrangements, and believed risk to be an inherent feature of social commitment. Contrariwise, physicians considered abortion as a violation of the medical mandate to save life, viewed the law as excessively constraining medical practice, and feared losing their ethical standing if involved in abortion. High and visible participation by clergy and low and invisible participation by physicians in the referral network were outcomes of these alternative constructions of the abortion phenomenon.

Early testing of the market concept produced only an imperfect fit between model and evidence. Clearly, though, such diverse events as market shortages, high prices, erratic distribution of legitimate services, and excessive social and psychological costs operated outside the control of any individual practitioner and agency. What did physicians have to say of the abortion "problem"? Did they ignore it, treat it as an unshareable professional burden, or view it as unspeakable dirty work associated with an illicit business operation? This example from an early interview with a sympathetic university physician indicates that professional knowledge about the abortion event is both highly personal and professionally risky.

Investigator: Do you see any women here asking for abortions?

Physician: I really can't speak for my colleagues, but I have two or three women a day in my practice asking for abortions. Frankly, I feel overwhelmed with personal responsibility. I think I'm really one of the few at _____ taking on this responsibility.

Investigator: Is there a policy here at _____ that covers this abortion situation?

Physician: No, there's no policy. In the professional system there is a tacit understanding that each man in his individual practice does his own thing, but not visibly.

Investigator: Are there any physicians with whom you talk about this part of your practice?

Physician: No, it's a difficult problem. There is little or no medical communication in this business.

Investigator: Do you have any idea how town doctors handle patient requests for an abortion?

Physician: I really don't know what's going on. I'm frankly confused. I don't get any information from professional associations, journals, or organized medicine. All I know is what I hear from the girls I deal with. The whole thing [abortion referral] seems to be handled only by indirection.

Investigator: What kind of problems does the abortion issue create for the practitioner?

Physician: (Snide laugh.) Some are making $100,000 a year take-home pay in New York. There really seems to be little sharing of this kind of burden. At the present time, there's a 50-50 split in the profession on the pros and cons of abortion. Professionals like to play God, and this makes it difficult to have any kind of rational discussion in this area. The way it's operated is [that] before New York there was the psychiatric route . . . that's the rich people's way out. The kids went to holes and came back with perforations and allied [gynecological] problems. That's when we saw them here at _____ for postabortion care after the damage was done. Things are safer now. It's still illegal to give abortions in Michigan, and, of course, it's unsafe for any doctor to be involved in this . . . Seems like a strange word, abortion.

Both this woman physician and other health workers were infuriated by a system in which profit-taking by a few and institutional indifference contributed to an inchoate structure, or one in which the abortion patient became the individual doctor's problem and not a general medical responsibility.

Although the scarcity model generated questions and hypotheses during the first five months of fieldwork, it produced only limited data. Spending 200 hours in the field and accumulating about 35 unstructured interviews (with physicians, clergymen, agency workers, feminists, et al) primarily served to sensitize me to the complexities of the changing abortion scene. Intuition and hunch necessarily prevailed over systematic procedures in those early months. When insiders hinted at the existence of a referral system, an elaborate trafficking of abortion clients across state lines that operated in defiance of the law, I could make little sense of reconciling this expansionary structure with the restricted legitimate one reported by most respondents. Despite my best efforts to sound out the depth structure, this clutter of suppressed knowledge remained submerged. After five months I could only conclude that abortion is a risky venture carrying high social costs for producers and even higher costs for consumers and the larger public.

PHASE II: FORMAL AND INFORMAL INTERVIEWING (FIVE MONTHS)

If the first stage of fieldwork involved seeking a model as a general guide for fieldwork, the second phase concentrated on generating data to support, reject, or revise the preliminary model. This required tapping occupational groups who provided service for abortion seekers (e.g., physicians, social workers, family-planning counselors, and the like) to gain data on the who, what, where, how, and why questions. Who provided legal (i.e., hospital) abortions, and who offered illegal ones? What organizations or occupations were involved? How did participants view the abortion issue in terms of the "risk" factor? Where were abortion seekers routed? How did mechanisms for regulating services operate among legitimate providers? Why did some professionals and agencies appear willing to be intensively involved in certain phases of abortion service while others rejected abortion clients altogether?

It was a big order. Freedom from time and personal commitments required of the organizational participant, though, meant that I could experiment with a number of alternative strategies for generating data. The basic problem was inefficiency; the methods search often entailed loss of time and yielded unproductive or repetitive data. In working with three main techniques—"snowball" sampling, participant observation, and interviewer-selected sample—I eventually learned to assess their utility and to shift techniques to adapt to the stage of the fieldwork and my increased ability to deal with high-status health professionals.

The snowball sample that had initially appeared so fruitful turned out to have serious defects. The method yielded colleague and friendship networks, not the organizational linkages I sought. Moreover, respondents tended to answer questions soliciting facts about their practice with tangential opinions ("I have nothing against abortion, but the woman should be using contraceptives"). Medical specialties were even paradoxically lined up on what appeared to be the opposite position expected on the abortion issue. One county medical association survey showed gynecologists expressing the most negative abortion values among all specialities sampled, whereas pediatricians were most favorably disposed to medical abortion. Did this imply that gynecologists rejected women for pre- and postabortion treatment or medical referral? Alternatively, were pediatricians seeing child-abuse cases resulting from unwanted pregnancies, leading them to favor abortion as a preventive medicine measure? My snowball approach did not reveal the answers.

One alternative I considered was to drop this circuitous route for seeking respondents and to join the abortion reformers. This would eliminate two problems—access and identity. On the one hand the access problem was the chief barrier to gaining insider's information; on the other hand my protective guise of "objective" investigator, masking a strong personal commitment to abortion reform, made me increasingly uncomfortable.

The open-commitment course appeared tantalizing but essentially impractical. If I pursued this course, I would end up with a study of the reform movement, not an investigation of the abortion market. This was confirmed by repeated interviews with a radical-reformer physician, who convinced me that his view of the world (which was similar to mine) was too restrictive and too "political" for an adequate understanding of multigroup conflict and change. After wrestling with a research identity, I chose to remain formally uncommitted to the movement, at least until I had established myself in the field as an independent investigator.[4]

A third technique entailed interviewing some leading medical practitioners and researchers by presenting myself as a neutral observer writing a research report in an area where documentation was either inadequate or lacking altogether (which, of course, was true). Data from highly knowledgeable and influential persons enabled me to reenter the agency and practitioner scene with a greater understanding and appreciation of the subtleties of medical control of abortion.

Another reason for interviewing prominent specialists was political capital. University credentials, while honorable, did not certify me as a credible person who could handle organizational secrets or verbal admission of less-than-ethical management of this stigmatized service.

As a woman, I believed that I had at least three strikes against me. First, most informants assumed that I favored abortion and abortion reform

and tended to play down negative statements. Doctors remained professionally "correct" but not very informative. Second, most physicians and agency
doctors (with few exceptions) make no distinction between a woman
sociologist and a woman social worker, or between researcher and practitioner. The difficulty of establishing an authoritative professional identity
became clear after one hospital chief of staff denied my request for access to
patient records. Third, there are few professional women in medicine or
medical research. For the most part male physicians deal with women as
subordinates (e.g., paraprofessionals or helping personnel). As a "paraprofessional" I was useful for listening to the practitioner's problems in dealing
with a troublesome client group (i.e., abortion consumers). Productive data
on concrete strategies of office or hospital management, however, was almost
nil.[5] To bypass the identity block I used data supplied by influential persons
and posed the interview in the following way:

> Investigator: Dr. _____ , president of the OB-GYN Association mentioned
> to me last week [month] that he has altered his former policy
> of having decisions lodged in a hospital abortion board. Do you
> think your hospital [or colleagues] would be willing to try the
> consulting system that he recommends for hospital obstretric
> departments?
>
> Gynecologist: Incredible! He can do something like that. Look at the
> situation he has there—a university teaching hospital insulated
> from the community with complete freedom to experiment in
> these programs. If we tried that here, the board would close us
> down tomorrow.
>
> Investigator: Why does the board have this kind of power?
>
> Gynecologist: It's not merely the board. It's the whole community. There's a
> resistance here to that sort of thing. We'd have the Catholic
> hierarchy on our necks. They'd get their lawyers and shut the
> hospital down.
>
> Investigator: But don't physicians react to this type of external control?
>
> Gynecologist: Most don't want any part of that kind of medicine. Those that
> do can go elsewhere. We're running a clean hospital here. How
> could we possibly control some of these people [physicians]?
> They would abuse the freedom. We'd end up running an
> abortion mill for county [noncommunity] doctors who don't
> have the credentials for determining these kinds of decisions,
> much less giving this type of surgery.

Using this interview tactic, expressions of opinion declined and statements
about patient management increased. Frank responses to professional prac-

tice were, I concluded, directly related to their perception of my role as an informed observer with ostensible connections to esteemed colleagues.

Another procedure-involved an open-ended interview guide adapted to different occupational groups. After the first dozen or so interviews with a specific professional group, I reworded the items to include information from other respondents. Questions were then phrased as information statements (as the above interview illustrates). As the number of interviews accumulated, the pattern of responses usually became repetitive (e.g., almost all gynecologists admitted to having "problem pregnancy" patients; few had direct experience with abortion procedures; most kept a list of agency or clergy referrals, and so on). Since I was not interested in a survey of attitudes or practices, but rather in identifying a pattern of professional conduct, I tested the limits of the interview situation. Now I was ready for more direct evidence of how the medical system operated. For this I needed to secure such data as patient records, abortion procedures, and doctor-patient interactions. But more fieldwork was necessary before I could decide how best to proceed.

Three crucial fieldwork tasks were completed during this phase: coding, developing multiple perspectives, and delineating network boundaries.

Before entering the field, I developed a flexible coding plan for categorizing theoretical and empirical indicators. This plan facilitated ongoing analysis by building on earlier materials as I formulated questions and hypotheses throughout the study. Categories were added, combined, or deleted as the fieldwork progressed. Because interviews were categorized on a number of dimensions (e.g., occupation, ideology, actor's market role, and so on), I was often frustrated by efforts to keep current files. Daily interviewing, nightly taping, and weekend typing were slow, laborious, data-retrieval processes. Time spent on organizing files meant time taken away from fieldwork, a situation eventually resolved by acquiring a part-time assistant.

Coding was related to the pattern-building task and entailed three activities: separating rumor from fact and uninformed or out-of-date information from informed and current data; categorizing new information as redundant, similar to, different from, and anomalous in terms of existing categories; and employing the multiple method check-recheck approach (e.g., informants, documents, interviews, observations) before accepting data as evidence.

Interviews provided the baseline data, but more crucial at this stage was that this method yielded trusted informants who could provide access to secret documents, translate the often cryptic codes insiders use for privileged communication, and clarify their occupational perspective. Acquiring informants is a slow and tedious process. After eight months in the field and 105 interviews (44 physicians, 28 clergymen, 15 law-enforcement workers, and 18 agency nurses and social workers) I acquired seven informants—two physicians, two clergymen, one agency worker, and two movement feminists. If gaining informants involves one set of activities, keeping them apprised of the study and "on your side" requires still another. Informants not only need to be "informed" of the investigation by mail or phone (What does this mean? Who will it help? Why are you doing *that*?); they also must be visited, so as to maintain the more open agenda of face-to-face contact. And because each informant represented a distinct "slice" of the structure, offering a different perspective, keeping the players in their appropriate categories required perpetual finesse and diplomacy (e.g., physician X was not on speaking terms with clergyman Y; to bring up the "wrong" name in this context would seriously diminish rapport and usually release either resentment or invective.)

Constructing the abortion event as a social structure required building a picture from the disparate viewpoints of people in many different locations.[6] For example, to generalize about physicians' responses to abortion clientele I needed to know how physicians *differed* in terms of social location, type of practice, and previous experience with abortion patients. Repetition was no longer a problem; it was now a guide enabling me to move into new interviewing settings.

Moving to unit analysis entailed interviewing all professional and administrative persons in 25 different organizations, a strategy that rapidly changed my first impression of the new referral system as anomic. Once perceived as a formless, uncoordinated set of individual professionals and discrete organizations having no connective ties, the system began to coalesce into meaningful patterns. Medical and social agencies began to "look alike," having similar rhetorics and strategies for managing the "crisis client," a nearly universal label for abortion seekers. Other agencies "looked different" in that evasive techniques to avoid abortion clients included antiabortion rhetorics and rejection of abortion seekers as "someone else's problem."

During this time I discovered the central role of the Michigan "problem pregnancy" counseling clergymen, who, as part of a national network of clergy reformers, were mobilizing physicians and agencies and routing consumers to medical and counseling services in Michigan and elsewhere. Similar to a complicated puzzle, the abortion structure began to emerge. Hospital emergency rooms picked up the medical wreckage of women who risked health and life to get an illegal abortion. Over the last decade police had become slack in enforcing the law, a condition that encouraged proabortion forces to push more openly for changing the law and medical practice. And the risk factor had changed, enabling laypersons and even law-enforcement persons to link into the quasilegal system. The referral network emerged as an integral feature of the Michigan medical scene, resisted by many professionals and surrounded by silence; nonetheless, it was a highly successful enterprise. Clergy records showed their organization yearly referred 15,000 women for out-of-state abortions (a low estimate, as some clergymen refused to keep records either because they feared recrimination from hierarchy or parishioners or because they rejected the bureaucratic procedures).

While initially identifying two sectors, legal and illegal, I now discovered a third sector—and all of them were operating simultaneously. With this evidence the model was revised to include referral activities, later termed the "broker" segment of the abortion market.

PHASE III: PARTICIPANT OBSERVATION (SEVEN MONTHS)

The participant-observer phase extended to the completion of fieldwork. This period was especially marked by accelerated fieldwork involvement, entailing nearly a total commitment to field activities.

The problem now involved filling in concrete details of the market pattern in terms of which conditions, causes, consequences, and social units existed for each market segment, and determining how these features were connected. With the closing of official doors on my proposed study of hospital abortions, I was unable to repeat interview ground already covered. Moreover, I was still hesitant about how to negotiate political contacts, essential for understanding power arrangements. The referral system seemed little more than a skeletal shape that lacked substance, and the theoretical threads—market and broker processes—seemed as disconnected as before. Without observational data on hospital abortions or interviews with black market practitioners, the broker arrangements appeared as relatively isolated phenomena. At this juncture I could only infer that the processes of hospital control limited therapeutic abortions drastically, and that criminal abortionists and clergy-agency brokers picked up the slack left by legitimate medicine. In other words, *stringent regulation of a high-demand resource generates alternative channels of exchange*. But what evidence could support or refute this hypothesis?

On the surface the solution seemed simple—use cooperative informants, especially among the proabortion group. But there were obstacles here as well. Being tied into a specific network could bar future access to neutral or hostile respondents, and a prematurely open commitment to the abortion "cause" could exacerbate personal and political conflict. The issue was not merely pro- versus antiabortion but also reform versus radical change. Reformers clearly were operating within established moral boundaries; feminists perceived the abortion movement as part of the crusade for women's liberation. For weeks I dangled between identities—"true believer," movement radical, and scientist. Viewed some years later, the entire episode has a fantasy quality. Staying aloof gave me "freedom," but being a free agent kept me from data sources. It was an agonizing paradox, without apparent solution, for even relatively sophisticated fieldwork training offered few guidelines.

Organizational realities had to be contended with. Factionalism was commonplace, and "oneupmanship" among opponents frequently led to intense antagonisms over tactics. Movement goals were often ignored or subordinated to petty rivalries and ad hominum disputes. Overlapping authority structures (especially between physician and clergy groups) within the movement and between movement members and community organizations confounded the situation, making it difficult to assess which persons were dependable for providing information or contacts. My "sentiment-for-the-underdog" commitment (using Howard Becker's model) had little impact on some allies, who clearly identified themselves as racists, sexists, and antiwelfare ideologists. In a word movement politics and personalities threatened to needlessly absorb energies that I believed would better be devoted to observing events and cross-checking data.

Inevitably fieldwork involved varying types and degrees of social participation. Lunches, cocktail parties, dinners, and extensive telephone and personal contacts helped establish the political connections necessary for gaining access to confidential records and setting up a survey study (described below). Once key informants understood that my commitment was ideologically supportive, if politically detached, I was allowed access to the closed hospital system and, with less success, to the criminal system.

Because abortion was now legal in New York State and elsewhere, both therapeutic and criminal abortion markets were declining in Michigan. If the Michigan referendum action was successful in legalizing abortion, it would transform the market before I could finish the fieldwork. A physician informant eventually demonstrated how legitimate and criminal systems mutually reinforced each other. Physicians and clergymen regularly referred patients to selective criminal abortionists on a negotiated-fee basis. In turn doctors inexperienced in abortion techniques were being provided training by illegal entrepreneurs in preparation for legal abortion. (One illegal abortionist in Chicago whom I interviewed was reported to have made three trips to Japan and at least two trips to Eastern Europe to learn updated abortion techniques.)

The participant-observer label is often a misnomer for many fieldwork projects. As the term implies, these researchers supposedly know their informants as persons "in the round," including job, home, and social events; this situation characterized my involvements. What is frequently ignored is that there is a crucial difference between genuine participation (involving daily routines such as organizational payrolls, deadlines, political defeats, victories, and the like) and marginal participation, wherein the aim is to write a research report and move into an unrelated work world. I lived with my marginality by redefining my ideological commitment in moral terms, while justifying my political detachment as pragmatically necessary for realizing my own career goals. (Participant-observations problems are described in: Denzin, 1970; Habenstein, 1970; Jacobs, 1970; Johnson, 1975; Lofland, 1971.)

The participant-observation stage was especially useful for revising the descriptive model through new evidence furnished by on-the-scene observations. A reversal in perspectives was often one result.

Here is an example of how I clarified the conflicting medical realities about abortion.

Investigator:	Why do doctors believe that abortion is such a dangerous procedure?
Chief of Staff	Because most physicians don't have any experience in giving them. Their experience is limited, when they do give them, to one or two a year, often on medically sick patients. Also, they are fearful of puncturing the pregnant uterus, now stretched and thinned like a blown-up balloon, with instruments in an area they can't see and haven't developed a touch for.
Investigator:	But don't we know that a very large number of women receive illegal abortions every year, and return to have normal pregnancies and deliveries?
Chief of Staff	Yes, but our physicians see only the wreckage of botched abortions in their offices or hospital emergency rooms. They see the gynecological cripples that result from this experience, and they want nothing to do with it.
Investigator:	Doesn't this finding lead to a demand by physicians for reform of the present law?
Chief of Staff	Not necessarily. Doctors don't like the idea of using abortion as a back-up for sloppy birth control use. Besides, giving abortions is not interesting medicine. It's too routine, and would limit their practice to a repetitive procedure. Once the word got out, they'd be running an abortion mill.

Many physicians further admitted that they regarded abortion patients as either promiscuous or mentally ill, an undeserving clientele who took up hospital resources and physician time better spent on "sick" people. This link between abortion and a degraded population, underworld operators, and unethical physicians explained why so few physicians were actively engaged in legal reform or in testing the law by openly giving abortions. Recognizing the reluctance of physicians and organized medicine to plunge into change or patient advocacy led to hypotheses about the role of the broker system and the physicians' tentative position at the boundaries.

PHASE IV: STRUCTURED TECHNIQUES (SIX MONTHS)

The structured-technique stage of data gathering entailed three studies within the study: (1) a two-hospital (Michigan) analysis of abortion patient records for 1971 (n=2000); (2) a 35-item questionnaire mailed to 109 consulting clergy, based on a geographically stratified sample (clergy membership=300), with 62 persons responding; and 42 retrospective interviews (56 open-ended questions) of abortion consumers (36 completed protocols) who had received abortions from 1964 through 1972. This section documents the problems, social context, and decision plan for collecting such survey materials.

After nearly 15 months of fieldwork, the data appeared adequate for mapping out the major institutional and market sectors (e.g., legal, medical, social agency, public health, and referral activities). Without survey data, though, it was impossible to judge which various practices or policies were widespread and which were restricted to only a few settings. Ambiguities were still pervasive and required more intensive rather than extensive data gathering. There were dangling questions. Were counseling clergymen in rural areas linked to the local health system (indicating a type of legitimacy for abortion referral)? Or did they send patients away to urban communities for necessary services? Was there really a link between therapeutic abortion and involuntary sterilization, as feminists claimed? How were abortion seekers coping in this organizationally untested, and apparently very complicated, broker system?

Scrapping one set of plans and settling for compromise solutions was a common experience. After failing to receive approval to observe various hospitals' abortion boards on grounds of patient confidentiality, I shifted to hospital records, a less direct way of discerning typical control strategies. I was not disappointed.

For example, a standard control strategy in the urban university hospital was psychiatric labeling, resulting in 80 percent of abortion patients being diagnosed as "psychotic" (although only a small proportion of the records showed previous psychiatric disability). Fully 44 percent of these patients were sterilized as part of the abortion "package." From these data it was clear that high rates of complication were genuine and in large part induced by the health care structure. Hospital records and interviews showed that a relatively large staff of low-experienced physicians (averaging five abortion procedures yearly) performed mainly mid-trimester abortions, procedures typically associated with high medical injuries. System quotas and delays, additional surgical problems associated with sterilization, and a relatively high-rise patient group (e.g., multiple pregnancy, illness, presurgical pregnancy complications, and the like) combined to make abortion a hazardous and expensive (averaging $800) procedure.

The rural hospital served a distinctly different clientele (e.g., young, never pregnant, early gestation), had no formal psychiatric screening, and performed low-cost (about $300), low-risk abortions with few or no medical complications. The physician who created the program had positioned himself on local hospital and community boards, convincing town elites that abortion was necessary for "mental health" reasons. Interviews confirmed that a carefully selected clientele eliminated the rationale for sterilization, and a healthier and younger patient group kept the complication rate down, a precautionary measure to safeguard the program.

Importantly, survey data would have made little sense without the earlier stages of interviewing and participant observation. I would have been unable either to translate the raw data into meaningful patterns or to interpret it in sociological terms.

Studying the counseling movement among the clergy proved fascinating, as both occupation and preoccupation. I had been interviewing this group for almost six months before I used the term *broker* to describe their activities. My early hope of constructing a natural history of the organization, in which I had been encouraged by clergy organizers, did not appear feasible. The research project was by this time a far more elaborate, time-demanding, and expensive enterprise than initially envisioned. Thus, time and cost constraints led to the decision to use a mailed questionnaire for studying changes in the clergy movement personnel and recruitment patterns (e.g., shift from crusader role to community resource role). But I was naive in believing that the clergymen would be willing to expose possibly contaminating information, even as anonymous subjects. There were many blank spots—personal networks, relationships with clients, troubled marriages, parish and administrative threats—and only sketchy returns on role-management strategies. Undoubtedly, clergymen were also responding to the questionnaire as an "official" document and to the investigator as an organizational volunteer; they did not use this opportunity to express personal experiences and sentiments. Clergy informants later assured me that the data were not misinformation, but lacked the intensive quality achieved in interviews.

Trying to get the woman's version of the abortion routing required months of tracking down false leads or broken promises. At one point, attempting to interview clergy-counselor clients, I discovered that the movement had no record of clients' names. To use this channel I would have to serve as a lay counselor, requiring training and of course more months in the field. I avoided this hurdle by using three university students to contact friends or associates; in turn these contacts furnished other leads.

During the search far more women (probably over half) refused an interview or failed to show up at the appointed time than were finally interviewed. We attributed this to the persistence of the abortion stigma, particularly for the unsophisticated or younger college student, a situation substantiated by discussions with students in my Sociology of Deviance classes.

PHASE V: RECONSTRUCTING THE MODEL (FIVE MONTHS)

In brief the evolving fieldwork strategy entailed multiple methods, which were adapted to fieldwork experience and avowed ideological commitments. Other considerations in choosing samples and techniques included stage of the study, theory development, and data clarification. My problem at this final stage included two related issues. The first was how to write up a narrative that had no logical conclusion, and the second involved incorporating the actors' model, my ideological perspective, and sociological model into a conceptually coherent statement.

Constructing a pattern means fitting together a number of episodes, events, incidents, and meanings—an inductive approach that usually violates standard textbook procedures of precision, efficiency, and verification. Rather than hypothesis "testing" in the classic sense, involving rules of deduction and statistical inference, hypotheses were viewed as tentative; initially a hunch, followed by trial-and-error methods of securing additional information before the speculation became a guiding question, then a hypothesis, and only after no disconfirming evidence, a "fact."

Data also had to be checked for flaws, errors, and inconsistencies before making the final model revision.

Researching changing social events involves substantial costs and delays. The most significant hold-up at this stage was the issue of "whose perspective" would be the core of the study—that of physician, clergy, abortion seeker, agency professional, or feminist.

For a brief time I considered taking the consumer point of view as the central focus, but I soon realized that this perspective could severely limit the study's structural scope. Because abortion seekers and patients had only superficial ties with clergy counselors and physicians, these consumers played only a marginal role in social change. Studying the powerless, I recognized, was not necessarily the best strategy for understanding the organization of power.

A second alternative was a pluralistic perspective—legal, medical, clergy movement, social service agencies, and consumer, without choosing "favorites." This required wrestling, first with the disparate evidence (i.e., contradictions and differences) to develop a consistent view of each segment, and second to integrate these segments into coherent sociological analysis of conflict and change. An early draft of the multiperspective approach showed me its weakness. I had captured the market phases (legal, illegal, and broker segments), revealing some intricacies of the changing system, but the study lacked focus.

Finally, I took the clergy movement as the principal drama, to examine how market activities (e.g., hospital management and agency activities) affected the clergy movement and were in turn influenced by that movement. The multiple-perspective approach was salvaged by rendering actors' constructions of the situation in terms of their organizational position and by incorporating my concern for social change and its consequences for enhancing options for women.

Some research involvements neither die nor fade away but continue to haunt the investigator. Abortion remains a vocation and avocation, despite the reality that advocates' passions and perseverance have generated few fundamental structural changes. Examining the current scene reveals physicians and administrators controlling access to abortion services, providing rhetorics for participation, unilaterally establishing costs, and offering questionable "treatment" programs for abortion repeaters or others violating established rules (e.g., teen-age pregnancy). This has invariably excluded consumers from rule-making and allocation decisions, an integral feature of movement goals. Because my "bandwagon" commitment to movement ideology caught me off guard, I could not adequately predict that decriminalization would institute an exclusively professional regime, eliminating the amateurs. It is apparent that research dealing with social change must also account for the way that systems maintain themselves by co-opting and absorbing alternatives. In the abortion case the "routinization of charisma," following the rise and legitimation of new structures, defused potentially threatening practices by translating moral issues into occupational mandates.[7]

NOTES

[1] I am grateful to Peter K. Manning, Michigan State University, for his critical reading, which contributed to useful revisions.

[2] Various terms used throughout this report denote distinct procedures. *Method* is the most general term, and refers to any logical, systematic inquiry. Thus fieldwork is a method, as are interviews, questionnaires, and content analysis of documents and organizational records. *Strategy* entails a relatively long-range plan or course of action for deployment of the investigator's resources to acquire data or data sources. The research stages explicated here indicate a series of strategic maneuvers for obtaining information or access. *Tactic* involves a specific plan or procedure for gaining data in fieldwork situations that require expedient or political approaches.

Technique specifies a technical activity, contingent on fieldwork know-how for acquiring data. The success of a given method (e.g., interview) for yielding data depends on the stage of the fieldwork (strategy), the specific fieldwork situation (tactic), and the ability to negotiate social contacts and personal identities for using technical skills (techniques).

[3] An excellent collection of papers dealing with the relationship between power structures and research enterprise is found in "Social Control of Social Research," *Social Problems*, 21 (Summer, 1973), entire issue.

[4] The subjective component as explicitly developed in this narrative is a device for clarifying the link between personal identity and methodological and epistemological issues involved in fieldwork. The separation between self, methods, and knowing—characteristics of the verification mode—is clearly inappropriate for the discovery process; *Verstehen*, or understanding, requires a reflexive mode. This includes a selx-consciousness of the investigator in role; or a conception of self as engaged actor shaped by social and historical forces. (These issues are examined in Becker, 1963, 1964; Erickson, 1972; Gouldner, 1971; and Lee, 1975.)

[5] Being a woman investigator, I later realized, had more positive than negative aspects for turning up data. In the first place I avoided counterproductive debates on the confused morality of abortion; second, a lack of professional identity may have been on occasions ego deflating when relating to high power-persons, but served to maintain open communication with equal or lower rankers (e.g., agency workers, medical students, etc.). And the imposed "paraprofessional" role sensitized me, far more than collegial status, to the sexist hierarchical nature of organized medicine and its incapacity to provide radical leadership for legal change. (See also Moore, 1973.)

[6] For analysis of two distinct models (actor's model and observer's model) and their use by social scientists, see Tyler (1969) and Ward (1965).

[7] Space limitations do not permit developing the critical theory, especially the perspectivist approach, that animated this fieldwork. For a formulation of these ideas, see Davis and Anderson (forthcoming).

REFERENCES

Becker, Howard. *Outsiders: Studies in the sociology of deviance.* New York: Free Press, 1963.

Becker, Howard. *The other side.* New York: Free Press, 1964.

Becker, Howard. "Whose side are we on?" *Social Problems*, 1967, *14* (Winter): 239-47.

Cicourel, Aaron V. *Method and measurement in sociology.* New York: Free Press, 1964.

Davis, Nanette J. Labeling theory in deviance research: A critique and reconsideration *Sociological Quarterly*, 1972. (Fall).

Davis, Nanette J. Clergy abortion brokers: A transactional analysis of social movement development. *Sociological Focus*, 1973, *6* (Fall).

Davis, Nanette J. The abortion consumer: Making it through the network. *Urban Life and Culture*, 1974 (January).

Davis, Nanette J. *Sociological constructions of deviance: Perspectives and issues in the field.* Dubuque, Ia: Wm. C. Brown, 1975.

Davis, Nanette J., and Anderson, Bo. "Ideological biases in an academic tradition." In Robert B. Smith (Ed.), *Handbook of social science methods,* Vol. I, *An introduction to social research.* Cambridge: Ballinger, 1982.

Denzin, Norman K. *The research act.* Chicago: Aldine, 1970.

Erickson, Kai T. "Sociology: That awkward age. *Social Problems,* 1972, *19* (Spring).

Filstead, William J. (Ed.). *Qualitative methodology: Firsthand involvement with the social world.* Chicago: Markham, 1970.

Gouldner, Alvin. *The coming crisis in Western sociology.* London: Heinemann, 1971.

Habenstein, Robert W. *Pathways to data.* Chicago: Aldine, 1970.

Jacobs, Glenn. *The participant observer.* New York: George Braziller, 1970.

Johnson, John. *Doing field research.* New York: Free Press, 1975.

Kitsuse, J. I. Societal reaction to deviant behavior. *Social Problems,* 1962 (Winter): 247-57.

Lee, Alfred M. Humanist challenges to positivists. *Insurgent Sociologist,* 1975 *6* (Fall): 41-50.

Lemert, Edwin. *Human deviance, social problems, and social control.* Englewood Cliffs, N.J.: Prentice-Hall, 1964.

Lemert, Edwin. *Social pathology.* McGraw-Hill, 1951.

Lofland, John. *Analyzing social settings.* Belmont, Calif.: Wadsworth, 1971.

Manning, Peter K. Deviance and Dogma. *British Journal of Criminology,* 1975, *15* (January): 1-20.

Moore, Joan. Social constraints on sociological knowledge: Academic research concerning minorities. *Social Problems,* 1973, *21* (Summer): 65-66.

Packer, Herbert. *The criminal sanction.* Stanford, Calif.: Stanford University Press, 1967.

Schur, Edwin M. *Crimes without victims.* Englewood Cliffs, N.J.: Prentice-Hall, 1965.

PART TWO
INTERVIEWS

The interview is a basic tool of social research; perhaps more books and articles have been written about the interview and interviewing than about any other technique of data gathering. It is often used to supplement other approaches. In experimental work subjects have been "debriefed" after experiments to ascertain what they understood to have been happening, to detect biases in the experimental conditions, or to correct misimpressions. In field studies interviews are often used to gather detailed data that may be obtained more parsimoniously in that fashion than through official records or observations. Interviews are even used in interview studies to check the quality of interviewers, to ascertain their level of performance, or to check on the validity of data. Whether interviews are *unstructured* (the respondents are free to discuss whatever they want at their own pace), *focused* (a limited subject is probed in depth without a fixed order), or *structured* (prespecified questions are asked in a fixed order), they are a major source of social science data. *216246*

In this section examples and discussions of these three rather different forms of interviews are presented. Blauner and Wellman describe their attempt to "decolonize" research by making residents and local community people a part of their research, hiring community people to work in the project, and obtaining the views and suggestions of these people by means of unstructured interviews as fundamental guidance in the developing work. Although this principle has long been a part of anthropological fieldwork, especially the use of "native" or resident informants, it has usually been assumed that the characteristics of the interviewer, the interviewee, the setting, and the questions did not have an independent effect on the pattern of response elicited in surveys. At very most it was considered as something to be controlled by hiring interviewers of different age and sex and comparing their data. Blauner and Wellman thus examine one kind of error that might be found in social research: the bias that comes from differences in social status and culture between the researcher and the researched, and from the unwillingness of local groups to answer questions in ways pertinent to the investigation.

In their chapter Zimmerman and Wieder suggest that they wish to find substitutes for "tracking"—actually following a person from day to day. Roger Barker's *One Boy's Day* (1951), an example of actual tracking, is tedious reading but does establish the fact that very detailed information can be produced by such a method. Unfortunately, it is atheoretical, unlike the Zimmerman and Wieder chapter, and does not contribute to our systematic understanding of social life. Tracking is an observational technique, and alternatives such as diaries or diary-interviews are ways of triangulating behavior with reported behavior. Zimmerman and Wieder paid their respondents to keep diaries of their activities, and then with information from these diaries as benchmarks, they utilized focused interviews to check the consistency of their diarists' accounts. This cross-check is necessary because there is ample evidence that what we say and what we do are often quite different things.

In attending to temporal, spatial, and interactional diversity, to diversity within roles, and to person-related differences in the positioning of an observer Zimmerman and Wieder outline some of the basic choices in undertaking a field role, as well as those aspects of social life that the diary, diary-interview method can illuminate. They emphasize in their work the connection between such a self-conscious process of research and the analytic-induction method evaluated by Manning in the last section of this volume.

The next chapter, by Somers and his colleagues, describes a survey of students who were participants in a youth culture not unlike that studied by Zimmerman and Wieder. This survey utilized a combination of structured interviews and questionnaires to assess the students' cultural and political views and usage of drugs, the same topics studied by Zimmerman and Wieder. Somers et al. not only provide an insightful report of their problem formulation, but also discuss the important ethical problems intrinsic to studies of sensitive topics such as these. For them the critical issues involved, if not total decolonization of their research, at least the following: (1) ensuring that the interview data could not be used against the best interests of the respondents, and, more positively, would help the respondents by providing enlightenment concerning the crucial topics of the study to policy-makers, the public, and the respondents themselves; and (2) minimization of bias by training the interviewers and controlling the quality of the data. The investigators feared that the sensitivity of their questions would lead many potential respondents to refuse the interview or to give invalid replies. The chapter shows how these problems were handled. Of particular importance is the authors' discussion of the technique that enabled them to maintain the anonymity of their respondents, while at the same time matching information about names and interview responses.

In each of the three chapters in this part the reader is given some critical material, some suggestions for research, and some rich examples of the actual data gathering and analysis that occupies the investigators.

REFERENCES

Barker, Roger. *One boy's day.* New York: Harper & Row, 1951.

Chapter Four
The researcher and the researched[1]

BOB BLAUNER and
DAVID WELLMAN

INTRODUCTION

During the 1960s many assumptions of the academic world were challenged by events both on and off campus. There was a growing tendency for powerless and excluded social groups to view academics and their activities politically, to criticize their relation to, and responsibility for, existing economic, social, and ideological arrangements. In Latin America as well as in Europe and North America debates raged on the political commitments of social science. Calls arose for a radical sociology and new political sciences, histories, and anthropologies that would identify with the interests of oppressed classes and groups.

The relationship of social research to ethnic and racial minorities came under particular attack. The idea of internal colonialism was advanced in Latin America as a framework for interpreting the subjugation of Indian populations, and in the United States it became an important paradigm with respect to the oppression of blacks, Chicanos, and other third-world people.[2] Though no one seriously questioned the positive contributions that social science had made in the past to the liberalized climate in which subjugated groups were presently intensifying their struggles, the new perspective indicated that social science research was itself caught up in the colonial relation between white institutional power and the communities of people of color. As ethnic and racial consciousness exploded in the black power movement, the social scientist began to look like another agent of the white power structure. Like policemen, storekeepers, teachers, and welfare workers social scientists were usually white outsiders who entered ghettos and barrios to advance personal and institutional goals that were determined outside the community of study. The authority of these outsiders to diagnose group problems and to interpret culture and life styles conflicted with the demands for group self-definition and self-determination that were central to the new consciousness of the racially oppressed. From such a perspective the fact that the major studies and analyses of third-world people in the United States have been carried out by whites took on a new significance.[3]

Movements toward decolonization that have shaken other areas of culture and politics thus confronted social research. Social scientists studying race and poverty in the 1960s found that the norms of pure, disinterested scientific investigation were no longer adequate. The "subjects" had changed from "passive objects" to active critics of the research process. The experiences of our own study, the subject of this paper, were profoundly influenced by this new dialog between social scientists and the racially oppressed.

In 1965, when the second author began work in the area of black-white relations, he was impressed by an apparent centrality of what might be termed "manhood issues" for understanding both racism and the comparative position of Negroes in American society. His initial theoretical approach to the low status and problems of black people was in terms of cultural and social determinants within the group, paralleling the sociologists' attempts to understand the relative mobility of various European and Asian ethnic groups in terms of distinctive group characteristics. He was struck by indications of strong tension between men and women in the black community and by a variety of data suggesting that women tended to be relatively more resourceful, assertive, and perhaps "less damaged" by the legacies of slavery and discrimination. An early hypothesis was that black lower class society had innovated a concept of manhood—a street or hustling ideal—that while viable as a survival technique, actually functioned to impede the integration and success of individuals—and by aggregation—the group as a whole into the larger society.

About this time Moynihan's report became public.[4] His perspective overlapped with our own in many ways, though there were significant differences. For our work the key point about *The Negro Family* was not any new facts or theories that it introduced, but the dialog that it opened up. The critical responses to this controversial document, both reasoned and emotional from the black community and its scholars as well as from white social scientists, were important to the clarification of our theoretical positions. The emergence of the black power perspective the following year, as well as our continuous involvement with groups and individuals in the ghetto, also sharpened our awareness of the complex theoretical and political issues of contemporary racism.

In addition our own staff members who knew racial oppression from firsthand experiences forced us to look more closely at the realities of race. We saw that such questions as manhood and male-female relations could not be isolated from the larger structural pattern of racial domination. To place the problem in its original fashion, no matter how sophisticated and sensitive our research, would have clear theoretical and political consequences. Our original emphasis implied a denial of the historical and contemporary power of racism, of power and privilege, as first causes of our racial arrangements. We therefore transformed our project's focus, giving primary interest to racism and institutional conflict and reshaping within this larger context our concerns with manhood and culture. We enlarged our concerns to deal with the interaction between minority individuals and the social institutions shaping their views of themselves and their possibilities in the larger society. We sought to uncover subcultural and social-psychological mechanisms developed by minority group members to protect their self-dignity and manhood.

Important as theory is, by itself it cannot resolve the contradictions inherent in studies of race relations and third-world groups that are conceived and directed by white social scientists. As our project progressed, we became more and more aware of these built-in conflicts between the colonial aspects of racial research and our identification with decolonization movements, between the institutional and professional context of social science and our critical posture toward established theory and practice in sociology. In this paper and in an earlier one (Blauner & Wellman, 1973) we attempt an understanding of these contradictions and at the same time discuss the attempts we made, only partly successful, to move in the direction of decolonization. The earlier essay focused particularly on the issue of white researchers in the black community and on problems within the university milieu. The present chapter treats in greater depth how we adapted our methods of inquiry and data collection to the systematic inequality inherent in the relationship between the researcher and the researched.

SOCIAL RESEARCH AS A REFLECTION OF SOCIAL INEQUALITY

Sources of the Problem

Scientific research does not exist in a vacuum. Its theory and practice reflect the structure and values of society. In capitalist America, where massive inequalities in wealth and power exist among classes and racial groups, the processes of social research express both race and class oppression. The control, exploitation, and privilege that are generic components of social oppression exist in the relation of researchers to researched, even though their manifestations may be subtle and masked by professional ideologies.[5]

Behavioral scientists' control over research enterprises, including all the intergroup interaction they set in motion, is supported by the norms of professional autonomy and expertise. According to this view only social scientists can define a suitable problem for research because they alone know enough about the theory of the field and the methods by which theories are tested. In this scientific model there is no place for the community-of-those-studied to share in the determination of research objectives. The theories, the interests, and the very concepts with which we work respond to the dynamics of increasing knowledge within our individual disciplines and professions, as well as to fashions and status concerns. The life problems and needs of the communities-under-study need affect the scholar only indirectly. A similar imbalance in control exists at the point of research production—the administration of a test or questionnaire, the conducting of an interview, even the moment when a participant-observer sees something in the field and makes a mental note for a diary. At every stage there is a gulf between the researcher's purposes and the subject's awareness of what the investigator and the research instrument are all about.

Consider the norm of the in-depth interview—the respondents are expected to reveal various aspects of their personal lives and of their social and political beliefs; interviewers are supposed to be neutral recorders, revealing nothing in return about their own lives, feelings, or opinions—this might "bias" the data. The monopoly of control continues through analysis and publication. The individual research subject's unique outlook and specific responses are typically lost in the aggregate of data, which are subjected to standardized statistical summaries, ideal type classifications, or some other operation. Because behavioral scientists write for other scholars and "experts," those who are studied usually cannot understand the research report toward which their own responses contributed. The communication gap between researcher and researched, which probably exceeds that between doctor and patient, serves to maintain the inequality of power between the two mutually interdependent parties and underlies the privileged status and elite outlook that social scientists enjoy in a class society.

Exploitation exists whenever there is a markedly unequal exchange between two parties and when this inequality is *supported* by a discrepancy in social power. In social research, subjects give up time, energy, and trust but typically get almost nothing out of the transaction. We social scientists obtain grants that pay our salaries; the research thesis makes our professional statuses legitimate; then publications advance us in income and rank, further widening the material status gaps between the subjects and ourselves. Thus, many of us know ghetto residents who have said—partly boasting, partly complaining—that they have put a dozen people through graduate school, so studied have been some black communities, e.g., Richmond, California. Of course, once a study is completed, the chances are that no one in the community will ever see the researcher again. There may be less unhappiness at being used in this way by a budding scholar from one's own ethnic group, but this does not change the essentially exploitive character of the relationship, since minority social scientists are still groping toward the forms that would relate their careers to their communities of origin in a meaningful way. All this contributed to the hostility to universities in many black ghettos during the 1960s and early '70s.[6]

What keeps behavioral scientists from sensing that their projects use people as objects, as things, as means to an end? Not ethical insensitivity, primarily, though it is true that professional socialization is notoriously indifferent to such philosophical issues. It is the ideology of science that provides the rationale. For we have been taught that the development of a science is a slow and cumulative process, and therefore no quick results should be expected. Only when our science gets it together will we have the theoretical knowledge to provide the basis for solutions to the social and human problems that poor and oppressed people face. Built into the deepest roots of the scientific attitude is the assumption that the accumulation and systematization of knowledge *must* be in the interest of the common good; in America social science has gained justification through its concern for the common man. Some scholars, perhaps many, retain this belief; perhaps it is defensible if one's view of science and society is sufficiently long-term. For the short run, the span of time in which people live their lives, it is seriously open to question.

The poor and the racially oppressed have been promised much from social science. Occasionally a study, a book, or a series of investigations does make a difference to a particular community or even to national policy. The 1954 Supreme Court decision on school desegregation responded to briefs that depended heavily on sociological and psychological research. But in the overwhelming number of instances there is no tangible change in the lives of the subjects—in either the short or the long run. The poor and oppressed, with their pragmatic sense and sensitivity to phoniness, knew this long before many of us. The lack of payoff comes from at least two sources—first, the distance between our theoretical and empirical concerns and the life problems and situations of those we study; second, and ultimately more crucial, our lack of power to implement and influence change in those cases where existing knowledge already suggests specific solutions or reforms.

Our Attempts at Reform

We began with a number of specific strategies aimed at transcending the one-sided and exploitive dynamics of the research process. First, the funding agency budgeted $2,500 to enable us to pay five dollars to each respondent. We stressed that this money was a wage for labor time, rather than a bribe for information. Though a ludicrous sum in today's era of inflation, in 1968 the five dollars sometimes made a difference and was appreciated. Still a surprising number of interviews took place freely, without any interest in compensation. The idea that funded research on low-income communities should include sizable grants to indigenous people or organizations seems to have gained support since the 1960s.

Second, we decided to deviate from conventional notions of the appropriate research staff. "Science" is usually restricted to "experts" who are traditionally selected by "objective" criteria—formal education, degrees, research experience. Of course these criteria can effectively exclude people of color from actively participating in studies of their own communities. We considered as "experts" those who had lived the lives we wanted to understand. In selecting the original staff, then, degrees and research experience were hardly considered. Of the five black research assistants in a group of seven only one had a university degree. Three had no association with any college or university. More pertinent to us were their ties to diverse segments of the black community. The five fieldworkers and interviewers included a working longshoreman, a community worker in the schools, a Bohemian-oriented part-time musician, a Southern-born civil rights veteran, and a graduate student from a middle-class Berkeley background, who was the one woman in the group. Their informal education included such schools as street hustling, new careers and other poverty programs, civil rights and nationalist movements.[7]

What impressed us about this original staff was their ability to talk about sensitive issues, to draw people out, and to understand the feelings of a variety of sectors in the black community. Training a conventional research team is not easy. The problems are magnified when you begin with a group of people with minimal exposure to sociological thinking. The problem was compounded by a commitment to use the assistants in conceptualizing problems as well as for data collection. Weekly seminars, which were also attended by other social scientists interested in race relations, were the format for both the training and for generating intellectual contributions from the staff. The seminars began with discussions on the aims and ideas of the project.

These seminars accomplished a number of purposes. They allowed the staff to participate actively in the ongoing development of the study. They were also concerned with specific issues of data collection, staff members sharing with each other the various problems faced in their work. We also related current issues to our emerging framework. Although time-consuming and often frustrating, the weekly seminars were successful. Besides developing a certain collective spirit, they served to formulate and reformulate the basic assumptions and concepts underlying our research. Because our staff was in daily touch with communities outside the university (especially black ones), they gave us a better grasp of the complexities surrounding race in America and helped us avoid at least some mistakes.

A third tactic was an attempt to be honest about the purposes of the research and the difference it would make. The approach was "no bullshit." We did not promise to save the world; we did make it clear that we were dissatisfied with the way some social scientists had approached race relations and described the experience of black people in America. We hoped to do better, and if we were able, it would be because we had been able to elicit depictions of the realities as perceived by the principal actors, ordinary people, black and white. We used two types of data to accomplish this— relatively unstructured, in-depth interviews and group discussions involving three to five people.

The data collection proceeded in two stages. We first organized the discussion groups and recorded them on tape; then we interviewed individuals who had participated in the group sessions. The discussions were conducted with formal and informal groups and focused on various aspects of racism. The groups were selected to represent a range of sex, age, class, and political and religious orientations. We spoke with business clubs, hippies, church groups, unions, street gangs, militants, college students, and professionals. To maximize rapport research assistants established contact with leaders of these groups or with trusted figures in them. They explained the aims of the study and asked them to participate in a discussion.

The format was flexible. We wanted the direction of the meeting to be influenced by the special concerns of its members, by the natural climate of the group, and by the rapport developed between the group and the researcher-discussion leader. Each meeting began with an explanation of the study. To ensure that there would be a basis for comparison among groups we prepared a number of standard opening questions. The form they took varied according to the composition of the group, but basically the questions were aimed at eliciting feelings about the crucial racial issues of the day and their causes. We also formulated a number of questions that could be used to shift the focus when an issue was exhausted.

We decided to use group discussions as a data-gathering technique because they had the potential to stimulate spontaneous and heated arguments about racial problems. The discussions also served a number of other functions. First of all they acted as "icebreakers." Touchy questions were raised more easily in a group context; the collective support of a group gave its members a greater sense of confidence than if they were facing an interviewer alone. We were concerned that in a climate of highly charged racial issues group meetings might encourage hostile and even demagogic responses rather than a more critical soul-searching. In many instances this occurred. Airing these views, however, cleared the way for participants to move onto other aspects of the problem. The heated airing of opinions also encouraged a variety of responses to issues. Group members were forced to confront and disagree with each other and were able to deal with issues without being overly concerned with conning researchers.

The group discussions opened up the subject, cleared away some of the ideological response-sets, and gave discussion leaders an opportunity to prove themselves trustworthy, or at least as people who could be spoken to frankly. This rapport established, the discussion leader could then ask members of the group for individual interviews, where issues were pursued in greater depth in a more private and confidential setting.

Most of the data we collected were from these in-depth interviews. Since we wanted depictions of racism as it is experienced by the people living it, our interviews were as open-ended as possible. We therefore developed an interview guide rather than a schedule with structured questions. The guide posed issues in terms of people's life histories. Thus, interviews were organized around a person's experiences with the major insitutions in American society—family, school, work, police, politics, welfare, etc. We wanted to find out where each respondent was "at," to get as full a picture of him or her as possible. The point was to be flexible—to get inside the person and evoke a sociological portrait in the respondent's own language. This meant many things: starting with a person's current job and working back to how they got there; talking about where they would like to be and where they expected to be in the future; or starting with a person's childhood memories, including first experiences with social institutions, racism, or minority groups, and letting them proceed from there.

Structured survey questionnaires were not used because we did not want to put respondents into categories based on our own preconceptions. The decision to use in-depth interviews was also based on the exploratory character of the research and the sensitive nature of its content. We felt that the variables under consideration were not sufficiently developed to permit the use of precision instruments like survey techniques.

To ensure spontaneity and looseness we conducted the interviews with tape recorders. The interviewer, thus freed from note-taking, was encouraged to participate in the discussion and exchange ideas with respondents. This helped counter the tendency for interviews to be one-sided affairs; with the interviewer contributing little or nothing to the discussion.

Although it should be emphasized that our field staff mostly listened to respondents, they sometimes discussed their own views on controversial questions—black men and white men, the facts of the Huey Newton murder trial, the causes of unemployment. Sometimes heated and very emotional exchanges took place. Although such involvement is risky and must be utilized selectively on the basis of an intuitive grasp of a situation, it is striking that such violations of interview "objectivity" almost always took place in the very best interviews, the deepest, richest, most honest.

The best interviews came out of rapport that had been largely established in advance. Because Hardy Frye had been active in grass-roots organizations and outspoken in battles with the local power structure, he had gained a trust and a respect from black community members that made them remarkably open and honest in the interview. Similarly, when Alex Papillon interviewed longshoremen, he was putting on tape men who had known his father for years, who had seen him (Alex) take on the union leadership, or whom he had befriended on the job. Lincoln Bergman had a direct line to San Francisco's Haight-Ashbury because his brother and sister were then "hippies," and some of Sheila Gibson's best interviews were with long-time family friends. Thus, neutrality and distance are not always the best recipe for in-depth interviewing.

After the interviews and group discussions were transcribed, we summarized them in terms of their uniqueness. The first reading gave us a picture of the respondents as individuals; it also contributed to the second stage of data analysis. The transcripts were incredibly cumbersome, since the interviews had lasted from one and a half to four hours, and the guide only staked out in general terms the issues concerning us. And people responded to the issues in a variety of ways, many of which were unanticipated. In order to compare respondents systematically it was necessary to develop a coding procedure that could include most of the thoughts they brought to our attention. After reading each interview and discussion once through, we developed 32 topic-categories that we felt captured the essence of the interviews. Our coding scheme was not preconceived; it emerged out of our interaction with the thoughts expressed to us in candid, spontaneous dialogues. Too often research conducted among people of color is analyzed in categories derived from the life experience of the usually white social scientist. Many distortions of the black and brown experiences can be attributed to this procedure.

The categories we developed reflect the concerns of our respondents. For example, we did not usually ask about intermarriage, because we had felt that its importance for race relations was in large part myth or stereotyped. Yet this topic was brought up spontaneously and passionately by a sizable number of the whites. So it had to become a categorical focus. And many black people related to us exciting accounts of how they had maintained their dignity in situations designed to undercut self-respect. Some people explicitly referred to this as "survival," others talked about "getting by" or "getting over." These discussions emerged in various contexts—while talking about work experiences, encounters with school officials, growing up in the South, etc. Rather than simply code the account under the category "work experience," or "school experience," we developed a category for "survival." Through this process many of our topic categories were devised; other categories were obvious from the start. We knew, for example, that work experience, police encounters, manhood orientations, political attitudes, and dealings with racist institutions and practices were either important to our respondents or crucial to our analysis.

With these categories in mind we then reread the transcripts in order to code them. This two-stage process provided both a portrait of individuals and groups as well as a basis for comparison. We could move to substantive aspects of the analysis once the data were organized in this fashion.

Our perspective is complex and not easily summarized; nevertheless, an example of our approach should be helpful. One of the issues concerning us was how conflict, aggression, and subordinated social position are handled among oppressed groups. We were unsatisfied with traditional formulations suggesting that the characteristic response to oppression is self-hatred. To ascertain how people regard themselves our interviews raised questions concerning their goals, ideals, orientations toward work or education, and self-conception. Many people responded to these issues in ways that suggested they had not internalized America's negative image of black people.

Some respondents, for example, talked about subtle or behind-the-scenes renunciations of this image. Analyzing these materials helped us to differentiate among types of responses to social subordination.

Although we made some attempt to relate these differences to social class, region, sex, age, and family instruction about race, in the final analysis we chose not to carry through such a systematic analysis. When one of us analyzed the orientations of the white respondents to racial inequality, he initially classified them and attempted to link them to standard sociological variables. But the nature of our data did not lend itself to the kind of clear-cut coding and categorization through which definitive statements could be made about our sample in aggregate terms. Presenting the material in the form of vignettes or portraits, however, enhanced the unique quality of the data, and the author was still able to enrich his analysis of individual case histories by means of the general themes and issues developed in the early categorical analysis (Wellman, 1977). And when the other author began working on a study of the racial crisis of the late 1960s, he chose to present the data primarily in the form of edited interviews. Experimenting with other forms convinced him that the varieties of racial experience and the unique consciousness of the era could best be evoked by letting people speak for themselves (Blauner, in progress).

CONCLUSION

Our attempts at "decolonizing our project" were only partly successful. Our understanding of the ramifications of the researcher-researched relationship came too late in the game, and we could not fully reshape our strategies and priorities. Some major transformations in theoretical focus and research techniques were the most we could accomplish. This was partly due to another problem, the limitations of our resources in money, time, and people. If research with communities of the poor and the racially oppressed is to approach reciprocity in exchange values, the cost will be great. And because of our limited resources our priority had to be data collection rather than social action and service to the community. In decolonized research these priorities have to be equalized, if not reversed.

In our earlier essay we advocated the founding of new organizational formats to cope with this problem: Centers or institutes might integrate social action, change, and community assistance with the theoretical and empirical goals of the researchers. Such centers would begin with a commitment to serve the interests of oppressed communities, as seen by their citizens and local organizations. Academic research projects would relate to these interests and be understood, discussed, and approved within the community. Collection of data and theory testing would go hand in hand with the work of the center's staff in dealing directly with the needs of a community—problem-solving, technical assistance, organizing, education, and of course allocating money. With the financial crisis of the public sector today, the prospects for such centers seem utopian. But they still seem to us the only truly adequate response.

The major innovation that has taken place is the concern of the federal government for the protection of "human subjects." The human subject guidelines provide some minimum safeguard against extreme abuse, but with bureaucratization they have tended to become almost tokenist and in some instances create more problems than they solve (Duster, Matza, Wellman, 1978). HEW rules focus on individuals; they do not encompass the group or structural dimensions of research that we have addressed: the imbalance of power between largely white professionals and third-world or other ethnic groups, and between universities and low-income communites.

In the late 1960s many of our problems seemed to stem from the fact that two white sociologists had initiated a study of blacks, were in effect the bosses and the only staff members with long-term responsibility and commitment to the research. Even our project, which focused on racism, reflected in its structure and function the prevailing patterns of racial domination. In response to this we advocated a racial division of research labor in the fields of race and poverty. Though we did not say that whites cannot study people of color, we pointed out then that there were

certain aspects of racial phenomena, that are particularly difficult—if not impossible—for a member of the oppressing group to grasp empirically and formulate conceptually. These barriers are existential and methodological as well as political and ethical. We refer here to the nuances of culture and group ethos; to the meaning of oppression and especially psychic reactions; to what is called the black, the Mexican-American, and Asian, and the Indian *experience*. Social scientists realize the need for a series of deep and solid ethnographies of black and other third-world communities and for more penetrating analyses of the cultural dynamics, political movements and other contemporary realities of the oppressed racial groups. Today the best contribution that white scholars could make toward this end is not firsthand research but the facilitation of such studies to minority scholars by people of color.[8]

In this spirit we advocated the opening of graduate schools to minority scholars and recommended that white sociologists, instead of focusing on people of color, should investigate how racism is embedded in American institutions, culture, and personality.

Since this was written, the number of miniority social scientists has increased—both in the professions and in the graduate schools—and a certain amount of ethnography and social history are written by these "insiders." In the society as a whole, unfortunately, the Great Retreat from Race has been reflected during the 1970s in a diminishing research interest in racism. Too many white sociologists, just like their counterparts in the public at large, believe that the reforms of the 1960s effectively eliminated racism. In today's atmosphere, therefore, the two of us, anyway, welcome the interest of anyone, of whatever color, in examining the realities of our racial arrangements and in striving to make the research relationship a more equal and more humane one.

NOTES

[1] An earlier version of this chapter was presented at a conference on Problems of Research with Low Income and Minority Groups in the United States, sponsored by the National Institute of Child Health and Development, New Orleans, Louisiana, March, 1970. A different version of the paper appears in *The Death of White Sociology*, Joyce A. Ladner (Ed.) (New York: Random House, 1973). We are grateful to Hardy Frye, Robert Somers, Lloyd Street, and Harold Wilensky for critical reactions to the early draft.

[2] It appears as if the Latin American and North American theories developed for the most part independently of one another. See Casanova (1965) and Stavenhagen (1965). For a statement similar in outlook to the present essay see Stavenhagen (1971: 333-357). For discussions of internal colonialism in the U.S. see Cruse (1968), Carmichael & Hamilton (1967), Allen (1969), Blauner (1969), and Barrera, Munoz, & Ornelas (1972).

[3] In the U.S. the most strategic expression of this clash took place in the community and academic response to the "Moynihan Report." In Latin America the pivotal case of research serving American imperialism was Project Camelot, a Defense Department-financed study of internal conflict that was attacked as a counterinsurgency operation. On the relatively more complete research colonialism in the study of Mexican-Americans as compared to Afro-Americans see Blauner (1972).

[4] Moynihan (1965).

[5] An upsurge of critical questioning of the social scientist's ethical and political role in the mid-1960s is indicated by Sjoberg (1967).

[6] For searching insights into the dynamics of this situation we recommend Memmi (1967) and Fanon (1967). Fanon also speaks to the fundamental irrelevance of the manifest purpose and professional goals of the colonizer in the colonial situation. Even though the French doctor in Algeria was committed to the cure of his patient, the structural and cultural conflict made it inevitable that the colonized Arab would react to him as an alien and an enemy.

[7] Of course there was nothing new in our critique of standard research qualifications. The idea of using "indigenous" community people in research was part of the widespread subprofessional or paraprofessional movement, sometimes formulated as "new careers for the poor."

[8] For a critique of this position, see Merton (1972), pp. 13-14.

REFERENCES

Allen, Robert. Black awakening in capitalist America. Garden City, N.Y.: Doubleday, 1969.

Barrera, Mario, Munoz, Carlos, and Ornelas, Charles. The barrio as internal colony. In Harlan Hahn (Ed.), *Urban Affairs Annual Review 6*, 1972.

Blauner, Robert. Internal colonialism and ghetto revolt. *Social Problems*, 1969, *16* (Spring).

Blauner, Robert. *Chicano writing: Racial oppression in America*. New York: Harper and Row, 1972.

Blauner, Robert, & Wellman, David. Toward the decolonization of social research. In Joyce Ladner (Ed.), *The death of white sociology*. New York: Random House, 1973.

Carmichael, Stokely and Hamilton, Charles. *Black power*. New York: Vintage, 1967.

Casanova, Pablo Gonzalez. Internal colonialism and national development. St. Louis: Washington University Monograph Series, Studies in Comparative International Development, I, no. 4, 1965.

Duster, Troy, Matza, David, and Wellman, David. Field work and the human protection of subjects. Unpublished paper. Institute for the Study of Social Change. Berkeley: University of California, 1978.

Fanon, Frantz. *A dying colonialism*. New York: Grove, 1967.

Memmi, Albert. *The colonizer and the colonized*. Boston: Beacon, 1967.

Merton, Robert K. Insiders and outsiders: A chapter in the sociology of knowledge. *American Journal of Sociology*, 1972, *78*, 9-47.

Moynihan, Daniel Patrick. *The Negro family: The case for national action*. Washington, Department of Labor, March, 1965.

Sjoberg, Gideon. *Ethics, politics, and social research*. Cambridge, Mass.: Schenkman, 1967.

Stavenhagen, Rodolfo. Classes, colonialism, and acculturation. *Studies in Comparative International Development*, I, no. 6, 1965.

Stavenhagen, Rodolfo. Decolonizing applied social sciences. *Human Organization*, 1971, *30* (Winter): 333-57.

Wellman, David. *Portraits of white racism*. New York: Cambridge University Press, 1977.

Chapter Five
The diary–diary-interview method[1]

DON H. ZIMMERMAN and
D. LAWRENCE WIEDER

INTRODUCTION

When sociologists decide to enter the field for a firsthand look at social behavior in natural settings, they typically identify themselves as researchers, at least to some of their "subjects." They then somehow contrive to plant themselves squarely in the thick of things; that is, the observers attempt to position themselves in such a way as to gain access to the activities and events they wish to describe.

Whyte (1955), for example, was able to initiate his classic study of street corner boys in Boston through an introduction to the leader of the Norton Street gang (who was to become his chief informant). Whyte explained his research to Doc and asked for his help, to which Doc replied:

Well, any nights you want to see anything, I'll take you around. I can take you to the joints—gambling joints—I can take you around to the street corners. Just remember that you're my friend. That's all they need to know. I know these places, and if I tell them that you're my friend, nobody will bother you. You just tell me what you want to see, and we'll arrange it. (p.291)

Before meeting Doc, Whyte had experienced some difficulty gaining entry to the community. With Doc to vouch for him, however, he not only gained entry but also access to many of the patterns of Cornerville life that he subsequently reported in vivid detail in *Street Corner Society*. Meeting Doc was a fortunate happenstance for Whyte, but little else in his study was so crucially dependent on mere good fortune. He followed the model of the anthropologist and lived amidst the people he observed. Although he was known to the people in the community as an outsider, someone "writing a book," he was also part of the community, a true participant-observer.[2]

It is not always possible to follow the demanding regime of the participant-observer, however desirable that might be. This chapter presents a technique of fieldwork that approximates this classic pattern of observational research and suggests how it may be employed when investigators are not able to make firsthand observations themselves or wish to supplement their own observations. We call this alternative procedure the *diary–diary-interview* method.

We briefly note that the diaries just referred to are not those "intimate journals" (Madge, 1965: 83) that persons ordinarily keep for their own varied and private purposes, although such spontaneously generated documents have been employed in sociological and psychological research (cf. Allport, 1942; Angell & Freedman, 1953: 300-309; Blumer, 1939; Gottschalk et al., 1945; Thomas & Znaniecki, 1927). The term *diary* is used here to refer to an annotated chronological record (cf. Sorokin & Berger, 1939) or "log" (cf. Allport, 1942). Individuals are commissioned by the investigator to maintain such a record over some specified period of time according to a set of instructions. The employment of diary materials in this sense, when coupled with an interview (or series of interviews) based on the diary, is similar to the "life-history" method (cf. Becker, 1966; Conwell & Sutherland, 1937; Denzin, 1970: 219-259; Dollard, 1935; Madge, 1965: 182-190; Shaw, 1930) but also contrasts with it in certain respects. The relationship between the diary—diary-interview method and the life-history approach (and other uses of "personal documents") will be pointed out as relevant to the discussion that follows.

Consideration of certain fundamental problems of observational research will help in our presentation of diary—diary-interview method. We begin by pointing out that a basis for the observer's presence in the setting must be established—i.e., some acceptable rationale for the presence of the observer within the social space of the target group must be devised. Whyte (1955) solved this problem through his relationship with Doc. There are other solutions to the entrance problem, depending on the nature of the setting in question and the strategy of observation adopted.[3] While the problem of entry can sometimes perplex the would-be observer, a more serious problem looms when entry has been successfully effected.

This is called the "positioning" problem, the "getting into the thick of it." Even relatively simple social settings exhibit a diversity of behavior patterns distributed in time and space and across different categories of persons. Solutions to the problem of *positioning* the observer in such a way as to accommodate this diversity will inevitably have consequences for the nature and scope of information that can be gained, given that the observer cannot be everywhere at once nor can he expect to achieve the same degree of rapport with all potential subjects. The ideal never reached in practice is that of the omniscient, omnipresent observer, free to travel in space and time, invisible to those observed, and possessed of the ability to read minds (cf. Arnold, 1975: 24-25). Short of such talents, ethnographers must devise means to get where they need to be, see and hear what they can, develop trust between themselves and the subjects, and ask a lot of questions.

One way of accommodating this diversity of behavior in settings may be formulated as a general ethnographic strategy we call tracking. The diary-diary-interview method is, in some of its features, similar to tracking and thus can be used as an approximation to it. Prior to discussing tracking in any detail, we need to take a closer look at the problem of the diversity of behavior in settings with which tracking, as a method of "positioning" the observer, can deal. Some of the most fundamental dimensions of this diversity may be illustrated by considering the problem of observing the university.

1. *Roles and other person-related differences.* The observer must come to terms with the fact that different people and different types of people engage in different activities and that they also behave, feel, and think in typically different ways. These differences are often organized into different *roles* or social categories—e.g., age, sex, race, etc. Observers generally decide to focus on some specified roles rather than observing everyone they happen to confront on a "catch-as-catch-can" basis. In observing the university observers would be likely to select some roles from the wide range of roles (from deans to students to gardeners) that are potentially available to them.

2. *Diversity within roles.* The extent to which ethnographers must concern themselves with differences in behavior, feeling, and thought among incumbents of the same role depends heavily on exactly how they circumscribe their subject matter. For example, if they define a problem in terms of the *role* of the student *in* the university organization as such, the fact that students differ in many ways may not be relevant to the study. It may be sufficient for ethnographers to set out to observe all the different ways that students can act *on campus* as students (what the range of possible behavior is while enacting the student role) and what they *must* do as students (what they must minimally do if they are to maintain their status as students as compared with what they could do to get themselves dismissed from the university). Other definitions of the topic of interest, however, will require that ethnographers be more deliberate in their sampling of the persons whose behavior and talk they observe, perhaps even requiring a representative sample. An interest in the variety of student life-styles, for example, is likely to require such a sample.[4]

3. *Temporal diversity.* Ethnographers must also concern themselves with the fact that behavior, feeling, and thought vary temporally in terms of (1) daily, weekly, seasonal, etc. cycles, (2) in terms of phases of activity, and (3) more or less idiosyncratically. The university, for example, presents a very different scene for observation at twelve midnight than it does at twelve noon. Classes on the first day look different from classes in midterm. The behavior of students who engaged in the practice of "cramming" might involve their not studying during most of the semester. Observation might also show that when they did study prior to examinations, the way in which they behaved changed progressively as the hour of the examination approached. That is, one could observe that their pre-examination behavior had definite phases to it. Furthermore, the temporal arrangement of some of their behavior might appear idiosyncratic. One student might appear outgoing and happy during some weeks of the semester and withdrawn and

depressed during other weeks without these mood shifts being associated with other temporallly organized features of his existence. Nevertheless, his behavior, especially vis-à-vis other students, might be markedly different during these periods. Ethnographers who observed only one of these periods would find their observations skewed. Somehow ethnographers need to take into account the cyclical character of the observational scene, the differences between various phases of activities that may go on within that scene, and the possibility of idiosyncratic temporal differences.

5. *Spatial or locational diversity.* Persons may behave, feel, and think in typically different ways, depending on the setting or subsetting in which they locate or find themselves. On the same university campus one may find a more or less standardized way that students act and even feel and think within classrooms which contrasts with the typical ways that they behave, feel, and think in the gymnasium, at a rock concert, in the student union, in the library, and in professors' offices. Ethnographers must position themselves relative to these various subsettings and know the relationships between them in order to make sense of what they observe.

5. *Interactional diversity.* How persons behave, feel, and think may systematically vary depending on who they are interacting with and who is present. For example, students may talk in one fashion when they are in a discussion group that is led by a faculty member and in another fashion when they are together in the student union without faculty present. Ethnographers must either position themselves in such a way as to permit them to observe these interactional differences or at least be aware that there are systematic forms of behavior that they are unable to observe.

Furthermore, observers must also "position" themselves in such a way that they not only observe what people do and say, but that they also observe what these same matters *mean* to the participants. Observers may find that the scenes of interest are organized in such a way that the participants are constantly commenting on the meaning of their activities. For example, in some universities one may find that "what classroom activities are all about" from the point of view of students is the principal topic in the student union. Observers who sit with students in the student union might hear all that they need to know. On other campuses, however, students' conversations in the student union might be largely devoted to talk of weekend and nighttime activities as well as the playing of bridge. Ethnographers of such a campus might have to form relationships with students that permitted them to ask about the meaning of classroom activities. We should also note that ethnographers who found students freely talking about the classroom might also decide that additional and private interrogation was also necessary, since the way students talk in public about lectures, faculty, and the like might be only a partial view of what these things mean to them.

Ethnographers, then, are faced with the task of (1) encountering and describing the repetitive events and activities that make up the routines of the group they are studying. They will attempt to position (and systematically reposition) themselves in such ways as to take into account role and other person-related differences, temporal and spatial differences, and interactional differences. Ethnographers also have the task of (2) positioning themselves socially so as to obtain information about the meaning of these activities from the point of view of those who engage in them. That is, they must either be in a position to overhear and be a participant in naturally occurring conversations in which the meaning of routine events is discussed by the participants and/or form relationships with the participants so as to be able to freely interrogate them.

We suggest, then, that to pursue an adequate investigation of social conduct in situ requires making observations on behaviors presumed to be distributed *across* roles, varying *within* roles across incumbents as well as through time and by location, and varying in response to the interactional combinations of roles and/or persons in the given setting. In effect these dimensions represent five basic sources of variation in conduct, at least in the sense that observers should *look* to determine whether or not some activity is uniform or variable over such features. A particular theory might mandate other features as well.

TRACKING

The features of social life outlined above pose a challenge to ethnographers who propose to describe some particular social scene. We view tracking as one response to this challenge. While we may have named this strategy, we did not invent it, for many of the features of tracking outlined below are to be found in the work of a number of participant-observers (e.g., Bitter, 1967a,b; Black & Reiss, 1970; Pilavian & Briar, 1964; Skolnick, 1967; Sudnow, 1967; and Zimmerman, 1969).

Tracking, first of all, provides a way for ethnographers to overcome the sometimes frantic urge to be everywhere at once, while at the same time it allows them to approach their goal. This is done by systematically following the routine of a succession of different role-incumbents over some time period. By periodicallly switching from one subject to another, observers are eventually able to encounter many of the patterned activities within the setting from a number of different role-bound perspectives.

In tracking, the ethnographers stay as close to the subjects as they can manage, attempting to see what the subjects *see* as well as noting what they do and what they say. Skolnick (1967: 33) provides an example of tracking police:

I spent eight nights with . . . patrolmen, mostly on weekends, on the shift running from 7 PM to 3 AM. All of this time was spent interviewing and observing, talking about the life of policemen and the work of the policeman. I understood my job was to gain some insight and understanding of the way the policeman views the world. I found that the most informative method was not to ask predetermined questions, but rather to question actions the policeman has just taken or failed to take, about events or objects just encountered, such as certain categories of people or places of the city.

Skolnick then shifted his attention to the vice control squad. While he does not describe much of the actual sequences of his observations there, what he does describe gives us an impression of the observer's closeness to his subjects in "tracking" work (1967: 35-36).

Under direct observation, detectives were cooperative. They soon gave permission to listen in to telephone calls, allowed me to join in conversations with informants, and to observe interrogations, In addition, they called me at home when an important development in a case was anticipated. Whenever they went out on a raid, I was a detective as far as any outsider could see . . . I looked enough like a policeman when among a group of detectives in a raid for suspects to take me for a detective . . . Even though I posed as a detective, however, I never carried a gun . . . As a matter of achieving rapport with the police, I felt that such participation was required. Since I was not interested in getting standard answers to standard questions, I needed to be on the scene to observe their behavior and attitudes expressed on actual assignments.

Tracking provides a systematic solution to the problem of positioning the observer vis-a-vis the diversity of behavior in settings.[5] As is evident in the examples above, tracking in the hands of Skolnick and others provides a way of positioning as to observe not only what people do and say but also what these matters mean to the participants. Furthermore, by systematically tracking the occupants of one role (e.g., a sergeant in the police department) and then tracking another (e.g., a lieutenant in the same division), etc., ethnographers are able to incorporate into the research plan and description the fact that persons in different roles act differently. If the definition of a research problem demands it, ethnographers may, if they choose, track a number (even a representative sample) of incumbents of the same role. By tracking the same individual over a sufficient period of time they are able to take temporal variation into account. Because they follow one individual over the full course of his or her day, they are also able to observe the differences in the individual's behavior that are related to, or caused by, the various settings in which he acts and the various persons with whom he interacts.

Tracking is of course a strategy based on the *overt* observer role. It presupposes the ability of an investigator to move across social boundaries in a given setting with some degree of freedom and the ability to ask questions and engage in conversation with a wide range of participants. Unless the social setting and its activities are tightly encapuslated and delimited in time and space—such as the "tea-room" setting in which anonymous, impersonal sexual activity is performed largely in silence (cf. Humphreys, 1970)— occupying a preexisting role in some setting constrains covert observers to the range of behaviors appropriate to that role and what Merton (1957: 368-70) calls role set.

While the use of tracking as a strategy of observation furnishes a way of dealing with the problems of positioning, it is not always possible to employ it. It is easiest to use when the activities of interest are bureaucratically circumscribed. If it is applied to more diffuse roles (e.g., "member of the counterculture"), ethnographers are likely to have more difficulty distinguishing between the role-relevant activities in the setting of concern and activities that are under the jurisdiction of other roles more peripheral to the scene. In highly organized settings ethnographers are typically able to assess some activities—e.g., an employee receiving a call from her husband—as not relevant to the role-bound behaviors they are studying or, as the case may be, as an instance of the intrusion of role behaviors supposedly excluded from the setting.

Observers of more diffuse roles are also likely to find that their presence alters the behavior they are observing to a greater extent than is the case with more highly specified roles. The latter often do not afford the role incumbent much latitude to modify their behavior. As Skolnick (1967: 36) argues, "they are hardly free to alter their behavior, as, for example, when a policeman kicks in a door in a narcotics raid" (see also Becker, 1970: 44-51). Not only do some diffuse roles permit subjects to alter their behavior more easily, but some roles and settings are of such a character that the ethnographer's presence profoundly alters the subject's social circumstances. For example, a housewife who typically spends much of her day in solitude or in the presence of young children would have, in the presence of the ethnographer, an adult companion with whom she could constantly interact as she went about her day. We might expcet her to alter her physical appearance, the manner in which she served meals, the character of occasions of taking coffee breaks, and many other matters.

In diffusely organized social worlds ethnographers frequently must make themselves, in effect, exactly or nearly like those they are observing, if they are to avoid heavy observer effects and, often, if they are to be tolerated by "the natives" as they constantly intrude themselves into the scenes (cf. Sullivan et al., 1958). Making oneself appear like one of the natives may have serious limitations. Sex and age differences may be impossible for some ethnographers to overcome. The moral, ethical (cf. Coser et al., 1959), or legal constraints that some ethnographers feel may prevent them from effectively participating with "the natives"—for example, as in participating in a burglary or engaging in homosexual activities (cf. Humphreys, 1970; Polsky, 1969). Finally, tracking in some settings may require profound alterations in scheduling, fulfilling family responsibilities, and the like on the part of an ethnographer. A situation that required staying up all night might be difficult for one who teaches during the day. In all these matters tracking may pose serious difficulties for the ethnographer, although the difficulties depend as much on what the ethnographer is willing and able to do as they do on the setting.

THE DEVELOPMENT OF THE DIARY–DIARY-INTERVIEW METHOD

In the development of a study of the counterculture (Wieder & Zimmerman, 1974, 1976; Zimmerman & Wieder, 1971) we would have preferred tracking as our method of observation, but because of the diffusely organized character of life in the community of interest and because of the difficulties that would have been posed by our attempting to make ourselves over into "natives" at least ten years our junior, we decided not to do so. Initially we tried a variety of alternative techniques.

The design of the study was based upon the utilization of sociologically trained, paid research assistants who by virtue of age and closeness to the counterculture scene would not only be initially more credible to informants, but could adjust more readily to their pattern of living. Our selection of more or less "native" assistants also provided a solution to the problem of establishing contact with informants—our assistants provided a way into the community by inviting their friends, and friends of friends, to participate in the study.[6]

Our initial data-collection techniques called for "seminars" in which we and our assistants engaged informants in unstructured discussions of various aspects of their lives, as well as both structured and unstructured interviews, organized biographically, by which we sought to reconstruct the course of individual experience and the social pathways that led our informants toward the counterculture life-style. We relied on our assistants' field notes for a picture of actual behavior in the community. While many valuable insights and a good deal of information were gathered in this way, we soon became uneasy about the progress of the research. Our most important questions had not yet begun to draw out the systematic answers required: What do these people do all day? What varieties of activities do they engage in? How many people do they interact with every day? What is the typical temporal sequence of events? And so on. Interviewing by itself was inadequate for the purpose of establishing a clear picture of such activities.

In the midst of this concern we came to the view that we had to get into the field with some approximation to the tracking procedure discussed earlier. We decided to experiment with the informant diary as a data-collection tool. The following section discusses the rationale behind this decision.

A Conception of the Subject as Diarist

With the exception of covert nonparticipant-observers (a sort of spectral presence) ethnographers never rely solely on what they can see and overhear. In the course of their research they typically employ some type of interview, structured or unstructured (along with a lot of casual chatter), to elicit information going beyond what they can obtain by keeping their eyes and ears open. By and large this information pertains to the point of view of the "natives"—i.e., their definition of the situation—and includes their attitudes, beliefs, evaluations, boasts, complaints, etc., all of which adds the critical subjective dimension to the naturally occurring activities being witnessed.

Granted that observers both observe and question, the targets of this scrutiny and interrogation function in two analytically distinguishable roles—native *performer* and reflective *informant*. As performer the native presumably moves through normal activities "as if" the observers were not present, which is to say that they behave naturally (cf. Becker, 1970: 43). As informant he reflects on his own and others' performances, specifies their purpose, enunciates standards of conduct, allocating praise and blame in terms of such standards as well as acting as critic of an ethnographer's attempt to formulate witnessed and recounted events. In a sense the participants qua informants are lay observers of their own and their cultural colleagues' activities—adjunct ethnographers of their own circumstances. In this role they thereby furnish an ethnographer's major resource in reporting the "view from within." A single individual can and most often does function in both roles in the course of field research. It should be evident that the tracking referred to above entails treating subjects as both performers and informants.

The rationale of the diary approach involves more fully exploiting the informant as observer. By requesting that subjects keep a chronologically organized diary or log of their daily activities, we in effect asked them to record their own performances as well as to report the performances of others with whom they interact. Completed diaries functioned for us in much the same way as did the field notes turned in by our regular research assistants. Diarists thus functioned as surrogate observers.

The next step in our procedure is perhaps the most crucial. The diarists, having furnished a report of their own and their associates' performances, were then cast in the role of informants—that is, they were subjected to lengthy, detailed, and probing interviews, based on their diaries, in which they were not only asked to expand their reportage but were also questioned on the less directly observable features of the events they recorded, on their meaning, their propriety, typicality, connection with other events, and so on. Thus, the diaries employed in our research were (1) done on request, (2) prepared according to a set of instructions, (3) limited to a span of seven days, and (4) employed as the basis of a lengthy interview with the diarist.

We view the diary *in conjunction with* the diary interview as an approximation to the method of tracking. While actual tracking is to be preferred *as an ideal* in every case, the diary—diary-based interview affords at least the possibility of gaining some degree of access to naturally occurring sequences of activity, as well as raising pertinent questions about their meaning and significance. The diary partially recovers features of scenes and events that, if witnessed through tracking, would have been the topic for on-the-spot interrogation. In many circumstances the diary offers the possibility of researching topics that would otherwise be inaccessible for the reasons we have already enumerated, e.g., the diffuseness of the social world being investigated.

The practice of having subjects maintain chronological records of their activity is not without precedent (cf. Sorokin & Berger, 1939),[7] nor is the coordination of some form of personal document (e.g., an autobiographical statement) and an interview or series of interviews (cf. Denzin, 1970: 228-31). Our approach differs from other applications of the life-history method in its emphasis on diarist as surrogate observer. That is, one way we treated the material generated from the diary—diary-interview method was as analogues of the field notes of a thoroughly debriefed research assistant. Treated in this way, the diary and diary-interview materials revealed the same sorts of located (i.e., perspectival) views of social and cultural objects that are observable through tracking. These "located views" of social and cultural objects, reported by an ensemble of diarists, are then combinable, in ways specified below, into coherent descriptions of the social setting under study. It is perhaps unique to the use of multiple, contemporaneous, or near contemporaneous diaries and diary-interviews that data may be obtained that are comparable to data from direct observation of such matters as socially structured patterns of action, norms, roles, and so forth. Character-istically, former uses of the general life-history method have yielded descrip-tions of an ensemble of similar or analytically identical *situations* in which the subjects are located, treated as those subjects' particular situations rather than their cultural or socially structured situations from which descriptions of "culture" and "social structure" could be obtained (cf. Angell, 1936; Cressey, 1953; Lindesmith, 1947).

THE DIARY FORMAT

While each investigator must devise a set of instructions for potential diarists that are congruent with his or her own research interests, the instructions we used are rather general, simple, and serve as a good example.[8] In brief, diary writers were asked to record in chronological order the activities in which they engaged over the course of seven days. We provided the formula: Who? What? When? Where? How? We asked them to report the identity of the participants in the activities described not by name, of course, but by relationship to the writer—e.g., roommate, girl friend, etc.—using initials to differentiate individuals and noting the sex of those involved. The "What?" was a description of the activity or discussion recorded in the diarist's own categories.[9] "When?" referred to the time and timing of the activity, with special attention to recording the actual sequence of events. "Where?" was a designation of the location of the activity, suitably coded to prevent identification of individuals or places. The "How?" was a description of whatever logistics were entailed in the activity—e.g., how transportation was secured, how marijuana was obtained, etc.

Diligence by the diarist in answering these basic questions in conjunction with the researcher's strategy for locating diarists provides a solution to the problem of positioning the observer vis-a-vis the diversities of behavior in settings. Although the solution is even better when the diary is taken in conjunction with a diary-based interview, the general character of the solution is more easily indicated at this point of our exposition.

1. The problem of role- or category-related differences in activities, feelings, and thoughts is resolvable for researchers who make their observations through diaries by the way in which they choose diarists. The roles of interest may be covered by choosing diarists among incumbents of each role. Since researchers need not collect their data all at once, they may wait for the results of the first diaries (and diary interviews) to display the setting so that they can rationally decide which other roles are of interest.

2. The diversity of behavior among incumbents of the same role is no special problem to researchers using this method. There is no principled limit to the number of diaries that researchers can collect. If the problem demands a representative sample of incumbents of the same role or social position—e.g., housewives—they may select a random or other representative sample of diarists in that role or social position.

3. Some aspects of temporal diversity are easily and more or less automatically accommodated by diaries, since the diarist records events sequentially and notes the time of day of their occurrence. Other sequences are made visible through the practice of having diarists keep diaries over a consecutive number of days. Researchers may request the same individual to do several diaries at different times during a year to deal with the typicality of any given time period for the diarist. Researchers may also invite different diarists to write their diaries at different periods during the year to "control for," or to describe, such matters as seasonal and other cyclical matters.

4. By asking diarists to note where they went through the day and to note where each reported occurrence happened, the researcher discovers the settings in which the reported events occur.

5. By noting who was present, the diarist gives the researcher an initial indication of interactional differences.

6. In describing who, what, when, where, and how diarists reveal *some* of the meanings of the reported events.

In our experience all of these matters tend to be barely indicated in the diaries as such. Because the diarist does tell the researcher some concrete details along all these "dimensions," the researcher is in a position to ask the diarist to elaborate any of the matters in the diary interview. Without knowing some concrete details to begin with, the researcher would not be in a position to ask any elaborating questions. But before we consider the diary interview as such, there are further details of the diary itself that should be noted.

Our diary writers were instructed to record as much of what transpired during a day as they could, and they were told that whatever was notable to them was of interest to us.[10] They were also instructed to avoid omitting events because they seemed mundane. We urged them to be frank and to include such things as sexual activity and drug use. Imposing no length requirement, we asked them to be as detailed as they could and suggested that they set aside regular periods during the day to write the diary. We cautioned them to avoid writing their diaries all at once and to make entries at least once a day. (We should note that if the diaries we collected were to be construed as exhaustive records of the diarists' activities, we would have to conclude that this group was characterized by extraordinary bladder and bowel capacities, since no instance of the elemental act of elimination was reported.) An excerpt from an actual diary resulting from following these instructions is presented here:

Thursday Evening: About 7:30 P.M. I was outside sitting on the bench in the front yard [of his rented duplex in the student community] playing my guitar and Bob [one of several roommates] came outside and said he thought he heard a band playing. As he went back in the house I noticed that he had a joint [marijuana cigarette] in his hand. I followed him in and helped him finish it off and then rolled one of mine for Bob and Vicki [another roommate] and I. Adequately ripped we followed the noise of the band, cutting through the blocks [between buildings] to Jackson Street. In an apartment complex's front yard was a small crowd of people (about 50-70 standing around listening). The band really sounded good. I wondered why they were playing there, but then just settled back to enjoying the experience. People in the crowd were moving in time to the music. There had been a couple of cases of beer passed out and wine was offered around. Finally the smell of pot filled the air and later a joint came my way which I toked on for all I was worth. Really stoned now, the music sounded better than ever. About 10:30 I got sleepy and went home and crashed.

For their efforts diarists were paid a fee of $10.00. We counted on three things to motivate a reasonably conscientious effort. First, there was the personal relationship to one of the research assistants, and so they were helping the assistant to "do his job." Second, the research assistants checked the diarists' progress within the first few days to encourage the writers to make regular entries and to deal with any questions that might have arisen concerning the task.[11] Third, there was the factor of the fee itself, and the fact that the task would not be complete and the fee paid until there was a completed interview based on the diary materials.[12]

The effectiveness of the diary method is undercut, we believe, if all that is collected is the diary. Our experience has indicated that there is considerable variation in the depth and detail reported in such diaries. Further, there is the ever-nagging possibility that some diaries would in whole or in large part be fabrications. Short of obtaining comparable observational data (cf. Becker & Greer, 1957a) the only check feasible is that of internal consistency. Since "consistency" is at best an amorphous concept, something more than an inspection of the diary is clearly called for (Dean & Whyte, 1958).

THE DIARY INTERVIEW

Hand in hand with the diary as a data-collection "instrument" is the "diary interview." Like the personal statement prepared by the "focal subject" of the life-history approach (Denzin, 1970: 226-28, 237), the diarist's statement is used as a way of generating questions for the subsequent diary interview. The diary interview converts the diary—a source of data in its own right—into a question-generating, hence data-generating device.

Preparation for the diary interview requires inspection of the relevant diary. In our own research each diary was read by at least two research personnel, who sought to formulate questions for the diarists based on the diary narrative. Then the two collaborated and noted all the questions on a single copy of the diary in question. One of these two persons would then interrogate the informant, "armed" with the prepared questions. For example, one of our diarists wrote in her diary:

Talked to S.H. about the bathing suit which she is going to batik for me. She "got it for me wholesale" from [local store], and I will probably trade something for her doing the suit.

The researcher first read this section of the diary to the diarist, hoping that she would "spontaneously" elaborate. But the diarist replied, "Mm-mm," requiring the researcher to be more direct in her questioning:

Researcher: Could you tell me more about that—is that a typical kind of thing that you, like, sort of exchange goods?

Diarist: Yeah, yeah, it's very typical. Ah, I live, around, and it always seems that I've known a lot of people who make things and do things, and so we just exchange one skill for another. Somebody made me a pair of earrings once, and I dyed some cloth for them, with natural dyes, and, ah, ah, especially in where I live now, you know . . . there are lots of people around that exchange skills, and nobody seems to have a lot of money, so we just, ah, L. gave me a drawing once, and I gave her some homespun wool so she could do a weaving, and then she did me—she did a weaving for me, and I crocheted her a hat and gave her some homespun to do some more weaving.

The researcher would then listen to the informant's response and then probe again for more detail if the developing description was relevant to the research concern. Sometimes these probes were also prepared; in other cases simple, nondirective (Rogers, 1942, 1945) probes were employed. The character of these nondirective probes can be seen in each of the researcher's queries to the diarist in he following transcript:

Diarist [In responding to a question about having children]: I don't know. I really don't know. I really like kids, and everytime I see a baby, I get this surge, you know, of maternal feelings, but, um, a lot of things, you know, come into it. Like, the population problem is just so incredible. Ah, you know, you can feel it so strongly here in three years. Just too many people, and it really gets to be a strain on you.

Researcher: Mm-mm.

Diarist: And I'd feel like it would be part of, mm, part of my job just to try to keep that down. And, ah, ah, also, things are, they're just really shaky. You know, it seems that nothing is terribly stable, or secure.

Researcher: You mean the world . . . or what?

Diarist: Yeah, the whole world. The world. The world.

Researcher: The world?

Diarist: In general. That's the way I feel about it at the moment, and that could also be part of my being shaky and insecure, feeling this. Um, but I don't think that can be discounted entirely. Um, and also, the other thing is that kids take a lot of your life . . . a lot of patience. Lot of years.

Our reading of these documents, guided by the general concerns of our research, represented a search for the relevant questions to ask of this particular group. Our notion of relevance was tied to the assumption that if we could clarify the detail of everyday life in the scene, we would in the process discover the structure of relevancies that inform, render sensible, and give value to such activities. We adopted the stance of one who was ignorant and needed to be told about the most trivial matters. We attempted to guard against assuming that we fully understood a particular entry, and indeed, we asked questions in the face of the conviction that we knew the answers.

In one aspect the diary interviews were a process of expansion, filling in details that were omitted. In another aspect they led beyond the particular events recorded, touching on attitudes, beliefs, knowledge, and experience of a more general character. Not only did we explore the community context of the seven days' activity, but we invited reflection on the connection between that context and the diarists' "world view." A five- or ten-page diary often generated over 100 specific questions, and diary interviews sometimes covered five hours of interrogation. While unimpeachable assurances were available that a given diary was not a work of fiction, the impact of this intensive interrogation was presumed to be such that maintaining a pretense would be difficult without falling into glaring inconsistencies, especially since the diary writers did not have access to their diaries after completion or during the interview.

USING DIARY MATERIALS: WORKING CRITERIA

Informant diaries and the interviews based on them yield a large amount of detailed and heterogeneous information. It is the investigator's task to transform this fund of data into a defensible representation of the social phenomena that are of interest. In simpler terms the investigator attempts to take a large amount of detailed information and make it into a "factual" and general story. The pertinent question here is how this can be done and can be justified on grounds other than the researcher's intuition, based on his or her familiarity with these details. While many ethnographic reports are formulated in terms of a researcher's general familiarity with the data, analyses of ethnographic materials, perhaps especially diary—diary-interview materials, can be subjected to relatively specific constraints that make the analysis more methodical and rigorous.

The problem facing the ethnographer is essentially this: Such social phenomena as roles, norms, values, socially organized patterns of behavior, and so on have the character that no single observation (without the context of other observations) is in itself clearly identifiable as an observation of the phenomenon of interest.[13] For example, the rulelike character of a rule partially resides in its repeated use. A pattern of behavior emerges *as a pattern* only through repeated observation. For example, the idea of personality or character structure as used in clinical psychology and in the field of culture and personality "refers to some observable consistency in behavior. An unrepeated type of action is not in itself made the basis for establishing a dimension of type of personality . . ." (Turner, 1961: 58). As we shall see, repetition is only one of many possible constraints upon researchers that demand some particular organization for their observations.

The form that the phenomenon of interest should have—as that phenomena is conceptualized within some discipline such as sociology—can be "translated" into guides or instructions for the researcher's observations, analyses, and theorizing. While guides or constraints should be derivable from any fundamental social scientific conception of some phenomena,[14] we will illustrate these matters with the fundamental conceptions of social organization and culture that define a very general stratum of sociological phenomena. The proper use of these two concepts, in effect, informs investigators what they are looking *for* and looking *at*. How these conceptions can operate as constraints on, or guides to, observations and theorizing can be seen by considering each of the them in turn.

SOCIAL ORGANIZATION

Regularities in conduct (alternatively, stable patterns of social interactions) that are systematically interrelated are referred to a social organization. This rather broad concept is defined in different ways according to the particular perspective adopted by the investigator. In general the notion is used to talk about a specifiable population of actors who are linked together through a network of social relationships and who engage in interdependent activities of a distinctive character within a bounded social territory. Under the auspices of this notion ethnographers attend to such particulars as the scheduling and sequencing of activities, the use of titles and other forms of address, the ways in which interactions are initiated and terminated, which actors can request or demand what of whom, and so forth. Such details constitute the basis of talking about more global patterns of conduct and their interrelationships.[15]

What must investigators observe if they are to claim that they have detected some form of social organization conceived of in this fashion? How can they use this basic sociological conception in the actual practice of their observational work?[16] In the case of diaries, how can a scientist claim to have detected particular patterns of organization in the reported performances and associated commentaries of diarists? The criteria we suggest are derived from explicit and implicit statements of classical sociological theory. Durkheim's (1962) conception of social fact provides for many of these criteria, but they are not unique to his work (cf. Wieder, 1974: 31-37).

Description: To begin with, any analysis requires that the phenomenon of interest be circumscribed and defined in some fashion. Sociologically interesting phenomenoa may arise from theory or from the researcher's empirical acquaintance with the subject matter. In either case some statement of the phenomena, couched in the "language of observables," must be made. In survey research such statements tend to be operational definitions. In ethnographies of all forms the phenomena may be circumscribed by the ethnographer's attempt to describe some *typical* social form (often based on the data) and then testing that described social form against (further) data.

How diary materials can be used to develop evidence that a particular pattern of social organization has a typical form may be illustrated by some materials drawn from our study of the counterculture. We illustrate this and other criteria with the practice of marijuana smoking as a unit of social organization—i.e., the use of marijuana as a socially constrained activity requiring a particular kind of interaction between participants (Zimmerman & Wieder, 1971: 42-72). It should be noted that we offer this particular practice as an example, not in the expectation that it is news, but by virtue of its simplicity. Through the use of diaries as well as other information (including limited firsthand observation) we evolved a description of one phase of marijuana use, the practice of "passing the joint" (when more than one person is involved).[17]

Having arrived at a description of a unit of interest, it was possible to inspect diaries for references to "smoking occasions," to note the features recorded by the diarist, to question the diarist further in the interview, and to compare this information with that available from the diaries of other informants or from field notes based on direct observation.

The process of searching the materials for instances of the practice thus defined affords the opportunity to confront the occurrence of the practice in a different form. The object of the search is to provide grounds for asserting that the practice, when it occurs, typically occurs in the way specified.

Recurrence: In order to gain confidence in its description, the search for reported instances of the phenomenon of interest is inseparably linked to the process of accumulating evidence that the phenomenon recurs as described. For example, it is well known that marijuana smoking is a widespread activity among college-age youth such as those who served as subjects in our research. The point, however, is that we wished to make the claim (trivial though it may appear when viewed in isolation from other aspects of marijuana use) that the practice or social form not only recurs, but that it recurs in a standardized fashion.

Distribution: The criterion of recurrence is also tied to the issue of distribution and cannot be fully explicated without reference to it. The phenomenon must be examined with respect to its distribution relative to the types of situations and types of actors making up the interaction settings of the group in question. Thus, the search of our material focused on the types of occasions in which the practice of "passing the joint" occurred and on the composition of the participants. Our conclusions were not surprising: The matter was reported by virtually every diarist; it was widely distributed with respect to different types of social occasions wherein it was possible to smoke without detection *or* effective actions by authorities; and it was almost universally engaged in by the individuals in question.

Transpersonality: The matters of recurrence and distribution lead us to another criterion: the independence of the practice or social form from the personalities of the individuals involved. In our research the issue was whether or not "passing the joint" was a custom that was passed on to each succeeding cohort of persons adopting the life-style, since this was central to the determination that the pattern under scrutiny was a feature of the social organization of the community rather than a feature attributable to the makeup of the individuals in the community. Also involved here is the notion of relative *persistence*; we distinguished between a transitory phenomenon (a fad or fashion) and something more enduring. The observation that persons are socialized to a pattern is one kind of evidence for its transpersonality.

To no one's amazement, our diary materials and other data indicated that "passing the joint" was indeed transpersonal in the sense specified above. Just as persons are taught to experience the effect of marijuana as pleasurable (Becker, 1953), they are also taught—largely by example—to "pass the joint," and in addition they may acquire certain common rationalizations for the practice—e.g., "it is more economical" or "it's a way of increasing solidarity," and so on. We might add that this practice is by no means unique to the community studied and that others besides counterculture youth also "pass the joint."

CULTURE

Culture is conventionally conceived as a more or less integrated system of norms and values that defines the desirable ends of action and the appropriate means of achieving them. Sometimes referred to as "designs for living," culture is one basis for the actor's definition of the situation. The relationship between culture and social organization is of critical interest in ethnographies. Within this scheme social organization is the result of norms and values being systematically translated into conduct: the fundamental patterns of social organization are culturally sanctioned.[18] There are of course some systematic patterns of action that are indirectly related to norms and values and are, in and of themselves, not specifically culturally sanctioned.[19]

From this general sociological perspective there is, then, the additional criterion for developing an empirically warranted description of social phenomena, and it goes hand in hand with the criteria for describing social organization:[20] The researcher must find evidence that the behaviors constituting the pattern of social organization are sanctioned and enforced within the group in question.[21] Such evidence can be marshalled using diary materials.

In the example of "passing the joint" one could well raise the question of whether the form in which it so regularly occurs is in fact culturally sanctioned—i.e., whether deviations are noticed and corrective action applied. No clear-cut instances of deviation were apparent in our materials, so we were required to employ hypothetical examples in certain diary interviews to explore this dimension as well as to examine closely those cases where certain participants refrained from smoking. While we cannot go into detail on our findings in this respect, our analysis suggested that (1) failure to pass a joint, should it occur, would be sanctioned; (2) persons expect to share a joint in his fashion if they are going to smoke at all; and (3) the ritual takes precedence over other concerns such as the communication of disease (Zimmerman & Wieder, 1971: 52-55).

Procedurally, the determination that a pattern is culturally supported rests on (1) encountering reported instances of sanctioning—e.g., a negative remark such as, "He's really on a power trip," or reports that a particular person is being avoided or is subject to derogatory comment by virtue of (a) a particular act or series of acts or (b) the view that he or she is the kind of person who will persist in certain undesirable behaviors—and (2) incidents in which persons are being explicitly instructed to behave in a certain way.

In general such indications will have to be pursued further in the diary interview, in order to expand the details of the case and to make clear the depth of the negative responses and the generality of the norms and values involved. The process of developing evidence for the cultural foundations of patterns of social organization will receive further attention below. We might note here that the criteria advanced for specifying elements of social organizational patterns (recurrence, distribution, and transpersonality) also apply to the adequate determination of the cultural bases of the pattern.

In concluding this section we might point out that the patterns or regularities reported by a particular ethnographer (or for that matter any investigator, regardless of the method employed) are always *more or less* recurrent, distributed, and so on. The quantitative or qualitative specification of these properties is always to the sophistication of the available observational and measurement procedures and the feasibility of their use in the particular study, as well as the level or precision required by the problem under investigation. For our purposes the properties we offer as indicative of stable patterns of culturally sanctioned social organization can serve as a set of guideposts for directing and evaluating ethnographic descriptions of social phenomena, whatever the scope of observation or level or measurement.

THE ANALYTIC PROCESS IN THE DIARY–DIARY-INTERVIEW METHOD

Our experience with the diary–diary-interview method recapitulates the basic structure of most ethnography: Ethnographers only partially know what particulars of conduct they are looking for before they see them, but upon seeing them, they know that they have found what they have been searching for "all along." Effective ethnographers are either constantly or intermittently operating as theorists over the course of the data collection. Ethnographers engage in a self-corrective, continuous process in which:

> ... analysis is carried on *sequentially*, important parts of the analysis being made while the researcher is still gathering his data. . . Further data gathering takes its direction from provisional analyses. . .
> (Becker, 1970: 400; cf. Lindesmith, 1947: 9)

This systematic use of a provisional working hypothesis bears strong resemblance to the process of *analytic induction* (Cressey, 1950, 1953; Denzin, 1970; Lindesmith, 1947; Robinson, 1951; Turner, 1953; Znaniecki, 1934; Manning, this volume) in that researchers alternate between formulating the phenomena and gathering new data, which they use to reformulate their ideas. At each stage the present formulation accounts for or encompasses all the observables at hand. Here, hovever, the end product is not causal theory, as it is in analytic induction, but empirically warranted, theoretically relevant description.

In our study of the counterculture we found that it was useful to formulate what we knew "as of today" once a week or so. We then used that formulation as a point of departure and as a schema of interrogation for the gathering of further data. Thus, at any given time we had "questions in mind" that we addressed to the diaries—looking at them to find answers to our questions. At the same time, as we read the diaries, we discovered new questions by seeing the written accounts and answers to some question. Furthermore, we often sense that a question or an answer was implied in a diary remark but was "not quite there," which motivated a request for further elaboration from the diary writer.[22]

Besides asking for further details of events, we also asked our informants about their feelings about the events they reported, their feelings about the other participants in those events, their sense of alternatives that were actually or potentially available to them as courses of action, how they choose one course of action over another, the consequences, especially social consequences, of choosing one course of action over another (in this way uncovering sanctionable structure), and their sense for the typical flow of events.

As we proceeded, we came to a sense of the typical and sanctionable flow of events in the life of counterculture youth. We found ourselves able to read the diaries in terms of expectable events that did not occur. Such discoveries permitted us to probe our informants about the reasons they had not done something—e.g., why had a particular diarist not gotten stoned before going to a Chinese restaurant, since this would have been a typical occasion for getting stoned? Replies to probes of this sort generated answers that were possible descriptions of the cultural conditions under which some event could and could not properly occur—i.e., we obtained descriptions of the conditions under which some event would or would not occur from the standpoint of our subjects' cultural knowledge.

Thus, although comparable data were gathered from many persons, and each person was asked many of the same questions as each other person, our use of the diary—diary-interview method was cumulative and more focused in character. That is, as more and more diaries were collected and the results of diary interviews inspected, each successive diary was subjected to increasingly specific and refined interrogation.

In addition, the process builds in a partially self-corrective mechanism. Each question directed at a diary writer, even if it is merely a request for additional detail, functions as an implicit, local hypothesis. Thus, the answers to such questions provide for the possiblity of disconfirming some previously held notion. For example, asking why some event did not occur is based on the investigator's expectation that it should have happened, given what he thinks he knows. Some answers could modify or even radically alter that expectation. Thus, the diary—diary-interview method is in part a continuous process of challenging and refining the investigator's conceptions.

In conclusion we must acknowledge that many issues relevant to the evaluation of this procedure remain to be addressed, among them the relationship of the diary—diary-interview process to standard conceptions of adequate hypothesis testing. Our concerns here have been with the use of this procedure to produce descriptive findings tied closely to the fine detail of daily activities. We can envision modifications in the procedure that would make it more useful to investigators with different aims, including the uses of sophisticated sampling techniques in the selection of diarists, more structured instructions to diarists, standardized questions to be administered during the diary interview, and so on. The procedure's most basic application is an adjunct to, or approximation of, the process of direct observation that is central to the ethnographic research tradition.

NOTES

[1] The ethnographic study on which this chapter draws was funded by Grant 70-039, Law Enforcement Assistance Administration, United States Department of Justice. The findings and interpretations presented in this chapter do not necessarily reflect the policies or official position of the funding agency. Portions of this chapter are reprinted from our article in *Urban Life* 1977, 6 (January): 479–498 by permission of Sage Publications, Inc.

[2] Sociologists often distinguish between types of observer roles. For example, *overt* participant-observers declare themselves to their subjects and openly assumes the role of sociologist in the midst of the ordinary social activities characteristic of the setting being studied. As overt *participant*-observers, they intervene in the routine of their subjects. Intervention may be minimal, involving conversations or even formal interviews, or they may assist with or join in the activities of the subjects. *Covert*

participant-observers are something like spies. They pretend to be something they are not—ordinary participants—and operate with an ulterior motive, namely, to report on the activities they observe. In some instances the masquerade is limited and involves the exploitation of very standardized conventional roles, such as bar patron (Cavan, 1966). A little further down the line is a type of infiltration—e.g., Humphrey's (1970) assumption of the role of "watch queen" in his study of sex in public restrooms. At the extreme is the manufacture of a biography, status characteristics, and even physical appearance to gain access to attitudes and actions otherwise difficult to observe. There is a unique and controversial study by a research team working for the U.S. Air Force in which an Air Force officer was converted into a basic trainee to study the morale of recruits (Coser et al, 1959; Sullivan et al., 1958; cf. also Erikson, 1967). Overt nonparticipant-observers are obviously known to their subjects as research scientists, but remain in the background and do not interact with subjects. It is difficult to locate a clear instance of this type outside the laboratory setting where subjects are viewed from behind a two-way mirror. The covert nonparticipant-observer mode is exemplified by research done by Sudnow (1972b), in which surreptitious photographs of individuals were employed as data for the analysis of "glance behavior." For this line of research it is neither necessary nor even desirable for the observers to declare themselves or participate. In part this is due to the nature of the social activities of interest, which are assumed at the outset to be highly standardized behaviors that are frequent and common and can be found in most public places where the observer has access as a member of the public. For more detailed treatments of various classifications of the observer role see, for example, Denzin (1970: 185-218); Gold (1958); Junker (1960: 35-40); Lofland (1971: 93-116); and Schatzman & Strauss (1973: 52-56).

[3] An obvious expectation of ethnographers is that the setting they enter is organized in definite ways (Humphreys, 1970: 24-26). From the outset would-be observers are anticipating the constraints imposed by the cultural and social organization of the group they have chosen to study. The ways these constraints operate pose the problem of initial access to the setting, which can be quite varied. For example, formal organizations are available as a research site contingent upon the approval of those in authority, and it is characteristic of such settings that there is a definite structure of authority. In contrast, such settings as bars and public restrooms are different kinds of possible research targets and are characterized by different internal organizations. Cavan (1966) exploited the fact that there are readily available roles that she, as an adult, could easily assume, and thus her access problem was trivial. She also discovered that certain bars were largely patronized by men, and her sex thereby became a liability. She was also constrained in her observation by the limits of normal bar-patron conduct. Humphreys' (1970) investigation of sexual activity in public restrooms capitalized on the fact that these behaviors were also organized into definite role relationships, among them the role of "watchqueen" or lookout who, by fulfilling the necessary function of warning those engaged in sex of the approach of "outsiders," could also observe what was going on in the restroom. Humphreys, by assuming this role, provided for his covert sociological purpose, observation, while at the same time avoiding full participation himself. Both Cavan and Humphreys opted for the covert participant-observer approach (see footnote 2). Most sociological field studies are undertaken in the overt participant-observer mode, in part for ethical reasons, in part for the reason that the covert mode constrains the

observers to the confines of the indigenous role they assume, whereas the creation of the observer role within a given setting typically allows greater latitude of observation.

[4] For a discussion of the elements of sample design see Sudman (1976). A very readable introduction to sampling may be found in Slonim (1960). Arnold (1970) discusses a nonprobability sampling frame for field research, which he calls "dimensional sampling."

[5] There is another sense in which tracking may be even more systematic. While Skolnick permitted the relevancies of his observations—the questions that he asked himself about his subjects about what they both were observing—to emerge out of the apparent concerns and interests the subjects had in the developing events—e.g., first they were worried about this, then they were pleased about that, etc.—there is another, more structured form of tracking that Reiss (one of its advocates) called "systematic observation of natural social phenomena" (Reiss, 1971). In this method the observer records the observations he makes while tracking in a prestructured manner. The standardized recording form instructs the observer to note certan predecided, hence standardized features of the episodes that he witnesses.

[6] The "snowball sample" resulting from this procedure is certainly far removed from a probability sample of the community, but nevertheless adequate for our qualitative interests (cf. Coleman, 1958). In evaluating the uses of available informants one might consider the following:

Informants are indispensable resources for most observational studies. The more articulate the informant, the greater his or her value, and great effort is usually expended to establish and sustain the rapport necessary to gain the cooperation of key individuals in a given setting. Lurking in the background is the possiblity that those persons who consent to be informants (or diarists) are, compared to others in the setting, atypical in one or more respects. Informants are seldom selected randomly, and the kind of relationship involved is difficult to generate under the constraints of sound sampling procedure. While this issue is too involved to treat in depth here, several rule-of-thumb guidelines for guarding against the distortion that can result from the atypicality of informants can be specified. Recalling the discussion of the problem of positioning, investigators should ask themselves: (1) Are my informants well distributed across the relevant roles in the setting? (2) Is their role behavior seen by others to be remarkable in some way, i.e., superior, peculiar, etc? (3) Are they situated in the routines characteristic of the setting so as to reflect the temporal and spatial diversity present? (4) Is the range of interaction between the informants' roles and other roles in the setting restricted in some way? (5) Do the informants stand to gain something from their cooperation with the researcher, and if so, how likely will this be to effect what they report? These considerations do not solve the problem of the typicality of informants, but they should serve to avoid a naive reliance on the word of a few "special" individuals. For a striking example of the consequences of uncritical reliance on readily available informants in the field of linguistics see Labov (1973). For other treatment of issues clustering around the use of informants see Back (1960); Becker & Geer (1957a, b; 1960); Campbell (1955); Dean et al. (1969); Dean & Whyte (1958); Lofland (1971: 111-113); Madge (1965: 81-87); Schatzman & Strauss (1973: 87-88); Trow (1957); Whyte (1960); and Zelditch (1962).

[7] For a recent example see Carey's (1968: 201) account of a limited use of diaries

for purposes similar to ours. Carey's report stimulated our interest in diaries, although he does not appear to have followed them up with interviews.

[8] All of our subjects had at least some college or university training, and many had bachelor's degrees. Moreover, the vast majority of them came from middle and upper-middle class professional and business backgrounds. Thus, the task posed for them was perhaps in keeping with the heavy emphasis on verbal skills characteristic of such a group; it might be problematic for other groups stressing different kinds of competency. Daily tape-recorded telephone interviews based on diarylike instructions might be used with less literate populations.

[9] Diarists' descriptive language was thus not standardized. A partial remedy for the problems involved in this potential heterogeneity of description is provided by the diary interview through which the investigators can, for all practical purposes, coordinate their understanding of the particular diary's terminology with that of the worker.

[10] This feature of the diary instructions is at first glance particularly hair-raising, since it means that what is reported in the diary is a function of the unknown system of relevancies of each diarist, and furthermore, this could be substantially different between different diarists. Thus, a good deal of activity of potential interest to the ethnographer runs the risk of being omitted by even the most open and truthful writer. Such a risk must be acknowledged, the only effective remedy being direct observation or, at minimum, a highly structured set of instructions. However, the more the diarist is instructed on what to observe, the greater the possibility of another obvious type of distortion—one that is probably the more serious, since it most often works in favor of the investigator's preconceptions.

[11] This procedure, while valuable, raised its own problems, largely revolving around the personal relationship between many of the diarists and the research assistants. It is quite conceivable that certain materials were omitted by diarists to conceal them from the assistants. It is difficult to say if such omissions occurred frequently or if they were significant.

[12] It should be stressed that the procedure for motivating diarists to comply with our instructions was tied to the particular circumstances of our study. It may not be possible (or even desirable) in all cases to pay diarists, and in other situations the personal ties between the research assistants and the diarist may not exist. For example, if diarists were to be selected by probability sampling techniques, the latter type of relationship is all but ruled out. What must be kept in mind is that the agreement to keep a diary and to be interviewed about it represents considerably more of a commitment in time and effort than completing a questionnaire or participating in a standard interview situation. Thus, attention must be paid to the practical problem of how cooperation can be secured in the course of planning research using this technique.

[13] The ethnographer *may* perceive a single occurrence as an instance of some type or class of occurrences, but this by itself is not evidence for the type or class.

[14] For an example of another phenomena see Turner (1961), for a somewhat similar treatment of personality. Since Turner was not primarily concerned with the problem of observing personality, his treatment is not as detailed as the one presented here.

[15] Our discussion of social organization is modeled after that of Garfinkel (1956).

See also Wilson (1970: 698ff) for a discussion of the relationship between social interaction and large-scale social structures.

[16] Our remarks here are pertinent to the use of any ethnographic data and to any such analysis of qualitative material that recommends itself on a factual basis.

[17] "Passing the joint" can be described as a definite sequence; the joint, once lit, is passed in either direction, hand to hand, around what is interactionally, if not always geometrically, a "circle," affording each individual in the circle an opportunity to smoke. Cf. Zimmerman and Wieder (1971: 42-72).

[18] One consequence of this proposal is that the ethnographer must construct a description of "basic" social organization patterns that is congruent with the actor's view of social reality. Since the notion casts the actor in the role of sanctioner or cultural agent at least some of the time, it must be supposed that instances of the pattern in question are recognizable to him as an instance of the way things should (or should not) be done.

[19] That is, it is possible to formulate patterns of behavior that are recurrent, distributed, and transpersonal that are not any direct sense culturally constrained although they may be derived from more fundamental patterns that are—e.g., differential crime rates, rates of residential mobility, motor vehicle accidents, and so on.

[20] Since the relationship between culture and social organization *appears* to be causal, the reader may wonder why we treat cultural features as criteria for an empirically warranted *description* of social phenomena. In brief, the causal connection between cultural elements such as norms and the patterns of behavior making up social organization is illusory. Partially formulated cultural elements frame the observations the ethnographer makes of patterns of behavior. Similarly, partially formulated observed patterns of behavior lead ethnographers to see that certain utterances of their informants are statements of and about their culture. Culture and social organization are thus aspects of the same phenomenon. (Cf. Wieder, 1974; Wieder and Zimmerman, 1976a)

[21] In alternative language the task is to show that such patterns *constrain* the conduct of the individual, either through internalized dispositions to comply or through institutionalized expectations of compliance enforced by sanctions (Wilson, 1970)

[22] Readers familiar with ethnomethodology may recognize that the procedure advocated here explicitly employs the use of the *documentary method of interpretation* (Garfinkel, 1967: 76-103). In every case the diary descriptions and the diarist's interview remarks "document" the "underlying pattern" of the form of the phenomena. In using these remarks as a constant source of questions we capitalized on their *retrospective* and *prospective* meanings. This explicit use of the documentary method of interpretation acknowledges the differences between observing physical events and the events of social and/or meaningful conduct. Since use of the documentary method of interpretation apparently cannot be avoided in the description of *substantive* sociological phenomena (Garfinkel, 1967: 94-103; Wieder, 1974; Wilson, 1970), it seems to us that the observation of substantive phenomena can be made more effective, efficient, and even more methodologically rigorous through the explicit and to some extent self-conscious use of this "method." The alternative appears to be the artful masking of the use of the "method" (often even from the

investigators themselves), which in a variety of ways hides the essentials of ethnographic work and obscures the character of the observed phenomena. Becker's recommendation (1970: 411) that ethnographers present the "natural history" of the processes whereby they arrived at their conclusions as the best "proof" available in ethnographic work appears to be directed to some of the same matters as our recommendation.

REFERENCES

Allport, Gordon. *The use of personal documents in psychological science.* New York: Social Science Research Council, 1942.

Angell, Robert C. *The family encounters the depression.* New York: Scribners, 1936.

Angell, Robert C., & Freedman, Ronald. The use of documents, records, census materials, and indices. In Leon Festinger and Daniel Katz (Eds.) *Research methods in the behavioral sciences.* Ill.: Dryden Press, 1953.

Arnold, David O. Dimension sampling: An approach for study of a small number of cases. *The American Sociologist,* 1970, 5: 147-50.

Arnold, David O. Qualitative field methods. (This Volume.)

Back, Kurt W. The well-informed informant. In R. N. Adams and J. J. Preiss (Eds.), *Human organization research.* Homewood, Ill: Dorsey, 1960.

Becker, Howard S. Becoming a marijuana user. *American Journal of Sociology,* 1953, 59: 235-42.

Becker, Howard S. Problems of inference and proof in participant observation. *American Sociological Review,* 1958, 23: 652-60.

Becker, Howard S. Introduction to Clifford Shaw, *The jack roller.* Chicago: University of Chicago Press, 1966.

Becker, Howard S. *Sociological work.* Chicago: Aldine, 1970.

Becker, Howard S, & Geer, Blanche. Participant observation and interviewing: A comparison. *Human Organization,* 1957, 16: 28-32. (a)

———Participant observation and interviewing: A rejoinder. *Human Organization,* 1957, 16: 39-40. (b)

Becker, Howard S., & Geer, Blanche. Participant observation: The analysis of qualitative field data. In R. N. Adams and J. J. Preiss (Eds.), *Human organization research.* Homewood, Ill.: Dorsey, 1960.

Bittner, Egon. Police discretion in emergency apprehension of mentally ill persons. *Social Problems,* 1967, 14: 278-92. (a)

Bittner, Egon. The police on skid-row: A study of peace keeping. *American Sociological Review,* 1967, 32: 699-715. (b)

Black, Donald J., & Reiss, Albert J., Jr. Police control of juveniles. *American Sociological Review,* 1970, 35: 63-77.

Blumer, Herbert. An appraisal of Thomas and Znaniecki's *The Polish Peasant in Europe and America.* In *Critiques of research in social sciences I.* New York: Social Science Research Council, 1939.

Campbell, Donald T. The informant in quantitative research. *American Journal of Sociology,* 1955, 60: 339-42.

Carey, James T. *The college drug scene.* Englewood Cliffs, N. J.: Prentice-Hall, 1968.

Cavan, Sherri. *Liquor license*. Chicago: Aldine, 1966.

Coleman, James S. Relational analysis: The study of social organizations with survey methods. *Human Organization*, 1958, *17* (4): 28-36.

Conwell, Chic, & Sutherland, E. H. *The professional thief*. Chicago: University of Chicago Press, 1937.

Coser, Lewis A., Roth, Julius A., Sullivan, Mortimer A., Jr., & Queen, Stuart A. Participant observation and the military: An exchange. *American Sociological Review*, 1959, *24*: 397-400.

Cressey, Donald R. *Other peoples' money*. New York: 1959, Free Press, 1953.

Cressey, Donald R. Criminal violation of financial trust. *American Sociological Review*, 1950, *15*: 738-43.

Dean, John P., Eickhorn, Robert, & Dean, Lois R. Fruitful informants for intensive interviewing. In George J. McCall and J. L. Simmons (Eds.), *Issues in participant observation*. Reading, Mass.: Addison-Wesley, 1969.

Dean, John P., & Whyte, William Foote. How do you know if the informant is telling the truth? In George J. McCall and J. L. Simmons (Eds.), *Issues in participant observation*. Reading, Mass.: Addison-Wesley, 1958.

Denzin, Norman K. *The research act: A theoretical introduction to sociological methods*. Chicago: Aldine, 1970.

Dollard, John. *Criteria for the life history*. New Haven: Yale University Press, 1935.

Durkheim, Emile. *The rules of the sociological method*. New York: Free Press, 1962.

Erikson, Kai T. A comment on disguised observation in sociology. *Social Problems*, 1967, *14*: 366-73.

Filstead, William J. (Ed.). *Qualitative methodology*. Chicago: Markham, 1970.

Garfinkel, Harold. *Studies in ethnomethodology*. Englewood Cliffs, N.J.: Prentice-Hall, 1967.

Garfinkel, Harold. Some sociological concepts and methods for psychiatrists. *Psychiatric Research Reports*, 1956, *6*: 181-95.

Gold, Raymond L. Roles in sociological field observation. *Social Forces*, 1958, 217-33.

Gottschalk, L., Kluckhohn, Clyde, & Angell, Robert. *The use of personal documents in history, anthropology and sociology*. New York: Social Science Research Council, 1945.

Humphreys, Laud. *Tearoom trade*. Chicago: Aldine, 1970.

Junker, B. H. *Field work*. Chicago: University of Chicago Press, 1960.

Labov, William. The linguistic consequences of being a lame. *Language and Society*, 1973, *2*: 81-115.

Lindesmith, Alfred R. *Opiate Addiction*. New York: Principia Press, 1947.

Lofland, John. *Analyzing social settings: A guide to qualitative observation and analysis*. Belmont, Calif.: Wadsworth, 1971.

Madge, John. *The tools of social science*: An analytic description of social science techniques. New York: Doubleday Anchor Books, 1965.

Manning, Peter K. Analytic induction. This Volume.

Merton, Robert K. *Social theory and social structure*. New York: Free Press, 1957.

Piliavin, Irving, & Briar, Scott. Police encounters with juveniles. *American Journal of Sociology*, 1964, *69*: 206-14.

Polsky, Ned. *Hustlers, beats and others*. New York: Doubleday Anchor Books, 1969.

Reiss, Albert J., Jr. The systematic observation of natural social phenomena. In

Herbert L. Costner (Ed.), *Sociological methodology*. San Francisco: Jossey-Bass, 1971.

Robinson, W. S. The logical structure of analytic induction. *American Sociological Review*, 1951, *16*: 812-18.

Rogers, Carl R. *Counseling and psychotherapy*. New York: Riverside Press, 1942.

Rogers, Carl R. The non-directive method as a technique for social research. *American Journal of Sociology*, 1945, *50*: 279-83.

Schatzman, Leonard, & Strauss, Anselm L., *Field research: Strategies for a natural sociology*. Englewood Cliffs, N.J.: Prentice-Hall, 1973.

Shaw, Clifford R. *The jack-roller: A delinquent boy's own story*. Chicago: University of Chicago Press, 1930.

Skolnick, Jerome. *Justice without trial*. New York: John Wiley, 1967.

Slonim, Morris James. *Sampling*. New York: Simon & Schuster, 1960.

Sorokin, Pitirim A., & Berger, Clarence Q. *Time-budgets of human behavior*. Cambridge, Mass.: Harvard University Press, 1939.

Sudman, Seymour. *Applied sampling*. New York: Academic Press, 1976.

Sudnow, David. *Passing on: The social organization of dying*. Englewood Cliffs, N.J.: Prentice-Hall, 1967.

Sudnow, David. Temporal parameters of interpersonal observation. In David Sudnow (Ed.), *Studies in social interaction*. New York: Free Press, 1972.

Sullivan, Mortimer A., Queen, Stuart A., & Patrick, Ralph C., Jr. Participant observation as employed in the study of a military training program. *American Sociological Review*, 1958, *23*: 660-67.

Thomas, William L., & Znaniecki, Florian. *The Polish Peasant in Europe and America*. (Vol. 1, 2nd ed.). New York: Alfred Knopf, 1927.

Trow, Martin. Comment on "participant observation and interviewing: A comparison." *Human Organization*, 1957, *16*: 33-55.

Turner, Ralph. The problem of social dimensions in personality. *Pacific Sociological Review*, 1961, *24*: 605-11.

Whyte, William Foote. Interviewing in field research. In R. N. Adams and J. J. Reiss (Eds.), *Human organization research*. Homewood, Ill.: Dorsey, 1960.

Whyte, William F. *Street corner society*, (rev. ed.). Chicago: University of Chicago Press, 1955.

Wieder, D. Lawrence. *Language and social reality*: The case of telling the convict code. Thettague: Mouton, 1974.

Wieder, D. Lawrence, & Zimmerman, Don H., Generational experience and the development of freak culture. *Journal of Social Issues*, 1974, *30*: 137-61.

Wieder, D. Lawrence, & Zimmerman, Don H. Becoming a freak: Pathways into the counter-culture. *Youth and Society*, 1976, 7 (March): 311-44.

Wieder, D. Lawrence, & Zimmerman, Don H. Regeln im Erklarungsprozess. Wissenschaftliche und ethnowissenschaftliche Sociologie, *Ethnomethodologie*, Herausgegeben von Weingarten, Sack und Schenkein, Surkamp, Berlin. (On explaining by rule: Scientific and ethnoscientific sociology. In F. Sacks *et al* (Eds.), *Topics in Ethnomethodology*. Berlin: Surkamp, 1976.

Wilson, Thomas P. Conceptions of interaction and forms of sociological explanation. *American Sociological Review*, 1970, *35*: 697-710.

Zelditch, Morris, Jr. Some methodological problems of field studies. In George J.

McCall and J. L. Simmons (Eds.), *Issues in participant observation*. Reading, Mass.: Addison-Wesley, 1962.

Zimmerman, Don H. Tasks and troubles: The practical bases of work activities in a public assistance agency. In Donald A. Hansen (Ed.), *Explorations in sociology and counseling*. Boston: Houghton-Mifflin, 1969.

Zimmerman, Don H., & Wieder, D. Lawrence. *The social bases for illegal behavior in the student community*. Washington, D.C.: U.S. Department of Commerce, 1971.

Znaniecki, Florian. *The method of sociology*. New York: Farrar and Rinehart, 1934.

Chapter Six
Structured interviews[1]

ROBERT H. SOMERS, DEAN I. MANHEIMER, MARIANNE T. KLEMAN, and GLEN D. MELLINGER

The successfully completed interviews reported on in this chapter were the first of two waves of observations for twin longitudinal studies. The surveys—one of nearly 1,000 male freshmen who entered the University of California (Berkeley) in the fall of 1970, the other of an equal number of senior men who graduated in the spring of 1971—were for the purpose of studying changes in the personal values and life-styles of these young men as they moved through and out of the university. The second wave was carried out by mail, with personal contact where necessary to enlist cooperation from as many students as possible.

Much personal information was sought in interviews lasting a minimum of one and one-half hours and in many cases continuing for two and one-half hours or more. Areas of questioning included personal experience in the especially sensitive areas of political dissent and the use of drugs. Since the interviews were conducted at a time when gaining the cooperation of respondents for studies of this nature was very difficult, we believe it useful to discuss the procedures we followed that helped us to obtain a high level of cooperation.[2]

Underlying the specific procedures, and probably the basis for our success, was a continuing commitment to two principles that bear on the ethics of social research. First, research procedures should be designed within a framework of sincere respect for the respondents as people and for their right to privacy. Second, the results of the study should be of interest and benefit to the subjects of the study (students in this case) and other persons with similar experiences (e.g., other students) as well as to researchers and other members of the public. Putting these principles into practice and communicating them to respondents required, in this instance, giving attention to a number of practical details in preparing interviews, in recruiting, selecting, and training fieldworkers, in protecting the rights of respondents, and so on. While the importance of such considerations is commonly recognized, it is less common to have sufficient resources and commitment to give these considerations the attention they deserve. Our efforts would, of course, have been impossible without the full support of the sponsoring agencies. The remainder of this paper describes our efforts.

In a longitudinal survey, where the same person is interviewed more than one time, the observations thus made over time make it possible to provide more than speculative answers to a number of questions about how a person's attitudes and values change and what factors influence those changes. In this instance, by obtaining data from the same student two and one-half years after the first interview, we hoped to learn how his academic and career achievements, personal feelings of well-being, social commitments, and political and social values had changed. We also hoped to learn how these factors were influenced by the student's academic and extra-curricular experiences and by his perceptions and evaluations of the social and political institutions of which he was a part.

One of the most crucial problems to be solved in any survey is that of obtaining the cooperation of a sufficiently large proportion of the designated sample so that the results will not be biased by nonresponse. This problem of nonresponse is especially great in a longitudinal study because it accumulates through each successive wave of the study. For example, in this study we set ourselves an ambitious target of 90 percent completion for each wave, which if fulfilled would still mean that only 81 percent (90 percent of 90 percent) of the originally designated sample would be represented in final analyses. Anything substantially less than this, we felt, would call our results into question.

Even without these special considerations of longitudinal study design, the decision to survey the Berkeley campus in 1970 posed a challenge to survey methodology for a number of reasons. Increasingly, various segments of the public were resisting studies that inquired into personal matters. This resistance partially grew out of a concern with invasion of privacy. This concern was often manifested in a fear that guarantees of anonymity for the respondent were either deliberately false or unintentionally misleading, because personal and perhaps incriminating information would inevitably find its way into the files of public or private agences (cf American Statistical Association, 1974). Among some groups there was also a feeling that society needed reformist action, not more studies. We already knew enough, they suggested, and money spent on studying issues would mean less money spent on reform programs. Moreover, most of these sentiments were frequently found among students and were very likely more pronounced on the Berkeley campus than at many other colleges and universities.

In spite of many dire predictions that our research effort would fail because of this sentiment and the rapidity with which campus opinion could be mobilized into organized opposition, we found it possible to obtain what we feel are valid data with very satisfactory completion rates: on the first wave we obtained the cooperation of 92 percent of the freshmen and 90 percent of the seniors. By intensive concern for each of the following aspects of data collection, we sought to maximize cooperation in the face of difficulties. (On the second wave we obtained lengthy questionnaires from 87 percent of freshmen and 83 percent of senior Time-1 respondents).

1. Protecting Respondent Anonymity.

Our first important concern was to protect the anonymity of respondents. The aim was to get all of the approximately 2,150 young men designated in the two samples to cooperate in being interviewed and to be honest and open in their answers. Furthermore, since we were collecting information on a number of sensitive areas, including drug use and political orientation, it was imperative to provide a system guaranteeing that all information would remain confidential.

The problem was thus to develop a foolproof system enabling us to assure students that their responses would remain anonymous and could in no way be identified by either our own staff or by any outside person or agency that might wish to identify individual responses. Yet the system also had to enable us to collate the data for each individual student, including information obtained from the same student at a later point in time. These seemingly contradictory requirements were accomplished by modifying a procedure used by Astin and Boruch (1970) of the American Council of Education.

To understand how this was done, it is first necessary to give a brief description of the field instruments. Early in the study design we recognized that for a number of reasons data collection during the second wave would have to rely largely on self-administered procedures. Yet we were reluctant to give up personal interviews, because they permit greater rapport with respondents as well as more useful qualitative information. These considerations led us to divide the first-wave instruments into two parts—an interview schedule and an accompanying self-administered form (SAQ). We placed in the SAQ all sensitive material and most of the material on which we were especially interested in observing changes. This permitted more rigorous control over the confidentiality of sensitive replies and also enabled us to collect the change-relevant data in the same manner at both times.

As a first step in developing anonymity procedures, each person selected for interviewing was assigned a permanent serial number, known as his "A" number, that we kept in our files together with names and permanent addresses. This number was placed on the respondent's interview schedule and on his SAQ.

As a second step, contact was established with a social scientist in Canada who was to become an important link in our procedures. This man had a special concern about precisely the issue of importance to us—the protection of personal rights to privacy in the context of social research—and was able to carry out the procedures we required. We sent to him a list of "A" numbers without names. Working under an explicit contract drawn up by us and approved by him, he randomly assigned a new number, a "B" number, to each "A" number. Thus each respondent had both an "A" number, which was linked only to his name, and a "B" number, which was used to identify his answers. The Canadian social scientist, who never received the names of respondents, maintained the only link between the "A" and "B" numbers.

The third step took place immediately after completion of the interview. Here the two parts of the interview were treated in significantly different fashions. Because all sensitive questions had been placed in the SAQ, we took special care with it. First, since we did not wish even the interviewers to obtain confidential information, we asked them to avoid looking at answers being entered by a respondent in the SAQ during the interview. Second, the SAQ was mailed directly to Canada by the interviewer. At this time the respondent was encouraged to accompany the interviewer to the nearest mailbox to satisfy himself that this procedure was being followed and that no one who read the answers would be able to identify them as his. Though respondents generally did not feel this necessary, we believe that the invitation provided them with convincing evidence of our earnest desire to protect their replies.

Upon receipt of the SAQ, our Canadian colleague removed the "A" number and returned the SAQ in a batch with some 15-20 others, each identified only by "B" number, to our office.

With one exception, this is the basic procedure that was followed for all other information about respondents, including their university records (obtained with their written permission) and their replies to the second-wave questionnaires. The exception is that, because we wanted to review the work of the interviewers, we asked that they bring the completed interview schedules, which were physically separate from the SAQ, to our office within a few days of completion. This brief return of the interviews to our office did not compromise our basic anonymity policy because the interview contained no sensitive questions. After supervisory review these interview schedules were mailed to Canada and handled like the SAQ, having the "A" number replaced by a "B" number and being returned to us. Only by going through the linking process in Canada were we able to connect these data with a student's 1973 replies and his other information.

These procedures for handling the data and in particular the SAQ, with its personal information about drug use, political views, and possibly even sexual deviance, had the effect of protecting not only the respondents but the researchers, too. We felt it important to have the information protected from court subpoena, and we did not wish to risk going to jail to protect the confidential information. Legal advisors assured us that our procedures provided this protection, since we had no way of identifying the replies of particular respondents. Further, the Canadian colleague was under contract not to reveal the list to anyone (including us) and could not be subpoened by an American court.

While one associate characterized this procedure as an "Abbott and

Costello" routine, and many respondents may have failed to grasp the essentials when it was explained to them, we believe that in addition to its major purpose it was very helpful in eliciting the trust of interviewers. It demonstrated to them that we would go to great lengths to protect the anonymity of respondents. And, in turn, this helped them to feel more confident in reassuring respondents that their anonymity would be protected and that information would not be used in ways that the students thought damaging to them or their interests.

We believe that procedures such as these are well worth the expense and effort they require. They protect the researcher as well as the respondent. By earning the trust of intelligent and skeptical students, they also encourage a high degree of cooperation.

2. Recruiting, Selecting, and Training Interviewers

Anticipating that interviewers would play an unusually substantial role in the success of this study, we took special care in selecting them. Of course, we needed their positive contribution in establishing rapport with respondents. But beyond this consideration an unfortunate choice could have jeopardized the study. For instance, we felt that it would have been possible for one or two antagonistic interviewers to thwart successful interviewing by arousing publicity against the study, perhaps distorting its aims and urging other students not to participate. Or an interviewer could have made improper use of confidential information obtained in the interview and, as a result of subsequent publicity, damaged our prospects.

Hence we decided against the usual procedure of advertising for interviewers and instead relied initially on nominations from colleagues. Later we found it necessary to seek qualified applicants from the university placement office. Since we were interviewing college-age males, we hired only male interviewers, giving preference to men in their twenties, but considering somewhat older ones if their experience and manner indicated they would relate comfortably to students. With effort we obtained a sufficient number of nominations and chose from this group about one in four, or approximately 70 young men we felt sure could establish effective rapport with our student sample and do a good job of honest interviewing.

Our efforts appear to have been successful, except in one unfortunate instance where an interviewer, after initial work of high caliber, began to deviate drastically from established procedure. In a later section we describe how we discovered the deviation that led to his eventual discharge and the discarding of his interviews. But we wish to emphasize now that things might have been far worse if our screening process had not been so careful.

The final stage of the selection process, which for some interviewers constituted the first portion of their training, began with a special practice interview the applicant undertook with someone of his choosing. A staff member discussed the completed practice interview with the candidate in order to evaluate his ability to handle abstract conceptions, to accept constructive criticism, and to understand better the extent to which he possessed those personality characteristics essential for effective interviewing.

All acceptable interviewers were carefully trained through a combination of techniques, including participation in all-day group discussions in which a large proportion of the time was spent on "mock" interviewing and review and criticism of practice interviews with friends and randomly selected strangers outside of the training sessions. Late in the training period interviewers also participated in the pretesting of questionnaire drafts, as described in the next section. When introducing inexperienced interviewers to the survey process, it is extremely helpful to utilize teachers who illustrate the human relations qualities that are essential to good interviewing. We were especially fortunate in being able to hire for a major portion of this training task a young woman with special talents in this area. In an effortless way she was able to convey a sincere and warm respect for the other person and a refreshingly relaxed feeling of openness, candor, and acceptance. These are obviously qualities of inestimable value in interviewing, and we believe that this fortunate choice contributed in important ways to the success of the whole enterprise.[3]

Early experience in the field suggested to interviewers that they needed a written list of brief answers to some of the common questions that respondents posed about the study. Students often wished to know who was sponsoring the study, how the results would be used, why we were interviewing only men, and so on, and interviewers found it useful to be able to leave a copy of these explanations with respondents.

In addition to the basic training described above interviewers attended briefing sessions with the senior investigators, qualified supervisors, and other interviewers to discuss the purpose of the study and procedures for handling any problems that might arise. To make this type of training more effective, interviewers were provided with a detailed, 30-page manual of instructions covering both general aspects of interviewing and the specific problems of this particular interview.

As part of this manual interviewers were provided with a general description of the form the interview would take and the importance of keeping records of attempts to contact the respondent. In addition, university records do not contain all the information we needed to select our sample (age, foreign birth, date of intended graduation for seniors), and so interviewers were instructed to conduct this screening on their first contact.

It is important that interviewers know when they have obtained an appropriate and complete answer to interview questions. To provide interviewers with this understanding, a portion of the training manual was devoted to detailed discussion of the intent behind questions in the interview schedule; this will be described later.

It is obvious that in reporting survey results high priority must be given to establishing the accuracy of the data. Thus, although we should establish a trusting relationship with interviewers, we must nevertheless verify the honesty of their work. This issue is discussed further in Section 6, below, but these obligations also present implications for supervision and training of interviewers. In order to undertake verification procedures and still retain the trust of interviewers, we believe it essential to be open and honest with them and to provide full information at the start of their training about techniques that will be employed to obtain an independent verification of their work.

One of the standard verification procedures used in this study was especially controversial: the use of "plants," who were actually not respondents at all but experienced interviewers. Our presentation of this idea in the training sessions generated much heated discussion in spite of the fact that the technique was intended primarily as a form of supervision rather than verification. The "plants" discussed the effectiveness of the interviewer's work with him and his supervisor in a later review session. In some cases a favorable report from a planted respondent helped to reassure the office staff about an interviewer's fieldwork. We do recognize, of course, that the knowledge of this procedure may have discouraged dishonesty on the part of one or two interviewers.

Another section of the training manual presented general information about the nature of the interviewing task. Here interviewers were provided with the kinds of exhortations and cautions that are commonly found, perhaps in a less detailed way, in textbooks. We developed our own set of instructions because we felt it to be a more personal way of introducing the interviewers to their tasks. Unlike textbook material, everything in these notes was directed to this specific study, making it both clearer and more meaningful. In this section we also described comfortable ways in which interviewers could deal with commonly occurring problems in the interview situation, including the appropriate manner in which to conclude the interview when all questions had been answered.

These notes were helpful in defining the role taken by an interviewer—one that is at once supportive and nonjudgmental, warm yet with a necessary distance. The manner in which thoughtful and respectful communication took place between interviewer and respondent when this role was comfortably assumed is a fascinating aspect of this study.

The manual of instructions for interviewers concluded with a detailed discussion of the meaning of specific interview questions. We provided some background and explanation of what we expected to accomplish with most questions. Without this understanding the interviewer would be unsure whether a respondent had given an adequate answer to the question, whether the question should be repeated because it had apparently been misunderstood, whether the answer should be probed for more detail, and so on.

As fieldwork commenced, special memoranda for interviewers were prepared on questions that gave special problems. Questions 45, for instance—"Now I would like to ask you what you would like most to get out of life. . . . What kind of life would you like to be living ten or twelve years from now?"—created considerable difficulty because of its openness. Interviewers felt that answers could be given in innumerable different areas and that, at minimum, they should be instructed to probe for a response in designated areas. This might include whether or not the respondent anticipated having a family or the type of work he might do or his preferred living circumstances. It was precisely this tendency to suggest answers that we wished to avoid in this question, and for this reason the interview instructions printed with this question say "Probe for clarity only." Further, we knew from pretest experiences, discussed below, that although the question was very open, it produced answers that were meaningful and in line with our purposes. The memorandum we prepared grew out of our lengthy discussions in the training sessions as well as early fieldwork, and emphasizes those points that were found to clarify the intent of the question. It also suggests ways of encouraging respondents who sometimes felt that, as young men just entering the university, they couldn't possibly know what their life would be like in 10 years. Interviewers were asked to remind the respondent gently that most people had some feelings about what they would *like* their lives to be like (which is what the question really asked).

Other procedures were used to ensure thoughtful and accurate interviewing. After completing his first two interviews, and then at regular weekly intervals, the interviewer reviewed his work with a supervisor. As preparation for review all completed interviews were edited for omissions and instances of inadequate or misplaced probing. We also used periodic memos and quizzes that brought to everyone's attention the most common mistakes and so helped the entire group minimize interview error. The quizzes also served the function of making sure interviewers periodically consulted the instructional manual.

In short, our training program was comprehensive. One of the indirect gains such thorough training provided our study was well expressed by an interviewer: "Wow! If you're going to so much trouble with us, this study *must* be important." To the extent that such enthusiasm was conveyed to respondents, it undoubtedly contributed to the success of the study.

3. Pretesting Data-Collection Procedures

Throughout this study we recognized the importance of testing the procedural plans we were formulating. Material we thus pretested ranged all the way from basic ideas about the study to details of the phrasing of particular questions and the manner of administering the questionnaire. At times these pretests took the form of discussions of alternative plans with people experienced in student surveys, with people who knew the student population well, or with students themselves. At other times we actually tried out alternative procedures with small samples of five to ten pretest respondents; then, as plans became final, we administered preliminary drafts of the questionnaire to groups of 30 or 40 students. To avoid influencing the students who would eventually become part of our actual fieldwork, we always went to other campuses for this pretesting and sought students who could be assumed to resemble our study population in attitudes and background.

  a. Testing basic assumptions about the content of the study. In the early stages—some six to eight months prior to the beginning of interviewer selection and training—members of our professional staff led discussions with various people to throw issues and ideas back and forth and to uncover salient areas to be included in the interview. Initially we assembled small groups of students and persons involved with the counter-culture, including colleagues conducting research in the Haight-Ashbury area. Later we conducted group sessions with young men who were about to become students at nearby colleges. We learned far more than expected from these sessions. The areas we intended to study had of course been outlined in our original research proposal, and we expected that the discussions would help us round out coverage of these areas. But we did not realize that only in these discussions would we begin to get a feeling for what issues were important to students.

  For instance, we had felt that students would welcome objective studies of drug use, but we soon learned that this topic was not seen by them as one in urgent need of research, perhaps because drug use was taken for granted by so many students. Nearly all with whom we spoke had experimented with one or more drugs, as had most of their friends. The number who became heavy users was very small, however, and students in general appeared to regard most drug use as an innocuous pastime, largely unrelated to major life events or experiences. The relative unimportance of drugs to these students was later supported by the survey results, in which only 8 percent of the freshmen users reported they would be bothered "quite a bit" or "a lot" by a sudden withdrawal of the supply of all drugs (except alcohol and tobacco) that they had ever tried.

  On the other hand, we found more preoccupation with and striving for personal self-understanding than we had expected. In many cases we also found a sense of frustration at the difficulty of evolving a meaningful set of goals and values and a firm sense of identity as adults in this society. We soon became convinced that to understand fully the problems facing these young men, and even to understand their attitudes toward drugs, we had to take account of fundamental aspects of their social and psychological development. It also seemed that students would be more interested in, and responsive to, the study and would provide us with more thoughtful answers to all the questions if we stressed these more basic issues. Further, this shift in focus would increase the educational value of the study results to both the public and to students themselves. Consequently, we expanded those sections of the interview that dealt with feelings of self-understanding, efforts to achieve better self-understanding, personal goals and values, and the relation of these to the student's anticipated occupation and life-style.

The shift in focus seems to have been effective. As we began to pretest interview schedules, the temporary interviewers we hired for this developmental work would often report that a respondent's closing remark was something like, "You know, you really hit a lot of things I've been thinking about."

   b. Deciding about response precodes.   Initially most draft questions were asked as open-ended questions. When we wished to establish precodes, pretest responses were helpful in showing the range and distribution of answers given by a sizable number of persons. If there was some tendency of the answers to cluster, we knew that we could precode such common replies and leave an "Other (Specify: _____)" response, in which the respondent could write a more idiosyncratic answer. For instance, we wished to develop questions about political or social-reform activities in which students had voluntarily participated. Pretests enabled us to obtain an idea of the range of activities that were common among students in 1970 and 1971 and so to establish satisfactory precodes. These questions on political activity as well as those on drug use were definitely to be precoded because, eliciting potentially sensitive information, they were destined for the more anonymous SAQ, where we precoded as much as possible on the grounds that respondents would not voluntarily write very full answers.

Other questions did not lend themselves to precoding because the range of answers was very large or because the precodes would suggest answers to the respondent or would encourage him to give answers that he felt to be socially acceptable. For instance, as noted in the preceding section, we resisted pressure from interviewers to precode the question: "What sort of life would you like to be living some ten to twelve years from now?" for precisely these reasons.

   c. Narrowing down the number of questions on each issue.   In developing questions for possible inclusion in the final instruments we soon had a far larger set than we could possibly have used. Early open-ended pretesting indicated which questions were yielding useful answers and which could be discarded. But even after this cutting the semifinal drafts of the schedule were quite lengthy, and we utilized pretest respondents at later stages to make estimates of the time it would take to answer each section. We felt that one and one-half to two hours was the most that we could ask respondents to give to the study and hoped that most would take less time. Although pretest estimates varied widely (as did the time taken for interviewing during the final fieldwork), they apparently helped us to avoid exceeding the bounds of patience; in the actual survey only one interview was broken off before the end.

Most of the pretesting discussed so far was qualitative and relatively unstructured. Another type was quantitative and provided us with estimates of the distributions of responses to be obtained from our target population. We wished to obtain such estimates for two reasons: (1) to eliminate questions where there was insufficient variation for analysis and (2) to make a preliminary exploration of correlations.

For these purposes we developed packages of pretest materials that, for practical reasons, were shorter than the whole draft. Each package contained two or three sections of the draft interview (relations with parents, political views, drugs, etc.) together with a personal background section. The packages were varied so that each of the eight sections was included in a portion of them. Since we didn't want to risk contaminating our sample by circulating copies of draft questions on the Berkeley campus, we prevailed on the interest and good nature of colleagues teaching at other universities on the West Coast and sent them packages to hand out to some 50 to 80 students in their classes.[4]

Although this method gave us little critical feedback about question wording or salience, it did help reduce the size of the instrument. Some items were found to be too skewed for analysis, such as yes/no questions with a 98-2 percent split, and were eliminated unless we decided to retain them for descriptive purposes. As an instance of the latter, only a very small proportion of the freshmen were married, but that question was considered of sufficient intrinsic importance to be retained. With quantitative data from these pretests we also carried out preliminary correlation and factor analyses. These were of great help in eliminating redundant questions, because the factor structure made this high correlation between items very apparent.

d. Clarifying the phrasing of questions.   One of the important reasons for pretesting is, of course, to ensure that questions are clearly phrased. We wished, for example, to learn whether some students recalled having bad experiences with drugs. At one point in the pretesting we attempted to learn about this by asking drug users, "Have you ever had a bad reaction to or a 'bad trip' on drugs?" One pretest respondent said:

What do you mean by 'bad trip'? You would really have to define it. Do you mean getting really emotional and crying, an excruciatingly painful experience, or a freak-out that puts you into the hospital? I think what people fear sometimes is that they can't come back. but I've had very painful experiences, though I think I've never bum-tripped. Also, you might include [as bad reactions] the problem of things happening when high—cops and so on. I really can't answer.

Another pretest respondent said that the unpleasant experience he had couldn't really be called a "bad trip" because he later realized that he gained some very useful insights from it. On the basis of these pretest responses it was possible to revise and elaborate the question to obtain more meaningful replies.

Pretesting also helped us make more refined and elaborate decisions about question wording. For example, we used the colloquial phrase "bad trip" in the question above in spite of a general policy emerging from earlier discussions with students and others to avoid the vernacular in phrasing questions. Many would see it, they said, as distastefully ingratiating and possibly as an attempt at cooptation, just as many students viewed President Nixon's use of the peace symbol in 1970. Another reason for avoiding the vernacular is that it undergoes continual change and is employed by some listeners to verify that a speaker has properly kept up with current fashion. Thus, to use in the interview the word *pot* for marijuana might have sounded somewhat out-of-date because the fashionable term had changed to *grass* in many places and, at least in the Bay Area, was giving way by the time of our interviewing to *dope* or *stuff*.

This clarification of the phrasing of questions was carried out in two ways. First, small groups of six to ten young men were invited to come in and, for a small payment, fill out the draft questionnaire, which included both interview and SAQ questions. After they completed their answers, we discussed with them what the questions meant, whether they were bothered by any of the questions or response categories, and how they felt in general about the questionnaire. Second, a staff member would work with an individual respondent as he answered those questions destined for inclusion in the SAQ, interrupting him as he checked off his answers to ask what his thoughts were, whether he had any conflicts or uneasiness in answering, and so on. This latter type of testing was done by a staff member well versed in the purposes of the study and the intent of individual questions, and so he was in a good position to spot misinterpretations.

e. Testing procedures for administering the interview.   Early pretest experience suggested to us the desirability of breaking up the interview by administering sections of the SAQ alternately with sections of the interview. In this way we would reduce the problem of respondent fatigue arising from a long personal interview and an equally long SAQ. With further testing of this procedure we found that it had other advantages as well. By permitting SAQ questions to follow immediately after questions on the same topic in the interview schedule, it made the whole interview more coherent. Further, it mollified those students who objected to the feeling that they were being "pigeon-holed" by precoded responses in systematic research. Since they had just explained how they felt in an open-ended interview, they had less objection to circling an SAQ response that didn't quite fit their opinions.

All other aspects of the administration of the interview were checked in later phases of the pretesting. In some instances individual staff members worked with individual respondents, testing the final draft to see if the form or content of questions and instructions could be improved in any way and to see that nothing had been overlooked. Just before final printing of the protocols we conducted a "dress rehearsal" with about 20 respondents to correct last-minute difficulties and to make a final check on all the procedures and instructions.

As noted in the preceding section, some of the final phases of the pretesting also became a part of the training of interviewers, providing a double benefit to the study. By participating in small-group assessments of the drafts of the interview schedule, interviewers obtained a sense of participation in the study even during their training. In addition, we gained helpful criticisms of the draft from young men who were presently or recently students undergoing the kinds of experiences we planned to study. These newly hired interviewers were also very useful in testing the final interviewing instructions because they were better able than experienced interviewers or staff members to identify ambiguities and gaps in these instructions.

Although these various pretest activities required an ambitious investment of time and energy, the success of our fieldwork convinced us of their worth.

4. Mobilizing Community Support for the Survey

For studies of this nature we routinely obtain supporting statements from community leaders who are known to, and are respected by, our respondents. In the present study we had to give special consideration to the sources from which we sought support. An endorsement from the university administration in 1970 might have labeled the study part of the "dreaded Establishment," a misapprehension that would have been a great handicap in persuading students to be interviewed. Instead, we discussed the study with, and obtained supporting statements from, a diverse array of community leaders, including respected faculty members, the student body president, the head of the local free church, and Dr. Eugene Schoenfeld (better known as Dr. Hippocrates, a local "hip" doctor and author of a nationally syndicated medical-advice column).

This support served a number of purposes. It gave us, and more importantly our interviewers, confidence that our research enjoyed the kind of broad local support that we had hoped for. Obviously, if interviewers are not convinced that a research project is important, they would not be likely to convince a respondent that his participation is important. Interviewers were also prepared with copies of these letters to show to skeptical respondents. This community support also gave the rest of our staff a needed feeling of security. We knew that if the study received any unfavorable publicity, we would call on these community leaders for help in clarifying the nature of the study.

We also discussed our study with the editor of the student newspaper, and this led to an unanticipated kind of advance publicity. An interview with a reporter for the paper was followed by a story describing our study as a survey of students' sexual habits. Our first reaction was consternation; our second, anxiety. We feared that the article's sensational undertones might alienate respondents. Instead, it apparently aroused their interest. Interviewers said that some respondents, after reading the article, welcomed the opportunity to take part in the study and were apparently not too disappointed that the survey was somewhat less sensational than they expected.

5. Obtaining and Maintaining the Respondent's Cooperation

A number of steps were taken to encourage the participation of respondents when fieldwork finally got under way. A few days before being approached by our interviewer, each designated respondent received a letter from us describing the study, asking for his cooperation, and explaining why his participation was important. Where this letter failed to convince a student to take part, we sent a second letter answering insofar as possible the questions or objections he had expressed to the interviewer who called him after the first letter was sent. An interviewer always made it clear to a reluctant respondent that he was not being forced to participate and that he had every right to refuse, but that we wanted a chance to answer his objections because we felt it was really important that he participate. This attitude alone convinced some respondents to participate, with a comment something like: "Oh, if I don't *have* to do it, then I will." In the case of more serious refusals interviewers were instructed to ascertain the reasons underlying the resistance. If a respondent would not divulge even that to the interviewer, we usually made no further efforts to persuade him. But if he was willing to voice his objections, then in most cases the interviewer or a member of the professional staff was able to answer his objections satisfactorily and the student would decide to complete the interview.

Because of the importance of a high completion rate and the real (though slight) possibility of collective protest against the study, a special element was added to the design of our fieldwork. Rather than selecting respondents to be interviewed in alphabetical order as they happened to appear on the list, we divided the entire sample into random subsamples and attempted to complete the interviewing of the earlier subsamples before turning to the next. In this way, even if the fieldwork was broken off before being completed, we could extract a representative sample of responses by utilizing one or more completed subsamples.

6. Establishing Procedures to Check on the Reliability and Validity of the Data We Were Collecting

We followed several routines as well as certain specially designed procedures to establish the reliability of our data. As noted earlier, we occasionally used a "planted" respondent whose task it was to observe the work of the interviewer. Also, we sent all respondents a note asking them to return to us a postcard verifying that they had been interviewed and making an estimate of how long the interview took, so that we could compare their estimates with the records given us by interviewers. If we consistently found a systematic difference between the time estimates of an interviewer and his respondents, we had reason to question the honesty of the interviewer. It was just such a consistent discrepancy that first led us to suspect the work of one interviewer. Our suspicions were justified as postcards began to come back from his respondents saying they had not even been interviewed. Further investigation and a meeting with the interviewer led us to the painful decision to discharge him and discard all his work.

Another standard verification procedure was to telephone a randomly selected 25 percent of the respondents. First assuring them that we didn't have the specific information they had given the interviewer—since this was being handled in an anonymous way—we asked how the interviewer had handled the interview, whether he had used the procedure of alternating between the personal interview and the self-administered form, and other easily ascertained matters. This personal contact with the respondent after the interview was helpful to supervisors and also provided convincing verification. As with other verification procedures, of course, we recognized the importance of informing interviewers about these matters early in their training.

Occasionally, in surveys of this nature, it is possible to check directly the validity of information given by respondents. One such check in our survey involved Scholastic Aptitude Test (SAT) scores, which we asked freshmen to report in their SAQ's. Since these scores are also on the college admissions records, which the respondents gave us permission to use, we were able to compare the two. In order to match a student with his admissions record and yet keep his anonymity intact, it was of course necessary to go through the "A" and "B" number routine described earlier. A comparison of the two sets of scores revealed that while there was a small bias toward claiming a higher SAT score than the one on record, in only a few cases did the respondent report a highly discrepant score.

7. Summary

This review of our activities in preparing and maintaining a large interviewing operation as part of a longitudinal study should make clear the need for attention to methodological details, the need for safeguarding respondents against possible misuse of the information they furnish, and the need for advance planning to make the survey results beneficial to those who are giving up their valuable time to participate.

NOTES

[1] Portions of the material discussed were presented in "Technical and Ethical Considerations in Data Collection," presented to the First International Conference on Student Drug Surveys, Newark, New Jersey, September 1971, and published in the *Proceedings* of that Conference and in *Drug Forum*, 1 (No 4), July 1972, pp. 323-333. While our surveys dealt with a broad range of personal experiences and attitudes, we included detailed questions about the extent, recency and level of use of drugs as well as attitudes about them. The entire study was supported by PHS Grants as follows: DA 00137 from the National Institute on Drug Abuse (formerly MH 17642 and MH 21425 from the National Institute of Mental Health), and DA 00647 from the National Institute on Drug Abuse. Dean I. Manheimer and Glen D. Mellinger were the Co-Principal Investigators.

[2] This growing difficulty in gaining the cooperation of respondents is recognized in "Report of the ASA Conference on Surveys of Human Populations," *The American Statistician*, February, 1974, Vol. 28, No. 1, pp. 30-34.

[3] We refer to Barbara Dorsey of West Coast Community Surveys (Berkeley). We are also indebted to Selma Monsky, Director of Field Operations, Survey Research Center, University of California, Berkeley, and formerly Director of West Coast Community Surveys, for invaluable assistance in many phases of the development of fieldwork procedures and instrument design.

[4] We are especially grateful to Professors Riley Dunlap and Robert Smith for their help in coordinating these pretests on their respective campuses.

REFERENCES

Manheimer, D.I., Mellinger, G.D., Somers, R.H., & Kleman, M.T. Technical and ethical considerations in data collection. In S. Einstein (Ed.), *Student drug surveys: Proceedings of the First International Conference*. Farmingdale, N.Y.: Baywood Publishing Co., 1972. Also appeared in *Drug Forum*, 1972, *1* (4), 323-333.

Mellinger, G.D., Davidson, S.T., & Manheimer, D.I. *Changing patterns in use of alcohol and marijuana among university males*. Paper presented at the North American Congress on Alcohol and Drug Abuse, San Francisco, December 1974.

Mellinger, G.D., Somers, R.H., Manheimer, D.I., & Skronski, M.C. *Drug use and academic achievement among university men: A longitudinal analysis*. Unpublished paper, March 1975.

Somers, R.H., Mellinger, G.D., & Manheimer, D.I. *Illicit drug use, alienation, and career choice: A longitudinal analysis of male university freshmen*. Paper presented at the Pacific Sociological Association, Victoria, B.C., April 1975.

Mellinger, G.D., Somers, R.H., & Manheimer, D.I. *Drug use and academic attrition among university men*. Paper presented at the Conference on the Social Psychology of Drug and Alcohol Abuse, Los Angeles, May 1975. Published in the *Proceedings* of the Conference.

Somers, R.H., Mellinger, G.D., & Manheimer, D.I. *Drug use and career choice among university men.* Unpublished paper, May 1975.

Mellinger, G.D., Somers, R.H., & Manheimer, D.I. Drug use research items pertaining to personality and interpersonal relations: A working paper for research investigators. In D.J. Lettieri (Ed.), *Predicting adolescent drug abuse: A review of issues, methods and correlates* (National Institute on Drug Abuse, Research Issues Series No. 11). Washington: Government Printing Office, 1975.

Mellinger, G.D., Somers, R.H., Davidson, S.T., & Manheimer, D.I. *Drug use, academic performance and career indecision: Longitudinal data in search of a model.* Paper presented at the Conference on Longitudinal Research on Drug Use, San Juan, Puerto Rico, April 1976. Published in D.B. Kandel (Ed.), Longitudinal research on drug use: Empirical findings and methodological issues. Washington: Hemisphere, 1978.

Somers, R.H., Mellinger, G.D., Manheimer, D.I., & Davidson, S.T. *Male drug use at a major university: Its implications for academic motivations, dropping out, academic performance and career indecisions.* Paper presented at the American College Health Association, Denver, April 1976.

Mellinger, G.D., Somers, R.H., Davidson, S.T., & Manheimer, D.I. The amotivational syndrome and the college student. *Annals of the New York Academy of Sciences,* 1976, *282,* 37-55.

Davidson, S.T., Mellinger, G.D., & Manheimer, D.I. Changing patterns of drug use among university men. Published in *Addictive Diseases: An International Journal,* 1977.

PART THREE
DOCUMENTS

Good social research synthesizes evidence from different sources. Surprisingly, field researchers, perhaps because they are so strongly motivated to explore firsthand the empirical social world, often neglect to gather and analyze existing documents that bear on their study. This section is directed toward correcting this fault. The three papers discuss historical evidence, journalistic evidence, and content analysis. Well-chosen vignettes from historical or journalistic accounts can give an interesting substantive flavor to qualitative or quantitative studies. Moreover, an element of quantification is introduced if statements gleaned from newspapers or narratives are systematically classified into various categories and then counted to provide unobtrusive or nonreactive measures of social variables. These measures can be analyzed statistically, as illustrated below in Danzger's chapter, or they can be juxtaposed with qualitative observations to provide mutual corroboration and specification.

Marienthal (Jahoda, Lazarsfeld, and Zeisel, 1971), a classic study of a community of unemployed workers near Vienna circa 1930, provides numerous examples of such juxtapositions of evidence. In one, reproduced below, the authors placed together a numerical count gleaned from the diet records of 41 Depression-wracked families and a statement from an unemployed man:

Here are the meat days of the 41 families:

Meat Days per Week	Percent of Families
0	15
1	54
2	19
3	5
4	7
	100

Of the families (54 percent) who had meat once a week, all had it on Sunday. Those who had meat more than once had it on Sunday and some other days. During the week, fifty-six of the meals eaten by these forty-one families contained meat; thirty-four of the meat dishes consisted of horse meat, eighteen of rabbit stew, two of beef, one of mincemeat, and one of pork. One unemployed man told us that cat meat was also eaten:

"Cats keep disappearing. Only a few days ago Herr H.'s cat disappeared. Cat meat is very good. Dogs are also eaten. But that began already before unemployment. At J. T.'s, for example, they once roasted a dog. A few days ago a man was given a dog by one of the farmers on condition that the animal be killed painlessly. The man went everywhere to find a basin for the blood and finally got one. But he had to promise a piece of the meat in return. The basin belonged to A's family."

The lesson to be learned from this is not that cat meat is delicious, but that the mutual use of qualitative observations and quantitative measures is a better strategy than relying solely on one source of insight. The qualitative data clarifies the meaning of the numerical data, vividly portrays the empirical reality being studied, and leads to new research questions and answers,thereby guiding the research process. Hopefully, the chapters in this section will foster such beneficial juxtapositions.

J. M. Reitzel and B. Lindemann clarify how historians evaluate and utilize documentary evidence. Since the logic of historical research is directly applicable to the analysis of any kind of document—field notes, transcriptions of interviews, survey questionnaires—this chapter is particularly pertinent. The authors stress a theoretically informed inductive research methodology. In the context of a specific research problem there is a reciprocal interplay between the gathering of evidence and the formulation of interpretations and hypotheses: The evidence leads to new theorizing, the new hypotheses stimulate the gathering of new data, etc. It is apparent that this process can begin in either of two ways—by reviewing a set of documents to establish which ones are useful, or by first establishing on theoretical grounds what kinds of documents are needed and then setting out to gather this evidence.

The authors discuss how to develop new sources of evidence as well as how to assess extant materials. They give a number of useful examples of how to ascertain validity through internal and external checks on documents and through checks on the generalization of findings, and of some of the limits built in by the absence of certain theoretically desirable data sources. They point out that historical research contains a limitation not present to the same degree for students of contemporary events. Some evidence may not exist and cannot be re-created (such as official records of births and deaths, diaries, newspaper accounts by on-the-spot observers, etc.). Their review is a useful model for assessing any set of studies on a subject where conflicting or incomplete data are present or where a fabrication is suspected.

In "The Use of Newspapers" Danzger makes an important point about the social organization of news gathering—cities without wire services may produce less valid or complete accounts than larger cities with multiple sources of news-gathering, including the major wire services. Thus, a study of events reported in or from those cities is likely to be less complete than events reported in papers in larger cities. As Danzger notes, an event reported in a newspaper is very likely to have occurred, but events that did not appear (and were obtained from other sources) will obviously be missed when one relies only on national newspapers such as *The New York Times*. (It should be pointed out that some of Danzger's conclusions are not fully supported by other research in the United Kingdom on the representation of events. Glasgow Media Group, 1976; Cohen, 1973). Newspaper reports continue to be questioned as to validity and reliability when one is not studying major national news events, and even then political biases are likely to exist. However, counts of newspaper reports of events such as riots or demonstrations may be the only feasible way of gauging the frequency of occurrence of these important social indicators of societal malaise.

The drudgery of building up such measures from newspapers or other texts can be reduced considerably by the use of the General Inquirer system for computerized content analysis. This ingenious system is described in the chapter by Ogilvie, Stone, and Kelly. If the General Inquirer is used to analyze the content of a daily newspaper, it can reveal trends in public opinion and salient public issues (De Weese, 1976). Thus it offers a method complementary to public opinion survey research for the study of changing public issues.

REFERENCES

Cohen, Stanley. *Folk devils and moral panics*. London: Paladin Books, 1973.

De Weese, L. Carroll, III. Computer content analysis of printed media: A limited feasibility study. *Public Opinion Quarterly*, 1976, *40* (Spring): 92-114.

Glasgow Media Group. *Bad news*. London: Routledge, Kegan Paul, 1976.

Jahoda, Marie, Lazarsfeld, Paul F., & Zeisel, Hans. *Marienthal*. Chicago: Aldine, 1971.

Chapter Seven
Historical evidence

J. M. REITZEL and B. LINDEMANN

INTRODUCTION TO HISTORICAL ANALYSIS

Reading maketh a full man; conference a ready man; and writing an exact man. . . . Histories make men wise; poets, witty; the mathematics, subtile; natural philsophy, deep; moral [philosophy], grave; logic and rhetoric, able to contend.

Of Studies by Sir Francis Bacon (1561-1626)[1]

The man who wrote this statement of educational philosophy, although not a scientist, heralded a new approach to knowledge about the physical world that eventually became known simply as "the scientific method." Application of this new method produced the technology that is so characteristic of modern Western culture. The distinctive feature of Bacon's methodology was a greater reliance upon replicable experiments and quantified data and less use of syllogistic reasoning. Because of his conviction that all true knowledge was also useful knowledge, Bacon tried to transfer the exactitude of the new methodology from the physical to the social sciences, to human events and attitudes.[2] Modern social scientists, in their attempt to refine rules of inquiry that will generate reliable knowledge about societies past and present, are directly involved with the same issues that concerned Bacon.

The above quotation comes from one of Bacon's short essays in which he outlined an educational program built around the new scientific method. His emphasis on the value of the traditional liberal arts seems puzzling at first, but Bacon was not trying merely to outline experimental techniques or rules for collecting data. He reckoned that the reliability of the new method was no better than the quality of the researcher's mind. It was the individual researcher who decided which facts and observations were relevant and then analyzed them, supplying others with data for further research. Bacon wanted to fashion the human mind into a scientific tool, to be used with the same precision which he expected of man-made tools. Twentieth-century social scientists have the use of a far wider range of technical aids than was available to their predecessors. Yet the one indispensable tool is still the trained mind; hence social scientists are concerned about methodology, for it is the study of the process by which the mind can become a reliable, flexible tool.

For Bacon, as for modern social scientists, this training prepares researchers to become "objective" in their discovery, analysis, and presentation of the social world. Objectivity in this sense does not mean to researchers what it often means in the popular mind, namely (in the words of Webster's *Third Unabridged Dictionary*) "existing independent of mind: relating to an object as it is in itself or as distinguished from consciousness or the subject." Social scientists today do not aim at total understanding of an object "as it is in itself," since they recognize that all knowledge is by definition a product of the human mind. The aim of social science researchers is instead to achieve that "objectivity" given as Webster's third definition of the word: ". . . observable or verifiable, especially by scientific methods . . . of such nature that rational minds agree in holding it real or true or valid." The objectivity of social science is that process of establishing methods of inquiry that will yield knowledge that is reliable in the sense that people of similar training can recognize its worth and use it in their own studies.

To physical scientists generally, and to many social scientists, one crucial test of objectivity, and hence of reliability, is their capacity to replicate findings. Can another researcher perform the same experiment or very similar experiments and get the same answers? For many social scientists this sort of verification is impossible. Historians, together with those sociologists and anthropologists who study the structure and functioning of one social group at a particular time—those who are termed participant observers—can never exactly repeat the same study. The social conditions that a researcher studies will never again be duplicated; they cannot be artificially reconstructed by another researcher. The degree of objectivity, and hence the validity of this sort of social research, cannot depend upon replication. The research must be tested on the methods used to collect data. The rules of evidence and the problems of organization will vary somewhat according to the subject of the inquiry and the kinds of materials used.

Historical research differs from much social science research in two factors—in the materials used as sources of data and in the subjects studied. Historians study anything about the past that can be analyzed—the arts, thought, the migration and assimilation of peoples, social change, the lives of individuals. History thus includes aspects of both the humanities and the social sciences. Most social scientists work within a single chronological period, the present or the most recent past. Within this single period they study group interrelations, changes of attitudes, and stratification. The range of their investigations is limited only by their training and interests. Historians work within a closed system. They depend upon data that happened to be preserved from the past. They can greatly expand the potential use of their available sources by varying their topics and questions, but they cannot create previously nonexistent sources by conducting interviews or by setting up controlled experiments with live subjects. Rarely, and only in studies of the recent past, do historians have a sufficient range of data to use accepted sampling techniques. Should an exhaustive use of their data prove inconclusive, they cannot compile another set by asking other people the same or different questions. Their approach to documents is analogous to the process sociologists call "secondary analysis" (Hyman, 1972). Many sophisticated research methods developed by contemporary social scientists cannot be used by practicing historians as a reliable way of organizing and verifying their data.[3] Consequently, historians use quantification less than do other social science researchers.

Even with these distinctions history and the other social disciplines use similar evidence and study similar phenomena. Furthermore not all sociologists limit their inquiries to the present or the recent past. One of the founders of modern sociology, the German scholar Max Weber (died 1920), became famous for his statements about the economic implications of the Protestant Reformation.[4] Lately other sociologists have been using an historical context as a means of enlarging both the number and the types of human societies they can study; for example, Erikson (1966) and Merton (1970) have studied the English and American Puritans, societies created by an early splintering within the Protestant movement. Similarly, sociologists who study present-day societies use newspapers, legal documents, and other artifacts of daily life—types of evidence also useful to historians. The aims of historians are also similar to those of other social scientists: to produce systematic, reliable statements that either increase the available pool of knowledge about a given topic or bring existing knowledge into a more precise focus by means of new interpretive patterns.

Because of these common materials, subject matter, and goals many of the techniques for handling narrative sources are common to all the social sciences, regardless of their different orientations. The special rules of inquiry that historians have developed as aids in the analysis of their documents are relevant to anyone engaged in nonquantitative social research. This article is not concerned with the theoretical structure of the social sciences or even that of history.[5] Detailed analyses of some of the practical problems of historical inquiry have been published by Bagley (1965), Fischer (1970), Hexter (1971), and Shafer (1974). This essay is intended as a brief introduction to these problems and methodological issues of history for the researcher who is not primarily a historian. Consequently, we have omitted some issues that are of value only to the historian, such as authenticating and collating manuscripts.

The process of documentary research discussed above in theoretical terms is followed by everyone in daily life. That is, everyone has some occasion from time to time to make a personal historical enquiry, and the procedure in such a mundane case is similar to that followed by professional historians. The hypothetical example that follows will illustrate this similarity and will furnish as well a brief overview of what historians do when they set out to write an account of the past. The rest of this essay will discuss in more detail the methods by which historians evaluate their evidence and guard against misinterpretation. We shall discuss three major aspects of historical research: types of evidence, the levels of analysis that historians use on their evidence, and the ways historians construct internal and external contexts to verify their analyses.

Put in its simplest terms, the aim of historical study is the recovery of the past. In this sense everyone practices history.[6] Consider as an example a situation that could confront any student: Three weeks after finishing a semester of college, a student whom we shall call Sam discovered that the registrar had recorded an F as a grade in one of his courses. Sam thought he had done well in this course, so he pondered a bit about the possible reasons for the F. Based on his knowledge (which in this case stemmed from his personal experience) he asked himself a few questions and formed several hypotheses. What grades had he received for the course before the final exam? If he had failed the final exam, would that have been enough to cause him to fail the course? Some preliminary calculations and research (checking on his previous grades and the percentage weight of the final exam) convinced him that he could not have failed the course even if he had failed the final exam. Therefore, he hypothesized, there must have been some mistake. Perhaps the professor had lost his final exam. Perhaps the professor or the registrar had recorded the wrong grade. Only further research would enable him to test the validity of these hypotheses. Accordingly, Sam went first to his professor, who took out her book of grades (a relevant historical document). She found that she had graded Sam's final exam and given him a C for the course. The record thus showed one of his hypotheses to be invalid. To discover what had happened, however, still more research was necessary. A check at the registrar's office proved that the professor had given the wrong grade to the registrar. One of Sam's hypotheses thus proved valid by the evidence.

This simple case presents elements common to any social science research. Researchers first make a mental catalog of their information and sources. Then they frame questions that will guide them in their preliminary research. On the basis of this research they form several hypotheses, or to use the term preferred by historians, interpretations. With these they try to analyze the preliminary data. Then they undertake more intensive research to check their interpretations. As they progress in their research, they discard some theories, and on the basis of the new information they refine their interpretations or frame entirely new ones.

In any major study this simultaneous process of fact-gathering and interpretation is carried on at many different levels and may at any one time involve masses of documents or only a single memo. For example, an historian trying to get information about a certain memo written by a presidential aide would make use of procedures similar to Sam's. The memo itself might then be one bit of evidence crucial to an historical understanding of an aspect of presidential policy. Before arriving at a broader explanation of this policy, the historian would frame new questions to guide further research, much of it on the same preliminary level. This research might include other puzzling, undated, unsigned staff sheets. Again the historian would form broader but still tentative conclusions before doing even more research and then finally incorporating all the findings into an integrated narrative.

Throughout this lengthy process the individual historian is guided by standards of scholarship that are recognized by all historians and that give the discipline its unity. These standards are learned not as methodological abstractions, but through analogy and practice in the course of a lengthy "apprenticeship." As graduate students historians first study examples of scholarship in their own and in different fields. Such examples offer analogies of good (and bad) methodology that help apprentice scholars with their research problems. They then develop analytical skill by writing papers in their specialties; these are submitted to both peers and professors for criticism and revision. Throughout their professional lives historians further refine their technique by subjecting their work to the exacting scrutiny of specialists. In the following discussion of methodology we will follow a similar method, introducing the reader to historical scholarship by setting out examples of methodological problems. Since every historian follows similar procedures in analyzing evidence, each of the examples could be used to illustrate several different points. However, a multiplicity of examples, ranging widely over time and subject, introduces the nonspecialist to the variety of contexts in which historians work.

PRACTICAL PROBLEMS IN EVALUATING EVIDENCE

Types of Historical Evidence

In searching for information about past societies historians, like all good social scientists, use every available kind of evidence. The evidence used in a particular historical inquiry depends on the information sought. Historians may write about one individual, search out the pedigree of an influential but anonymous tract, or determine the activities of certain legally, socially, or economically defined groups. They may be interested in the composition of certain political parties or in the dichotomy (if it exists) between individual and group attitudes and actions.

Some of the evidence historians use is official—that is, it was meant to be preserved for future use. This includes all sorts of governmental files, financial records and titles to property (whether truthful or forged), court cases, memoranda, laws, propaganda, literature, minutes of the meetings of public corporations, and newspapers (or those documents that had a similar function before the age of print, such as local chronicles and annals). Historians also have access to other materials, including both physical artifacts and written sources, that had not been collected with any purpose of preservation but had existed primarily as adjuncts to everyday life. They include clothing, dishes or furniture, marginal notes in books or letters, private correspondence and memoirs, household accounts, and other scribblings and jottings.

Social researchers, whether they study the past or the present, whether they analyze individual documents or conduct surveys and random samplings, begin by framing questions that will give structure to their research. The insight and care they bring to this initial task determine the reliability of their findings. It is not enough simply to be rigorous in analyzing data, for the data gathered depends partly upon these initial questions. Researchers who study aspects of a contemporary social group often frame questions and then decide what kinds of data will best answer those questions. They then proceed to collect data. The only limit to the kinds of questions they raise is their ingenuity in generating new data. They choose from a variety of methods, either observing subjects directly or constructing clinical experiments, the conditions of which are carefully controlled. They decide what part of the population to study and how best to do their sampling. Each of these decisions involves the framing of questions. Hence they must be concerned that the questions asked and the techniques used to answer them do not predetermine their answers.

For historians this problem is somewhat different. They may have abundant information about a subject, but they do not work with a potentially unlimited amount of data. They may even have trouble learning about existing sources because of incomplete archival catalogs, because many private collections are closed to public scrutiny, or because they are insufficiently acquainted with certain types of foreign and specialized scholarship. No matter how well they have mastered the necessary technical skills, they cannot add to the total number of surviving diaries, charters, wills, and other written and physical sources from mankind's past that have been preserved. Therefore, the sorts of questions they can ask successfully depend on the type and quantity of material available as a result of preselection by the accidents of time. In examining child-rearing practices, for example, they cannot ask if toilet training varied according to social class in 17th-century Virginia because they have no way of determining what toilet-training practices were in any given class at that time. Chance references in diaries or letters might give some clue as to practices among the literate—that is, the upper classes—but the information would be too sparse to allow the historian to generalize even about these classes. Evidence of toilet-training practices among other classes simply does not exist.

Because historical questions are framed around the use of a restricted amount of data, historians are aware that some questions cannot be answered by the surviving evidence. They mold their questions to the kinds of information that they can expect to find in their sources. Most documents can be used in a variety of ways, depending on the focus of the particular inquiry. Asking the right kinds of questions can sometimes lead historians to look for information in documents previously used for other purposes. In the following section we shall (1) examine ways in which historians use the same document or set of documents for many different purposes; (2) show ways in which historians can frame new questions and thus be led to previously overlooked sources of information; and (3) discuss the nature of documentary "finds."

Creating New Evidence

Historians are trained to use a variety of sources and to use each type of source in many ways. Historians reading a statesman's memoirs may by only incidentally concerned about the career or attitudes of that person: they may use the statesman's chatty remarks to find out where another person was at a certain time or whether there was a shortage of some commodity in a certain locale. The statesman's descriptions of town and country areas may provide information on the spread of urbanization and of people's reaction to it, on changes in the lifestyle of others, or on the changing ratio of sheep to cattle ranching. Similarly, historians may be interested not so much in the content of a document as in the use of individual terms or names. Such word analysis is often tedious but fairly straightforward, as when historians work out modern equivalents for medieval measures (see pp. 181–183). Or it can begin with detailed lists. For example, personal names can be used as clues in locating and dating the popularity of the earliest French epic, *The Song of Roland*. French nobles increasingly named sons "Roland" or "Oliver" after the heroes of this epic. They shunned the use of "Ganelon," a name that had been popular before its association with the villain (Bloch, 1964b: I, 102).

Good history, along with all good social research, integrates every known piece of evidence from every known source. In so doing research methodology must deal with the further problem of allowing for indecisive results or even for results that disprove the initial organizing assumptions. Researchers may even get results that they find personally repugnant. Sometimes the organizing assumptions of scholars are such that important sources of evidence are overlooked. By questioning these assumptions other scholars often will be able to make dramatic revisions in a field. The following example involves our understanding of medieval craftsmanship. The first scholars to study medieval art and architecture were antiquarians and art historians; their main sources of evidence were the art objects themselves. Most of these are unsigned, and few schematic drawings exist that can be attributed to a definite individual (for a famous exception see

Honnecourt, 1959). In addition, we have few medieval writings about art, and they seldom comment upon or name an outstanding artist. Scholars thus concluded that medieval people took little pride in individual achievement. It was further supposed that medieval artisans had beeen drawn from a pool of unspecialized laborers. Patronage, mainly by ecclesiastical corporations, was assumed to be fitful and disorganized.[7] This social pressure toward anonymity and amateurism was especially striking when contrasted to the Renaissance and its cult of the outstanding individual.

As historians who were not working in art history began to question the assumptions behind this theory, they found information on the subject in sources other than art objects or writings on art (Harvey, 1969; passim, esp. 25 ff., 39 ff. 59 ff.). Local histories, letters, and household accounts had references to the careers of medieval craftsmen, construction processes, and activities of patrons. Taken together, these tidbits were evidence that people in the Middle Ages did take pride in the work of artists and builders even if the scope of their pride did not reach Renaissance proportions. Furthermore, manuscript illustrations were found to show examples of medieval cranes, pulleys, scaffolding, and the grouping of workmen into hierarchies—all indications that professional sophisticated builders were involved in medieval construction. By questioning standard generalizations about medieval artisans historians were led to use different sources written by men who were only incidentally concerned with the art of their times.

Contributions to historical knowledge, whether in modern or premodern history, generally depend upon a revised analysis of known sources, not upon a discovery of new or hitherto unknown material. The "new" sources used by revisionists were usually known to the scholarly world, although their use may have been restricted to scholars within a certain field, or they may not have been read with the "new" perspective. Thus, these known sources can generate "new" evidence.

The existing documentation on any problem is relatively less abundant in premodern history than in modern history. Even in the earlier periods little-known or previously forgotten documents are sometimes found. A scholar may edit for publication a series of letters, diaries, or financial accounts that had been virtually lost because they were in manuscript form in some local archive. Or historians can use documents that had been overlooked by previous researchers. On rare occasions sources are found that are actually "new" to the scholarly world. Dramatic finds were made shortly after World War II in the Egyptian desert near the Nile and at Qumrân, on the northwest bank of the Dead Sea (Cross, 1958; Doresse, 1960; Freedman & Greenfield, 1969; Gray, 1965). It is likely that the desert will yield still more in years to come. Together with archaeological evidence, these scrolls and papyrus booklets are allowing scholars to answer questions about Judaism and early Christianity that they could not previously consider because of the scarcity of evidence. Occasionally, documentary discoveries are made that are less dramatic than the Egyptian and Qumrân finds and involve the puzzling out of bits and pieces of previous research, to see if it is possible to identify sources that once were known to have existed but have dropped from notice (for literary examples see Altick, 1966).

Similarly, advances in modern technology have made available to historians new sources in much the same way that archaeology and radio-carbon dating have helped scholars of prehistory. Aerial photographs enable historians to trace field systems, trade routes, land reclamations, and urban growth (Beresford & St. Joseph, 1958; Orwin & Orwin, 1967). Technology has also had the effect of generating new historical data; scholars in modern social and economic history use films, cartoons, and photographs; potentially these are far more informative than their earlier counterparts, which were marginal sketches and handbills. Occasionally, historians uncover forgeries by supplementing textual or stylistic analysis with techniques such as X-rays, spectroscopy, and chemical analysis of inks and paints. Recently discovered frauds include both manuscripts and works of art. (von Bothmer & Noble, 1961; Knight, 1974; Metropolitan Museum of Art, 1968)

Sometimes historians combine physical and written evidence in order to understand the total culture of a period. So far the periods studied in this way have been those that were unusually dynamic in all the arts (Antal, 1948; Hauser, 1960; L'Orange, 1965; Meiss, 1951; Panofsky, 1966, 1972; Pickering, 1970; von Simson, 1964, 1965; Sypher, 1955). Thus, Meiss examined the effects on Renaissance Florence and Siena of the dislocations brought about the Black Death (bubonic plague). Historians have had trouble assessing the plague's psychological impact because of the number of variables involved. For example, scholars still do not agree on the death tolls.[8] Meiss expanded the range of his evidence from documents to art. He related visual themes and images to those found in prayers, letters, diaries, and tracts. The frequency and similarity of certain motifs suggested that Renaissance society had been so deeply affected by the plague as to express its dislocation and despair in both visual and printed media. In this case artistic evidence helped substantiate interpretations that previous scholars had drawn solely from written evidence.[9]

Technology, "new" uses of known documentary and physical evidence, or the recovery of lost documents lead less frequently to major reinterpreta-tions than might be expected. The discovery of previously forgotten letters, the opening up of police archives, or the declassifying of secret documents can clarify issues or events or test existing studies. New documentary sources can also open entirely new areas for study, as with the Qumrân scrolls. Rarely, however, is it the new technique or the documentary find in itself that leads to a reinterpretation so fresh as to change the terms of historical debate on a problem. This is so because the earlier historians who worked on the problem, if they were well trained, were capable of recognizing the limitations of whatever evidence they had.

LEVELS OF HISTORICAL ANALYSIS

From the surviving evidence, sometimes abundant and sometimes discouragingly sparse, historians try to get a clear understanding of a part of the past. They generalize from facts that are themselves statements about the past, often varying widely in scope. A fact can be explicit and limited, as in the statement that Thomas Jefferson died at Monticello, Virginia, on July 4, 1826. Or a fact can be broader, as in the statement that Charlemagne was the first of the medieval Western emperors. Historians are concerned about the generalizing process because of their need to communicate their findings in ways that are at once accurate and broadly useful. They want to be sure that their generalizations accurately describe, and do not go beyond, the details found in the documents available to them. At the same time they want their findings to be significant—that is, they want to squeeze out of their documents the greatest possible amount of information. Often this desire to generalize forces historians to decide whether their documents describe only a particular case or are instead "typical" and "representative" of a larger set of phenomena. The section that follows will consider some of the methods historians use to establish the broader significance of their specialized studies while ensuring the accuracy of their generalizations. We shall discuss three research puzzles that confronted the issue of typicality: (1) to what extent historians can generalize from documents that express the views of a single social class; (2) how studies of individual communities can be used to describe society at large; and (3) how seemingly atypical documents can be used to study social structures that are smaller than total societies.

Generalizing from Class Specific Documents

Before the present century only a limited number of people in any society could read and write. In using written records, particularly personal materials such as diaries, letters, memoirs, and tracts, the historian sometimes tries to decide whether the opinions expressed in these works or the life-styles portrayed there were widely held by the entire society. Were they "typical"? It is possible, for example, to exaggerate the extent to which ecclesiastical corporations controlled the countryside in northern France during the early medieval period simply because their documentary collections tended to be the ones to survive.[10] Similarly, most secular writings until recently came from the pens of members of the social and economic elite, since only they were literate.

Let us examine how historians determine whether writings by an educated minority represent the total society. The issue involves not only practical problems of evidence but also the social philosophy of the researcher. Some researchers do not deem it necessary to study the views of the masses in order to generalize about the society of a period. They do not believe that the working-class person—whether an unskilled or semiskilled laborer, an artisan, small shopkeeper, factory worker, or traveling salesman— has ideas that differ from those held by the contemporary elite. Still others assume that only part of the elite shape opinion for society at large at any one time. In order to construct a synthesizing theory about a particular society, historians who hold these views will examine (depending on the historical period) the attitudes of the relevant elites, whether they are churchmen and noblemen, merchant bankers, generals, or executives. The rest of the people in society, insofar as they are presumed to think about such questions at all, are held to share the views of the articulate elites.

This is a common procedure in historical writing about the American Revolution. The governing elite in 18th-century America consisted of clergymen, lawyers, merchants, and large landowners. Historians have traditionally analyzed the American Revolution on the basis of the writings and speeches of this segment of society.[11] Participation of the lower classes (generally in mob riots), when noted at all, is interpreted as being the result of upper-class propaganda and manipulation, not the spontaneous expression of lower-class grievances (for bibliographic discussion see Lemisch, 1967: 19-29).

Some historians have recently questioned these assumptions and this approach to historical evidence. One of these, Jesse Lemisch, has called for a new history of the inarticulate that will incorporate the lower classes into any general study of social tension in Revolutionary America. He believes that historians should proceed "from a point of view which assumes that all men are created equal, and rational, and that since they can think and reason they can make their own history."[12] Such a generic proposition requires historians to determine what reason the poor themselves gave for their actions. Were the Stamp Act riots, for example, mere excuses to plunder shops, as scholars have maintained? Or is this interpretation overly influenced by the comments of contemporary observers who belonged to the colonial elite? Perhaps the riots were political actions of protest against measures that hurt the poor directly.

Any historian who poses the question as Lemisch does immediately confronts a methodological problem in that the poor were inarticulate. They were not pamphleteers; if they spoke publicly before crowds, their speeches were never recorded. Accounts of their actions, which can furnish circumstantial evidence of their motives, are found largely in letters and newspapers that reflect an upper class bias. How can historians study their motives?

Jesse Lemisch's account of the Stamp Act riots can be taken as one illustration of the problems involved in writing a history of the inarticulate. Historians have long known why colonial leaders protested sharply against this British law that required all legal transactions to be stamped. It was a form of taxation that was especially hard on lawyers, importers, and merchants—the very groups that dominated colonial governments. When colonial legislatures met to declare themselves opposed to the Stamp Act, they agreed to force repeal of the tax by stopping all business that required the use of stamps. At the same time rioting broke out, to the alarm of British officials, who thought that the riots were organized by colonial leaders, already known to be hostile to the new tax. Many historians have adopted this view, although no direct evidence exists that can identify the leaders of the mobs—if indeed these mobs had leaders.

The historian who questions the traditional interpretation must first ask whether urban laborers had any possible reasons of their own for opposing the Stamp Act. Lemisch studied the pattern of mob activity. Using descriptions written by British and American officials, he plotted the route taken by the rioters. He pointed out that they bypassed richly stocked shops to threaten the lives and homes of those officials most responsible for enforcing the Stamp Act. He concluded from this that their actions were motivated by political concerns, not by the desire for plunder. Lemisch's research thus expanded historical knowledge about the activities of the poor. He used observational data that originated from the articulate segment of Revolutionary society as a means of studying the actions of the inarticulate mob. In order to do this Lemisch had first to distinguish between the events and the upper-class evaluation of these events. This kind of evidence, while informative, is hardly conclusive. The motives and leadership of the poor are still obscure. New analytical strategies are needed if historians are to decide between the traditional and the revisionist views.

Lemisch was restricted in his analysis because the existing documents did not answer many of the questions he wanted to pose. In the absence of their own writings the motives of the poor can only be surmised. However, other questions about the inarticulate can be answered by the use of demography.[13] Demographic historians study growth and changes in populations: births, deaths, marriages, changes in job status and property ownership, and geographical movements. They primarily use records kept by public agencies such as census reports, local records of cities and counties, wills, tax rolls, and records of the sale and transfer of property. If they ask the right questions, demographers can make quite accurate generalizations about the inarticulate from this kind of official documentation.

The advantages and limitations of the demographic method have been summarized by one historian (Greven, 1970: 18):

Many questions cannot be answered by using such sources as local records, probate records, land records and vital records. Questions involving the innermost workings of families—their emotional life, their methods of child nurture, discipline, and acculturation, their motivations, personal viewpoints, and values—are particularly difficult to answer or to document from such records. What can be done with the records we have is basically to determine what men did, what actions they took, and how they behaved . . .

One important demographic study of the inarticulate used census records of Newburyport, Massachusetts, for the years 1850-1880. Stephan Thernstrom (1964) was limited to this particular thirty-year span because only for these years of the 19th century were appropriate census records available in Newburyport. His purpose was to discover the degree of social mobility that existed in this New England town in a period when it was widely believed, by contemporaries as well as by later historians, that the laboring man could and did rise from rags to riches. The census records were taken at 10-year intervals. They "provide the historian with a primitive social survey of the entire population of a community; occupation, place of birth, property holdings, literacy, and other useful information about every inhabitant is listed" (Thernstrom, 1964: 5). These particular census records also furnished the name of each person polled, which made it possible to trace the members of a family through the 30-year period and to collate census information with contemporary banking records. Thernstrom concluded from his study that the degree of social mobility was less than commonly believed. Laboring men did make modest gains in acquiring property but generally not in job status. There was, however, some social mobility on the part of sons, who generally had a slightly higher job status than the fathers.

Just as Lemisch used accounts of the articulate to determine the actions of the inarticulate, so Thernstrom used demographic methods to the same end. He assumed that letters or newspaper articles expressing the viewpoint of the articulate classes did not necessarily reflect the views of the inarticulate masses. His generalizations, like Lemisch's, were thus carefully framed around the kinds of evidence available to him.

Generalizing from Community Records

In making meaningful generalizations demographers face a problem that is methodologically similar to the one discussed earlier. Just as historians must be cautious in using class-restricted documents to generalize about society as a whole, so demographers must not assume that findings in one community are true of the larger society. Demographic historians limit themselves to specific communities in order to make an exhaustive use of the available data. Their analyses may be perfectly accurate but insignificant because they are true of such a small segment of the total population. How can such studies have more than local interest? How can one generalize from them to society at large? In order to determine that the findings from one community are typical, historians use the same methods as do other social scientists. They look for corresponding evidence from other, similar communities. Unlike other social scientists, however, historians cannot generate additional, comparative studies if the basic documentation is lacking.

The ideal way to study the social structure of a larger society would be to collect representative samples of all communities found in that society. Such a study of contemporary society is theoretically possible, if impractical. Researchers could generally find the needed information about whatever communities they chose. Historians cannot always freely choose the communities that they expect to be representative. They can study only the communities and the years for which documentation is available. Sometimes the evidence is abundant. New England towns in the 17th and 18th centuries, for example, kept the vital statistics of all their inhabitants, and most of these records have survived. Thus, historians like Greven (1970) can compare their findings in one community with those describing other New England towns.[14] If the findings from one case study are replicated in other studies, then the historian can conclude that the original findings are characteristic of the period.

By contrast, Thernstrom was the first to use demographic methods to study mobility patterns in a 19th century city. He could not compare his findings with other, similar studies, nor could he, as a careful social scientist, assume that patterns in Newburyport were in any way typical for the century. He did, however, develop some tentative generalizations about mobility patterns in the United States by comparing his study with other dissimilar studies (Thernstrom, 1964: 196 ff, for following discussion).

The one other study that had been done of an American community in the same years, 1850-1880, had involved a region very different from Newburyport. The historian Merle Curti had studied the population of Trempealeau County, Wisconsin, a frontier, agricultural region where there were few unskilled day laborers of the sort found in Newburyport. Thernstrom noted that Curti had found the population turnover to be high in Trempealeau County; however, it was only a little higher than that in Newburyport. The extent to which unskilled day laborers purchased property was similarly little different from that in Newburyport. Only in one respect was the unskilled laborer's opportunity for upward mobility greater on the Wisconsin frontier than it was in the eastern industrial city: Many unskilled laborers improved their status by buying and operating farms. In frontier society the acquisition of property also involved a change in occupation and thus a change in status. In Newburyport the purchase of property involved buying a house, which made little difference in the social status of unskilled laborers because they remained unskilled laborers. Thernstrom concluded that upward mobility for laborers was not much greater in this frontier community than it was in Newburyport, an eastern industrial community. These two studies thus furnished evidence that was contrary to both scholarly opinion and the popular belief that many common laborers in the 19th century improved their social position.

In order to get more persuasive evidence Thernstrom needed to compare Newburyport to other eastern towns. Although no other detailed study existed, Thernstrom did find fragmentary evidence about a variable that in the Newburyport study had proved to be closely related to mobility— population turnover (Thernstrom, 1964: 198ff). The frequent changes in population that were so characteristic of Newburyport were found also to be characteristic of selected New England cities and of all of Massachusetts, the most highly industrialized state at that time. Thernstrom reasoned from this evidence that if other industrializing cities were similar to Newburyport in this related measure, then they probably were also similar with respect to mobility. Using the clear evidence from Trempealeau County in the West and the indirect evidence from industrial regions in the East, Thernstrom inferred that the low mobility rate of day laborers in Newburyport was typical for the time. His tentative conclusions will be strengthened, however, only when additional studies are done of a variety of cities during these years.

Using Limited Documentation

The preceding examples showed how historians work with the problem of typicality, how they test whether findings about a particular group are also true for the larger society. The examples demonstrated the use of class-biased documents to discover the actions of various classes in society, and the use of individual studies to gain insight into the total society of a period. Historians who work in the more remote past often find that their more limited evidence keeps them from directly comparing the results in one case study with similar or contrasting evidence from other case studies. Even so, an isolated set of documents can be gleaned for information about the larger society as long as evidence can be pieced together with other evidence taken from dissimilar sources of the period. If not, the documents can still be analyzed internally for information about that one community.

The following example of this type of limited, intensive analysis comes from the historical literature on the medieval French peasantry. Medieval peasants are even more obscure and anonymous than the urban poor of colonial America, and they, too, must be studied through class-restricted documents. Consequently, we know far more about their servile obligations and farming routines than about their personal attitudes or lives as individuals; medieval lords typically recorded only data that was directly connected to their rights of lordship.

This restriction is particularly true of estate surveys. The earliest and fullest of these is a ninth-century document that was drawn up on the orders of the abbot of the wealthy Benedictine monastery of St. Germain-des Prés (St. Germain-in-the-meadows), at that time located just outside Paris (Guérard, 1844). The survey is incomplete but still lists 10,026 dependent peasants in 2,088 households on 22 different estates or manors that the abbey controlled. The area represented is encompassed by a 10-mile radius from the abbey (Duby, 1968: 13, 17, and map, 367). The compilers intended to record the services owed the abbey for plots held by each peasant household, the names of those responsible for the services, the numbers in each peasant household, and the types of land parceled out on each estate, with some indication of the crops or livestock that each could support.

The survey is detailed and comprehensive enough so that historians can draw out data that they can compare with data from other contemporary surveys, charters, and laws. Because the language is technical, historians must study closely the meanings of particular words and the contexts in which each is used. A typical entry from the survey reads:

Ebrulfus, a *colonus*, and his wife, a slave, . . . dependents, of St. Germain; they have 4 children. Ermenoldus, a slave, and his wife, a *colona*, . . . dependents of St. Germain; they have 4 children. . . . Teutgardis, slave of St. Germain; she has one child. . . . These three hold a free manse having 4 *bunuaria* and one *antsingam* of arable land, 4 acres of vine and 2 of meadow. They work 8 acres [of the abbey's] vine. They owe 2 *modios* of wine for the right of pasture and 2 *sestarios* of mustard. . . . Maurus, a slave, and his wife, a freedwoman, . . . dependents of St. Germain; they have 2 children. . . . Guntoldus, a *colonus* of St. Germain. These two hold one servile manse, having 2 *bunuaria* of arable land, 2½ acres of vine and 1½ of meadow. They work 8 acres [of the abbey's] vine and owe 4 *modios* of wine for right of pasture; 2 *sestarios* of mustard, three hens and 15 eggs; also manual labor, corvees and cartage.[15]

The italicized Latin words, untranslated from the survey, refer to legal titles or common measures that were well known to the compilers. Thanks to the comparative work of previous historians, they can be translated into modern approximations.[16]

By carefully examining many discrete bits of evidence, historians can learn about stratification and family size and other features of medieval peasant life in the Paris basin. Historians can also learn about legal status, as the compilers carefully noted this information for each adult, grouping the peasants into three categories: the *colonus* or *colona* (depending on the sex of the peasant), the slave, and those who were termed "freed." The quoted entry above suggests that regardless of this stratification no rigid correlation existed between legal status and either the obligations of peasants or the size of their holdings. Moreover, slaves and nonslaves were free to intermarry. This blurring between legal and actual economic status would be confirmed by studying other entries of the survey. Taken together the evidence suggests that legal distinctions had a quite different use for the ninth-century compilers than we would initially expect, and that modern English words such as *free* or *slave* carry with them social and economic distinctions that are misleading when applied to the society of a very different period.

Other entries in the survey mention agricultural innovations and building schemes the abbey was undertaking; they indicate that the abbey was wealthy and efficiently administered.[17]

Linguistic historians are interested in noting the popularity of certain names and of studying names as clues to the ethnic origins of the population. The survey, then, can be used to draw out information on a variety of subjects beyond those pertaining to peasant tenures and obligations. By an intensive analysis of many such official documents, historians have been able to construct a good profile of peasant life in medieval France even though they have had to tailor their inquiries to the surviving evidence (Duby, 1968: 556-85; the size and range of the bibliography often surprises nonmedievalists).

DEVELOPING HISTORICAL CONTEXTS

Thus far we have discussed various sorts of evidence historians use, and we have shown by example the kinds of generalizations they derive from their evidence. We have seen how historians establish the significance of their specialized studies—that is, how they check the validity of broader generalizations by comparing their particular study to the existing body of research and knowledge on the same general subject. We are now going to study in more detail the earliest stages of research in historical projects, the painstaking analysis of documents that leads to an accurate description of past events or ideas.

As historians critically analyze individual documents or groups of documents belonging to the same category, they simultaneously develop a broader context—that is, they fit the documents into historical settings. These two parts of the contextual frame are complementary, and historians work with both at the same time; an increased understanding of the external context often modifies initial interpretations of a document, and a close analysis of a document contributes to an understanding of its historical context. In the following section we shall discuss some of the methods historians use to work out wider contexts for their documents. By refining their analysis of these contexts they are finally able to frame valid or reliable descriptions. In order to focus the types of problems that historians solve in creating historical contexts, we have selected examples from especially problematical sources, such as laws and personal narratives. These sources are problematical because often their contexts and hence their significance are unclear.

Internal and External Analysis

Historians realize that even the most ordinary words, both their own and those of their written sources, carry a range of connotations and meanings. The problem is also familiar to survey researchers and participant observers. The interviewers must try to get a precise understanding of the ways in which informants use words to express their attitudes. The interpretative problem remains even if researchers try to be nondirectional in their interviewing, or if, like Oscar Lewis (1961) and Robert Coles (1967-1971), they try to create autobiographies for their subjects by the use of extensive quotations. In each case the observer or those who read accounts of the interviews must try to understand the informants in their own terms. They must establish for themselves an interpretative context that will take into account possible inconsistencies in attitudes and other important though largely unexpressed differences in perception that separate them from the social world of the informants.

When historians use eyewitness or personal accounts of the past—memoirs, diaries, letters, and chronicles—they must consider more than the attitudes and world-view of the writer of each source. They must also determine how that writer related to his or her period. In order to use this kind of source historians first examine the internal context, the specific words and phrases. Then they compare the source with others of its time and type or with contemporary public records. They create both an internal and an external context for the source before integrating it into historical narratives.

Internal analysis is easier with long narratives simply because the writers give more detail. They may write about several subjects or about the same subject in several ways. Thus, when reading what the medieval French chronicler Ralph Glaber (Ralph the Hairless) wrote about the evils of his own time, the modern historian first evaluates Ralph as an eyewitness.[18] It is possible to accept Ralph's gloomy portents as proof that 10th-century France was anarchic, one of the bleakest of the "Dark Ages." Careful historians note, however, that Ralph's purpose in cataloging the ills of his day was to urge a higher standard of morality. Ralph saw himself as a moralist, not as a neutral observer. The fact that his comments are uniformly pessimistic does not in itself prove that the times were bad.

In evaluating Ralph as a useful documentary source the historian takes note of the nature of his complaints. Some do indeed indicate that the period was far from being a secure one for large segments of French society. However, some offer definite signs of increasing stability. Expensive stone churches were being built even though the existing ones were in no need of repair; Frenchmen from the south were pouring into Paris, bringing with them new styles of dress. Nobles were more frequently joining together in peace associations. Since Ralph feared all change, he viewed these phenomena as dangerous novelties. Yet his own statements offer evidence to contradict his evaluation, and the historian can thus modify Ralph's assessment of his times.

Historians use a similar approach to literature—including folk tales, epics and poetry—beause these are also personal sources. Sometimes the writer's attitudes are clear, whether the work itself is signed or anonymous. This is often the case in political poems, as they state a grievance or comment upon an event or person. Historians then use other evidence to find out whether the writer's attitudes were widely held and were reliable portrayals of the subjects and events described. Using literature as a historical source involves determining each work's broader interpretative context. For example, novels of manners and society, such as those of Charles Dickens, Leo Tolstoy, and Honoré de Balzac, must be examined with the possibility that the situations depicted bear more relation to the author's imagination and the requirements of the story than to an exact portrayal of the societies they describe.[19]

One of the most ambiguous forms of literature is satire because its meaning depends upon its intended audience, and their attitudes may have been quite different from those of modern researchers. Historians need to determine just what is being satirized. What is the nature of the discord between the actual norms of that sóciety and the literary caricature of those norms? And what was the audience's anticipated reaction—laughter, anger, shame? Recently, scholars have begun to restudy the interpretive contexts of certain problematical literary works such as the medieval tales of courtly love and Niccolò Machiavelli's *The Prince*.[20] They want to find out if these works were intended as satires. From this perspective *The Prince* is not political theory but an embittered blast at what Machiavelli thought was the increasingly despotic and ineffectual character of Florentine government. The book has been a puzzle—some would say a scandal—ever since its first printing, posthumously, in 1532. One problem for Renaissance scholars is that the political ideas of *The Prince* are plainly at odds with Machiavelli's actions as a civil servant and with his other writings (for recent studies see Anglo 1969; Gilbert, 1965; Hale, 1963). Whatever the final evaluation, historians who analyze Machiavelli's attitudes in *The Prince* must also consider its Renaissance audience; they must also study the reception of the book by those who had known the author and who were familiar both with the conditions under which the book was written and with the man who wrote it.

The Need for External Contexts

Even though historians adopt a cautious attitude toward eyewitness accounts and literary works, they still do not dismiss them as valueless. Ralph's chronicles and *The Prince* remain valuable sources of information about society of the time as long as they are carefully analyzed. In order to do so, historians train themselves to be independent of the world-view of their sources and to use to advantage their chronological distance from the societies studied.[21] This independence is particularly important when dealing with judgments on a society that were made by a member of that society. The alternative forces historians to remain fixed to the same prejudices and fears that biased eyewitness accounts, whether these were written by chroniclers, landholders, or satirists. Conversely, historians are careful not to allow their own world-views to cloud their understanding of personalized accounts. Especially tricky are analyses involving words that seem meaningless within the internal context of the document. In these instances an external context is needed from the beginning in order to avoid misinterpreting the evidence. The following two examples come from both personal and legal records. They show how words can be problematical and how historians learn to analyze these words.

Some of these value-loaded words should be easier to recognize than others because they have especially broad connotations. Just as societies change their values over the years, the words used to reflect these values also change their meaning. The difficulty comes when connotative political terms used by past societies also have present connotations. Consider, for example, the term "democracy" as used by 18th-century writers.[22] A British general, Thomas Gage, sent a letter home to England from Massachusetts shortly before the beginning of the Revolution. He reported: "from what has been said, your lordship will conclude, that there is no government in Boston, there is in truth, very little at present, and the constitution leans so much to democracy that the governor has not the power to remedy the disorders which happen in it" (quoted in Pole, 1962: 633). A modern American uses the term *democracy* with approval; generally, it refers to governments based on a very wide, if not universal, suffrage. Thus, Gage's statement and similar ones by crown officials in other colonies seemed to indicate that colonial governments were popular democracies. One historian, Robert E. Brown, wanted to determine whether the observations by these officials were well-founded; as a good historian he did not want to rely solely on their narratives, so he looked for other kinds of evidence. He studied suffrage qualifications in Massachusetts and Virginia and discovered that property qualifications for voting were so low that most white men could reasonably expect to acquire enough land to become enfranchised. And those men who were not qualified to vote sometimes did so anyway. Using such evidence Brown concluded that these two colonial governments were middle-class democracies based on a nearly universal white manhood suffrage (Brown, 1955; Brown & Brown, 1964).

Brown's methods, particularly his use of statistics, have been criticized from many directions (Lemisch, 1967: 6-9; Pole, 1962: 630-34). But what is of concern here is his understanding of the word *democracy*. Brown established an external context of one sort to verify eyewitness accounts; that is, he examined suffrage records as one index of democracy to see if Gage and other observers had correctly perceived the degree of democracy in Massachusetts and Virginia. However, Brown failed to make the internal textual analysis necessary to determine what people of the 18th century understood by the term *democracy*. He accepted uncritically the modern American meaning of the term, and accordingly took the broad suffrage in the two populous colonies to be sufficient evidence that these colonies enjoyed democratic government. His view was seemingly reinforced by the narratives of 18th-century observers like Gage, who had not bothered to define the word *democracy* because its meaning was understood by contemporaries.

To determine what Gage meant it is necessary to examine the internal context in which he and other writers used the term, and to compare their political concepts with views portrayed in contemporary treatises on political theory. Also necessary is an understanding of the structure of colonial government and of the nature of colonial society. A careful analysis of the use of the term *democracy* in the broader context of 18th-century political thought, both British and American, reveals that their concept of it was very different from ours. The idea of popular government in the sense of popular control by a majority of the people was an idea held by only a few radicals.[23] Colonial leaders agreed with British officers in condemning government by popular majority. Democracy was supposed to be only one element in government, and it was located in the popularly elected assemblies. Thus, when British officials complained that democracy (or more commonly "the democracy") was becoming too powerful in the colonies, they meant that the colonial assemblies were usurping the authority of the governors and councils (Lokken, 1959; Buel, 1964).

Furthermore, a close examination of colonial government, politics, and social structure indicates that even if a wide suffrage existed (and this in itself is a matter of dispute), it did not mean that colonial assemblies were controlled by the people or even that the assemblies were particularly sensitive to popular pressure. Those habitually elected to colonial assemblies were, in the phrase of the times, "the better sort"—merchants, lawyers, large property owners. Furthermore, members of the same families appeared with significant regularity in the same governmental posts over several generations. In theory, and to a great extent in practice, colonial society was a deferential society. Social order depended, it was thought, on a government by the aristocracy of wealth, education, and birth. The average voter was expected to elect his betters to office. To ensure that he did so, nominations of candidates were generally made by and from the ruling oligarchy, elections were by voice vote, and the electorate was often manipulated by threats or bribes. In practice colonial government could hardly be considered to be democratic in the modern sense even if the suffrage was broad by European standards (Pole, 1962: 635-44).

It is not only because meanings change over time that historians approach with caution terms like *democracy* and *socialism*. These words have come to have so many connotations that they are meaningless unless carefully defined. Furthermore, they carry emotional charges that are not entirely predictable. Even recent documents that have employed these terms would therefore have to be analyzed with the same care with which one analyzes documents of the Revolutionary period. In all such cases a variety of documents must be examined to determine what contemporaries understood by a word and to find the range of connotations it had for them.

If historians are careful about possible ambiguities in the words found in their sources, they may occasionally be forced to admit that, given the lack of sufficient evidence, certain sources remain enigmatic. In these instances they will have to be content with partial explanations. By letting other historians know about the sources, however, they may eventually be able to get corroborating evidence that will permit a fuller explanation. We may take as an example a case from the legal records of early-14th-century England, a suit involving a broken contract.[24] Contemporary records are full of similar cases. What makes this one unusual is its language. It was alleged that one John Baker seemingly had "sold" his wife to a couple in return for a pig of a specified value. Shortly after this arrangement was made, John became dissatisfied and asked to have his wife back, promising to pay two-thirds the value of the pig. When he failed to pay, the couple sued him. Historians are puzzled, and not simply because of the wife's "depreciation." Despite the document's clear reference to a "sale," a reference that was repeated twice in successive stages of the suit, the purpose and nature of the transaction remain obscure. Whatever the transaction, the recording scribe felt no need to include details not immediately related to the litigation. Considerable investigation suggests two possibilities. The "wife-sale" may have been a service arrangement in which the pig represented wages. The difficulty with this interpretation is that other cases of such contracts are not written in terms of a sale. The case may also have been an attempted "divorce" that the husband later regretted. The couple may have been the parents of John's wife, and the compensation merely a legal requirement for making the contract valid. John Baker's "sale" is still mysterious because of the difficulty historians have in establishing an external context for the case, specifically in deciding what the words, "he sold his wife" meant in this context. That the source is a legal record also contributes to the difficulty of interpreting it.

Legal records are commonly either court cases, as in the above "sale," or laws. Court cases only outline the situations they record; their purpose is to preserve written evidence of the type of case, the participants, and the final decision. A law's purpose is somewhat different, as it is a statement of policy toward a given situation. In either record, however, extraneous detail, so necessary for establishing an interpretive context, is omitted for the sake of efficiency. Thus, when historians attempt to generalize from a particular law to the social conditions that produced the law, they need external information. For example, a law passed by officials of the city of New York in the colonial period regulated garbage disposal; it specified a scaled system of fines for various offenses (Fischer, 1970: 44-45). By itself the law could mean that the city's government was energetic enough to see that streets were kept clean; one could assume that the law was enforced and was possibly not the first of its kind. The law also could be used to substantiate the opposite conclusion—the city's extreme filthiness had shamed officials into making a tardy attempt at corrective action, an attempt that may or may not have been successful.

Such a law is a source of historical fact about the society that drafted it, but only when used with reference to an external context. Additional information could come from contemporary descriptions of the city by both inhabitants and travelers, other similar laws, or fines and court orders. In the absence of such external data the law is meaningful only in a restricted context, the context supplied by an intensive internal analysis of its details— e.g., distinctions that are made among the fines, provisions for the law's expected enforcement, names of officials and the like.

The interpretive limitations of a single case or law and of a single personal or literary narrative also apply to a series of documents. If the series comes from a single source, as it would in a collection of letters written by one person, historians need to use other related material in order to make reliable generalizations and to weigh all the potential interpretations.

The dangers of relying on a single type of source are further illustrated in a study of presidential foreign policy in the 1930s by Charles Beard (1948). The author's interpretative bent was reflected in the book's title, *President Roosevelt and the Coming of the War of 1941*. Beard's central thesis was that Roosevelt had been so eager to take the United States into war that he ignored the mandate for peace that had been given in the election of 1940. Beard believed that Roosevelt tried to manipulate various incidents with both Germany and Japan in such a way as to heighten tensions and thus force a declaration of war; Japan's attack on Pearl Harbor was the final, successful result of this policy.

Beard based his interpretation on a close textual analysis of Roosevelt's speeches without reference to other sources such as White House records, preliminary drafts of speeches, or foreign policy programs. A good example of his method is found in a passage in which Beard maintained that Roosevelt distorted the meaning of the preelection Democratic platform. The platform had promised that, "We will not participate in foreign wars . . . except in case of attack" (Beard, 1948:134). Because of this strong statement Roosevelt had to justify his decision to declare war by redefining the word *attack*. According to Beard,

Evidently, President Roosevelt did not in July, 1941, regard the word "attack" as necessarily implying an act of war at all against the United States, . . . for he said: "an attack *begins* as soon as *any* base had been occupied." . . . Since he added that this base might be thousands of miles away from our shores, he evidently meant that he could regard an attack on the United States as *beginning* . . . if made on the territory of some foreign country. (Beard, 1948: 137)

Beard's conclusions are suspect because his research was not thorough. He made an internal analysis of Roosevelt's speeches to determine what was "evidently meant," often finding that "the text of his [Presidential] statements afforded no answers" (Beard, 1948: 138). In these cases Beard conjectured as to the meaning. To check that his interpretation of Roosevelt's speeches was accurate, and to answer questions not provided by the text, Beard should have turned to other sources. He was not sensitive to the interpretive limits of his evidence, a skill necessary to historical objectivity, as that word was defined earlier. Both internal and external contexts are needed for an exhaustive interpretation of sources, whether these are speeches, laws, poems, or letters.

This chapter has discussed in some detail the basic rules of historical inquiry that are used by all practicing historians. Our examples of research problems, drawn from widely different fields of history and from historians with very different points of view, are representative of the diversity of the field. Practicing historians have such different interests and periods of research that they are often unfamiliar with each other's work. The scholarly world of the medievalist who studied the legal status of a French village (see above, pp. 30 ff.) is far removed from that of the Americanist who studied revolutionary mobs (see above, pp. 21-2). Yet each can understand and appreciate the other's work because they were trained in the same methods of documentary analysis. It is this common understanding of the rules of inquiry that gives history its unity as a discipline. Historians measure each work of scholarship by the same general standards: Does the work clearly state its purpose, persuading readers that the questions asked are worth asking? Are its sources the ones most relevant to the study, and are they examined exhaustively? Finally, does the argument or analysis use evidence in ways that are coherent and persuasive? (Hollinger, 1973: 380, 383). We have discussed by means of detailed examples each of these standards of scholarship that historians demand of themselves and of their colleagues.

Historical research is kin to puzzle solving. It needs the same mixture of patience, ingenuity, and logic, as well as the capacity for enduring tedium. Sir Francis Bacon, author of the statement at the head of this article, stressed the rigors of scholarly research, as we have done also throughout the previous pages. The reward, the attraction of history for the scholar, is the adventure involved in solving research puzzles. As an English gentleman of the generation after Bacon observed, scholarly activity has a "direct incontinency of the Spirit which hath a pleasure in it like Wrestling with a fine Woman" (Altick, 1966: 15). Changing the "Woman" to "Man," we fully agree.

NOTES

[1] Bacon (1955: 129). For information about Bacon see Palmer and Colton (1965: 262-65).

[2] Bacon (1955): especially selections from *Novum Organum* (1620), *The Advancement of Learning* (1623), and *The New Atlantis* (1627). For modern assessments see Butterfield (1965: 108-28) and Hall (1966: 164-69).

[3] For an introduction by both sociologists and historians to the controversies surrounding historical methodology see Cahnmann & Boskoff (1964); Erikson (1970); Landes & Tilly (1971); Lipset & Hofstadter (1968); Phillips (1971). Attention to the general problem of synthesis in history and other social disciplines resulted in two reports of the Social Science Research Council (1946: Bulletin 54; 1954: Bulletin 64).

[4] Weber's initial studies in the sociology of religion were published as three articles in 1904-1906 and used the work of the economic historian Werner Sombart, who had published *Der Moderne Kapitalismus* in 1902. The resulting controversies, to which Sombart also contributed, are summarized in Green (1959).

[5] The literature is vast. For introductory bibliography and articles that include the views of historians as well as other social scientists see *History and Theory* (1961-present); recent general assessments such as Nash (1969) and Rickman (1967). For some historians' views see Leff (1969), Marsak (1970) and these issues of *Daedalus*, 99: 2 (1970); 100: 1 (1971a); 100: 2 (1971b).

[6] The analogy was originally put forward by Becker in his presidential address to the American Historical Association in 1931 (1966: 233-55 and note, 233). For a slightly contrasting view see Hexter (1971: 22-23). Ambiguities in the use of the word *history* have been discussed by Gottschalk (1963: v-x).

[7] This assessment of medieval individuality got its most famous exposition from a Swiss historian, Jacob Burckhardt, in 1860 in his *Civilization of the Renaissance in Italy;* however, similar attitudes were held by Renaissance humanists. See Ferguson (1948: 19-20, 27-28, 179-252 passim). A recent article on medieval architectural skills is Shelby (1972).

[8] The scholarly literature on the effects of the plague is vast. A representative study of one of the towns in Meiss' work is Bowsky (1964).

[9] Meiss' conclusions are still being evaluated as scholars have revised the dating of certain artworks used in his study. For a comprehensive treatment of the issues involved see Oertel (1968).

[10] For examples of available documentation, which suggests that this is an issue, see Duby (1968: 556-85).

[11] Bailyn (1967, 1968) analyzed works of Revolutionary theorists and polemicists, assuming that the views expressed were shared by most Americans to such an extent that they helped explain the Revolution. Lemisch (1968a) offers a critique.

[12] Lemisch (1967: 29). The Stamp Act discussion that follows is based on Lemisch (1967). For a more convincing study of the inarticulate see Lemisch (1968b). A study demonstrating that scanty evidence about working-class groups can also suggest quite contrary conclusions about their Revolutionary motives is Hutson (1971).

[13] An introduction to historical demography is in *Daedalus*, 97: 2 (1968) and Wrigley (1969). These have specialized studies and general bibliography.

[14] Lockridge (1970: 181-99) has a bibliographic discussion.

[15] Excerpt of the *polyptyque* of Abbot Irminon from Guérard by White (1965: 281).

[16] Fisher (1968). The rendering of such specialized terms is complex; frequently, the accepted ratios of conversions are large enough to invalidate attempts at quantification. For an example, using the term *bunaria*, see Duby (1968: 554) and White (1965: 280-82). Duby (1968: 17ff) offers examples of the need for caution in using these surveys for the purposes of wide generalizations.

[17] For some account of possible interpretations attached to the single term *manse* in the Carolingian period see Bloch (1966: 69-70 and passim, 150-63); Duby (1968: 7, 12-13, 28-33, 116-18); Herlihy (1960).

[18] Excerpted in Lopez (1959: 10-12; for an introduction, 1-4). The entire work is useful for background information and primary material on the period.

[19] Literature has been used frequently as an historical source; for examples, which also discuss the broader problems involved, see Laslett (1965); Lukács (1962); Vance (1970).

[20] Newman (1969) and Mattingly (1958: 482-91). Mattingly's article was reprinted together with other historical assessments in Jensen (1960).

[21] These observations, well known to historians in general, were succinctly made by Bloch (1964c: 62-64) and Hexter (1963: 1-13).

[22] Palmer (1953: 203). For the political implications of ordinary words see Orwell (1954).

[23] Examples are Thomas Paine and John Woolman. Lemisch also suggests that the populace was not so compliant as the "better sort" wished (1967: 10-29).

[24] We owe the following reference to Professor John S. Beckerman of Haverford College. The document, from the manor court of Lewishman, Kent, is preserved in the Public Record Office, London, SC2/181/58.

REFERENCES

Altick, Richard. *The scholar adventurers*. New York: Free Press, 1966. (First published London: Collier-Macmillan, 1950.)

Anglo, Sydney. *Machiavelli:* A dissection. New York: Harcourt, Brace, 1969.

Antal, Frederick. *Florentine painting and its social background*. London: Kegan, Paul, 1948.

Bacon, Francis. *Selected writings* (Hugh G. Dick, ed.). New York: Modern Library, 1955.

Bagley, J. J. *Historical interpretation: Sources of English medieval history, 1066-1540*. Baltimore: Penguin Books, 1965.

Bailyn, Bernard. *The ideological origins of the American Revolution.* Cambridge, Mass: Harvard University Press, 1967.

Bailyn, Bernard. *The origins of American politics.* New York: Alfred Knopf, 1968.

Beard, Charles. *President Roosevelt and the coming of the war, 1941.* New Haven: Yale University Press, 1948.

Becker, Carl L. Everyman his own historian. In *Everyman his own historian.* Chicago: Quadrangle, 1966. (First published New York: F.S. Crofts, 1935.)

Beresford, Maurice W. & St. Joseph, J.K.S., *Medieval England:* An aerial survey. Cambridge: University Press, 1958.

Bloch, Marc. *Feudal society* (L.A. Manyon, trans.). *From La Société féodale.* . . . 2 vols., Chicago: University of Chicago Press, 1964. (First published Paris: A. Michel, 1939-1940.)

Bloch, Marc. *The historian's craft* (Peter Putnam, trans.). New York: Vintage, 1964. First published as *Apologie pour l'histoire; ou Métier d'historien.* Paris: A. Colin, 1949.

Bloch, Marc. *French Rural History* (Janet Sondheimer, trans.). Berkeley: University of California Press. First published as *Les Caractères originaux de l'histoire rurale françaises.* Cambridge, Mass.: Harvard University Press, 1931.

Bothmer, Dietrich von, & Noble, Joseph V. *An inquiry into the forgery of the Etruscan terracotta warriors in the Metropolitan Museum of Art.* New York: Metropolitan Museum of Art, 1961.

Bowsky, William M. The impact of the Black Death upon Sienese government and society. *Speculum,* 1964, *39* (January): 1-34.

Brown, Robert E. *Middle-class democracy and the revolution in Massachusetts, 1691-1780.* Ithaca, N.Y.: Cornell University Press, 1955.

Brown, Robert E., & Brown, Katharine. *Virginia, 1705-1786: Democracy or aristocracy?* E. Lansing, Mich.: Michigan State University Press, 1964.

Buel, Richard, Jr. Democracy and the American Revolution: A frame of reference. *William and Mary Quarterly,* 1964, *21* (April): 165-90.

Butterfield, Herbert. *The origins of modern science, 1300-1800* (rev. ed.). New York: Free Press, 1965.

Cahnmann, Werner J., & Boskoff, Alvin, eds. *Sociology and history: Theory and research.* New York: Free Press, 1964.

Coles, Robert. *Children of crisis* (3 vols). Boston: Little, Brown, 1967-1971.

Cross, Frank Moore. *The ancient library of Qumrân and modern biblical studies.* Garden City, N.Y.: Doubleday, 1958.

Daedalus. Historical population studies. *Journal of the American Academy of Arts and Sciences,* 1968, *97* (Spring).

Daedalus. Theory in humanistic studies. *Journal of the American Academy of Arts and Sciences,* 1970, *99* (Spring).

Daedalus. Historical studies today. *Journal of the American Academy of Arts and Sciences,* 1971, *100* (Winter). (a)

Daedalus. The Historian and the world of the twentieth century. *Journal of the American Academy of Arts and Sciences,* 1971, *100* (Spring). (b)

Doresse, Jean. *The secret books of the Egyptian gnostics.* . . . (rev. ed.). Philip Mairet (trans.). New York: Viking, 1960.

Duby, Georges. *Rural economy and country life in the medieval West.* Cynthia Postan (trans.). Columbia: University of South Carolina Press, 1968.

Erikson, Kai T. *Wayward puritans: A study in the sociology of deviance.* New York: John Wiley, 1966.

Erikson, Kai T. Sociology and the historical perspective. *The American Sociologist,* 1970, 5 (November): 331-38.

Ferguson, Wallace K. *The Renaissance in historical thought. . . .* Boston: Houghton Mifflin, 1948.

Fischer, David H. *Historians' fallacies: Toward a logic of historical thought.* New York: Harper & Row, 1970.

Fisher, John L. *A medieval farming glossary of Latin and English words. . . .* London: National Council of Social Service, 1968.

Freedman, David N., & Greenfield, Jonas C. (eds.). *New directions in biblical archaeology.* Garden City, N.Y.: Doubleday, 1969.

Gilbert, Felix. *Machiavelli and Guicciardini: Politics and history in sixteenth-century Florence.* Princeton: Princeton University Press, 1965.

Gottschalk, Louis R. (ed.). *Generalization in the writing of history:* A report of the Committee on Historical Analysis of the Social Science Research Council. Chicago: University of Chicago Press, 1963.

Gray, John. *Archaeology of the Old Testament world.* New York: Harper & Row, 1965.

Green, Robert W. (Ed.). *Protestantism and capitalism: The Weber thesis and its critics.* Boston: D.C. Heath, 1959.

Greven, Philip J., Jr. *Four generations: population, land, and family in colonial Andover, Massachusetts.* Ithaca, N.Y.: Cornell University Press, 1970.

Guérard, B[enjamin] E.C. (Ed.). *Polyptyque de l'abbé Irminon. . . .* (2 vols.). Paris: Imprimerie royale, 1844.

Hale, John R. *Machiavelli and Renaissance Italy.* New York: Macmillan, 1960.

Hall, A. Rupert. *The Scientific Revolution, 1500-1800:* The formation of the modern scientific attitude (rev. ed.). Boston: Beacon Press, 1966. (First published London: Longmans, Green, 1954.)

Harvey, John. *The Gothic World, 1100-1600.* A survey of architecture and art. New York: Harper & Row, 1969. (First published 1950, London: B.T. Batsford.)

Hauser, Arnold. *The social history of art,* (4 vols.). Stanley Goodman (trans.). New York; Vintage, 1960. (First published New York: Knopf, 1951.)

Herlihy, David. "The Carolingian *Mansus.*" In *Economic History Review.* 2nd ser., 1960, *13* (August).

Hexter, J.H. *Reappraisals in history. . . .* Evanston, Ill.: Northwestern University Press, 1961.

Hexter, J.H. *Doing history.* Bloomington: University of Indiana Press, 1971.

Hollinger, David A., T.S. Kuhn's theory of science and its implications for history. *American Historical Review* 1973, 78 (April): 370-93.

Hutson, James H. An investigation of the inarticulate: Philadelphia's White Oaks. *William and Mary Quarterly,* 3rd ser., 1971, *28* (January): 3-25.

Honnecourt, Villard de. *The sketchbook of Villard de Honnecourt* (Theodore Bowie, ed.). Bloomington: University of Indiana Press, 1959.

Hyman, Herbert H. *Secondary analysis of sample surveys: Principles, procedures and potentialities.* New York: John Wiley, 1972.

Jansen, De Lannar (Ed.). *Machiavelli: Cynic, patriot, or political scientist?* Boston, D.C. Heath, 1960.

Knight, Michael. Yale Says prized 'Vinland Map' of North America is a forgery. *New York Times*. January 26, 1974, pp. 1, 38.

Landes, David S., & Tilly, Charles (Eds.). *History as social science*. Englewood Cliffs, N.J.: Prentice-Hall, 1971.

Laslett, Peter. *The world we have lost*. London: Methuen, 1965.

Leff, Gordon, *History and social theory*. Montgomery: University of Alabama Press, 1969.

Lemisch, Jesse. The American Revolution from the bottom up. In Barton J. Bernstein (Ed.), *Towards a new past: Dissenting essays in American history*. New York: Random House, 1967.

Lemisch, Jesse. What made our revolution? *The New Republic* (May 25, 1968): 25-28. (a)

Lemisch, Jesse. Jack Tar in the streets: Merchant seamen in the politics of Revolutionary America. *William and Mary Quarterly*, 3rd ser., 1968, 25 (July): 371-407. (b)

Lewis, Oscar. *The children of Sánchez: Autobiography of a Mexican family*. New York: Random House, 1961.

Lipset, Seymour M., & Hofstadter, Richard (Eds.). *Sociology and history: Methods*. New York: Basic Books, 1968.

Lockridge, Kenneth A. *A New England town: The first hundred years*. New York: Norton, 1970.

Lokken, Roy N. The concept of Democracy in colonial political thought. *William and Mary Quarterly*, 3rd ser., 1959, 16 (October): 568-80.

Lopez, Robert S. *The tenth century: How dark the Dark Ages?* New York: Holt, Rinehart and Winston, 1959.

L'Orange, Hans P. *Art forms and civic life in the Late Roman Empire* (Dr. and Mrs. Knut Berg, trans.). Princeton: Princeton University Press, 1965.

Lukács, György. *The historical novel* (Hannah and Stanley Mitchell, trans.). London: Merlin, 1962. (First published 1937.)

Marsak, Leonard M. (Ed.). *The nature of historical inquiry*. New York: Holt, Rinehart and Winston, 1970.

Mattingly, Garrett. Machiavelli's *Prince*: Political science or political satire? *The American Scholar*, 1958, 27 (Autumn): 482-91.

Meiss, Millard. *Painting in Florence and Siena after the Black Death*. . . . Princeton: Princeton University Press, 1951.

Merton, Robert K. *Science, technology and society in seventeenth-century England*. *Osiris*, 1938, 4 360-632. Also New York: Fertig, 1970.

Metropolitan Museum of Art. Art Forgery. *Bulletin*, 1968, 26, (February): 241-76.

Nash, Ronald H. (Ed.). *Ideas of history* (2 vols.). New York: Dutton, 1969.

Newman, F.X. (Ed.). *The meaning of courtly love*. Albany: State University of New York Press, 1969.

Oertel, Robert. *Early Italian painting to 1400*. New York: Praeger, 1968. (Translation of a work first published in 1953, Stuttgart: Kohlhammer.)

Orwell, George. Politics and the English language. In *Collected Essays*. Garden City, N.Y.: Doubleday, 1954.

Orwin, Charles S., & Orwin, Christobel S. *The open fields* (3rd ed.). Oxford: Clarendon. (First published 1938.)

Palmer, Robert R. Notes on the use of the word "democracy," 1789-1799. *Political*

Science Quarterly, 1953, *68* (1953): 203-26.

Palmer, Robert R., & Colton, Joel. *A history of the modern world* (3rd ed.). New York: Alfred Knopf. (First published, 1950).

Panofsky, Erwin. Gothic architecture and scholasticism. New York: World, 1966. (First published 1951, Latrobe, Pa.: Archabbey Press.)

Panofsky, Erwin. *Studies in iconology: Humanistic themes in the art of the renaissance*. New York: Harper & Row, 1972. (First published, 1939, New York: Oxford University Press.)

Phillips, Bernard S. *Social research: Strategy and tactics*. New York: Macmillan. (First published, 1966.)

Pickering, Frederick P. *Literature and art in the Middle Ages*. Coral Gables, Fla.: University of Miami Press, 1970. (Translation of a work published in 1966.) Berlin: E. Schmidt.

Pole, J[ack] R. Historians and the problem of early American democracy. American Historical Review, 1962, 67 (April) 626-46.

Rickman, Hans P. *Understanding and the human studies*. London: Heinemann, 1967.

Shafer, Robert J. (Ed.). *A guide to historical method*. Homewood, Ill.: Dorsey, 1974.

Shelby, Lon R. The geometrical knowledge of mediaeval master masons. *Speculum*, 1972, 47 3 (July): 395-421.

Simson, Otto G. von. *The Gothic cathedral. Origins of Gothic architecture and the medieval concept of order. . . .* New York: Harper & Row, 1964. (First published, 1956, New York: Pantheon.)

Simson, Otto G. von. *Sacred fortress: Byzantine art and statecraft in Ravenna*. Chicago: University of Chicago Press, 1965. (First published in 1948.)

Social Science Research Council. *Theory and practice in historical study:* A report of the Committee on Historiography. Bulletin 54. New York: 1946.

Social Science Research Council. *The social sciences in historical study:* A report of the Committee on Historiography. Bulletin 64. New York: 1954.

Sypher, Wylie. *Four stages of Renaissance style: Transformations in art and literature, 1450-1750*. Garden City, N.Y.: Doubleday, 1955.

Thernstrom, Stephan. *Poverty and progress: Social mobility in a nineteenth-century city*. Cambridge, Mass.: Harvard University Press, 1964.

Vance, Eugene. *Reading the Song of Roland*. Englewood Cliffs, N.J.: Prentice Hall, 1970.

White, Donald A. *Medieval history: A source book*. Homewood, Ill.: Dorsey, 1965.

Wrigley, Edward A. *Population and history*. New York: McGraw-Hill, 1969.

Chapter Eight
The use of newspapers[1]

M. HERBERT DANZGER

This chapter evaluates newspapers as a source for data in social science research. Examples of use are presented, as well as guidelines for research, with *The New York Times* as a model. The validity of newspaper reports, and particularly those of *The New York Times* is assessed. This is done by exploring the basis of the credibility of newspapers, by examining the network of information gathering and dissemination, by comparing reports of events appearing in different media using broad quantitative data, and finally by a statistical comparison of possible bias in reporting at those points where some biases might be thought to exist.

The concern for validating sources in such a manner stemmed from a study of civil rights conflict in the U.S. between 1955 and 1965 (Danzger, 1968a). That study involved an attempt to assess the effect of community characteristics (particularly power structure) on the occurrence, duration, and pattern of conflict. The study itself was divided into two aspects. One part dealt with all cities in the U.S. with populations over 25,000, and attempted simply to determine whether or not a city had experienced conflict, and if so, how long it had persisted. Another section dealt with patterns of conflict and characteristics of the participants in a subsample of 19 cities in which close to a thousand conflict events had occurred. Here the impact of power structure on conflict was assessed.

The data on conflict were drawn from *The New York Times*. Elements of the stories in the *Times* were coded and then analyzed with the assistance of computers. The use of computers enabled us to get at patterns that tended to recur in civil rights conflict yet would not be visible to participants in a conflict, who could only have been acquainted with a limited range of experience. The scope and design of the study dictated the need to use computers.

Given the sheer volume of the data, it would have been impossible to validate each story. Perhaps for this reason researchers on conflict have simply ignored the problem of the validity of their data.

For example, the classic and path-breaking study of community conflict by James Coleman (1957), used a bewildering diversity of source material from the mass media and elsewhere without attempting to validate any part of it. But without techniques for validating and quantifying such data, any findings on community conflict different from those described by Coleman may all too easily be dismissed as resulting from different data, rather than a call to reconsideration of earlier findings.

Studies of other forms of conflict have also used news reports. Rummel (1966) and Tanter (1966) study the dimensions of intra- and international

197

conflict. Both use *The New York Times* as their data source. Neither attempts to assess the validity of the *Times*'s reportage of conflict outside the United States. It may well be that the data were suitable for Tanter's or for Rummel's purposes and that their conclusions were not affected by weaknesses in news-gathering processes. Nevertheless, an examination of the data source was in order.[2]Similarly, reports on urban riots, student riots, and conflict over fluoridation or urban renewal have utilized such data, but again without any attempt at validation of the source.

It is our contention that what researchers require is a strategy that will enable them to validate great numbers of such reports without the need to validate each story separately.

EXAMPLES OF USE

Newspapers may of course be considered a source of sources. For instance, stock market tables, results of political polls, births and deaths, and summaries of official government reports are all found in the daily paper. The *New York Times Almanac* and the *World Almanac* are among the additional valuable sources of information that are provided by newspapers. Also helpful is the *Gallup Opinion Index*, which summarizes information provided to newspapers by the American Institute for Public Opinion. Should the researcher wish to go further, most reports give the reporter's provenance for the information. Researchers also value their use for sensitizing observations. Trends can be detected that might suggest legitimate research problems.

A variety of possibilities in the use of such data is available—from simple description, (i.e., Senator Jones spoke to a crowd in Yankee Stadium) to suggesting hypotheses as in a study on reactions to the Vietnam War. Tanter and Horowitz (1969) used data taken from the U.S. Department of Defense and from *The New York Times* to chart national trends. Figure 1 combines some of their data. It suggests that increased antiwar protests may have been a consequence of increased troop strength in Vietnam.

But researchers must be alert to a diverse range of quality in newspapers. For instances, the *Wall Street Journal* will most often provide the best data on the business community; and, despite its proximity to a local event, the community newspaper might not be as complete a source of data as the regional paper in the nearby large city (or vice versa).

PROBLEMS OF VALIDITY

The techniques for validation most widely used by social scientists are those developed by historians. These techniques are useful in qualitative analysis or in case studies. But they do not permit validation of great

Figure 1. Size of Antiwar Demonstrations and Number of U.S. Troops in Vietnam.

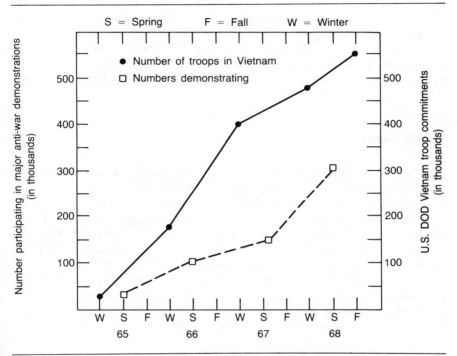

S = Spring   F = Fall   W = Winter

● Number of troops in Vietnam
□ Numbers demonstrating

Number participating in major anti-war demonstrations (in thousands)

U.S. DOD Vietnam troop commitments (in thousands)

Source of Data: Number of troops in Vietnam, Raymond Tanter (1969; Table 16–1); Numbers demonstrating, Jerome Skolnick (1969, Chart 1)

amounts of data that might lend themselves to the statistical analysis so typical of much of modern social research. (Interestingly, on the basis of our examination of the data, it is precisely this qualitative data that is most likely to be inaccurate.) An alternative to historiographic techniques of validation is required.

What follows is an examination of sources of error and bias in newspaper reporting and an attempt to validate a certain *range of data* appearing in the *Times.* The reader should note that these techniques might require modification when applied to other media and/or other social issues.

SURVEILLANCE, COMMUNICATION, AND GATEKEEPING

The role of the mass media is twofold—surveillance and communication, i.e., the gathering of news and the transmission of it. In each of these operations there is considerable room for omission and distortion. Following David M. White's (1950) classic discussion the process is examined as one of information input and output through various "gates" and "gatekeepers." Paradigmatically, this flow may be described in terms of the following elements: (1) the event itself; (2) the process by which the reporter comes to be alerted to the event; (3) witnessing or reconstructing the event by the reporter; (4) writing the story; (5) publication in the local newspaper; (6) publication by other newspapers.

1. The Event

Obviously, only a fraction of those events that occur are ever written up. The first criterion for the reporting of events is that they be "significant" or "important." Subjective as this may seem, its meaning appears to be "having impact on some large group," or as not being of purely personal interest to a small group. A generalization that applies here is that the more people who are affected by, or interested in, an event the more likely is the event to be newsworthy. The criteria of effect and of interest both apply. And the more critical the effect or the greater the interest, the more likely is it newsworthy, even if the group interested or effected is small. It is this range of information that is the "target" of media.[3] The range of these events constitutes an enormous narrowing of the total range of events.

2. Alerting the Reporter

If an event is or may be of mass range, how does the reporter come to be informed of it? For one thing, the news media regularly monitor critical sources of news. On the local scene this might be the town clerk's office, the local court, or the sheriff's office. In large cities the police teletype operates right into the news offices, and reporters are permanently assigned to city hall or to courts. On the state level the same monitoring occurs, and reporters are permanently assigned to state legislatures. This is true on the national level, too.

But one should note here that the model of the media as involved with surveillance tends to be misleading, for it focuses attention only on the efforts of the media to gather information. While this is an important part of the process, at this stage it is less important than that of the agents outside the media structure who are interested in passing on information. Informants range from passersby who happen to observe events and wish to inform the media, for whatever satisfaction this may bring them, to organizations that wish to publicize their activities. There is an enormous amount of information that is passed on to the media in hopes of publicizing it. The media's job here is more one of screening than of surveillance. So much information inundates newspapers that, as those seeking publicity know, it is quite difficult to get attention. Hence the development of "public relations" specialists, who probably produce a bias in terms of making more "favorable" news available.

On the other hand, injured parties in an intramural conflict at times bring in the news media in hopes that the power of the community at large can be brought to bear to their advantage or to hurt their opponents. Hence, "unfavorable" stories also get out. The balance between the two is unclear.

This problem is considered by Warren Breed (1958), who attempts to identify those stories within the range of newsworthy events that are nonetheless not found in news reports. He notes a number of themes reported by sociologists engaged in community studies. Under each of these themes newsworthy stories could conceivably be written, but generally are not. Under "business ethics" one should find stories such as "property interests prevent tax increases, force low physical and educational standards in high school" or "power and light company . . . remains smoke nuisance"; under religion, "upper-class resentment at lower-class membership in their church," or "low attendance at services"; under patriotism, he contrasts press reaction to United States intervention in the Guatemala Revolution of 1954 with the treatment of the Cuba intervention of 1961. Similar stories might also have been written on the family, the community, health and doctors. Breed's data provides underpinnings for the argument that newspapers are unreliable sources of information.[4]

But it is important to note that Breed's criticism refers to "soft news" (Danzger, 1976), those stories describing patterns that require digging, interpretation, and analysis. He is not suggesting that "hard news," i.e., descriptions of events such as a conflict or a demonstration—clear cut, open, and somewhat unusual events—might be omitted.

3. Witnessing the Event

The examination of events by reporters and their decision that something is or is not newsworthy is the next step. Here Breed (1955) points out that the news is to some degree censored. The experience of having editors consistently "blue-pencil" (edit) stories, of being called in by the editor or the publisher to discuss stories, informs the reporter informally but effectively as to what may or may not be published. Reporters soon come to learn that newspapers have different editorial policies (Tuchman, 1972: 672-74).

But Breed also points out that there are counterbalancing forces as well. For example, the norms of policy regarding a particular issue may not be clear. Or executives may be ignorant of particular facts, so that staffers who do the legwork can use their intimate knowledge of a story to subvert policy.

The staffer can decide whom to interview and whom to ignore, what questions to ask, which quotations and which items to feature (Tuchman, 1972, 668-69). To force publication of an article a reporter may "plant" the story in other papers or the wire services and then claim that the story is too big to ignore. And finally, Breed points out, it is the policy story and the assignment story that may most easily be subjected to decisions by superiors as to whether or not something ought to be pursued. But it is difficult to do this for beat stories and for stories initiated by the staffer.

A key point to consider is that it is highly irregular for executives to exercise censorship openly. The ethical norms of journalism forbid this. Breed says (1955: 327) that "no executive is willing to risk embarrassment by being accused of open commands to slant a news story." Although it does occur, the censorship itself is therefore rather limited in effectiveness.

4. Writing[5]

The writing of the story is another "gate" (and a major hurdle) to be passed between the story and its publication. The situation here is such that distortion seems inevitable, and experimental evidence indicates that it probably occurs.

There are two patterns here. Either reporters may themselves write a story, or the story may be phoned in to the rewrite desk at the office. That first pattern is likely in smaller papers where rewrite staff may not be available. On the other hand, larger papers use the rewrite pattern for quick-breaking stories that must be reported immediately.

Where a reporter on a large paper commands such respect that the rewrite staff will not dare to change the story phoned in (as was the case with Meyer Berger of *The New York Times*), or again where a reporter is working on some special assignment and has the time to carefully write his own copy, there may be no rewrite. On the other hand, for reporters of less than star stature working on quick-breaking stories, the rewrite staff reorganizes and rewrites the material for publication.

From the rewrite "gate" the copy is then passed to the desk for a particular area of news—for example, city desk, science desk, etc. The story may be killed at this "gate" or passed on either with or without further rewriting. From there it goes to the news editor or assistant managing editor. The news editor scans the article and then assigns it the appropriate headline to indicate its importance in the news or "kills it" if he doesn't like it.

If it gets through that gate, it then goes to the copy editor for correction of errors in fact, style, grammar, etc. Then it goes to the composing room.

All the above takes place under the enormous pressure of the news deadline for that edition, so that the entire pace is hectic, especially as the deadline approaches. The possibility for error increases under these circumstances of constant, rapid handling and passing from one individual to another. Experimental studies in the transmission of rumor have shown the kinds of distortions that may creep in under these circumstances (cf. Alport & Postman, 1955). The possibility for error is recognized by everyone connected with a newspaper, and certainly it appears to reporters that the amount of material discarded in the process of moving from reporter to copy desk may be four to five times as much as is published.

Some less obvious possibilities for bias in this process have also been pointed out by researchers. Bauer (1958) has documented the effect of the audience on recall in an experimental situation, in particular he found that this applied strongly to journalism students (as they were not involved in the subject matter but were more attuned to the "audience"). De Sola Pool and Shulman (1959) have pointed out that some reporters seem to write with an eye to "wreaking vengeance" or "righting wrongs" on some segment of the population, while others seem more concerned with telling a "happy story". Their experiments indicated that these "mind sets" make it likely that errors will be made in writing stories that are not congruent with a reporter's perspectives.

5. Publication[6]

Even if the story survives all these pressures intact and is indeed newsworthy, it may not be published if it comes in too late. Even if it comes in before the deadline, other news of apparently equal value may have preempted the available space. In other words, had it come in before that space was taken, it might have been published. And not only is this a hazard on any particular day, but it seems to be a systematic hazard on certain days of the week. On Mondays it is apparently easy to get things published, as not much of interest generally occurs on Sundays. But on Tuesdays it's much more difficult to get news published. Certain stories will appear at certain times of the year (holidays, for example), and will not be run at other times. New Year's, for example, may "knock out" news that might ordinarily be published, due to the year-end recapitulations of the year that are so prevalent.

CORRECTIVE PROCESSES

Doubt is cast on newspaper stories because they are viewed as though they operate as independent units, when in fact they do not. It is our view that it is the *interdependence of news-gathering and publication agencies that lends to newspapers a high degree of veracity*. In this section this factor of interdependence will be explored.

AN INTERACTIVE NETWORK MODEL OF
NEWS-GATHERING AGENCIES

The Wire Services[7]

The primary sources of domestic news for all newspapers in the United States, including the *Times*, are the wire services—The Associated Press and the United Press International. According to one expert (Hohenberg, 1960: 197) the most knowledgeable estimates are that 75 percent or more of national news published in the American press is provided by the wire services, and many newspapers accept at least half their statewide stories from the wire services as well. This figure would probably not apply to *The New York Times*, given their own enormous staff and widespread contacts, but this does indicate the importance of wire services of which the *Times* also avails itself. Both wire services provide news to more than 7,000 outlets, which consist of newspapers, radio and TV stations, newsmagazines, government agencies (including military intelligence), and even private companies. Each of the wire services maintains several hundred thousand miles of leased wires in the United States.

Both AP and the UPI compete for news on a global basis and service foreign as well as American mass media, including radio and television. John Hohenberg, a critical observer of the enterprise, writes (1960: 198):

[The wire services] . . . They must meet the standards of thousands of editors of all shades of political and religious beliefs, all nationalities and sympathies. The wire services, therefore, ordinarily take great care to present all sides of a story that is controversial. . . . They are impartial sources of information for all sides.

Not only do the wire services attempt to be reliable and unbiased, but they make every attempt to report the news in full. The APME Blue Book records the complaints of editors who called attention to "vast amounts of trivia in AP reports" (Hohenberg, 1960: 198). David M. White reports (1950: 384) that editors use about *one tenth* of the wire copy available.

The UPI has bureaus in every state of the union except Alaska.[8] Each state has from two to five bureaus. Each bureau has a number of full-time workers as well as a retinue of stringers, people who write for the wire service on occasion and serve as important sources of information. The stringers are often employed on local papers, but need not be. In 1967 the UPI employed about 5,000 full-time people in the United States, and in addition they had as many as 10,000 additional stringers. The latter figure is hard to estimate precisely because stringers are employed by the story, hence only on occasion. The UPI had staff not only in every state capital, but in principal towns and county seats. (In some states, such as Alabama and Georgia, county seats are important centers of news).

Major government departments are sources of news for the agencies. For example, the Department of Justice is an important source of information for UPI on civil rights. Leads emanating from Washington are then followed up on the local level.

The Associated Press is a cooperative association, wherein all members of the association supply news to each other. Each newspaper, radio, or TV network associated with this group acts as a source of news. AP has fewer people solely devoted to its activities than UPI, but the scope of its activities as a whole is more formidable. Of the roughly 1,700 newspapers in the United States, about 1,300 belong to the AP Cooperative. In addition, about 3,000 radio and television stations around the country are members of the association. AP also maintains about 100 offices in the United States.

On the other hand, United Press International is an independent entity, not an association of news agencies as is AP. This may make UPI a good check on those local events that might not appear in local papers. The possibility of UPI coverage may push a paper to publicize events even though they may be distasteful.

Both AP's and UPI's surveillance operations are enormous. Police and stock market teletypes along with teletypes from other agencies constantly pour information into these offices. Although AP and UPI are competitive organizations and do not cooperate with each other officially, neither can hide the news from the other for very long once information is on the wires. In reality, then, both operate almost as a single news-gathering network, with competition spurring both on to get the news first and best. A signal to this network brings in a flock of reporters from both agencies and other news-gathering groups.

With regard to civil rights, executives of both AP and UPI indicated that in addition to the news-gathering efforts already described above, special efforts were made to gather news. For example, Douglass Lovelace, AP bureau chief in New York, stated that AP had developed a "racial task force" comprised of experts with long experience and useful contacts in the field of civil rights. The task force consisted of seven top reporters scattered throughout the country (New York, Atlanta, Memphis, New Orleans, Chicago, Los Angeles), some of whom might be called together if important stories broke.

Jesse Bogue of UPI conceded that before the Little Rock, Arkansas, confrontation in 1957 there had been little coverage in depth, i.e., few interpretive stories had been written and incidents were covered only as isolated events. He argued that from 1957 onward, however, the entire effort had become more systematized and in-depth coverage sought.

As will be indicated in our statistical examination of wire service reporting below, the wire services are not infallible. Even "hard stories" are in fact missed. However, it is clear from the foregoing discussion that wire services do not simply pass news along a line of communication. Rather they use their massive network as a tripwire that signals the central agency when and where to send reporters or even teams of news-gatherers to cover stories.

The *Times* as News-Gatherer

For *The New York Times* the wire services act not only as a supplier of news but also as an alarm system. They function this way for any major newspaper with sufficient staff and for major newsmagazines, television groups, and the like. But the *Times*, with its enormous staff, is more likely than most other news groups to send its own reporter out after a big story. Hence for the *Times* in particular the wire services are not simply news suppliers.

This is not the only element in the system that operates as an alarm. Government agencies also often supply the *Times* with stories directly. And civil rights groups frequently call stories in to the *Times*, as it is the most visible major newspaper. Its influence, and the impact from publishing important stories there, are believed to be great.

In addition *The New York Times* has its own field offices where there are one or several reporters whose jobs are to obtain news that may be gathered at the same time by the wire services. For example, both wire services and the *Times* have a large number of reporters covering Washington, D.C., the state government agencies in New York, and at a number of other points. On the civil rights story the *Times* had, and continues to maintain, a regional office in Atlanta. This group operates in close liaison with the Southern Regional Council.[9] Two reporters are assigned to this office most of the time, and more may be assigned if the story should require it.

The liaison with the Southern Regional Council puts at the disposal of the *Times* the considerable resources of this organization. The Council maintains files on many communities, does research in the area of civil rights, explores attitudes, reports community changes, and attempts to keep track of groups, both pro- and anti-integration, of their areas of influence, activities, and the like. The Council of couse has its liaison with AP and UPI also, but the *Times* is not dependent on these wire services for information gathered by the council. There is no "gate" here. Once the "alarm" has gone off, and if the story seems important, the *Times* is likely to send in its regional staff on civil rights.

The Reporter as Witness

Granted that the "alarm system" is working well and that the *Times* is informed of the story, the next question is, How accurate are the reporters on the beat in covering a story? How do they know where to be, where the most important events are likely to occur? How accurate is the report of a single eyewitness in any case? We are aware of the difficulties of eliciting evidence from eyewitnesses in court cases. Their reports are full of omissions and distortions. We are aware also from observational (Tuchman, 1972) and social psychological work (Alport and Goodman, 1947; Molotch and Lester, 1975) of the possibilities for distortion. What makes a story accurate? How is a reporter able to avoid distortions?

An interview with Fred Powledge, formerly of *The New York Times* and assigned to the "civil rights beat," provided some insight into the question. The view expressed by Powledge was generally confirmed by others in the field. He pointed out that reporters for mass media found themselves on assignments with the same colleagues from other media again and again. Collegial relationships often developed into friendly ties, and these people would seek each other's company. They would stay at the same hotels, have their meals together, and drink together.

For example, in covering civil rights in the South, Powledge was frequently in the company of Claude Sitton, also of the *Times*, Joseph Cummings of *Newsweek*, Herbert Kaplow of NBC, Hughes Rudd of CBS, and a number of others. Inevitably, as they were covering the same stories, they would exchange information. Differences of fact would be examined and often later explored and ascertained. This exchange of information resulted in every reporter having a far more detailed and current view of a wider variety of relevant facts than any could have on his own.

Such an arrangement might also produce common errors, particularly if the reporters simply accepted the stories of others without checking on their own. It has been said that a situation of this sort developed in 1964 among reporters of the Vietnamese conflict, who stayed in their hotels in Saigon, bent elbows with other reporters for their stories, and never got out into the boondocks. I pressed Powledge on this possibility and on the possibility that the group might have been acting as a "pool" (in newspaper jargon a "pool" is a formal arrangement between reporters for sharing information).

Powledge strongly denied this and argued that while some information was exchanged, the reporters got the stories on their own. Without attempting to judge the complete accuracy of Powledge's statement, it seems that given the large staff of reporters from the variety of news media assigned to cover civil rights, little chance for real distortion existed. The real weakness of pool reporting occurs in two situations: (1) where access to the situation is limited or dangerous; (2) where the action is so spread out or so unpredictable that it cannot adequately be covered everywhere. The latter situation results in reporters being spread so thin that a single reporter's account is all there is to go on.

In the civil rights situation publicity was sought once conflict broke out.

Media were contacted by the civil rights groups in particular in an attempt to use publication of stories as weapons to achieve their ends. Demonstrations, boycotts, etc., could therefore be more adequately covered, as there was advance notice of these events.

A NEWSPAPER OF RECORD

The New York Times conceives of itself as a historical record—in fact, as the only newspaper that provides a historical record. It makes every effort to supply the details of the news that it believes important. Violence, demonstrations, and any "unusual" events were likely to be reported. The *Times* published between 75 and 90 percent of all stories appearing on the wires.[10] The stories may not report in full the details of the original wire story, but will get in if only in some shortened form.

If a story should be missed one day, it may pop up the next day. For example, a series of demonstrations may take place, and though one may be missed, for lack of space, it may be picked up the next day. Where stories have continuity, the "lost" stories may be recovered and be published together with the newer development. Stories lacking continuity may be missed, particularly if they appear to have no appreciable long-term impact. But for an important wire story to be missed by the *Times* it must not only be discarded by the wire service but also other news agencies as well. (There are 1,700 other newspaper and about 3,000 additional news agencies.) The interaction among news agencies provides a pressure toward publication of events.

Odd as it sounds, stories of great significance may be missed at first. The cause of this is the tendency for newspapers to report the "routinely unroutine," the kinds of events that are expected and whose significance may easily be known. When the stories are so unusual that their significance is not guessed, they may go unreported.

The fact that significant stories are occasionally overlooked is at times taken as evidence of the unreliability of news reporting. But this is likely to be rectified as the significance of the events becomes known.

A STATISTICAL TEST OF SUPPRESSION[11]

The foregoing describes how news that has been published locally gets to be known nationally and how the pattern of interaction of reporters and of newspapers tends to generate accuracy in the reports of events that are published.

Yet the weak link in this chain is the possibility that a local newspaper may not publish stories that it wishes to suppress, and so the story never gets on the wires. Under these circumstances the mechanisms of news media interaction that exert pressure for accuracy may never be activated.

To determine whether this has in fact occurred—i.e., whether stories might have been suppressed at the local level—we compared cities that have either AP or UPI offices (not simply outlets or stringers of affiliations with AP, but independent offices) with all other cities. Our hypothesis is if newspaper reports are suppressed, then more stories will be reported in cities with AP or UPI central offices than in other cities. The logic behind it is that the central offices, being independent news-gathering groups whose function is to transmit news, will be highly unlikely to suppress news. They are under pressure, not to suppress, but to disseminate.

If we find no difference in reports of conflict when cities with wire service offices are compared to those without such offices, this would indicate that news is not suppressed. For it would then appear that whether or not a city has a wire service office, the chance of a given story being published in the *Times* is about the same.

Data

To test the above hypothesis our procedures were as follows: *The New York Times Index* was scanned for the period 1955 to 1965. All stories under a variety of headings (e.g., civil rights, Negroes, education, sit-in) that related to civil rights conflict between blacks and whites were Xeroxed, clipped, and pasted onto index cards. Care was taken to preserve the page, and column on which the story had appeared in the *Times*. These cards were then sorted by state and city and arranged in sequence by date. Well over 10,000 were identified in this manner.

Out of this mass of conflict reports we selected only those related to cities with populations of 25,000 or more.[12] These reports consisted of descriptions of events such as demonstrations, marches, sit-ins, the posting of guards around schools to facilitate or prevent integration, and so forth. Our universe consisted of 644 cities in the continental United States having populations of 25,000 or more by the count of the 1960 U.S. Census.[13]

For each of these cities we simply counted the number of conflict reports published without regard to number of participants involved, intensity of conflict, and so forth. As the data were extremely skewed, however, we transformed the simple count of conflict events into the log of conflict events. In the analysis below "log conflict events" is utilized.

Results

The correlation between AP-UPI and log conflict reports is .524. This would seem by itself to indicate that the reports are an artifact of the location of AP-UPI offices. Moreover, using a step-wise regression we note that the bulk of the variance is "explained" by the existence of an AP/UPI office that appears to confirm that reports of conflict are no more than an artifact of the location of these offices. See Table 1.

It is of course possible that cities with wire service offices report conflict more frequently because they have other characteristics that in fact cause conflict. Hence, the greater reporting of conflict in these cities may reflect the reality of these other factors rather than the artifact of reporting patterns. In other words, more conflict may in fact take place in wire service cities.

To test this possibility we forced into the regression those factors that we have elsewhere argued (Danzger, 1968 and 1970) are highly related to conflict reports. Nevertheless, as the reader can see, AP/UPI still provides a substantial proportion of the variance. See Table 2.

It seems clear that research attempting to identify factors producing conflict will be utilizing contaminated data if newspaper reports are used. (Yet studies of civil disorder that attempt such statistical analysis do in fact use news reports as their data.) Conclusions based on such data are very likely to be misleading. Is there a way out of the dilemma?

It will be recalled that wire services function as an alarm, calling the news media to an event. In response reporters or even news teams are dispatched by other newspapers and even by the central offices of the wire services themselves. Even though the wire service may not have an office in a given city, once the word gets out about a newsworthy story, the wire services will not depend on stringers or the local paper for a report, but will send their own teams of reporters to investigate the matter further. We therefore expect that if we make comparisons among cities with wire service offices, we will find no difference in the number of conflicts reported. Once the alarm has been tripped, reporting will be equally good regardless of whether or not a city has a wire service office.

A single story, however, is not sufficient to bring in a substantial number of outside reporters. As Table 3 indicates, even though the effect of AP/UPI is reduced, it still remains.

Table 1. City Characteristics and Log Conflict Reports:
Step-Wise Regression for Cities with Populations of 25,000 or more

	N = 644
	R Square
1. AP/UPI	.275
2. South - Non-South	.132
3. Number Nonwhite	.107
4. City Age	.033
5. Unemployed	.021
Nine additional factors add only .013 to R square	
Total Variance Explained	.576

Table 2. City Characteristics and Log Conflict Reports: Forced
Step-Wise Regression for Cities with Populations of 25,000 or more

N = 644

Forced Step-Wise Regression

Number of nonwhites	*1st*
South-non-South	*2nd*
City Age	*3rd*
	R Square

1. Number Nonwhite	.270
2. South - non-South	.139
3. City Age	.081
4. AP/UPI	.054
Ten other factors add only .028 to R square	
Total Variance Explained	.572

Table 3. City Characteristics and Log Conflict Reports:
Step-Wise Regression for Cities with Populations of 25,000 or more

Only Cities with One or More Conflict Reports

N = 223

	R Square
1. Nonwhite	.247
2. South-non-South	.128
3. AP/UPI	.071
4. Unemployed	.020
Ten additional factors add only .050 to the R square	
Total Variance Explained	.510

However, if we take those cities that have reported *five or more
conflict events* over this 11-year period, we find that the effect of AP/UPI is
eliminated entirely (Table 4).

In sum, the statistical comparisons indicate that utilizing newspaper
reports of conflict as the basis for analysis is likely to be misleading, as these
data are contaminated by the factor of wire service office location. *But they
also show that if one uses only those cities that have already reported some
conflict, there seems to be no such contamination.*

RECENT DEVELOPMENTS

In 1975 I raised the problem of the validity of news and argued
that it is necessary for studies of conflict to explicitly consider the possibility
of bias and determine the parameters within which data could be accepted

Table 4.   City Characteristics and Log Conflict Reports:
Step-Wise Regression for Cities with Populations of 25,000 or more

Only Cities with Five or More Conflicts	
	N = 117
	R Square
1. Nonwhite	.249
2. South-non-South	.062
3. City Age	.034
4. Capital	.045
5. Number of Manufacturing Establishments Employing 25 or more	.014
6. AP/UPI	.010
Nine other factors add to R²	.040
Total Variance Explained	.463

as valid, before developing conclusions regarding conflict. This touched off a controversy. Tuchman, whose research has been in the area of mass media, argued (1976) that I did not go far enough in criticizing the use of such data for the study of conflict. Snyder and Kelly, whose work has been in the area of social conflict argued (1977) that I had overstated the problem. In their view, news reports are a valid data base where conflict is intense.

Thus, at present, rather than finding a convergence of views based on the accumulation of data, the perspectives of the fields of mass media and of social conflict appear to be moving toward polar views regarding validity of news for the study of conflict. As I have already suggested (1976) the question that needs to be examined is not whether news reports are "valid." Rather the key question is "valid for what purpose?" Different analytic perspectives and different theoretical interests require the validation of different *ranges* of data. For example where the theoretical interest is in identifying the characteristics of cities that experienced conflict, a count of conflict events of a given intensity may be sufficient. In this case, conflict is a crudely identified dependent variable. The researchers interest lies in identifying the relevant independent variables, i.e., the demographic factors associated with the occurrence of conflict (Danzger, 1968a, 1970).

Where the theoretical interest lies in the explication of the process of conflict, more refined description must be utilized. Here researchers will be interested in the organizational structure of participants, in the legitimacy or unusualness of the tactics utilized, in the issues involved (Coleman 1957, Danzger 1968a, 1968b, 1970). Interest has also been directed to the incidents antecedent to the outbreak of conflict and to cooperative and conciliatory gestures of participants in the conflict (Monti 1979). In all these latter cases, not only are the more subtle data required, but more refined techniques for the validation of data must be developed.

The Snyder and Kelly approach validates a range of data so narrow as to make it impossible to examine the antecedent events leading to intense conflict as well as the process and stages by which conflict "winds down." The approach I have suggested, is inherently capable of validating a broader range of data. Rather than approach validation by limiting the data to intense events I argue that sources of data should be examined for comparability. I have concluded that accounts of conflict events for cities with wire service offices or with substantial reports of conflict are comparable. Within this limited although large (i.e., minimally, more than ninety cities) group of cities, a wider range of events than those involving "intense conflict" may be compared. Of far more critical importance, however, is the fact that the broader approach permits the research to take into account the impact of the actions by those in pivotal social positions who neither use violence nor act in groups. The actions and statements of church leaders, police and business groups, the courts and even the intervention of the President of the United States cannot be taken into account when the Snyder and Kelly approach to conflict is utilized. Such data as may be validated by the Snyder and Kelly approach are so limited as to result in a sterile approach to the study of conflict.

Thus the preferred strategy is the comparison of accounts in the *Times* with those in local papers and with accounts of participants. Such a comparison will identify the special characteristics of the range of events and actors involved in conflict events that come to be published in the national media in contrast to those which are "lost" in the process of transmission.

SUMMARY

Newspapers can be a valuable source for data in social science research. Newspapers of record, like *The New York Times* and the *Washington Post*, provide descriptions of events and numbers for raw data.

Our analysis of the methods and procedures by which news is gathered and transmitted indicates that a news report that something did occur is highly likely to be accurate not only in its assertion that an event did occur, but also in its description of the elements of the event. (Interpretations and evaluations of events, as well as emphasis, will vary, however.) This accuracy derives from corrective processes that are embedded in the structure of news-gathering and reporting.

Current beliefs that all news reports are suspect on this account do not appear to be warranted when one considers that the news-gathering process actually contains corrective processes against suppression. The model of news-gathering is described in terms of a series of convolutions and circles. Distorted reports are corrected; omitted reports are inserted; a given reporter may be corrected by his colleagues; a given event may be observed by several reporters.

Nevertheless, statistical comparisons of events, particularly those that attempt to deal with the reasons why events occur in one place but not another (civil rights conflict, for example), are highly unreliable. It appears that cities without wire service offices may suppress news. One might then say, that while newspaper reports may be accepted as data that an event did occur, the lack of such report may not be an indication that events did not occur.

Statistical comparisons that attempt to determine why events took place in one city rather than in another must begin by ascertaining that new-reporting networks are similar in the cities compared. Comparing only cities with wire service offices would be one possibility. Alternatively, as we have shown in the case of civil rights, one may add to such a base other cities for which several reports of conflict have been published even if over an extended time period. Where conflicts have been reported, one may rely on news networks to be accurate also as to whether many or few conflicts have actually occurred.

Statistical analyses that do not examine the news networks or attempt to assess their validity should be viewed with wariness. But the facts of civil rights conflict (i.e., demonstrations and the like) as reported in the *Times* seem reliable enough to be used as data.

APPENDIX

How to Use *The New York Times*

The first step in using the *Times* should be an inspection of the data available in *Facts on File* and in *The New York Times Index*. Even in this cursory inspection, where the researcher is interested in nothing more than the volume of the data available, care should be taken to inspect all related categories. Failure to do this may result in a gross underestimation of the volume of material available. It would be wise to pick the brains of colleagues, librarians, and if possible, the staff of the *Times Index* for related categories. Each of the categories inspected should be recorded, along with the volume of material available in that category on a yearly basis. For example, "1964, pages nnn to kkk in the index under category x," etc. Such a list will prove valuable in pinning down the magnitude of the data and in planning the research.

Our study involved gathering data on civil rights conflict in the United States between 1955 and 1965 in every community in the United States. This required that the data be grouped together for each city for this 11-year period. But the *Index* does not present data in this form. We therefore Xeroxed every page of the *Index* on which this data appeared, and then cut out each of these stories separately. Each story was pasted onto a three-by-five card on which the year of the story and the city in which the event occurred were also recorded. At the bottom of the card a record was also kept of the page number of the *Index* from which the story was clipped. Care was taken in cutting the stories to include the date and page listing in the *Times*. Stories were then sorted by city and by date. As additional searching turned up more data, other stories were added in a similar manner. The remaining scraps of the xeroxed *Index* pages were kept for further inspection. Records were maintained on all categories searched and all pages Xeroxed.

Culling the stories was an immensely time-consuming job,[15] and one that had to be done systematically and carefully. A key category overlooked might substantially alter the character of the data. Wherever possible we checked our data against available reports (We were fortunate in that there were numerous histories of the civil rights movement available at the time this study was undertaken, including one by Anthony Lewis (1964), which leaned heavily on *The New York Times*.

The possibility of utilizing the data effectively, particularly if large numbers of such stories are to be utilized, depends heavily on the development of an effective coding scheme that will permit one to break the story down into theoretically relevant component parts. A scheme for the coding of protest had already been developed by Irving Goldaber (1965). It provided a helpful starting point in developing a code for the study of conflict. A fairly flexible and highly useful code for the study of such conflict has been developed. For the study of other phenomena, a rough coding scheme should be developed and then tested and modified before the study is actually undertaken. Whatever coding scheme is developed, the researcher ought to build an instrument with sufficient flexibility to permit substantial expansion or modification of the categories once the research is underway. Invariably it will be found that even a good test of the instrument will fail to hold all the data that might be important.

The data for the study of civil rights were taken from the microfilms of *The New York Times*, which are widely available. A detailed code book was developed, and coders were trained in its use. The accuracy of coders was checked by having each story separately checked by the research supervisor. Such checks were facilitated by brief summaries of the stories, which appeared in the *Index* (possibly as many as 50 percent of the dates we used appeared in the *Index* summary). We were also able to, and in fact did, use other checks on the coding, such as having two or more coders code the same set of stories. This provided a useful training experience, pointed up the obscurities of the coding scheme, and forced us to elaborate fully the rationale behind the code.

The coding scheme utilized for the study of civil rights conflict has not been published as yet. A preliminary report on the use of an earlier version of the code has been published (Danzger, 1968b) and is available on request.

NOTES

[1] A number of people assisted in this work by supplying valuable information and useful insights: Fred Powledge, formerly of the *New York Times*; Jesse Bogue,

Assistant Managing Editor, and Irving Peck, Promotion Manager, of U.P.I.; Austin Scott and Douglass Lovelace, New York City Bureau Chief, of A.P.; Gerson Jacobson of the *Day-Morning Journal*; Luther Jackson, formerly of the *Washington Post*; Irving Horowitz, Assistant National News Editor of *The New York Times*; Philips Davison, Professor of Journalism, School of Journalism of Columbia University; Benjamin Holman, Assistant Director for Media Relations, and Fred Wright, Director of Research, Community Relations Division of the U.S. Dept. of Justice (in Washington, D.C.); Jean Roberts and Roy Reed of *The New York Times* Atlanta (Ga.) office, assigned as liaison to the Southern Regional Council. Interviews were conducted from the summer of 1967 through the early spring of 1968. Jeffrey Hadden graciously provided the census data used here. The author is indebted to Babs Green Zimmerman for her editorial assistance.

Funds for this research were made available by the Faculty Research Award Program of CUNY (Grant No. 1090) and by the National Science Foundation (Grant No. SO 0905 R).

[2] The news-gathering and reporting capability of *The New York Times* outside of the United States does not match its capability within the U.S. In fact, foreign news correspondents (Lichtheim, 1965) have on occasion been highly critical of *Times* reporting on issues with which they are familiar.

[3] The precise definition of "target information" has long been a question that mass media have tried to answer. Reader and listener preferences have been surveyed countless times, information has been gathered on newspaper and magazine circulation and on TV and radio audience size, with a view to defining those issues that "affect and/or interest" people. Clear and definitive answers are not available.

[4] Breed (1958) excludes the "quality press" from his analysis and specifically mentions *The New York Times* and *Harper's* as examples of quality press. Nevertheless, we present a conservative argument for the validity of the *Times* and assume here that *Breed's* evaluation of mass media in general applies to *The New York Times* as well.

[5] The discussion in this section leans heavily on Hohenberg's (1960) work.

[6] The discussion in this section benefitted from several discussions with Professor Philips Davison, March 1968.

[7] In addition to published materials, particularly Hohenberg (1960), this discussion draws on interviews with executives of AP and UPI (Winter 1968 cited in acknowledgement).

[8] Information presented here was obtained in interviews cited above (Winter 1968).

[9] From interviews with Jean Roberts and Roy Reed, both of *The New York Times*, at the offices of the Southern Regional Council, Atlanta, Ga., August 1968.

[10] Telephone interview with Irving Horowitz, March 1968.

[11] The argument here follows Danzger (1975). Note that Table 4 here shows that 5 conflict reports over the 11 year span are sufficient to eliminate the effect of wire service offices in the regression, rather than 10 as reported earlier.

[12] Keyes (1958) has argued that it is at this population level that communities acquire the characteristics of urban cities. Below this level their character is not urban.

[13] In 1960 there were in fact 672 cities in the continental United Statesswith populations of 25,000 or more. But 28 cities were eliminated from the study because of insufficient data on census characteristics. These data were generously made available by Jeffrey Hadden.

[14]The Washington Post might be considered assthe "paper of record" for research on government affairs; the researcher must decide which paper best serves the data needs.

[15] This entire process has been immensely simplified by a service The New York Times began offering in 1973 called "The New York Times Information Bank." This service utilizes computers for search and retrieval of information.

REFERENCES

American Institute of Public Opinion. Gallup Opinion Index. Princeton, N.J.

Alport, Gordon W. and Postman, Leo F. The Psychology of Rumor. New York: Holt, Rinehart and Winston, 1947.

Bauer, Raymond A. The communicator and the audience. Journal of Conflict Resolution, 1958, 2 (March): 66-77.

Breed, Warren. Social control in the newsroom: A functional analysis. Social Forces, 1955, 33 (May): 326-35. (a)

_____. Mass communication and sociocultural integration. Social Forces, 1955, 37 (Sept.): 109-16. (b)

Coleman, James. Community conflict. New York: Free Press, 1957.

Danzger, M. Herbert. Civil rights conflict and community power structure. New York: Columbia University, unpublished Ph.D. dissertation 1968. (a)

Danzger, M. Herbert. A quantified description of community conflict. American Behavioral Scientist, 1968, 12 (Nov.-Dec.): 9-15. (b)

Danzger, M. Herbert. Critical mass and historical process as factors in community conflict. Paper read at Annual Meeting of the American Sociological Association, Washington, D.C., 1970.

Danzger, M. Herbert. Validating conflict data. American Sociological Review, 1975, 40 (October): 570-84.

Danzger, M. Herbert. Reply to Tuchman. American Sociological Review, 1976, 41 (December): 1067-71.

De Sola-Pool, Ithiel, & Shulman, Irwin. Newsmen's fantasies, audiences and newswriting. Public Opinion Quarterly, 1959, 23 (Summer): 145-58.

Gerbner, George. On content analysis and critical research in mass communication. Audio-Visual Communication Review, 1958, 3 (Spring): 85-108.

Goldaber, Irving. The Negro protest against the New York City Board of Education. Journal of Intergroup Relations, 1965, 4, 199-208.

Hohenberg, John. The professional journalist: A guide to modern reporting practice. New York: Holt, Rinehart and Winston, 1960.

Keys, Fenton. The correlation of social phenomena with community size. Social Forces, 1958, 36 (May): 311-15.

Lang, Kurt & Lang, Gladys Engel. *Collective dynamics*. New York: Thomas Crowell, 1961.

Lewis, Anthony, and *The New York Times*. *Portrait of a decade*. New York: Random House, 1964.

Lichtheim, George. The New York Times: All the news that's fit to print. *Commentary*, 1965, *40* (Sept.): 33-46.

Long, H. Luman (Ed.). *The world almanac & book of facts*. New York: World Almanac, annual.

Meyer, Sylvan. The press and the schools. Atlanta: The Southern Regional Council, 1962.

Molotch, Harvey L., & Lester, Marilyn. Accidental news: the great oil spill. *American Journal of Sociology*, 1975 *81*: 235-60.

Monti, Daniel. Patterns of conflict preceding the 1964 Harlem and Bedford-Stuyvesant riots. *Journal of Conflict Resolution*, 1979 (January).

New York Times Company. *New York Times almanac*. New York: annual.

Rummel, R. J. Dimensions of conflict behavior within nations 1946-1959. *Journal of Conflict Resolution*, 1966, *10* (March): 65-73.

Skolnick, Jerome. *The politics of protest*. Washington: U.S. Govt. Printing office, 1969.

Spearman, Walter. Racial issues in the news. Atlanta: The Southern Regional Council Atlanta, 1962.

Snyder, David and Kelly, William R. Conflict intensity, media sensitivity and the validity of newspaper data. *American Sociological Review*, 1977, *42* (February): 105-23.

Tanter, Raymond. Dimensions of conflict behavior within and between nations, 1958-1960. *Journal of Conflict Resolution*. 1966, *10* (March): 41-64.

Tanter, Raymond. International war and domestic turmoil. In Hugh Davis Graham and Ted Robert Gurr (Eds.), *Violence in America* (Vol. 2). Washington, D.C.: U.S. Govt. Printing Office, 1969.

Tuchman, Gaye. Objectivity as a strategic ritual: An examination of newsman's notion of objectivity. *American Journal of Sociology*, 1972 *77* (January): 660-79.

Tuchman, Gaye. Making news by doing work: routinizing the unexpected. *American Journal of Sociology*, 1973 *79* (July): 110-31.

Tuchman, Gaye. The news manufacture of sociological data. *American Sociological Review*, 1976, *41* (December): 1065-67.

White, David Manning. The gatekeeper: A case study in the selection of news. *Journalism Quarterly*, 1950, *27* (Fall): 383-90.

Chapter Nine
Computer-aided content analysis

DANIEL M. OGILVIE, PHILIP J. STONE and
EDWARD F. KELLY

It is a common notion that if the medical sciences were at the same
level of advancement as the social sciences, leaches would still be
prominent in prescriptions for cure of disease. Aside from unrealistically
glorifying the state of medical science, this analogy is painfully accurate
when one considers the primitive stages of development of some areas of
social science. We are beset with ridiculously oversimplified models, blind to
cultural biases that mask critical variables, and handcuffed (or made
overzealous) by second-sister conceptions of our status within the sciences.
However, there is one area, the broad area of technology, where notable
advances have been made in the behavioral sciences. The development of
high-speed computers has played a central role in the quantum leap of
technology. Very few social scientists have remained unaffected by the new
technology, for it has greatly increased our capacity to collect, store, analyze,
and reanalyze data.

These developments have not been met with great jubilation by all
interested and concerned parties. The satisfaction experienced by many
researchers who now have a powerful instrument at their disposal that
enables them to accomplish research they could not have conceived of
undertaking a few years ago has been countered by the troublesome
knowledge that quantity and speed are not synonymous with quality and
understanding.

As a case in point, this chapter considers the relationship between
quantitative and qualitative issues that arise in applying a computer-aided
system for content analysis. It neither glorifies the technique nor underplays
it. No attempt is made to simplify or to smooth over the difficult and
unsolved problems encountered in the process of building and revising the
procedures to be described and discussed. It is hoped that in the attempt to
involve the reader in the various issues that have been raised and the various
solutions, part solutions, and mistakes that have emerged, we will also be
exposing him or her to issues that are common to the field of content analysis
as a whole.

In this chapter we will not attempt to present a history of content
analysis or to review a large number of studies. This task has been admirably
accomplished by others who have treated these subjects at length. (See
Gerbner, 1969; Holsti, 1969; Pool, 1959; and Stone, 1966). In addition we
cannot undertake a fair treatment of *all* issues relevant to a truly comprehensive view of content analysis. Instead we have selected those issues that have

impinged most heavily on the development of the system of computer content analysis dwelled on herein. In following this strategy we recognize the danger of ignoring what may become the most critical content-analysis issues from some researchers. This is unavoidable here and in a treatise of almost any length, for it is impossible to anticipate the special and sometimes idiosyncratic problems researchers may encounter.

The final consideration that weighs against an urge to be comprehensive is the fact that certain absolutely basic issues must be made evident and resolved before the next line of issues can be faced intelligently. Too often researchers agonize over advanced issues when in fact they cannot afford the luxury of assuming that primary issues have been handled in a satisfactory manner.

AN INTRODUCTION TO CONTENT ANALYSIS

Nearly every time something is read, it is being content-analyzed. Whether the message is an instruction manual for the operation of a new washing machine, a speech by a presidential candidate, a novel, a description of a holiday in the Caribbean, or a cartoon, information is being processed and sometimes stored in the mind according to some principle, no matter how disguised or haphazard the principle may be. Often conscious and sometimes unconscious judgments are being made about the message according to some frame of reference. One may judge a message on the basis of how informative it is and whether or not it is interesting, funny, agreeable, radical, enjoyable, frightening, or boring. One may scan an article or a book for some specific information, such as names and dates or a description of an event of historical importance. A letter from a friend or relative may be studied with an eye toward noting any subtle indication that the writer's attitude about the recipient has changed. The survey researcher scans the comments made by interviewees for emerging viewpoints and mention of contextual factors not easily assessed by the questionnaire's fixed-response alternatives. Though it would be dull to suggest that reading is really nothing more than a form of content analysis, this point is true enough so that the term *content analysis* should not be clouded by mystery.

Of course there are major differences between casual reading and formal content analysis. Content analysts must systematically apply an objective set of rules to the messages under scrutiny, while readers can be much less rigid and less explicit about their manner of perusing a document. Berelson's influential definition of content analysis makes this point clearly: "Content analysis is a research technique for the objective, systematic, and quantitative description of the manifest content of communication." (Berelson, 1952; 18).

The requirements conveyed by the words *systematic* and *objective* are part of the requirements of any science. Without these requirements replication of procedures and informed evaluations of assumptions would be impossible. While the human memory is such that the reader may best recall what was most salient or what was read last, the content analyst systematically assigns controlled weightings to text, uncovering patterns that might otherwise go unnoticed.

A more recent definition of content analysis was developed jointly by Stone and his associates and Holsti: "Content analysis is any technique for making inferences by objectively and systematically identifying specified characteristics of messages" (Holsti, 1969; Stone, 1966). Again we find emphasis placed on objectivity and system. However, unlike Berelson's inclusion of quantification, this definition does not make counting an absolute necessity, nor does it specify that only the *manifest* content of a message is appropriate for content analysis.[1]

Another important feature of Stone's and Holsti's definition is their statement that content analysis is a research *technique for making inferences*. Stated simply, this means that content analysis is undertaken in order to reach a conclusion about something related to the researcher's interest. Often the inferences are in the direction of enabling the investigator to make a statement about the source of the content-analyzed message—e.g., "Based on the pattern of word associations we judge the patient to be in an acute state of schizophrenia." In other research designs conclusions are made about the antecedents of (or conditions that led to) a certain configuration of results—e.g., "The historical pattern of predominant value concerns follows a repeated sequence over the last century in England and America that partially reflects economic cycles." More rarely, inferences are made in the direction of the effects of a message—e.g., "Anti-smoking advertisements that make repeated and direct references to death are less effective than those suggesting a curtailment of sexual activity." It will be evident that problems of inference penetrate content-analysis research directly or indirectly at nearly every stage of an investigation.[2]

The systematic feature of content analysis is important in using content analysis for policy decisions. For example, an analysis was made of a new Mississippi state history manuscript, comparing it with the ninth grade textbook already adopted by the State. The analysis found the new manuscript gave a more equitable portrayal of Blacks; however it also found that the new manuscript gave considerably less attention to women, so that a revision was warranted. As we will see, a computer has the advantage of systematically checking many features at once, so that an investigator may take note of aspects of the text that otherwise would have gone unanalyzed. Moreover, systematic content analyses are just as likely to uncover an absence or fading away of a theme as well as a new emergence; for example, Johnson et al (1971) have used content analysis to study "black invisibility," or the absence of news about Blacks in the press compared to Whites, and argue that the impact of invisibility in creating urban dissatisfaction makes it a significant policy issue.

THE COMPUTER AS AN EFFICIENT CLERK

Imagine yourself as having been given the responsibility of counting the number of times hostility toward other countries is expressed in the Sunday editorials of five leading United States newspapers from 1970 to 1980. The editorials have been collected, and you are faced with between four and five million words of text to read. The first task is to decide what kinds of expressions are to be included as hostile statements. "The recent atrocities of the Viet Cong are sufficient cause for an all-out effort to destroy the enemy" would be a clear enough statement, but the sentence "The United States government has expressed disappointment over France's continued sale of weapons to potentially hostile forces" is less forceful and may be the source of some ambiguity. Some steps are taken to resolve instances of ambiguity, and after considerable preparation you begin to read the editorials. The editorials are interesting enough to keep the task above the threshold of boredom for the first few days, but gradually you become lethargic, drink more coffee, and begin to complain to your friends about your job. At first you were conscientious about your assignment, pondering ambiguous statements and examining your rules for inclusion before making decisions, but now you realize that there are so many decisions to be made that one or two (or 80 or 90) misclassifications will not be disastrous—and besides, who will ever know? It has occurred to you that had someone else been given the job, the results would probably be somewhat different anyway. Your final emotion may be one of anger at your employers for giving you such a tedious job in the first place.

Eventually the job is completed; the results are interesting but inconclusive. Your employers have looked over the results, and a few new ideas have occurred to them. These include going back over the editorials and locating expressions of conciliation, appeasement, and friendship plus recording the names of the countries that are the objects of the friendly and hostile attitudes. At this point it occurs to you that even if you were to agree to begin again, there is no guarantee that after another month's work your employers will be satisfied—they may well suggest a new set of variables for another round of reading.

Without belaboring this example, our major point has been made; most content-analysis tasks are time-consuming, tedious, unexciting, demanding, dull, hateful, and boring.

In the early part of the 1960s it occurred to some researchers that computers could take over some of the more tedious tasks, and a new era for content analysis was launched. To understand how computers can be helpful one should know a little about the general capabilities of the machines for handling textual materials. At the risk of offending those knowledgeable about computers, and with the assurance that no living or deceased clerk is in any way being depicted, we find it convenient to compare basic computer operations with the skills of an efficient but unintelligent filing clerk. To elaborate, imagine an individual who is capable of recognizing certain kinds of information, filing it, moving that information from file to file, retrieving it when it is called for, and in addition is able to add and subtract. What makes this person special is the fact that he (or she) can perform these operations with almost unbelievable speed and efficiency. The clerk's major drawback is the fact that none of those operations can be accomplished without very specific instructions from a supervisor. The clerk must be taught everything in great detail, and the supervisor must specify every movement with precise instructions in a language that the clerk understands, or else the employee will become confused, make mistakes, run around in interminable circles, or just give up.

The analogy with computers should be clear. The clerk becomes a computer, the supervisor becomes programmer, and the detailed set of instructions to the clerk become a program. All computers are not replicas of one another and that some have certain capacities others do not possess. So we ask the reader who has an image of one kind of clerk to make that image more flexible to include clerks of various sizes, shapes, and areas of greatest efficiency.

One of the simplest but most tedious content-analysis tasks that can be done slowly by hand and rapidly by computer is locating and counting specific words. Returning to our earlier example of the analyses of editorials, if it was decided that the occurrence of the words *war, battle, revenge, enemy, insurgents* (etc.) could be used as foolproof indicators of hostility toward other countries (a dubious assumption, to be sure), a computer could be programmed to recognize these words and to count the number of times they occur in each of the 2500 editorials. It could then be programmed to compute relative frequencies, controlling for newspapers, time, or whatever. Of course, in addition to programming the computer to recognize these words and pass over all others, the researcher would have to see to it that the editorials were transformed into symbols recognizable to the computer (e.g., patterns of holes in IBM cards or spots on a magnetic surface). The transformation is not performed without cost, but once completed, the gain is substantial. That is, the investigator could revise the list of words, program the computer to recognize and count the new ones, reprocess the editorials, and receive the results all in a few hours or days.

Often a content analysis is interested in the occurrence of more than just a few words. For example, consider the possibility of the editorial study growing to the point where 1400 words have now been identified as part of the investigation. The computer is programmed to count the number of times each word has been used in the many documents, and the results are printed. The researcher is now confronted with a cumbersome and bewildering array of results and wonders whether the data have been reduced (an initial aim) or expanded! Struggling through the printout, the researcher begins to cluster certain words together on the basis of meanings they have in common. Though the meanings assigned to some words may deviate from standard conceptions, the researcher assumes that, *for the purpose of this investigation*, the meanings are satisfactory. For example, one interest is in words that denote limitation of action. Among others, the researcher has located the words *arrest, bind, encircle, restrict*, and *surround*. These words are listed together under a category that might be named CONTROL. Other categories are generated, and eventually the 1,400 words are placed in 55 or 60 categories. Each category now makes up a *variable* in the researcher's theory, and together these categories may be called a *content-analysis dictionary*.

The computer is now programmed to store the 1,400 entry words along with their definitions (i.e., the categories to which the investigator has assigned them.) As the text is processed, each word is looked up in the dictionary, and if it has been assigned a definition, the score for the defining category is incremented by one. Now, instead of printing scores for each word, only the total score for each category may be printed for every document, making the data much more manageable.

The procedure of assigning words or phrases to content-analysis categories is the central feature of a computer system for content analysis called *The General Inquirer*. (Stone et al, 1966). This system will be our focus during the remainder of this chapter. To repeat what has been said above, the important elements of this system include *entry words* that are described by *content-analysis categories* (frequently called *tags*). The categories represent *variables* of an investigator's *theory*.[3] Together the categories make up a *content-analysis dictionary*.

Some other features of *The General Inquirer* should be described at this point. After documents have been processed (i.e., after each word has been looked up in a content-analysis dictionary by the computer), the results can be listed in one of several forms. For one, an investigator may want to receive a listing of all sentences plus a record of all tags (definitions) applied to words in each sentence. Or that operation can be bypassed, and the researcher can go straight to the "tag tally" procedure, whereby all tags applied to each document are totaled. These results can be printed on paper and/or submitted directly to computer programs that perform various statistical operations—such as correlations, t-tests, analysis of variance, etc. Finally, the researcher may desire to look at only those sentences to which a certain configuration or sequence of tags have been applied. In such cases the computer can be instructed to retrieve all sentences that match the specifications.

It should be understood that all these computer operations *could* be accomplished by hand. But among the obvious advantages of programming a computer to perform those menial tasks is its exceptional speed. Given the correct conditions (i.e., no programming errors and accurate keypunching and preparation of text) the computer is completely reliable in its matching of text words to dictionary entry words, whereas a human scorer is very likely to make mistakes. Finally, a distinct advantage of the General Inquirer computer-content system is its capacity to assist—force—an investigator to follow the dictates of *objectivity*. That is, the definition of words is an objective task; once it is accomplished, the investigator can be assured that the computer will *systematically* apply the definitions to all texts submitted.

Sloppy Dictionaries and the Problem of Mechanical Limitations

Though computers are magnificent servants, not only is their intelligence limited by the degree of imagination of their masters, but, due to their nature computers often restrict their masters' capabilities. This is especially true in the context of dictionary construction. The pleasure derived from the possibility of giving different words the same definition and thereby reducing data to a more manageable size is countered by at least two worrisome facts. First, the meanings of many common words change according to the context in which they are used. Second, the assumptions involved in grouping certain words under a single definition (a) may not be made explicit and (b) may not be valid. Recent versions of the Inquirer incorporate workable procedures that for most practical purposes resolve much of the semantic context problem. The latter problem of assumptions involved in dictionary construction will be discussed here.

Nearly everyone admires simple conceptual elegance. Some General Inquirer dictionary makers have constructed category systems that, on the surface, order the world in a delightfully elegant way. It was noted earlier that dictionary tags or categories represent variables of an investigator's theory. Ideally, the hypothesized relationships among variables are specified. For descriptions of three dictionaries that were developed from different perspectives and justified according to reasonably logical systems of thought, the reader is referred to chapter 5 of *The General Inquirer* (Stone, 1966).

When one gets beyond the categories themselves and takes a detailed look at the words that constitute them, the real problems emerge. To make these problems vivid we shall explore a study and discuss the findings, first in the context of a few tag scores, second in the context of the words that define these tags.

As part of a larger study of delinquency an investigator studied a depression-elation pattern that he argued was part of the psychology of delinquent gangs. His data were gathered in two parts. First he asked each gang member, in private, to make up stories to describe the thoughts and actions of persons depicted in thematic apperception pictures that are open to a variety of interpretations. He then brought the gang members together and asked the entire group to make individual contributions to a collective story about the same stimuli.

These data were then prepared for computer content analysis, and then the researcher processed them using a dictionary that had been written by another content analyst but included several categories relevant to the present researcher's focal concern. Important among these tags were two: SIGN-EXCITEMENT and SIGN-DEPRESSION.

The researcher hypothesized that, when alone, individual gang members are depressed; the purpose of the gang is to relieve this depressed state by engaging in a group search for excitement and thrills. Therefore, individual stories should include many words defined by SIGN-DEPRESSION. By contrast, group compositions should change this pattern, giving a significant boost on SIGN-EXCITEMENT scores.

The results supported this hypothesis and in addition revealed another pattern of interest. When individual contributions to the collective stories were separated and compared with the stories composed by the same individuals in private, it was discovered that gang leaders showed the most dramatic shifts from SIGN-DEPRESSION words in private stories to SIGN-EXCITE-MENT words in group stories. The researcher concluded that gang leaders are best able to express the depressed side of their personalities or are in fact the most depressed. In group situations these same individuals are best able to deny their depression and take the lead in the expression of excitement.

The interpretation of the results in this content-analysis study is not without interest, for it both has an intuitive appeal and is rich enough to generate additional research ideas. One could say with some certainty that it is "publishable"—our hallmark of acceptability.

But when we look beneath the surface of the summary findings and read the words actually defining the tags SIGN-EXCITEMENT and SIGN-DEPRES-SION, we are confronted by unsettling information. (These words appear in Table 1.) First, one must agree that the gestalts that emerge from the two lists are very different. Unfortunately they are not the opposites we had assumed they would be on the basis of what is conveyed by their titles. Instead, nearly all the words under SIGN-EXCITEMENT are adjectives that describe the grand nature of an object or event. Immensity of size, the greatness or unusual quality of something, are apparently assumed to be indicative of an aroused state on the part of the user of such symbols. This may be true, but it needs to be demonstrated. A *swell* guy, a *superb* meal, a *giant* redwood, a *perfect* sphere, an *outstanding* performance, a *massive* traffic jam, can be exciting things, but they may not be related, even indirectly, to an emotional state. In fairness to the analyst who constructed this category it should be noted that the "sign" part of SIGN-EXCITEMENT may

Table 1.   Words Tagged Sign-Excitement and Sign-Depression.

Sign-Excitement		Sign-Depression		
dizzy	novelty	afraid	helplessly	sadden
ecstasy	outstanding	anguish	hopeless	sadness
enormous	perfect	burden	hopelessly	scare
exaltation	sensational	crave	impossible	scaring
exotic	splendid	cried	insecure	shock
extraordinary	splendor	cry	insecurity	sob
extreme	startling	deject	lack	sorrow
fantastic	strange	depress	lament	sorrowful
giant	stupendous	dependence	lamentation	sorry
gigantic	superb	dependency	lone	suffer
glorious	supreme	dependent	lonely	tragedy
grand	swell	depression	loneliness	tragic
great	terrific	despondent	lost	unhappy
greater	unusual	desire	melancholy	unhappiness
greatest	vibrant	despair	miserable	upset
greatness	vivid	disgust	misery	vulnerable
immense	weird	distress	mourn	vulnerability
magnificent	wild	downcast	panic	weak
marvel	wildness	exhaust	passive	weakness
marvelous	wonderful	fatigue	regret	weary
massive		fear	regretful	weep
		gleam	relieve	wept
		gloomy	remorse	woe
		grief	remorseful	woeful
		grieve	sad	yearn
		helpless		

have been intended to convey the connotative nature of the category. As it stands, however, the increase in SIGN-EXCITEMENT words in group storytelling may be a measure of gang members' tendencies to exaggerate in the company of one another.

Having now become more familiar with the first tag, we expect to find the words defined by SIGN-DEPRESSION to be at approximately the same level of abstraction. But they are not. Instead, most of the words (e.g., *miserable, sad, unhappy, despair*) are close to synonymous with depression and therefore are more denotative than connotative.

The entire study is now in a rather confused state, whereas before it seemed clear and intellectually satisfying. Had the study actually been more fully completed (and some studies of unknowing but equally deceptive and therefore poor quality have been carried out), the author may well have proceeded to the second line of issues referred to at the beginning of this chapter without having resolved absolutely fundamental issues. In summary, let the reader be forewarned that increased manipulative power, intelligent use of computer output options, sophisticated statistical transformations, and similar technical innovations are meaningless if categories are poorly constructed and words are inappropriately and inconsistently defined. There are many ways to handle garbage. It can be slopped into an open bed truck and sloshed into a dump or it can be scented with perfume, wrapped in clean bags, tied with a bow, and disposed of mechanically. The end products may impress you differently, but trash is still trash.

It should be noted that most dictionaries are more carefully constructed than the one used in the above example. But more satisfactory dictionaries are not end-alls in content-analysis work. In fact, researchers who know their dictionary and use most words appropriately may convince themselves that they need no longer look at the text being tagged. Instead, they may feel that they can concentrate on the tallies and interpret their findings (or make inferences) solely from summary scores. In carefully controlled research this sometimes falls within the range of satisfactory procedures. But often, however, tag-tally output provides investigators with a kind of projective test on which they can exercise their imaginative skills—convincing themselves all along that they are conducting scientific research.

A case study of a college student recorded in chapter 13 of *The General Inquirer* provides an example of the kinds of error that can be made when tag tallies are the sole referents or inferences. Briefly summarized, a student with a pseudonym Windle was a participant in a course on small groups. The course was organized in such a manner that its members were responsible for bringing up and discussing topics of interest to themselves and others and from time to time discussing their own processes of becoming a group. Throughout the year the interactions among members were scored by observers using a system called Interaction Process Analysis developed by Bales (1959).

When Windle's interaction scores were compared with the scores of other group members, it was discovered that he (1) showed more positivity than others, (2) agreed a much greater number of times, (3) was not dominant, (4) submitted to others frequently, and (5) expressed little negativity. The author of the study summarized these findings in the following manner:

[Based on the subject's pattern of interactions scores], he looks like an agreeable, pleasant person. . . He appears to be submissive and non-obtrusive. It is probably easy to get him to go along with just about anything. In fact, he has a self-admitted need to be liked, to be one of the boys. His attempt to be liked comes out in the form of a general orientation to please the other person. (p. 456).

In addition to accumulating interaction scores for the students in Windle's group, each member had agreed to provide a research team with short reports written after each group meeting. The students were given freedom to discuss a wide range of topics. Most often they described their feelings about the group or about an individual member, the relevance of an assigned case or reading to events in the group, or their thoughts about the instructor's comments or lack of comments. In Windle's case these data provided the researcher with the opportunity of further describing and exploring evidences of his apparently strong desire to be liked.

With little more than a search for congruity with the pattern of his interaction scores to guide the investigation, Windle's reports were content analyzed by the General Inquirer and compared with content analyses of the other member's reports.

The dictionary used at the time for this study was the Harvard Third Psycho-Sociological Dictionary. Several years of work had been put into this dictionary, and it had survived (and had been improved by) a considerable number of debates engaged in by a number of contributors from diverse disciplines. This dictionary characterized 3,504 words by one or more of 83 tags. Among other areas, the tags covered divisions of roles (e.g., AFFECTION, ANGER), actions (e.g., APPROACH, AVOID, COMMUNICATE), institutions (ECONOMIC, RELIGIOUS), and psychological themes (STRENGTH, WEAKNESS, AUTHORITY). It had been used extensively by researchers. For example it had been central to analyses of presidential acceptance speeches, social change in small groups, psychotic language, suicide notes, and various studies of literature.

Compared to the tag scores of the other group members, Windle consistently used more words defined by SELF (e.g., *I*, *me*), MESSAGE-FORM (e.g., *art*, *book*), AROUSAL, (e.g., *awaken*, *felt*), DISTRESS (e.g., *alarm*, *conflict*), COMMUNICATE (e.g., *answer*, *tell*), ATTACK (e.g., *annoy*, *beat*), AVOID (e.g., *abandon*, *absent*), SIGN-STRONG (e.g., *powerful*, *sturdy*), SIGN-WEAK (e.g., *shy*, *postpone*), and SIGN-REJECT (e.g., *anger*, *jealous*). Windle's high scores on AROUSAL, DISTRESS, ATTACK, AVOID, SIGN-STRONG, and SIGN-REJECT were viewed with particular alarm, and the author of the study states:

Here we are confronted with a list of tags that could not possibly have been applied to words from the pen of Windle. What has happened to IDEAL-VALUE, AFFECTION, PLEASURE, GOOD, APPROACH, and FOLLOW? Certainly they would be more congruent with our record of his pleasant, agreeing, and submissive external behavior . . . (but soon enough, the incongruity is resolved. Windle is compensating for his submissiveness, for being pushed around, by attacking the other group members. Secretly he despises them. Underneath his pleasant mask he is seething with anger and he expresses his revenge in his reports.

Again, like the interpretation of results in the delinquency study, this interpretation has a certain amount of charm. Perhaps it's not quite publishable, but it would warrant a decent grade on a course paper. At this point the author of the study appears to have succumbed to the inviting temptation of never having to look at his raw data again.[4]

When the results are looked at in some detail, the first inference is discovered to be erroneous. This more careful scrutiny of the results is greatly assisted by the retrieval portion of the General Inquirer package of computer programs. Under the guidance of appropriate instructions the computer will locate and print all sentences that contain characteristics specified by the researcher. These characteristics include words, phrases, coded portions of text, and tags in any combination. For example, with respect to the above "seething anger" inference, retrieving sentences including words tagged by SIGN-REJECT should be informative. Expecting to find sentences like "My *anger* today was intolerable" or "I *reject* Mark's stupid remark" we confront statements like:

The group had been *rebelling* against Steve.
Then Burgess finally suggested we *"kick* him *out"* of next week's meeting.
As if, as Dr. . . . put it, we were considering the remains of a *deposed* God.
The analytic forces *criticized* him today.

Instead of finding slashing attacks on others, the sentences with words defined by SIGN-REJECT are written more in the context of reporting the day's events—"the group rebels," "analytical forces criticized," etc.

Noting that Windle not only obtained higher scores on some individual tags but also could be distinguished from other group members through his use of sentences tagged by certain combinations of tags, sentences containing these specific tag combinations were retrieved. For example, two sets of retrievals were composed, such that the computer located and printed all sentences with words tagged by ACADEMIC and AVOID (set 1) and SELF and AROUSAL (set 2). Table 2 lists examples of the sentences retrieved.

From the first set of retrievals we note a rather compulsive concern over the cases used as teaching devices in the course. Again the "seething anger" inference finds little to support it. Any anger that is expressed is in the form of criticism of those who block case discussion, of those who lead the group away from case analysis.

In the second set of retrievals it is evident that variations of the words *felt* and *feeling* are responsible for most increments in Windle's total score on the tag AROUSAL. In fact 24 of the 28 retrievals on SELF, AROUSAL, were matched by reason of the appearance of *feel* and its variations, plus references to self. Had retrievals not been made, we might have assumed Windle had used words like *arouse, impulsive, excited, restless, energetic,* and so forth. Instead, Windle chose to tell the researchers how he felt, how his feelings fluctuated with changing events.

Juxtaposing the requirements of the course with these two sets of retrievals it is noticed that Windle's central concerns matched special features of the course. That is, students were expected to (1) benefit educationally from the discussion of human relations case material and (2)

Table 2. Sample Sentence Retrievals

Sample Retrievals on ACADEMIC, AVOID

The group succeeded in *avoiding* the *case* for 40 minutes.

The *absence* of five members of the group produced the topic of *discussion* of today's meeting.

In my opinion we were actually *avoiding* the *cases*, the *reading*, etc.

Some members of the group desire to *escape* from the tasks of the course and to *avoid* being confronted with the great amount of *knowledge*.

Their *discussion* was *avoiding* the type of conversation and *analysis* I am interested in relation to this course.

Today, however, I did feel that more people . . . agreed with me and shared my frustration and annoyance toward Steve for his continued *avoidance* of case *analysis*.

Sample Retrievals on SELF and AROUSAL

And it is the same *feeling* or worry about exclusion that makes *me* fear my own absence.

I *felt* a sudden pang of guilt at what I had done.

I may have *felt* I had let him down.

I *felt* a tremendous degree of relief.

My feeling today was again one of frustration.

I *felt* disgust at myself and the rest of the group.

become more aware of their feelings. After systematically retrieving Windle's statements, then ordering and comparing them with the reports of other members, it becomes increasingly apparent that Windle generalized his desire to be accepted by writing passages that demonstrated his attempt to follow the dictates of the course. The author of this study concurs when he writes.

Our earlier "seething anger" hypothesis can now be viewed as the result of faulty inference. We had inferred that Windle's documents contained the results of frustrating submission, false positivity and superficial pleasantness. But in retrospect we wonder why we expected his interpersonal tactics to be different in the two situations. He wanted to be liked by his fellow group members. He also wanted to be viewed as a good cooperative likable student by the researchers. A more thorough consideration of the situation might have made us more aware of the level at which Windle would approach his writing task. (p. 466)

The reader should be made aware that the above example of an inference made with insufficient information is one of several that could have been selected. Of course the problem of poor (in some cases just plain wrong) inferences is especially severe in descriptive studies—studies in which no predictions are made in advance—for the temptation to describe a little and speculate a lot (and call the speculations "findings" or "results") is attractive in a young science. Content analysis is particularly well suited for descriptive studies, and there is no reason why such studies should not hold a respected position in every science. But descriptive studies must be done well, and this requires that data reduction be performed with utmost care and constant monitoring.

Sequential Co-occurrence of Tags (The Approximation of Meaning)

All the examples of content analysis studies referred to thus far have made inferences on the basis of the relative frequency with which various text characteristics have appeared within the documents studied. The assumption underlying these studies (in fact, the assumption underlying most existing content-analysis studies) is that frequency is a measure of degree of concern or importance. But there are some highly developed content-analysis scoring systems that do not rely so completely on frequency. One system of this type partly duplicated by a computer program is the Need Achievement scoring system developed by McClelland et al. (1953).

One reason for describing portions of this system is that it represents a partial solution to the problem of basing inferences on tag scores without intimate knowledge of the context in which tagged words are being used. In the case of Windle, just described, this problem was handled by retrieving and reading sentences that could support or not support the initial inference concerning Windle's supposed expression of hostility. Another way to deal with this problem is to specify word or tag sequences that identify the themes under investigation. Each portion of the predetermined sequence must be present before evidence that the theme actually exists is considered sufficient.

For example, one of McClelland's criteria for scoring the presence of achievement imagery in brief stories composed to projective stimuli is stated in the following manner:

One of the characters is involved in attainment of a long term achievement goal. Being a success in life, becoming a machinist, doctor, lawyer, successful businessman, and so forth, are all examples of career involvement which permit the inference of competition with a standard of excellence. (p. 113).

Examples of sentences that fulfill this one requirement include: "The boy desires to become a famous surgeon," "Esther is dreaming of becoming the first woman supreme court justice," "Greg wants nothing more than to become a world decathlon champion.

In every sentence there is an expression of a NEED (*desires, dreaming,*) combined with TO-BE (become, becoming) and ROLE-POSITIVE (*supreme court justice, world decathlon champion).* Part of the computer simulation of the hand scoring method is based on this sequence. Tags labeled NEED, TO-BE, ROLE-POSITIVE were used to define words such as those appearing in the parentheses above. When the computer locates these tags in the appropriate order, the story is scored for achievement imagery. If just one or two of the tags are used to define words in a sentence, the sentence is not scored for achievement. If this were not the case, sentences like: "He *wants* (NEED) to see the *doctor* (ROLE-POSITIVE)" or "She expressed no interest in *becoming* (TO-BE) a well known *musician* (ROLE-POSITIVE)" would be scored when they clearly fall outside the boundaries of achievement related imagery.

The 14 tags and nine rules combining them that were developed for the computer scoring system appear in Tables 3 and 4. An example of a story processed and printed by the program is given in Table 5. Even though quite elementary, this scheme of pattern evaluation produced high correlations with ratings made by independent scores for the thematic apperception test.

The requirement that two or more different tags appear in a strict order before achievement imagery is considered to be present decreases the damage done by mistagging ambiguous words. For example, the word *train* is classified as VERB-POSITIVE in the Achievement dictionary. This means that every time the noun *train* is used, it is mistagged. But no harm is done unless *train* is followed by a word tagged ADVERB-POSITIVE—e.g., "He would *train* (VERB-POSITIVE) *conscientiously* (ADVERB-POSITIVE) for every track meet."

However, it is not safe to assume that an appropriate string of tags corrects all errors caused by occasional mistagging due to word ambiguity.

Table 3.   Tag Names and Sample Words.

Tags	Examples	Number
NEED	wants, desires, hopes, yearns	57
TO-BE	become, becoming, to become	6
COMPETE	win, pain, overtake, surpass	28
VERB-POSITIVE	doing, making, inventing, working	136
ADVERB-POSITIVE	carefully, properly, cautiously, thoroughly	50
ADJECTIVE-POSITIVE	great, powerful, promising, splendid	166
VALUE-POSITIVE	discovery, creation, curiosity, intelligence	142
ROLE-POSITIVE	surgeon, lawyer, executive, professor	38
BLOCK	broken, damage, crises	53
SUCCESS	fame, success, glory, honor	23
FAILURE	error, incorrect, mistake, blunder	43
AFFECT-POSITIVE	joy, happy, cheerful, delighted	27
AFFECT-NEGATIVE	sad, anxious, sorry, worried	82
TIME	lifetime, life, years, weeks	4

Table 4.   Summary of Rules.

Rule 1:   NEED + COMPETE

"He wants to present a clear-cut synthesis of these two conflicting philosophies, to satisfy his own ego and gain academic recognition from his professor."

Rule 2:   SUCCESS + AFFECT-POSITIVE (within-and cross-sentence routine)

"The worker wanted fame and got it. He died a happy man."

Rule 3:   FAILURE + AFFECT-NEGATIVE (within-and cross-sentence routine)

"The invention will be a failure. Discouraged and financially bankrupt, the man will drown himself with liquor."

Rule 4:   VERB-POSITIVE + ADVERB-POSITIVE

"The operator is hoping that everything will pan out properly."

Rule 5:   VERB-POSITIVE + VALUE-POSITIVE

"The first man wants to get it fixed and do a good job."

Rule 6:   ADJECTIVE-POSITIVE + VALUE-POSITIVE

"He will wander from this steadfast purpose but eventually achieve it."

Rule 7:   NEED + TO-BE + ROLE-POSITIVE

"For a long time he has wanted to become a mechanic."

Rule 8:   NEED + TO-BE + ADJECTIVE-POSITIVE

"All he wanted was to become great at something."

Rule 9:   TO-BE + SUCCESS (last sentence routine)

"Mutual compromise and the machine will be a success."

The sentence "He *concentrated* (VERB-POSITIVE) daily and years later unveiled a high *quality* (VALUES-POSITIVE) painting," fulfills Rule 5 (Table 4) and is correctly identified as containing achievement imagery. But to our embarrassment the following portion of a punch recipe would satisfy the same rule: "Finally one cup of concentrated (VERB-POSITIVE) lemon juice will give the mixture a *quality* (VALUES-POSITIVE) certain to be preferred by your more rugged guests."

It would make a computer content analyst's life much simpler if all dictionary entries could unconditionally assign text words to content categories or tags, i.e., if the word *train* always referred to a series of attached cars with metal wheels pulled by a locomotive on two parallel rails, we could get on to more important practical and theoretical problems; or, if the word *concentrated* was always used in the context of "thinking about or working

Table 5. Example of Story Scored AI.

Sentence 1:
"The student is *dreaming* about *becoming* a *great inventor*." — NEED TO-BE ADJECTIVE-POSITIVE ROLE-POSITIVE SENTENCE SUM = AI

Sentence 2:
"After *years* of *labor* the crucial moment arrives." — TIME VERB-POSITIVE SENTENCE SUM = UI

Sentence 3:
"He *hopes* everything will *turn out well*." — NEED VERB-POSITIVE ADVERB-POSITIVE SENTENCE SUM = AI

Sentence 4:
"But the *experiment* will *fail*." — VALUE-POSITIVE FAILURE SENTENCE SUM = UI

Sentence 5:
"*Displeased* but still *confident* he will modify his procedures and try again." — AFFECT-NEGATIVE VALUE-POSITIVE SENTENCE SUM = AI

°°°°°SUMMARY+++++THIS DOCUMENT CONTAINS ACHIEVEMENT IMAGERY.

---

hard on something," we could rid ourselves of the gnawing concern about lemon juice. But lexical ambiguity abounds in all natural languages and cannot be ignored by computer content analysts.

To make matters worse, the word sense of interest to the content analyst is often not the most frequent usage. For example, an investigator may be interested in the use of the word *kind* as in "he is a kind man", but in fact it usually means "sort" or "degree" as in "a kind of evergreen tree" or "kind of lazy".

Consequently, recent versions of the General Inquirer have added sophisticated subroutines for disambiguating the meanings of over 1,000 common, multiple-meaning English words. The strategies for accomplishing this, based on searching word context, are too involved to be reported here, but they are described completely in Kelly and Stone (1975). Once developed, the procedures were statistically validated by testing them on a large new corpus of text representing many kinds of language usage. For each homograph, a helpful, improved accuracy gain, of known average magnitude, is attained in assigning descriptors.

Such increased accuracy in assigning descriptors, however, is only for common elements of English as they appear in most spoken and written productions. Additional problems occur when the research compares productions from different sociolinguistic communities, where some words may be used in ways quite different from what a general content-analysis dictionary writer anticipated. Similarly, if the study involves samples drawn from over a long time period, for the purpose of analyzing time trends, there is also the problem of language change. Some words referring to features of the political system or to social processes are especially likely to have relatively short periods of being in vogue. A salient feature may be missed by the computer because the investigator did not carefully check to ensure that such words were correctly indexed in the content-analysis dictionary.

Our examples of potential trouble spots at different points in the content-analysis chain of inference, together with ways to keep them in check, have focused on individual productions. Studies at this level may be predominantly concerned with whether the content analysis truly reflects the conscious intentions and unconscious motives, as well as the cognitive style, of the particular speaker or writer. If studies instead make inferences to a society, then there is an effort to bypass the idiosyncracies of one or a few individuals; documents from many different writers instead may be pooled to represent a sector of society at a particular time. For example, if the documents are newspaper editorials or song lyrics, then care may be taken so as not to avoid sampling too much from one newspaper or one songwriter. Indeed, for some purposes the number of cases in each sample (that is, the "N" used in statistical tests) may well be the number of different sources in each sample rather than, say, the number of editorials or songs. Even so, the cases within a sample may hardly be independent, for the editorial writer at paper X may have been trained at paper Y, and so on. The content-analysis investigator must wrestle continually with these problems of inference and should clearly report the choices taken.

THE INQUIRER AS AN EVOLVING SYSTEM

Over the years, newer versions of the Inquirer tend to offer expanded routines for increasing assignment accuracy as well as enlarged sets of categories and entry words. A recent dictionary contains 5,714 entry words, compared to the 3,564 words of its predecessor; more important, the addition of disambiguation makes for over 8,700 different words or word senses. In considering the number of tag categories associated with each dictionary entry word or word sense, the dictionary represents over 40,000 decisions. In general an attempt has been made to be more conservative and cautious, thus avoiding some of the categorization problems exemplified in the analyses of delinquent gangs or the study of Windle; yet obviously an analytic tool of this size will require years of testing and revision. This recent general dictionary, developed by D.C. Dumphy and associates at the University of New South Wales, is called the Harvard IV; its further revisions are indicated by a following number—for example, Harvard IV-4.

Prior editions of the Inquirer content-analysis system were constrained by the computers then available. Earlier computers were designed for manipulating numbers more than text materials. Computer memories were limited, thus constraining dictionary size.* Today dictionaries of 10,000 or 20,000 or more entries are quite feasible; the main restriction is the fatigue of the dictionary designer. After a dictionary contains four or five thousand entries, we know from Zipf's word frequency law (1945) that many additional entries are needed in order to obtain slightly better coverage, unless the investigator knows that certain infrequent words will be common in the texts being studied. Similarly, further disambiguation rules could be added for ambigous low-frequency words, but many such rules would be needed to increase accuracy significantly. In any open-ended task like this, there comes a time when the designers call a halt and leave further improvements to others, especially when a moderate size endeavor can accurately cover 95% or more of the text.

Although the availability of the disambiguation and an enlarged dictionary permit a finer-grained mapping of text words into tags, it cannot be emphasized too strongly that this new tool must be used just as cautiously as anything else in the system. Investigators are not thereby absolved of their duty to return constantly to the raw data; indeed, the analytic interplay between data and theory-building is a fundamental requirement in all good scientific work.

FUTURE CONTENT-ANALYSIS CHALLENGES

Most computer-aided content-analysis studies to date have been concerned with samples of text selected to test hypotheses. In most cases, the samples were fairly limited in size, mainly because all the text had to be keypunched on IBM cards.

Now reconsider the task of our content analyst bent on measuring hostility toward other countries as expressed in the Sunday editorials of five leading U.S. newspapers from 1970 to 1980. Suppose that instead of specific measures to test hypotheses, we wanted social indicators describing how tabloid and elite newspapers, both daily and Sunday, in different sections of the country have changed in hostility toward each major foreign country over the past 70 years? Certainly the size of the task would fatigue a battery of keypunchers or cause the efficient content analyst clerk to seek another job.

As computers become more efficient but wages rise, the proportion of content-analysis budgets absorbed in manually transcribing documents to "machine-readable" formats (such as the IBM card or magnetic disk)

---

*Today, some pocket-sized electronic word translators for use by tourists have a larger dictionary storage on chip than the largest commonly available computer core memories permitted in the mid-1960s.

becomes larger. Unfortunately, the all-purpose optical readers to take over this task have not yet appeared. Some machines, particularly those developed by Kurtzweil, Inc. are remarkably adept at reading a variety of printing fonts or even the poor reproduction quality of "third generation xerox." But they are just beginning to have the accuracy and low enough cost to make it practical for most research to put in books, newspapers, magazines, and the *Congressional Record* at one end and get our reels of magnetic tape at the other.

On the other hand there are machines that are quite adept at reading documents typed with a special typeball, first impression, on standard paper. Several recent content-analysis studies in Europe have used such typing to prepare materials for the computer, finding it easier both to make corrections and to prepare work at field sites. Often it might help greatly if documents that may be later used for content analysis (for example, interoffice memos for studies of information flows in organizational networks) could be prepared with such a typeball in the first place.

Another strategy that may be particularly useful in developing social indicators of communications content is to capture documents while they are machine readable as part of the publishing process. An increasing number of newspaper and other publishers now use the computer as part of the preparation process; reporters, for example, type their stories directly into the computer, and editors review them on a screen before they are electronically typeset. A project by Carroll DeWeese (1976) has captured the entire "news hole" of a major Detroit daily newspaper for over two years by tapping into this machine-readable stage.

For DeWeese's project the news hole was captured by setting up a minicomputer that pretended it was a second printing plant and received all stories sent for printing. This computer selected out the final "take" of what might be several transmissions and edited out many of the editors' directions specific to the final layout and printing. The minicomputer then stored the selected materials on magnetic tape for later content analysis.

As magnetic storage and retrieval costs decrease, we may expect more documents to be routinely archived in machine-readable form. Some newspaper wire services have already converted to archiving machine-readable formats and have made such archives available to communications researchers. *The New York Times* produces a machine-readable archive as part of their information services, summarizing information gleaned from newspapers around the world. Some large companies now use "electronic mail" for communications between different sites with automatic computer archiving as part of the process; entire computers have been dedicated, using computer communications networks, to the handling of such mail. Thus, rather than using the final typed or published documents, more researchers may turn to the machine-readable archive created as part of the production process.

Although the idea of creating systematic social indicators from communications content has been around for a number of years (see, for example, Stone, 1972), various national and international committees that have been set up to deal with social indicators have been unfortunately lethargic in spearheading any policies that would capture textual productions. More often than not, the machine-readable record is never created, or it disappears once the document is printed. Such important resources as the *Congressional Record* or the transcripts of foreign news broadcasts have continued for an unnecessarily long time to be prepared without a machine-readable record or to be printed in a way that makes optical reading unnecessarily difficult.

In most cases machine-readable formats do not just serve the needs of future researchers. Instead, they can also provide a basis for immediate automatic indexing, replacing manual procedures or making materials more useful. As electronically based word-processing systems become more common, the machine-readable record also simplifies preparing copy and making corrections. Thus, the all-purpose optical reader may soon be needed less than it once was, especially if machine-readable production becomes coordinated with some systematic machine-readable archiving.

One important focus of the recent evolution of the Inquirer has involved preparation for going beyond studying relatively small samples of text and instead towards creation and analysis of social indicators based on large volumes of communications content. In addition to improving technical capabilities, several studies have served as pilot explorations for developing indicators of changes over time or between different sectors of society.

Compared to much social indicator research, which tends to be weak on theory, indicators of communications content may in some cases have a better theoretical grounding. As mentioned in the editor's introduction to the next section of this volume, communications content may indicate a working through of phase sequences that reflect adaptive, productive, expressive, and integrative stages. Weber (1978) hypothesizes that the orderings of phase sequences are inherently likely to depend upon priorities of feedbacks, such that the order of phases differs in a multinational corporation, a democratic government, or a Marxist-Leninist organization. Following upon Namenwirth's (1973) uncovering of American value cycles using Lasswellian theory, Weber investigates phase sequences in England. Using British speeches from the throne between 1689 and 1972, he shows that the repeated phase order in the mercantilist era is quite different from that in the capitalist era and that each phase determines the terms by which current events tend to be interpreted.

In similar ways, many content-analysis studies may refer to a working through of phases, whether they are the problem-solving achievement sequences in children's readers, the sequence of power relations reflected in interoffice memos, changing forms of intimacy expressed in song lyrics, or the resolution of structural problems symbolized in tribal myths. In studying sequences of life cycles within a cohort or societal changes there may be somewhat similar strategies relating verbal productions to their contexts. Using Erik Olin Wright's (1978) terminology, the range of possible verbal productions may be constrained by "structural limitations," such as the economic system. Within this range further "selections" may occur as a result of other conditions within these limitations, such as the type of state. Whether there is continuation as is depends on "reproduction/nonreproduction" capabilities, as they prove compatible with different aspects of the situation; Wright considers ideology an integral factor in this process, both reflecting context and affecting selections within it. The content analyst, whether studying societal, organization, or life-cycle sequences, may look to textual productions as indicating approaches taken to working through problems, including what goals, motives, constraints, resources, opportunities, cognitive styles, and abilities are being given attention. Weber's study indeed illustrates how the contents reflected in textual productions may influence their own sequence of change, as Weber argues, directly transforming the situation or mediating transformation processes.

With such expanded analyses in mind the Inquirer system has been completely reprogrammed in newer computer languages for successive generations of computers, thus making earlier descriptions of technical procedures obsolete. A more recent effort has been made to embed the Inquirer procedures in a data-management and statistical processing environment, so that analysis of textual materials may be coordinated with other kinds of numerical processing (such as background information describing the documents or their contexts) and that files may be regrouped through sorting and merging. By making the disambiguating and tagging procedures efficient, their combined processing costs are under a twentieth of a cent per word, thus keeping open the possibilities for processing larger amounts of text.

While the availability of better procedures and higher speeds for computer content analysis should facilitate research, we continue to have fears that it will also promote a lot of bad, poorly thought-out data grinding. Today's alchemist in science is the person looking for the magic match between sets of data and data-analysis techniques. Often one sees the same set of data worked over by almost all the data-analysis techniques available at the local computing center. Today these alchemists submit their numbers to factor analysis, path analysis, small space analysis, tree procedures, etc., in the hopes that one of these methods will spell out the social science insight of the century.

When working with text, our alchemists are rarely interested in the tedious task of thinking through a theory and attempting to make the theory operational for content-analysis purposes. Instead, they argue, why not just *try* all the existing dictionaries and statistical techniques on their data? Who knows what pleasant surprise might result?

After seeing this kind of approach again and again, it can only be concluded that, despite the enthusiasm of the moment, the results are almost never worth the effort. Without theory many of the statistically significant results tend to be fortuitous. A certain number of statistically significant results can always be expected by chance, and users generally can select those they like from the thousands of numbers produced by the computer. Further, the issue in research is usually not the null hypothesis. Simply to say that the world is not random is not saying much.

THE MORE DISTANT FUTURE

At the beginning of this chapter we noted that people do an informal content analysis in their everyday reading and listening activities. So far we have described how the computer handles the formal counting aspects of this process. What about considering how the computer can be extended to be more like the human reader and listener? What do people do that computers don't?

One big difference, of course, is that the computer content-analysis system continues on and on without any change as a result of what has been previously analyzed. If you use a program again on the same data, you will get the same results, no matter what the computer program has been used for during the period in between. Passing over the data has no effect on the program. Of course, people are in a sense a cumulative product of their experience.

More recently there has been considerable interest in computers that improve themselves. The goal is to build up a cumulative store of information that will be relevant to making better analyses in the future. For example, 20 or 30 years from now, we might expect computers to write and continually modify their own disambiguation routines as well as make suggestive content analysis inferences based on their experience with other data. Initial investigations along this line have already been started by Schank and Abelson (1977) using artificial intelligence techniques to analyze certain kinds of stories as they come over the wire services. One caution however is in order. Even though such investigators in artificial intelligence such as Winograd (1972) have been able to create some sophisticated demonstrations, they are invariably effective for only a very limited domain of tasks. Artificial intelligence researchers have found again and again that it is necessary to provide an immense amount of "world knowledge" specific to a domain, in addition to general heuristics, in order to have an effective system.[5]

Another caution is that many artificial intelligence procedures use considerable amounts of computer time in order to accomplish their goals on a small amount of text. Eventually, computers may be so inexpensive that this will not make much difference, but at present the Inquirer has been designed to produce social indicators on large computers at speeds approaching 20,000 words of text per minute. Shure (1978) and his colleagues have borrowed Inquirer procedures and combined them with syntactic analysis capabilities developed by Woods (1970) in order to achieve additional thematic analysis capabilities for analyzing standardized political messages, thus illustrating the application of more advanced techniques (albeit at somewhat lower speeds) for certain relatively well defined tasks.

The main determinants of future directions, in our opinion, do not lie in technical capabilities as much as what investigators conceive to be the future goals for social science. Following the radical era of the late 1960's and early 1970's there has been less interest in analyzing the texts stemming from different sectors of society than in examining the material conditions constraining these sectors. Furthermore, instead of being a bridge between qualitative and quantitative research, content analysis has often been caught in a disfavored middle, as qualitative-oriented researchers eschew all numbers and quantitative-orientated researchers in some fields give priority to "hard data", especially from more experimental research designs. Then, too, content analysis has been caught up in the fortunes of the more comprehensive frameworks, with many investigators shying away from the theoretical bases provided by Freud, Parsons, Lasswell, or Levi-Strauss or the more empirical bases provided by Osgood or Bales and their colleagues.

Clearly reflecting the times, content-analysis studies of the 1970s, both of visual and written messages, have tended to take a renewed interest in issues of life-styles and interpersonal relationships. For visual messages, Goffman (1979) has studied gender relationships in advertisement photographs. For written materials, Aires (1973), for example, used the Inquirer to analyze transcripts of discussions by all-female, all-male, and mixed-sex groups to determine how the sexual composition of a group affects the ways it approaches and handles various topics, while Herbert (1976) followed this with a comparison of transcripts from black and from white working-class female discussion groups. Walker (1975) and Milburn (1979) examined changing models of interpersonal relationships as reflected in the texts of "top ten" songs in the American black and American general popular music markets over a decade. At Rice University, Gordon and colleagues created an elaborate special dictionary that focused on adjectives and phrases for analyzing descriptions of persons. This "person conception" dictionary is most typically used for situations where the respondent is given a stimulus such as, "I think of the U.S. President as . . ." or "I think of myself as . . ." and a set of lines to fill in multiple responses.

Although content analysis has been criticized for being descriptive and static, it may in the long run prove to be a better approach for uncovering underlying dynamic collective processes than other methods. As survey costs rise, content analysis may prove to be a subtle, cost-effective tool for tapping views at key nodes in a society. Moreover, it may well prove that the time frame of the survey researcher or experimentalist is too short to reveal the major interdependencies among underlying processes. Many survey reports, such as those studying voting behavior, that attempt to explain dynamics on the basis of trends over the previous decade may prove to have little explanatory validity in the next decade. Content analysis allows the time perspective to be extended back to a point before the survey researchers or the experimentalists were on the scene, thus examining interdependencies in a variety of contexts.

Unfortunately, some critics of content analysis have incorrectly assumed that because content analysis examines textual materials, the causal inference must only be to ideology. Even worse, some assume that in examining textual productions the investigator is taking what is said at face value as an explanation. Macro-sociological studies of the processes of dilemma resolution may in fact explain them in terms of structural-materialist causes, just as much as other kinds of events may be so explained. The text is regarded as data, without assuming that assertions being studied have validity either as universals or in describing the situation at the time. Instead, content analysts uncover underlying patterns in the different ways alternatives have been construed.

On the other hand, textual materials are but part of the historical trace, and we would encourage sociological investigators to examine such productions in the context of, and as a complement to, other non-textual data. To rule out content analysis, as some have done, by citing early Marx (particularly Marx and Engels, *The German Ideology*) wrongly equates the inference chains of modern content analysis with those of the German philosophers Marx & Engels criticized. To rule out considerations of textual productions beforehand—for whatever reason—as irrelevant to understanding social processes is an arrogant posture toward the human beings being studied. A mere change in thought does not transform a social situation. But content analysis may very well show how it is an important part of social processes.

For all its inadequacies and fuzziness content analysis thus may be as productive in uncovering underlying patterns of psychological and social dynamics as other research techniques, especially if it is used in conjunction with other indicators. The archives of textual materials are immensely varied; content-analysis studies include such documents as old school essays or advertisements. As larger machine-readable files become available for research, content analysis enables a repeated combing through the materials to test hypotheses by employing modern statistical procedures to unveil complex regularities.

Like all social science techniques of any power, however, content analysis may also carry with it social dangers that need to be approached with caution. The early mail plane may seem rather inconsequential compared to today's large jet planes, but the mail plane demonstrated that planes could not only fly but also be useful. Yet just as the jet plane also brought with it significant problems of pollution, so too the use of content analysis procedures for monitoring textual productions may bring with it possible negative consequences of invading human privacy. As more and more textual productions leave a machine-readable trace, there is always the possibility that these traces may be misused against people. Any optimism and endorsement, as should be evident, must thus include a warranted dose of skepticism and concern, together with a willingness to face such consequences realistically. The ideas and thoughts of an individual represents disaggregation in one domain. As the social sciences in many domains demand more depth than is posssible from aggregated data, they must ensure the responsibility and respect for the individual that goes with it.

NOTES

[1] Our general position on the manifest-latent controversy is that Berelson's exclusive emphasis on manifest content is too restrictive. For example, the word *red* certainly refers to a color, but under some conditions it symbolizes anger. However, a major problem arises when one attempts to discern under just what conditions red symbolizes anger. There is a great temptation to be liberal and include both manifest and latent content in a definition of content analysis, but to do so flippantly would be irresponsible. There is no adequate theory of language at the level of the single occurrence that can guide one on these matters, and the prospective content analyst should be cautioned accordingly. On the other hand we resist the charge that content analysis patterns only reflect the manifest aspects of a social system and not its latent functions. Inasmuch as content analysis can compare *manifest* productions stemming from different segments of society and compare different time periods, it can serve as a basis for inferences about *latent* structural dynamics.

[2] For thorough discussions of research designs as they bear on problems of inference the reader is referred to chapters 6 and 7 by Marshall S. Smith in *The General Inquirer* (Stone, 1966) and chapter 2 of *Content Analysis for the Social Sciences and Humanities* (Holsti, 1969).

[3] Some investigators, instead of specifying a theory, have used computer-clustering techniques to derive empirical categories. These strategies are debated in G. Gerbner et al (1969), one important such approach being that of Iker (1969).

[4] At this point it might be noted that many social scientists seem to have been seduced into thinking that manipulation of numbers is the highest obtainable goal of any science. There is some virtue in this belief. But the goal may be so inviting that it is achieved in a manner that moves the researcher a substantial distance from his original data. Pathetically, the researcher and his or her audience may never know when this occurs. This is especially true when the audience has no choice but to believe that the manipulations of the data (manipulations that many of them probably do not fully understand) have been appropriately chosen and executed.

[5] For a useful overview, see Boden (1977).

REFERENCES

Aires, E. J. *Interaction patterns and themes of male, female, and mixed groups.* Unpublished Ph.D. dissertation, Harvard University, 1973.

Bales, R. F. *Personality and interpersonal behavior.* New York: Holt, Rinehart and Winston, 1970.

Berelson, B. *Content analysis in communication research.* New York: Free Press, 1952.

Boden, M. *Artificial intelligence and natural man.* New York: Basic Books, 1977.

DeWeese, L. Carroll III. Computer content analysis of printed media: a limited feasibility study. *Public Opinion Quarterly*, 1976, *40* (Spring): 92-114.

Gerbner, G., Holsti, O. R., Krippendorff, K., Paisley, W. J., & Stone, P. J. (Eds.). *The analysis of communication content.* New York: John Wiley, 1969.

Goffman, E. *Gender advertisements.* Cambridge: Harvard University Press, 1979.

Herbert, J. C. *Manifest and latent constructions of power in black and white working class women.* Unpublished Ph.D. dissertation, New School for Social Research, 1976.

Holsti, O. R. *Content analysis for the social sciences and humanities.* Reading, Mass.: Addison-Wesley, 1969. (See also Holsti, O. Content analysis. In G. Lindzey and E. Aronson, *Handbook of social psychology.* (Vol. 2, rev. ed.). Reading, Mass.: Addison-Wesley, 1968.)

Iker, H. P., & Harway, N. I. A computer systems approach to the recognition and analysis of content. In G. Gerbner et al. (Eds.), *Analysis of Communications Content.* New York: John Wiley, 1969.

Johnson, P., Sears, D., and McConahay. Black invisibility, the press and the Los Angeles riot. *American Journal of Sociology*, 1971, *76*: 698-721.

Kelly, E., & Stone, P. *Computer recognition of English word senses.* Amsterdam: North Holland Press, 1975.

Leary, T. *Interpersonal diagnosis of personality.* New York: Ronald Press, 1967.

Milburn, M. Dependency and its reflection in popular song texts. In *Popular Music and Society*, in press.

Namenwirth, J. Z. The wheels of time and interdependence of value change. *Journal of Interdisciplinary History*, 1973, *3*: 649-83.

Osgood, C. E., Suci, G. J. & Tannenbaum, P. H. *The measurement of meaning.* Champaign-Urbana: University of Illinois Press, 1957.

Pool, I. de S. (Ed.). *Trends in content analysis.* Stanford, Calif.: Stanford University Press, 1959.

Schank, R. C., & Abelson, R. P. *Scripts, plans, goals and understanding: An enquiry into human knowledge structures.* Hillsdale, N. J.: Earlbaum, 1977.

Shure, G. Technical report. Department of Psychology, University of California, Los Angeles, 1978.

Stone, P. J., Dunphy, D. C., Smith, M. S., & Ogilvie, D. M. *The General Inquirer: A computer approach to content analysis.* Cambridge, Mass.: M.I.T. Press, 1966.

Stone, P. Standards for computer-aided content analysis: The Pisa conventions and recommendations. *Social Science Information* 1975, *14*: 127-37.

Stone, P. Social indicators based on communication content. *Proceedings of the Fall Joint Computer Conference*, 1972, 811-17.

Walker, A. W. *The empirical delineation of two musical taste cultures.* Unpublished Ph.D. dissertation, New School for Social Research, 1975.

Weber, R. P. *The dynamics of value change, transformations and cycles:* British speeches from the throne, 1689-1972. Unpublished Ph.D. dissertation, University of Connecticut, 1978.

Winograd, T. *Understanding natural language.* New York: Academic Press, 1972.

Woods, W. Transitional network grammars for natural language analysis. *Communications of the ACM*, 1970, *13*, 591-602.

Wright, E. O. Methodological introduction. In E. O. Wright, *Class, crisis and the state.* London: NLB, 1978.

Zipf, G. K. The meaning-frequency of words. *Journal of General Psychology* 1945, *33*, 251-266.

PART FOUR
INSPECTION AND
PATTERNING:
THE SEARCH
FOR BASIC
SOCIAL PROCESSES

The most difficult aspect of qualitative work is attempting to analyze and then fit together those things taught as analytically separate: data, concepts, and relationships. This process of inspection and patterning will be facilitated to the extent that the researcher searches for and documents basic social processes by gathering and thoroughly analyzing data. Field notes, transcriptions of interviews, and documents must not merely be read, they must be analyzed! A copy of the original observations should be available for cutting, pasting, coding, and sorting. Interesting vignettes can be pasted to index cards and then coded and sorted to discover patterns and relationships. A fruitful way to organize the data is to discover and document underlying social processes. The chapters discussing and illustrating inspection and patterning all have this social-process orientation.

The first of these, by Bigus, Hadden, & Glaser, argues for the utility of the study of basic social processes as (a) a mode of theory generation, (b) a focus of data gathering, and (c) as a means of reducing the gaps between the various substantive specialties (occupational, medical, political, etc.) within sociology. A social process studied in one substantive field may be generalized to guide research and theorizing in another. Using examples from their own and others' work, they suggest that this focus combines the often disparate operations of sampling, gathering, conceptualizing, and analyzing data. Once a process is outlined, such as recruitment, it can be studied in a variety of places and times and within disparate groups.

Manning's essay discusses and evaluates analytic induction, a qualitative methodology closely akin to reason analysis (Lazarsfeld & Rosenberg, 1955: 387-490; Zeisel, 1968: 153-89; Kadushin, 1968: 338-43), a methodology that bridges qualitative and quantitative methods. Both analytic induction and reason analysis focus on subjects who have performed a particular type of action—embezzling money, having an abortion, going to a psychiatrist, moving, etc. Both methods attempt to discern the reasons why the action was performed. These reasons often are structured to form a social process explanation.

The two approaches differ in that analytic induction attempts to find a covering law that universally holds for every observed case, whereas reason analysis attempts to find a parsimonious set of determining variables, some of which explain the action of one individual and other subsets explain the actions of others, and so on. The process explanations of analytic induction and reason analysis both tend to be invariantly time ordered for all individuals—first A occurs, then B, and then C.

As Donald Cressey practiced analytic induction in his classic *Other People's Money*, he first formulated a tentative hypothesis about the causes of embezzlement. Then he carried out a series of detailed interviews with imprisoned embezzlers and reviewed his case studies to see if his formulation held true for all cases. He found exceptions, so he formulated a new rule and gathered more data. After several iterations through this process of hypothesis formation and cross-checking against data, Cressey discovered a social process explanation that held universally for all of the cases in his study. He found that the preconditions for an act of embezzlement, for those in a position of financial trust and possessing the requisite knowledge, are: (1) awareness of an unsharable financial problem; (2) further awareness that this problem may be solved by embezzlement; and (3) the construction of a rationalization that permits both the criminal act and the maintenance of a self-conception as a law-abiding citizen. These three sequentially ordered, dichotomous attributes are prerequisites for the act of embezzlement—if they are present, then embezzlement takes place; if one or more are absent, then this act is not performed.

Interestingly enough, a process explanation such as the above, which often is thought to be antithetical to classical functional analysis, is actually very similar to the functional-prerequisites approach of Talcott Parsons and associates (Parsons, Bales, & Shils, 1953). For example, Parsons reasoned that before a social system can function effectively (that is, to survive), four dichotomous functional prerequisites must be fulfilled. These are: (1) *adaptation* to social, economic, and other environments; (2) allocation of resources for *goal attainment*; (3) *integration* and coordination of interrelated units in the system; and (4) *latency*—pattern-maintenance and tension-management—or, more simply, socialization of new participants into the institutionalized culture and maintenance of morale. If any of these prerequisites is missing, then the social system will break down. Although this AGIL scheme of Parsons' is often applied in static formulations, when it was first presented (Parsons, Bales & Shils, 1953: 163-269), the process of phase movement from one prerequisite to the next was emphasized.

This volume concludes with Smith's chapter "Enumerative Induction: Quantification in Symbolic Interactionism." First, it discusses a recent controversy between Howard Becker and Blanche Geer, who stress the virtues of participant observations, and Martin Trow, who argues for the articulation of qualitative and quantitative methods. Instructive examples of successful quantifications of symbolic interactionist problems are then briefly reviewed. Quantitative systematic observations, surveys, experiments, computer simulations, grounded theories and typologies have advanced knowledge about definitions of situations and the development of the social self, which are key problems of symbolic interactionism. These quantitative methods are presented in subsequent volumes of this Handbook.

REFERENCES

Cressey, Donald. *Other people's money.* New York: Free Press, 1953.
Kadushin, Charles. Reason analysis. In *International encyclopedia of the social sciences.* (Vol. 13). New York: Macmillan and Free Press, 1968.
Lazarsfeld, Paul F. & Rosenburg, Morris. *The language of social research.* New York: Free Press, 1955.
Parsons, Talcott, Bales, R. F., & Shils, E. A. *Working papers in the theory of action.* New York: Free Press, 1953.
Zeisel, Hans. *Say it with figures* (5th rev. ed.). New York: Harper & Row, 1968.

Chapter Ten
Basic social processes[1]

ODIS E. BIGUS, STUART C. HADDEN and
BARNEY G. GLASER

INTRODUCTION

One of the fundamental tenets of sociology is that social life is not random, that it exists as sets of behavioral uniformities which occur and recur over time. One of the primary tasks of sociology should be to systematically study these patterned regularities and their major variations as *social processes*. Although process has been addressed throughout the history of sociology,[2] it has too seldom been studied in a methodical manner in and of itself. This is not so much because of a lack of concern about social process as it is an absence of specific and systematic means of approaching its study.

Recognizing this dilemma, we would like to introduce a specific and systematic approach to the study of social process. We propose that one way social process might be studied is by way of a theoretical construct that we shall refer to as *"basic social process."*[3] The basic social process *conception* (hereafter referred to simply as "BSP") is a generic theoretical construct of the same genre as Weber's (1964) "ideal type" and Schutz's (1971) "homunculus." Unlike these conceptions, however, the idea of BSP was developed within, and is systematically tied to, a specific methodological program for generating theory.

Formulation of the BSP conception arose as a by-product of the ongoing development of what Glaser & Strauss (1967) refer to as "grounded theory" methodology. It is important to underscore the fact that the conception is not a preconception of the methodology, but rather is a product of its empirical application. Consistent with the reasoning to be advanced throughout this paper, the BSP notion was conceived *in the process of doing* grounded theory research.

Briefly stated, BSPs are conceptually developed to account for the organization of social behavior as it occurs over time. That is, BSP sociology is concerned with *dynamics*. Also, BSPs capture both micro- and macrophenomena through a conjoint consideration of both social psychological and social structural variation.These two analytic dimensions are integrated in BSP theories so as to reflect their empirical relationship in the social world. Although either structural or social psychological variation may have primacy in a particular research undertaking (empirically determined), in rendering a structural process theory social psychological variation will be accounted for, and vice versa.

Furthermore, although BSP theories are generated within substantive arenas, they are easily separable from them. The primary concern of BSP sociology is with the *generic*, and only secondarily with the substantive. Since the analytic focus is a *generic process*, formalization of theory can also be readily accomplished. As will be developed more fully later, BSP formal theory is generated from substantive formulations in a manner similar to the development of the original substantive process theory.

Although we are using the term "basic social process" to delineate a particular approach to the development of qualitative theory, we are by no means claiming novelty in this approach. Much work has been produced in qualitative sociology which, to varying extents, is compatible with the BSP notion. Notable examples are Davis' (1961) conception of the "deviance disavowal" process, Lofland's (1966) model of the "conversion" process, and Matza's (1964) conception of the process by which juveniles "drift" into delinquency. In addition, there are numerous studies on what might be termed the "becoming" process, such as Becker's (1953) "Becoming a Marihuana User," Olesen and Whittaker's (1968) "The Silent Dialogue," and Weinberg's (1966) "Becoming a Nudist."[4]

Neither are we claiming novelty in our concern for grounded studies which focus on generic variables and on process (cf. Blumer, 1956). These are concerns that have endured in sociology. However, the paucity of field studies which clearly and specifically illuminate generic processes testifies to the fact that not all has been said about these concerns. Generic processes are evident in many qualitative field studies, but in too many instances they remain conceptually underdeveloped.[5] Furthermore, most of the generic conceptualizations in sociology, e.g. functionalism, symbolic interactionism, are not well grounded in field studies. When used in field studies, such conceptualizations are usually used in an appended and/or force-fitted manner. It is our hope that the BSP conception will help focus field studies toward the theoretical development of grounded generic processes.

In this chapter we shall explore the utility of the BSP approach for generating sociological theory. We shall do this by first comparing process sociology (specifically BSP sociology) with what we shall refer to as "unit sociology," with respect to durability, generalizability, relationalability, and coverage. Second, we shall discuss in general terms the methodology of BSP development. We shall close with a discussion of what effects a well-developed process sociology might have on perspectives and conceptions in sociology.

UNIT VERSUS PROCESS SOCIOLOGY

It is sometimes unavoidable in making conceptual distinctions between real phenomena to oversimplify them for heuristic comparisons. The reader is advised to so view the distinction made in this chapter between unit and process sociology. Unit and process are tendencies in sociology, with some sociology sharing characteristics of both. Most sociology, however, tends toward the unit side of this distinction.

We use the term "unit sociology" to refer to work in which the basic analytic focus is on a specific sociological unit, such as a population unit (e.g. "Americans," "drug users," "scientists"), or cultural units (e.g. "skid row," "mental hospitals," "universities"), or combinations thereof (e.g. "deviants" as a conceptual category of prostitutes, drug users, check forgers, etc., or "occupations and professions" as the general category for nurses, milkmen, lawyers, and so forth). As currently practiced, unit sociology is generally concerned with developing static descriptions and/or conceptualizations of such units and their properties. The imagery suggested by such an approach is one of discrete entities which can be studied and understood in spatial and temporal isolation. In assuming this orientation dynamic, cross-contextual properties of behavior remain, almost unavoidably, undiscovered.[6]

For example, a researcher with a unit orientation would likely view the recruitment and orientation of nudists, nurses and marijuana users as qualitatively distinct phenomena, each requiring separate research efforts. Such research often results in separate and distinct explanatory schemes, emphasizing the properties of each unit *per se*. This approach is limiting in that it promotes a tendency to overlook the generic properties of each unit, while developing the substantive properties.

In contrast, BSP sociology takes generic process as its basic analytic focus and consequent endeavors are directed towards formulating theories about social processes. The referent is the process itself, not the particular unit or units in which it is isolated. Thus, a process sociologist would view the recruitment and initiation of nudists, nurses, and marijuana users as instances—"strategic settings"—of a generic process like "becoming." Within this orientation, the researcher would search each of these settings for phenomena related to the process of becoming, such as opportunity, acquisition of knowledge, skills and beliefs, justification rhetoric, and so forth. The focus would be on *becoming*, not on nudists, nurses, or marijuana users *per se*. BSP theories are, of course, developed through research conducted within such units, and will certainly lend understanding to these units. For example, a study of how people become nurses would add to the understanding of nursing schools and the nursing profession, even though the focus might be on becoming.

In themselves the foci of either unit or process sociology are not intrinsically meritorious. The test of their worth lies in how well they lend themselves to the development of sociological knowledge and theory. In this regard we will argue that BSP sociology produces significant advantages with respect to the durability of formulations and propensity for theoretical development. By durability we mean the capacity of a conceptual formulation to remain viable through time. Theoretical development refers to (1) the ability of formulations to be generalized and formalized, (2) the extent to which formulations can be related to other formulations in similar contexts, and (3) the ease with which conceptualization occurs.

Within this foreshortened universe of concern, we will deal only peripherally with the formal issues of interest to the philosophers of science—e.g. axiomatizing a body of knowledge, formal cumulative procedures, etc. (cf. Freeze, 1972, Mullins, 1974). Our concern, rather, is in dealing with the effects of analytic focus on the ability to generate durable conceptualizations with the capacity to be cumulated. In short, we wish to illustrate that as analytic foci "unit sociology" and "process sociology" have particular consequences along the dimensions outlined above.

Durability

It is perhaps axiomatic to say that the world changes. In recognition of this, sociologists have parceled out a portion of their domain to deal with such matters—to wit, "social change." It seems somewhat incongruous, however, that in recognizing social change as a crucial sociological concern, we often fail to consider it when pursuing research from a unit orientation. By focusing our efforts on substantive properties of units, we condemn our formulations to eventual obsolescence.

Since units will undoubtedly undergo siginificant change over time, the most that can be said for most unit formulations is that they illuminate a temporally circumscribed and thus particularized set of conditions. Explanations of behavior under such conditions rest upon a configuration of variables that may or may not be so aligned in the future. On a descriptive level, a statement about a unit remains intact only so long as the unit itself remains relatively static. As the unit changes, the description becomes increasingly obsolete.

Unit *theories* likewise may become obsolete over time. For example, a cursory review of the sociological literature on opiate addiction, merely one facet of the unit "drug use," shows an enormous change in the characteristics of the substantive unit. From Terry and Pellens' (1970) compendium of drug studies prior to 1928 through the most recent National Commission Report (1973), it is apparent that many variables attributed to opiate addiction— e.g. ethnicity, age, sex, drug of choice, etc.—have undergone radical transformation. It should not be surprising, then, that the only theoretical proposition to survive the quicksilver of the changing drug scene is Lindesmith's (1938 and 1968) analysis of the role played by withdrawal distress— perhaps the only durable static property of opiate use.[7] Such is the fate of unit-dependent theories; as the unit undergoes transformation, theory must be developed anew.

Many other examples of unit descriptions and theories are available, but they would only belabor the point. Durability is seriously undermined when descriptive and theoretical formulations are dependent upon such capricious properties as are found to constitute a particular unit at a particular time.

In contrast to unit descriptions and theories, BSP theories are quite durable (BSP sociology does not concern itself with description apart from theory). BSPs as generic processes are part of the basic fabric of social organization; they do not radically change or expire as time passes. Thus, the theories that reflect them merely become extended, deepened, and most importantly *modified* as the data which suggest them change. The manner in which BSPs exist in particular units may change over time, as conditions may change, but the fundamental core process and its essential properties will remain essentially intact.

This durability is enhanced by the fact that it is not merely the explication of generic properties that is the focus of BSP sociology. One is concerned, as well, with the conditions under which such properties may vary across units and through time. That is, BSPs are developed such that change is an oriented-to feature of the analysis. Examples of both a formal and substantive process theory will serve to illustrate this durability.[8]

From Glaser & Strauss' (1971) formal theory of "status passages," it appears that, as generic processes, status passages have always existed and always will exist in all cultures at all times. Furthermore, the essential formal properties of status passages are also durable. Status passages will always be repeatable or non-repeatable, voluntary or involuntary, undergone alone, collectively or in aggregate, and so on. Status passages at any time, in any location (i.e. in any unit) may be analyzed in respect to such properties.

In regard to more substantive BSP theory durability is reduced, but it is nonetheless much greater than with static unit based conceptions. The unit within which a substantive theory was developed may undergo change, but the theory need only be slightly modified to account for such change.

Bigus' (1972) substantive process theory regarding how milkmen "cultivate" relationships with customers and prospective customers will serve to illustrate. One of the essential stages of relationship cultivation is the development of trust. Milkmen at the time and location where this study was conducted utilized several "trust-inducing" tactics. If conditions changed such that a particular trust-inducing tactic lost its usefulness, the theory could easily be modified to account for the changed *conditions* and whatever resulted (the development of a new tactic, the increased use of already existing tactics, or whatever). If conditions in the retail milk business changed so radically as to eliminate the need for cultivating relations, a great deal of the original conceptualization of relationship cultivation would still remain useful. Even with a substantive BSP theory, the focus is on generic phenomena (e.g. trust development as it relates to relationship cultivation). If relationship cultivation were to be eliminated from the context of the home delivery milk business, it would nonetheless exist elsewhere, under conditions similar to those which originally gave rise to its presence in the milk business (such as low demand and high supply of a service or product, power asymmetry in relationship, and so forth). And, the understanding gained from its study in the context of the milk business would remain essentially intact. We would know at least some of the essential properties of relationship cultivation, some of the conditions under which it occurs, and so forth. In other words, we would have gained permanent knowledge about the dynamics of a probably universal form of social relationship, not merely fleeting knowledge of milkmen and their customers.

Generalizability

The foregoing example illustrates the potential generalizability and propensity for formalization of substantive BSP theory. The cultivating process and its essential properties occur in other substantive units (particularly those related to servicing such as automobile repair, undertaking, hairdressing, etc.). The existence of BSPs is not bound by, or dependent upon, their status in any particular unit. Although a BSP theory might have been originally derived from a particular unit, the conditions, properties, and consequences, of the process transcend the unit. Thus, the conceptualization developed in the original study of the cultivating process as it occurred in the context of the home delivery milk business remains intact when the BSP is applied to other units in which relationship cultivation occurs.

Unit theory is not so unbound. It is limited in its generalizability because a theoretical statement about a unit is bound by the particular configuration of conditions in the unit at a specific time.[9] As such, it cannot be lifted intact to another unit with a different configuration of conditions, much less a different class of unit, without obscuring the relationship of the theory to the obdurate world. The theory remains "trapped" in the unit within which it was developed, and it will always be read as a descriptive statement about that particular unit at a specific time.

Historically, the development of unit theory has been along lines of generalizing to larger units of the *same type*, rather than through densification and integration of the concepts themselves.[10] Such generalization is typically attempted in two ways: (1) through enlargement of the same class of population units (e.g., from marijuana users to users of other types of drugs), (2) through conceptual escalation from a substantive unit to a formal conceptual unit (e.g., drug users as an example of deviance). This type of theoretical development seldom achieves adequacy because variation in the form of fresh data from different units, undermines a developing unit theory. Such variation frequently functions to contradict the theory as it currently exists, rather than to contribute to its modification and elaboration.

Imagine, for instance, a theorist who develops a theory of LSD use that is to be used as a foundation for developing a theory of drug use in general (a larger unit). Comparative data from other units (barbiturate users, amphetamine users, for example) are collected for inclusion in the analysis. In short order the analyst discovers instances in the data, however, that are counter to the original theory. In the original work, it may have been found that LSD use occurs almost exclusively in subcultures which encourage LSD use. It was concluded, therefore, that LSD use is directly related to membership in such subcultures. However, the data from the comparative unit of amphetamine users indicates (hypothetically) that amphetamine users have a very strong tendency to shy away from drug subcultures. The analyst thus concludes, correctly within the framework of unit analysis, that the theory does not pertain to amphetamine users; a theory of amphetamine use must be developed apart from LSD use. The case for escalation of the original theory to a general, or more formal, theory of drug use has been weakened.[11]

The outcome of the above hypothetical example resulted from the researcher attempting to generalize a theory that was originally developed through focusing on substantive properties of a particular unit (LSD use), rather than on phenomena related to generic processes occurring therein. By using a substantive property of the unit (subculture affiliation) as the explanatory variable, the researcher has undermined the generalizability of the developing theory, and has failed to discover similarities in comparative units. If the focus had been on processes occurring within the units—such as getting into drug use (cf. Becker, 1953), getting out of drug use, or whatever—one would more likely have discovered similarities as well as variations between the units which could have been conceptualized and related to a generic-process core variable. Within this alternative framework, drug subculture affiliation would be conceived merely as one variation of getting into drug use. Further, similarities between this particular mode of introduction and other variations may also be discovered through closer comparison—which is encouraged, rather than undermined, by the generic process approach. For example, by focusing on avenues into drug use rather than on absence or presence of subculture affiliation, it may be discovered that the persuasion of friends is a key variable in acquiring knowledge about the availability and desirability of a particular drug and its use. One class of users—young persons, for example—may frequently be introduced into drug subcultures and hence into drug use by friends. Similarly, another quite different class of users, middle class housewives, for example, may also commonly be introduced to drug use through friends. In this instance, the friend may urge the housewife to see her family doctor, or another doctor who perscribes liberally, for a barbiturate prescription to "calm her nerves down." She may argue, "I did it, and it worked for me." Either of the above instances of introduction to drug use through friends could result in the routine use of a drug. Additionally, by using a generic process approach, a researcher would more easily avoid being conceptually misled by such common sense categories as "illegal" and "legal" drug use.

We do not argue that it would be impossible for unit-oriented research-ers to discover such variations and similarities as suggested above. We do argue, however, that it would be unlikely, because of the tendency in unit research to focus on substantive properties of units. Even if unit researches were to discover such variations from a unit perspective, not having a dynamic core variable which cuts across the units would retard the theoreti-cal linkages being seen. Such researchers would probably end up with a largely descriptive comparison of the units, with possibly an *appended* theoretical scheme.

The focus on generic process allows BSPs to transcend the boundaries of units and common sense categories; such a focus facilitates the elevation of the core theoretical properties to a more formal level, as was demonstrated in our previous example of "cultivation relationships." Further, the general-izability of BSPs data and findings from specific units are cumulative, thus allowing for the development of an integrated, dense theory. The process of "status passage" occurs, for example, in contexts of religion, education, marriage, aging, health and illness, alcoholism, and so on. Much of what is found in a study of the status passage process, as it occurs in religious settings, may be carried over to education settings in a cumulative fashion. The findings of further studies of status passages in yet other settings, may dings also be integrated into the developing theory of status passage. As findings from each study are integrated into the theory, the formal properties of the status passage process will emerge. In this manner each study will have contributed to the development of the formal process theory.

Integration and densification of a BSP theory is further enhanced because, not being unit dependent, variation in terms of fresh data from new units does not undermine a developing theory. To the contrary, it contributes to its generation, because it gives greater theoretical coverage and allows for modification and extension of the theory. An example from a BSP-oriented study can illustrate this point.

In research conducted in a small community (Hadden, 1973) it was found that local officials relied on a particular evidentiary form in order to provide a "basis" for their assessments of the "extent" of the drug menace in the community. Conceptualized as "evidentiary notions" this form entailed taking a supposed qualitative feature of the phenomenon (e.g., marijuana causes conduct problems), assessing it quantitatively (e.g., no incidents noted), and then asserting a qualitative appraisal of the phenome-non qua problem (e.g., minimal). From the data available in that particular research site this evidentiary form could be taken to be an invariant pattern in the creation of such problems.

A year after this first study information on the "rise" of a rape problem in a Southwestern city was reviewed and a second evidentiary form was noted—the patterning of idiosyncratic events. Here an unusually brutal rape/murder was widely publicized and immediately seized upon as an indicator of a more pervasive problem. The originally noted evidentiary form isolated in the drug study was only selectively employed in the initial stages of the career of the rape problem.

In comparing the careers of the two separate substantive problems, it can be noted first that the evidentiary form present in the rape career *does not* negate the prior form found in the drug study. Rather, it extends the concept of evidentiary notions to include another pattern. Second, in looking at this new variation we can isolate the conditions under which one form will predominate. Such a comparison in the present example indicated that the dictating features of an evidentiary base were conditioned by the degree of visibility of the phenomenon (i.e., how much information was readily available) and the degree of control over how much of this information was available to interested parties. In the drug case officials were dealing with a virtually invisible phenomenon (for the general public) where they held primary control over the availability of information. In the rape situation, however, the original "event" was highly visible through intense media coverage; officials had little direct control over public access to information. Correspondingly, the evidentiary bases for the problems took different forms.

From the foregoing example it is evident that in constructing a process theory new data collected from comparative units, whether different or similar, merely function to elaborate and extend the theory, rather than to undermine it. Thus, the avenue to generalization and formalization remains open.

RELATING CONCEPTS

With unit sociology there is typically no theoretical nexus with which to relate separate units to one another in an analytically significant way. Units are ordinarily seen as separate entities with definite boundaries; they can be understood in isolation, but they do not relate in any theoretically important manner to other units. In this sense theorists create unit theories that operate within a vacuum and imply unwarranted logical assumptions about the scope of the subject matters when generalizations to other units are attempted. For example, most studies of deviant behavior carry with them the implicit assumption that "deviant" behavior is somehow fundamentally different from "normal" behavior, that the "causes" of deviant behavior are also fundamentally different from the "causes" of non-deviant behavior rather than being two consequences of the same BSP.[12]

Such assumptions do not result from empirical investigation; they derive, instead, from the fact that sociologists have somewhat arbitrarily divided social behavior into two units, "deviant" and "normal."

The most superficial investigation shows that deviant behavior does not occur in a vacuum inhabited only by "deviant" persons who engage only in deviant behavior. What sociologists refer to as "deviant behavior" ordinarily develops and is acted out in the same setting as "normal" behavior (cf. Lofland, 1969: 62-69). Furthermore, it often develops in interaction with "normal" persons as consequences of the same BSP—e.g., "achieving prestige," or "achieving upward mobility" (cf. Bell, 1953). Despite rather obvious relationships, many theories of deviant behavior disregard phenomena which are not deemed to be direct properties of "deviants" or "deviant behavior." Theoretical integration between "normal" and "deviant" behavior as two dimensions of a BSP thus remains unachieved, despite the potential empirical relationship.

We realize one can argue that instances of deviant behavior share at least one commonality that would facilitate theoretical integration—presumed rule violation of some sort.[13] Even if we ignore that this is probably more of a legalistic or moralistic description of a unit, however, the "rules in use" nature of the phenomenon (Garfinkel, 1967) are typically taken in most research as an unexplicated, defining feature of the subject being studied. Consequently, the relationship(s) such behavior may have with more fundamental patterns of behavior is again obscure.

A partial exception to this general trend, the labeling perspective, takes as an object of study the interaction between rules, rule-making, rule-enforcement, and rule-breakers—in short, a process. Yet it is one of the consequences of the way we delineate the sociological world, and a testimony to the channeling of research dictated by unit analysis, that even when process models or theories (such as labeling) are advanced they are still taken as descriptive of a particular population or conceptual unit.

We would argue that labeling is a BSP (however ill-defined or specified at the present time) with strong carry-through outside the substantive field of deviance. However, since labeling was conceived from deviance studies, it is primarily taken as tied to that conceptual unit. In our analysis labeling (or some variant thereof) could indeed become a major theoretical contribution if this process were studied in the manner advocated in the final portions of this paper.[14] One of the problems with "labeling theory" at present is that it is the result of studies where the primary concern has been the explanation of the conceptual unit, deviance. Hence, the referent for the theory has been a unit to be explained in process terms and not *the process itself*.

The paucity of well-integrated propositions stems in our view from the failure to systematically focus on process—analyzing conditions, properties, consequences, etc.—regardless of the common-sense categories and predetermined conceptualizations about the nature of the social world. By cutting across and transcending the boundaries of separate units, BSP's provide a way of relating different units to each other. In our one example above, for example, cultivating a clientele is a way of relating the activities of milkmen to those of doctors.

Besides BSP theories relating diverse units to each other, analytically distinct BSPs relate to one another through the empirical world of units. Often one BSP is a property or condition that affects another BSP within a particular unit. For instance, the longitudinal study of the career of a "drug problem" in a small community, referred to earlier, yielded the conceptualization of an "alarming process." This process was characterized as the movement of a phenomenon from a position of little or no concern for the community through its "discovery as a matter of 'concern,'" the mobilization of resources to meet the situation, and finally the "demise" of the phenomenon qua community problem (Hadden, 1973). One of the major properties of this broad processual model was the notion of "pronouncing prevalence." This term refers to the social dimensions associated with certain behavior being made problematic—who can, under what conditions, successfully promote a phenomenon as worthy of attention. While the notion of "pronouncing prevalence" was isolated and developed within the context of the larger concern with the alarming process, it may also be developed in its own right as a BSP.

Pronouncing prevalence of phenomena is pervasive within social life as individuals, organizations, and their leaders furnish evidence to themselves and others of the "good life," decide on appropriate courses of action, and in general elevate phenomena from mundane to noteworthy status. If one were to develop this BSP theory of "pronouncing," it would certainly pertain to all problem areas including social problems. Sampling in other areas, however, would yield a wider applicability of the process as one would be specifically looking for the conditions under which pronouncing takes on different dimensions.

For example, in the original research where pronouncing was used to inform the alarming process, a notion of vulnerability was seen as necessary for successful pronouncements. Such pronouncements were couched in a rhetoric that connoted an inevitable spread of a problem on both a territorial and personal basis, unless social action was taken. In other words "everyone" was depicted as potentially affected. However, in developing the process of pronouncing in different contexts (i.e., non-alarms) we would probably find this "vulnerability" requirement to be but one of a number of strategies under which pronouncing took place.

The discovery of empirical relationships between BSPs within units, whether similar or diverse, can lead to a new development in theory. Through the discovery of pronouncing practices, as a major property of the alarming process, it became evident that pronouncing was itself a basic social process worthy of individual development.

THEORETICAL COVERAGE

One remaining aspect of theoretical development in which BSP sociology possesses major advantages over unit sociology concerns the problem of "immaculate coverage"—the emphasis in unit sociology on developing fully the properties of the unit under study to satisfy criteria of either logical or descriptive completeness. This emphasis is not of any necessity related to theoretical coverage; such a requirement impedes rather than fosters theoretical development.

Consider again the area of drug-using behavior. With the emphasis on the unit drug use, a well-developed theory would logically have to include the isolation of variables on the physician-addict, the garden-variety street user, the occasional marijuana smoker, the barbiturate abusing housewife, et al. The enormity of such a task is staggering. The difficulty for well-developed theory does not lie in the work requirements; rather, it would appear that many properties of the unit are simply not theoretically related to one another. On a common sense level only one property seems to bind the above-mentioned housewife to the marijuana smoker to the physician as a unit. They all ingest substances called "drugs." Despite this, a theory would somehow have to relate fundamentally diverse properties to account for all facets of the area under study. For this reason most unit analysis produces a few concepts, perhaps a stunted theory, and a tremendous amount of substantive description.

When conducting research and analysis, process theorists need only attend to those phenomena occurring in the unit(s) which appear to be theoretically pertinent to the process being studied. Although the research is conducted within particular units, *one is not studying the units per se; incumbent process(es) is the focus.* Therefore, that which does not relate to the BSP does not relate to the study. This allows the theorist to achieve sufficient theoretical coverage of the subject matter without researching the unit to immaculate *descriptive* detail. It also frees one from having to account for the great amount of behavioral variation (much of it theoretically unrelated) found in the unit.

METHODOLOGY OF BSP DEVELOPMENT

Having outlined the advantages of BSP sociology in regards to theoretical development, we now turn to the methodology of BSP development. As mentioned earlier, the BSP notion was developed in the process of *doing* "grounded theory" research; it is thus both methodologically and theoretically linked to that particular methodology. While this is not an appropriate forum for entertaining a programmatic account of "how to generate grounded theory," a slight digression into the methodology is warranted in order to demonstrate not only its departure from more traditional modes of research within the unit orientation but, more importantly, its congruence with the logic of basic social processes.

Briefly stated, the intent of grounded theory methodology is in the inductive generation of theory "from data ... systematically obtained and analyzed in social research" (Glaser and Strauss, 1967:1). In such formulations the hypotheses, conceptual categories, and their properties are derived, tested, and refined through a detailed and continuous inspection of comparative collected data. A "discovery" model of research is employed in generating BSPs in contrast to the more usual verification and descriptive model used in unit-oriented research. The general rationale for this type of research in an elemental science is succinctly captured by Glaser and Strauss in their advocacy of an inductive methodology. For them:

Verifying a logico-deductive theory generally leaves us with at best a reformulated hypothesis or two and an unconfirmed set of speculations; and at worst, a theory that does not fit or work... A grounded theory [read BSP theory] can be used as a fuller test of a logico-deductive theory pertaining to the same area by comparison of both theories, than an accurate description used to verify a few propositions would provide. Whether or not there is a previous speculative theory, discovery gives us a theory that 'fits or works' in a substantive or formal area (though further testing, clarification, or reformulation is still necessary) since the theory has been derived from research data, not deduced from logical assumptions about it. (Glaser & Strauss, 1967:29-30).

Consistent with this notion of an inductive methodology, researchers employing grounded theory will not preconceive the important properties and processes of the study area. They do not enter the research arena as a blank slate; rather, the BSP conception provides the researcher with an initial focus *without* having to preconceive eventual theory. The researcher has something specific to look for (a process), yet sufficient latitude to allow the theory to emerge inductively. Since there is an attempt to discover some sort of BSP, the researcher will begin the search for the process (i.e., core variable) that accounts for the most variation in the data and to which other variables appear to be related. In accomplishing this end data collection, coding, and analysis occur jointly,[15] such that freshly collected data informs the emerging theory, and in turn the emerging theory guides further data collection. Glaser & Strauss (1967: 45) refer to this process as "theoretical sampling."

Theoretical sampling is the process of data collection for generating theory whereby the analyst jointly collects, codes and analyzes his data and decides what data to collect next and where to find them, in order to develop his theory as it emerges. This process of data collection is *controlled* by the emerging theory, whether substantive or formal.

Congruent with the BSP conception, theoretical sampling involves sampling for variation to achieve *theoretical coverage*, and not descriptive or population (i.e., unit) coverage. For example, in his study of milkmen Bigus (1972) discovered that most of the milkmen's time and energies of the job were consumed with "cultivating relationships" (the BSP) with customers and prospective customers. This was the major "problem" confronting the milkmen on a day-to-day basis, and almost everything that transpired was related or affected by cultivating relationships. Consequently, Bigus' analysis was directed toward discovery of the generic properties of this process and *not* toward characteristics of milkmen, the occupation milkman, and the like. At this point the concern with the social phenomenon we call *milkman* was limited to the theoretical insights it could shed on the cultivating process. In this sense milkmen and their occupation had become a "strategic" research arena in which to study the emerging theory on cultivating.

As implied in the above example, theoretical sampling is not concerned with fully describing any particular unit or units in the conventional sense. Its primary function is to provide analysts with the opportunity to discover properties of the core variable being studied (which in the case of the process analyst will be a BSP), so as to densify or fill out the emergent theory. When generating a grounded theory, the sample size is determined only by the necessity of theoretical coverage. When sampling no longer produces new ideas (i.e., when "theoretical saturation" is reached), the need for further sampling ceases. Under this scheme it is not uncommon for major categories to begin manifesting themselves during analysis of the first several interviews or observations. The task at that point is to sample the research arena so as to provide the constituent properties of those categories, accomplishing at the same time intra-research verification on the emerging theory. It should not be surprising that a seemingly small sample (from a conventional perspective) would enable the process theorist to achieve sufficient theoretical coverage to generate a dense, well-integrated grounded theory, since each stage of research is being guided by a parsimonious search for variation around emergent process characteristics.

It should be noted that at times more than one BSP may be found to be important in a given situation or set of data. The choice of which to study as the major focus of a particular project is both an empirical and personal decision. On the empirical level one looks for the variable that accounts for a great deal of variation in the data. In other words, can its properties be sufficiently developed. On a personal level the choice becomes more arbitrary; quite simply, one chooses whatever is of personal interest. The choice made, analysts develop the second process only insofar as it relates to the one commanding primary attention. The other(s) may of course be similarly developed at another time.

Once a particular substantive unit or area is sufficiently exploited to discover a BSP and its major properties, a theorist is then free to sample theoretically in other diverse kinds of units to begin formalizing the theory. This can be specifically accomplished in a number of ways, the details of which are beyond the scope of this chapter.[16] Generally, however, formalization of a BSP theory can be achieved through analyzing data from a number of diverse classes of comparative groups and drawing out variables and properties that are shared by and vary within all comparative units, because of differing underlying conditions. In this manner the most general, cross-contextual (i.e., formal) properties of the process may be discovered. For example, the theorist constructing a formal theory of "cultivating" may discover that in all comparative instances, one stage of relationship cultivation concerns the establishment of trust. Trust may then be seen as a formal property of the theory of "cultivating." Similarly, a theorist may develop a formal theory of status passage and discover that in some units with some types of status passages the individual has no control over whether or not he/she enters the status passage, while in other units the individual maintains a high degree of control over the process. Even though events occur differently in each comparative unit, the theorist can ascertain that the extent to which a status passage is voluntary (or involuntary) is a formal property of the process of status passage. Thus, although great variation occurs, a common property is present—the extent of voluntariness. Concommitantly, the conditions under which status passage is voluntary or involuntary and the consequences of that variation further illuminates the process "status passage."

As previously mentioned, our discussion of the manner in which BSP is generated must necessarily be truncated. However, the foregoing discussion should demonstrate the general manner in which such theory is capable of being generated. Our sketch of the inductive procedures of grounded theory methodology as they relate to the development of BSPs should further sensitize one to the quite different appearance sociological renderings of the world might take if BSP analysis were pursued. It is on this topic that we now focus attention.

SOCIOLOGY ALONG PROCESS LINES

We have suggested that focusing on process as opposed to units will facilitate theoretical development. Implicit in this argument is the notion that generic process, as an explicit focus of any research inquiry, will alter the conceptual world of the discipline by cutting across and transcending traditional sociological boundaries. Again, a comparison with unit analysis should serve to underscore this point.

Much of unit sociology is delineated along lines that are *not* theoretically contiguous, although they are treated as such. For example, a unit sociologist beginning a study of "whorehouses" would probably place the study in the conceptual category of "deviant behavior" or possibly "social problem" (*apriori*, static conceptions). In doing so the presumption is that the essence, or at least a primary property, of the behavior to be studied is that it is deviant or socially problematic. Concomitant results will explain the motivations, attitudes, or other social characteristics of a person who engages in such practices as distinct from non-practitioners (i.e., "normals"). In categorizing whorehouse activities as merely another instance of deviant behavior, however, perhaps other more central characteristics of the phenomenon are denied serious consideration by the researcher.

If we hold in abeyance the deviance assumption about whorehouses, we note that the area to be studied is an organized activity, established for the expressed purpose of exchanging a "service" for remuneration. Viewed in terms of process, it would be found that the structural properties of the whorehouse are akin to servicing operations in general—a basic social process.[17] Quite simply, the whorehouse exists to provide a service(s) which happens to be sex. *One property* of a servicing process in this particular context is that the service being provided is generally considered deviant in the everyday world. The "fact" that it is so conceived may have some consequences for the organization of some of its publicly visible activities, such as making it necessary to maintain a low profile, putting limits on public advertising, necessitating payoffs to the police, and so on. However, the deviant conception of whorehouse activities is only one among many conditions and properties in this and other servicing contexts. Compared to other possible characteristics of the general process of "servicing" (such as power symmetry, role of expertise, specialized knowledge, rights of grievance, etc.) the primacy afforded the role of deviance in a unit analysis seems more reflective of common-sense considerations than theoretical fit. Conceptualized from a generic process orientation, the behavior of prostitutes and their customers has more in common, theoretically, with the behavior found in garages and beauty parlors than it does with check forgery, alcoholism, and the vast array of other instances ordinarily conceptualized as deviant behavior.

One further observation seems warranted. From our example of whorehouse activities it might be concluded that we have merely transposed a hypothetical social psychological study into one focusing on organization. We would answer that this is again an *a priori* characterization.[18] One of the strengths of BSPs is their ability conjointly to render both structural and social psychological variables in terms of social process. It may be the case that either structural or social-psychological variation has primacy in a given area, but that is a data-related question.

Essentially, what we are arguing is that regardless of the usual sociological interests—whether it be deviance, religion, collective behavior—or the usual primary focus as either organizational or social psychological, the referent for BSP theory is always generic process and *not* the particular substantive or conceptual unit involved. This does not mean that the analyst will be unable to explain how the particular research unit functions. Quite the contrary! Theoretical renderings in terms of BSPs contribute substantial insights into the practical realities of the day-to-day world by explaining its variation. However, as mentioned earlier, the analytic focus seeks theoretical coverage and not descriptive completeness (which is seen as impossible). No claim is being made that "servicing" in our prior example, as such, is the only theoretically significant feature of whorehouses. The only claim being advanced is that "servicing" explains much of the variation to be found in the actions, interactions, and perceptions found in the collected data from that research site. The process illuminates organizational features about the house, interactional patterns between prostitute and customer, prostitutes' conceptions of their roles, and a wide variety of less obvious variables. "Servicing" is not to be taken as a "theory" about whorehouses (or deviance), as such, but rather as a theoretical statement about processes which occur therein and in other areas of social life as well.

SUMMARY

In this chapter we have tried to accomplish three tasks. First, we introduced the concept of Basic Social Process (BSP) as a generic theoretical construct and argued for its utility in building theory in sociology. Part of this argument was a critique of what we characterized as unit sociology. From our view unit sociology is inherently limited in its capacity for theoretical development, since referents are not provided to transpose features found in one arena to other arenas, thus forestalling cumulative development of theory. Further, we argued one of the prime reasons for this incapacity to integrate unit theory in a cumulative fashion is that the subject matter involved is more reflective of common-sense considerations than theoretical fit—behavior in the world does not seem to be divided into discrete units of deviance, religion, and so on. BSPs, in contrast, are trans-situational and sensitized to temporal considerations, thus allowing theoretical development through comparison of generic process under different conditions.

Second, a strength of the BSP conception is its linkage to a specific methodological program—grounded-theory methodology. We have attempted to provide an encapsulated account of this linkage to illustrate the manner in which process can be investigated without relying on logical elaboration, intuitive insight, or other quasi-mystical techniques. In other words grounded-theory methodology provides a means by which BSPs can be a consistent analytic focus rather than a serendipitous finding.

Finally, we have attempted to illustrate the consequences BSP sociology would have for the manner in which the discipline theoretically divides the empirical world. In doing so we argued that BSPs as basic uniformities of social life cut across the boundaries by which sociology has traditionally been subdivided. If they didn't, the world would be infinitely more intricate and unpredictable. It seems reasonable, then, that one of the major ways in which we render the world sociologically should reflect this fact of uniformity.

NOTES

[1] We would like to express our appreciation to Martin S. Weinberg and Allen Grimshaw for helpful comments on an earlier draft of this paper. Marilyn J. Lester deserves special thanks for her extensive contribution to the content and clarity of the final draft.

[2] Concern with social dynamics is found in the works of many early sociologists, such as Comte, Marx and Simmel. For surveys of earlier studies of cyclical processes see Sorokin (1927, 1928). For a short survey of American conceptions of process see Buckley (1967: 17-23).

[3] The basic social process notion was originally conceived by Barney Glaser.

[4] The *becoming process* is, of course, a socialization process. The term *becoming* is frequently used by those who study the process (the aforementioned studies, for example). We prefer the term as a substitute for the more general term *socialization*. The term *socialization* is generally used in the framework of larger social and cultural units (usually socialization into "society"), and particularly in reference to childhood socialization. We think the term "becoming process" is appropriate to distinguish a particular type of socialization process. The studies which have used the term *becoming* share several commonalities which differentiate them significantly from the broader usage of the term *socialization*. First, they invariably concern adult socialization. Second, they concern socialization into relatively small social and cultural units (nursing profession, marijuana smokers, nudism, etc.). Third, the participants are ordinarily undergoing socialization into the particular role or setting voluntarily. Fourth, the socialization process is characterized by a constant interpretive process, in which candidates are continually faced with moral dilemmas and choice ("Is becoming a nurse worth all this work?" "is a marijuana high pleasurable" "is going naked in front of others immoral?"). And, fifth, as Olesen and Whittaker (1968: 13) point out, "From the standpoint of the candidates' progress and outcome, the movement forward is constantly and continually problematic."

[5] For a discussion of "Styles of Reporting Qualitative Field Research," see Lofland (1974). The BSP orientation would fall under Lofland's classification of "the generic style."

[6] While it is conceivable that generic unit theory and concepts can be developed, they would usually remain static (and probably reified) formulations, unable to systematically account for change. Cicourel (1970) has made an observation similar to the one here in arguing for the insights afforded from an ethnomethodological perspective. An explicit task of this latter perspective is the discovery of invariant practices—a direct reflection of our concern for generic process. As argued elsewhere

(Hadden & Lester, 1976), the ethnometholologists could reasonably profit (especially with regard to theoretical development) from the analytic procedures developed later in this paper.

[7] McAuliffe & Gordon (1974) suggest a modification of Lindesmith's theory so as to include the desire for euphoria in explanations of opiate addiction. Their study, citing a study of a small sample of addicts in Baltimore and reinterpreting previous research findings they found consistent with their own position does *not* undermine Lindesmith's proposition concerning withdrawal distress but does address this latter proposition's universality. At this point, given available contradictory evidence, McAuliffe and Gordon's proposition is best viewed as suggestive.

[8] We use the terms *substantive* and *formal* in the sense that Glaser and Strauss (1967: 32-33) used them.

> By substantive theory, we mean that developed for a substantive, or empirical, area of sociological inquiry, such as patient care, race relations, professional education, deliquency, or research organization. By formal theory, we mean that developed for a formal, or conceptual, area of sociological inquiry, such as stigma, deviant behavior, formal organization, socialization, status congruency, authority and power, reward systems, or social mobility. Both types of theory may be considered as "middle-range." That is, they fall between the "minor working hypotheses" of everyday life and that "all-inclusive" grand theories.

[9] Generalization from a "representative sample" to a population may appear to be an instance in which statements about one unit (i.e., the sample) may be generalized intact to another unit (i.e., the population). However, this is not the case. The sample is not the unit of analysis, the population is. The sample is merely assumed to be representative of the population in that it supposedly possesses the same properties and conditions. In short, the sample is presumed to be a microcosm of the population unit, not a separate unit in and of itself.

[10] The term *densification* refers to the proliferation of concepts—the development of the subproperties, conditions, consequences, and other aspects of a particular concept. The term *integration* refers to the process of drawing the relationship(s) between conceptual categories—demonstrating how they relate to one another in a systematic fashion.

[11] If formal unit theory cannot be generated from substantive theory (which has its roots in actual behavior) in the above manner, or through densification and integration of concepts, the only recourse left open for formalization is logical elaboration. The end result is reified theories. Such logically elaborated theories are more the products of vivid imaginations and personal genius than the products of systematic empirical research. We believe this accounts in large part for the lack of integration between substantive and formal unit theory, as well as for the tremendous gap between formal unit theory and actual social behavior.

[12] This assumption is so strong in some instances that the "cause" of certain types of nondeviant behavior are not even considered as pertinent sociological concern. Sociologists frequently interest themselves in the "cases" of homosexuality, for example, but seldom question the "causes" of ordinary heterosexuality, which is implicitly assumed to be "natural" and therefore presumably not of sociological concern. A noteworthy exception to the above assumption is found in Simmons (1969: 51), who states:

> Since virtually any behavior is deviant from the moral perspective of some judge, virtually everything causes deviance. That is, since deviant behavior includes virtually all human behavior, its causes are the causes of all human behaviors.

Another noteworthy exception is found in "differential association" theory (Sutherland, 1939: 4-9), which asserts that persons become deviant through essentially the same process as they become conformist.

[13] As many have noted, *rule violation* is not unique to deviant behavior, but also characterizes other conflict situations. e.g., Democrats vs. Republicans. See Lofland, (1969:13-16) for this basic argument.

[14] Work in this direction has been done by symbolic interactionists (cf. Strauss, 1959: 15-30 and Foote, 1951) and ethonomethodologists (cf. Garfinkel, 1967 and the various articles by Douglas, 1970), in their studies of *naming, identification*, the *documentary method*, and related terms that refer,essentially, to the process by which meanings and their resultant actions are constructed. This process is probably the most basic of all basic social processes. See Hadden and Lester (1976) for a further discussion of this point.

[15] The actual coding and analytic procedures are discussed in detail by Glaser (1966). These procedures are referred to as *the constant comparative method*.

[16] For a more elaborate account of the process by which substantive theory can be generated into formal theory see Glaser & Strauss (1967: 79-99) and Hadden and Lester (1976).

[17] Much of the following discussion on the dimensions of whorehouses draws upon a rudimentary analysis of data collected by Lee Stewart (for Stewart's own rendering of segments of this set of data see Stewart, 1972).

[18] In line with our previous discussion one could develop a social psychological process from the whorehouse data that would transcend this unit. But again, this is a data-related decision.

REFERENCES

Becker, Howard S. Becoming a marihuana user. *The American Journal of Sociology*, 1953, *59* (November): 235-42.

Becker, Howard S. *Outsiders*. New York: The Free Press, 1963.

Bell, Daniel. Crime as an American way of life. *Antioch Review* 1953, *13* (Summer): 131-54.

Bigus, Odis E. The milkman and his customer: A cultivated relationship. *Urban Life and Culture*, 1972, *I* (July): 131-65.

Blumer, Herbert. Sociological analysis and the 'variable.' " *The American Sociological Review*, 1956, *22*.

Buckley, Walter. *Sociology and modern systems theory*. Englewood Cliffs, N. J.: Prentice-Hall, 1967.

Cicourel, Arron V. Basic and normative rules in the negotiation of status and role, in H. Dreitzel, *Recent Sociology*, 2, New York: The Macmillan Co., 1970.

Davis, Fred. Deviance disavowal: The management of strained interaction. *Social Problems*, 1961, *IX* (Fall): 120-32.

Douglas, Jack D. *Understanding everyday life*. Chicago: Aldine, 1970.

Foote, Nelson N. Identification as the basis for a theory of motivation. *The American Sociological Review*, 1951, *16* (February): 14-21.

Freeze, Lee. Cumulative sociological knowledge. *The American Sociological Review*, 1972, 37 (August): 412-28.

Garfinkel, Harold. *Studies in ethnomethodology*. Englewood Cliffs, N.J.: Prentice-Hall, 1967.

Glaser, Barney G. The constant comparative method of qualitative analysis. *Social Problems*, 1965, *12*: 436-45.

Glaser, Barney G. and Strauss, Anselm L., *The discovery of grounded theory: Strategies for qualitative research*. Chicago: Aldine, 1967.

Glaser, Barney G. and Strauss, Anselm L. *Status passage*. Chicago: Aldine, 1971.

Hadden, Stuart C. *The social creation of a social problem*. Unpublished Ph.D. disseration, Washington State University, 1973.

Hadden Stuart C. & Lester, Marilyn. Ethnomethodology and grounded theory methodology: An integration of topic and method. American Sociological Association Meetings, New York, 1976.

Lindesmith, Alfred R. A sociological theory of drug addiction. *The American Journal of Sociology* 1938, *43:* 593-613.

Lofland, John. *Deviance and identity*. Englewood Cliffs, N.J.: Prentice-Hall, 1969.

Lofland, John. Styles of reporting qualitative field research. *The American Sociologist* 1974, *9* (August): 101-11.

Lofland, John. *Doomsday cult*. (Enlarged edition) New York: Irvington Publishers, 1977.

Matza, David. *Deliquency and drift*. New York: John Wiley & Sons, 1964.

McAuliffe, William E. & Gordon, Robert A., A test of Lindesmith's theory of addiction: The frequency of euphoria among long-term addicts. *The American Journal of Sociology* 1974, *79* (January): 795-840.

Mullins, Nicholas C. Theory construction from available materials: A system for organizing and presenting propositions. *The American Journal of Sociology* 1974, *80:* 1-14.

National Commission on Marijuana and Drug Abuse. *Drug use in America: Problem in perspective*. Washington, D.C.: U.S. Gov. Printing Office, 1973.

Olesen, Virginia L. & Whittaker, Elvi W. *The silent dialogue*. San Francisco: Jossey-Bass, 1968.

Schutz, Alfred. *Collected papers, Volume I*. Edited by Natanson. The Hague, Netherlands: Martunus Nijhoff, 1971.

Simmons, J.L. *Deviants*. Berkeley: The Glendessary Press, 1969.

Sorokin, Pitirim A. A survey of the cyclical conceptions of social and historical process. Social Forces (September), 1927.

Sorokin, Pitirim A. *Contemporary sociological theories*. New York: Harper & Row, 1928.

Strauss, Anselm L. *Mirrors and masks: The search for identity*. New York: Free Press, 1959.

Steward, George Lee. On first being a john. *Urban Life and Culture* 1972, *I* (October): 255-74.

Sutherland, Edwin H. *Principles of criminology*. Philadelphia: J. B. Lippincott, 1939.

Terry, Charles E. & Pellins, Mildred. *The opium problem.* Montclair, N.J.: Patterson-Smith, 1970.

Weber, Max. *The theory of social and economic organization.* New York: Free Press, 1964.

Weinberg, Martin S. Becoming a nudist. *Psychiatry: Journal for the Study of Interpersonal Processes* 1966, *29* (February).

Chapter Eleven
Analytic induction[1]

PETER K. MANNING

In spite of the diversity of problems, approaches, and conclusions in the writings of sociologists in qualitative research and analysis, all would seem to support one general position: Qualitative research is a preliminary, exploratory effort to quantitative research, since only quantitative research yields rigorously verified findings and hypotheses. The source of this position is that these sociologists appear to take as a guide to being "systematic" the canons of quantitative analysis on such issues as sampling, coding, reliability, validity, indicators, frequency distributions, conceptual formalization, hypothesis contruction, and presentation of evidence. Thus, these sociologists overemphasize rigorous testing of hypotheses and deemphasize the discovery of what concepts and hypotheses are relevant for the substantive area being researched.
—Glaser & Strauss (1965: 5)

Sociology is now passing through a crisis as deep as any science ever passed through. It was established as a synthetic science of "society" or "civilization," using the results of several other sciences to draw such comprehensive generalizations as none of those sciences could or cared to draw for itself. It is changing into an analytic science investigating directly and independently particular empirical data, formulating its own results in a vast monographic literature, not only avoiding hasty conclusions, but often mistrusting generalizations more than other sciences do, and more than is good for any science. In this crisis it needs all the light that methodological studies and discussions can throw on its present and future.
—Znaniecki (1934: v-vi)

INTRODUCTION

Analytic induction, a method of sociological research, contains in its procedure a vision of science and of the empirical world. George Herbert Mead, the canonical spokesman of the symbolic interactionist version of social psychology, elaborated a position on the nature of science that was to become central to practitioners of scientific induction.[2] Mead argues, ". . . there can be no scientific data without meanings" (Reck, ed. 1964:

273

206). As meanings change, the nature of the scientific world to which scientists direct their attention changes.

Scientific method is indifferent to a world of things-in-themselves, or to the previous condition of philosophic servitude of those to whom its teachings are addressed. It is a method not of knowing the unchangeable, but of determining the form of the world within which we live as it changes from moment to moment. . . . Science always has a world of reality by which to test its hypotheses, but this world is not a world independent of scientific experience, but the immediate world surrounding us within which we must act. Our next action may find these conditions seriously changed, and then science will formulate this world so that in view of this problem we may logically construct our next plan of action. . . . Science advances by the experiences of individuals, experiences which are different from the world in which they have arisen and which refer to a world which is not yet in existence, so far as scientific experience is concerned. But this relation to the old and new is not that of a subjective world to an objective universe, but is a process of logical reconstruction by which out of expectations the new law arises to replace a structure that has become inadequate (Mead, in Reck, ed. 1964: 210-11).

Mead's thesis is that science can never be divorced from the laboring, thinking, interacting, individual scientists who employ scientific methods to build up a response to a problematic situation that arouses their interest because of its exceptional properties. Once they identify this exceptional situation, they may build up alternative modes of response to it and attempt to rationalize, integrate, and bind together their findings with previously known laws, propositions, and hypotheses.

The scientist approaches a world mediated through symbols, the principal symbols being the shared framework that is science. Doing science is a symbolic act involving *attitudes*, or propensities to act; *values*, or objects desired; and a *framework of meanings*, or methodology.[3] *Methodology* refers to the generalized norms of scientific procedure, not to be confused with *techniques*, or the means employed to execute a study once a problem and a general approach have been established. Analytic induction is a methodology drawing on a vision of the scientific enterprise in part described by Mead.

How do we proceed from this very broad panorama of "science" to the actual work of sociology, and from there to the more specific concerns of analytic induction? First, sociology is clearly an *independent empirical* science that relies on objects that can be touched, felt, smelled, seen, or heard. Sociological research, as a symbolic act or series of symbolic actions, as the creative response sociologists make to the problematic, is typically a search for the empirical—that which can be verified, manipulated, and, if formulated adequately, proven or disproven. "Independent" means that sociology cannot rely on concepts and theories developed to deal with the problems of such other disciplines as behavioristic psychology, economics, medicine, or the natural or physical sciences.

Second, the creative response of the sociologist to the world is never simply physiologically "released" by an outside stimulus; it is a *process* involving the symbols of language, of self and other indications, and of symbolic interaction between scientists and the subjects of their concern. Sociology is not therefore simply a "behavioral science"; it involves both *"spatial knowledge"*—i.e., the "development of sense knowledge into knowledge of things"—and *"social" knowledge*, which is derived from contacts with the minds of other men, through communication, which invoves us in their sentiments and enables us to understand them. Spatial knowledge is mensurative, while social knowledge is dramatic (Cooley, 1926).[4]

Third, scientists must see their own scientific actions as a product, at least in part, of their social perspectives and quite distinct—analytically, at least—from the social perspectives of those they study (Cicourel, 1964: 23-24, *et passim*). Finally, sociology must be open to interpretation of experience and meanings as a product of processes and interaction, not as given in the nature of the empirical world. Any effort at interpreting the nature of the social world should reflect these assumptions about an "equation" involving the observer, the observed, and the framework of science. Analytic induction adopts this symbolic-interactionist conception of science. In the following essay the method of analytic induction will be described and illustrated, an example from my own research will be presented, the strengths and weaknesses of the method will be described, and an assessment will be made.

ANALYTIC INDUCTION: PROCEDURE AND ANTECEDENTS

Induction can be best understood by a comparison with deduction. Deduction is the process of reasoning from general tenets to more particular conclusions. Kinch provides an example of deductive reasoning in his discussion of a formal theory of the self concept (see also Zetterberg, 1965, for the deductive approach to theory).

KINCH'S BASIC PROPOSITIONS OF A
FORMALIZED THEORY OF THE SELF-CONCEPT[5]
(Derived from Symbolic Interactionism)

1. The individual's self-concept is based on his perception of the way others are responding to him.

2. The individual's self-concept functions to direct his behavior.

3. The individual's perception of the responses of others toward him reflects the actual responses of others toward him.

(These postulates are not expected to hold under all conditions: The formalization procedure described below allows us to consider under what conditions they will hold).

These three statements make up the postulates of the theory. Within these propositions there are four basic concepts or variables:

1. The individual's self-concept (S). (Defined above.)

2. His perception of the responses of others toward him (P). (The response of the individual to those behaviors of others that he perceives as directed toward him.)

3. The actual responses of others toward him(A). (The actual behavior of the others—that is, in response to the individual.)

4. His behavior (B). (The activity of the individual relevant to the social situation.)

By the use of simple logic we may take the three basic propositions and deduce from them three more. For example, from postulates 1 and 2 we can conclude that the way an individual perceives the response of others toward him will influence his behavior, for if his perception determines his self-concept and his self-concept guides his behavior, then his perception will determine his behavior. In symbolic form,

$$\text{if } P \rightarrow S \text{ postulate } 1$$

$$\text{and } \underline{S \rightarrow B \text{ postulate } 2}$$

$$\text{then } P \rightarrow B \text{ proposition } 4$$

Therefore, the fourth proposition of the theory (call it a derived proposition) is:

5. The way the individual perceives the response of others toward him will influence his behavior.

In like manner from postulates 1 and 3 we deduce a fifth proposition:

6. The actual response of others to the individual will determine the way he sees himself (his self-concept).

And, finally, by combining either propositions 5 and 2, or 3 and 4 we get the sixth proposition:

7. The actual response of others toward the individual will affect the behavior of the individual.

Our theory so far can be summarized in the following statement: The actual responses of others to the individual will be important in determining how the individual will perceive himself; this perception will influence his self-conception which, in turn, will guide his behavior. Symbolically,

$$A \rightarrow P \rightarrow S \rightarrow B \quad \rightarrow = \text{ ''leads to''}$$

Conversely, induction is the process of inferring a more general conclusion from the observation of a number of discrete facts. Public opinion polling is an example of popular induction—e.g., the newspaper columns of Gallup, Harris, and others. These two procedures are by no means mutually exclusive, and in research and theorizing there is a clear interplay between the two.[6] Few sociologists now begin with a closed, rationalistic, deductive system as a basis for hypothesis testing; most begin with a somewhat narrow, substantive problem (how do medical students learn to be physicians?) and attempt to specify the limits and scope of their hypotheses. Most sociologists thus use induction to a greater or lesser degree (McKinney, in Becker and Boskoff, eds., 1957: 197).

Two forms of induction may be identified—*enumerative induction* and *analytic induction*. In the enumerative-induction approach statistical generalizations are developed on the basis of a limited sample of cases that have been chosen to represent the known population. This incomplete induction of the universe allows a series of conclusions, or abstractions, based on generalization from those apsects of each case examined that resemble each other. If these generalizations are to culminate in a body of theory, they must refer to socially meaningful units (groups or individuals). Averages deal with aggregates or statistically created units; thus, the central problem is the relationship between the statistical findings and meaningful—i.e., *social*—groupings (Turner, 1948). These inferences are always qualified by a statement of the probability or likelihood that such associations exist in the larger population or universe. Probability enters not only because the universe is sampled and not completely enumerated, but also because a great many effects that are revealed in given relationships may not have been previously conceptualized nor explained.

Analytic induction seeks to develop *universal* statements containing the *essential features* of a phenomenon, or those things that are always found to *cause* or lie behind the existence of a social occurrence. The essential features are revealed, it is argued, when they are always present when the phenomenon is present; when they are absent, the phenomenon is itself absent. The definitional aspect of science is critical in analytic induction, and in the procedure redefinition and reconceptualization are often required to narrow the range of applicability or the scope of the theory. Exceptions or negative cases assume a major significance, since the explanations aim for completeness and universality. Traditionally, only a few selected cases are subjected to careful scrutiny (persons and families have been used). The first formal statement of this method is found in Florian Znaniecki's *The Method of Sociology* (1934: Chap 6). Prior to Znaniecki's statement several works using an inductive method had been published. In each case, reviewed in more detail below, slight variations on the method appeared[7] Now let us review some of the historical background and analogous developments in sociological methods.

The first American empirical sociological study of major significance was Thomas & Znaniecki's now classic *The Polish Peasant in Europe and America* (1927; originally published, 1918-1920, five volumes). Ostensibly a cultural ethnography with a concern for the development of concepts, it is more importantly a comparative analysis of the impact of social change on the Polish family, primary groups, and communal ties in two settings. The first volume contained a methodological note in which the concepts of *value*, *attitude*, *definition of the situation*, and the *four wishes* were defined and illustrated. Thomas & Znaniecki analytically distinguished *sociology*—the study of systems of *values*, particularly those that have the binding stature of rules—from *social psychology*, the study of *attitudes*. Explanation according to their scheme would be based on laws of becoming, including both values and attitudes. Changes detected in the Polish family in America were not simply changes in their values or in their attitudes, but in the synthesis of the two, called a *definition of the situation*. The source of both family and social disorganization was primarily a breakdown in the homogeneity of the attitudes toward the rules, hence a redefinition of the rules in the direction of greater individualism. Both the subjective and the objective aspects of social life were not only changing, but coming into fundamentally new relationships with each other. Thomas & Znaniecki argued that previous static conceptions, based on an analysis either only of rules or only of attitudes, could not deal with the massive changes they discovered. Hence, they suggested the need for a *situational social psychology*, which could take into account both the objective and subjective and was more appropriate for the study of modern, industrialized, changing, individualistic society (cf. Ball, 1971, and Janowitz, ed., 1966).

The theory evolved in the *Polish Peasant* required a method of equal scope and imagination. The fault of many previous works was, according to their perspective, the failure to deal with the subjective, concrete, and experimental dimensions of personal and group life. They proposed to remain as close to human materials as possible, to constrain their interpretations to an elaboration of what could be culled from what they called human documents. They were concerned with the subject as he tried to find his way through *his* world, and the feelings, confusion, definitions, and meanings constructed by the actor in response to the world (Thomas & Znaniecki, 1927, vol. 2: 1846-47). Seeking the actor's perspective, they collected newspaper files, letters, biographies, and autobiographies (one autobiography was published as vol. 3 of the five-volume edition), magazine files, community and organization records. Approximately 50 sets of letters exchanged between families in Poland and the United States were central to the work. These human documents, collected both in the United States and in Poland, were aptly suited to the methodological aims of the authors: they were an expression of human feelings, were close to the everyday experience and perceptions of their subjects, and were at the same time "objective" in that they could be analyzed and reanalyzed without damage to their content or meanings.[8]

It is likely that Thomas developed or worked out his style of analysis through his trained sensitivity to the problems inherent in the life crises he saw mirrored in the human documents.[9] He had previously used the inductive approach in an early form in his *Source Book of Social Origins*

(1909) and later in *The Unadjusted Girl* (1923) and in Thomas & Thomas (1928). It was, however, his colleague and friend Florian Znaniecki, who published the first systematic statement of analytic induction in *The Method of Sociology* (1934).[10] By the time this appeared in print, the sociology department at the University of Chicago was deeply committed to involvement in social life and to attention to its subjective elements as they could be extracted from human documents.[11] Robert Park and Ernest Burgess at this time wrote the "bible" of the "Chicago School" of sociology (1921) and were urging their students to see society as collective action, and to take part in it both as participants and observers.[12] The social-psychological framework developed by Park & Burgess and the ecological framework of Park, Burgess, & McKenzie loosely integrated this host of studies into a mosaic in which each part contributed to a larger understanding of community and society (Becker, 1966).[13]

In the late twenties a debate was carried on at the University of Chicago concerning the relative merit of the case-history-human-documents approach and the statistical-enumerative induction approach. During the twenties and on through the thirties, after the debate was no longer a major issue, members of the department had made major contributions to both modes of analysis. Clifford Shaw wrote his series on deliquent boys (1930, 1931, 1938), which had been preceded by Thrasher's *Deliquent Gangs* (1927) and Reckless' *Six Boys in Trouble* (1929). Burgess used both techniques in his work on marriage (Burgess & Cottrell, 1939; Burgess & Locke, 1945), although his sympathies seemed to favor the life-history method (Burgess, in Gurvitch & Moore, 1945). On the other hand the leading statistician of the day was Ogburn, keynoter for the empiricist-operational view of sociology that was being touted at the time by Lundberg, Chapin, Ogburn, and others. According to Faris (1967: 114-15), the debate revolved around the extent to which human experience and meanings were inaccessible to the statistical method. If this maxim were true, the case study would be not only an essential sociological tool, but perhaps the only way to tap "subjective facts." It was argued by some that attitude scales then being developed did not measure the same dimensions extracted from case histories by skilled researchers (Faris, 1967: 114). The issue was joined by Samuel Stouffer in his dissertation on student's attitudes toward prohibition and alcohol. Students were asked to write autobiographies and to include everything in their life experiences relating to alcohol and Prohibition law; additionally, they were asked to fill out questionaires designed to form a Thurstone type scale. Judges' rankings of the life histories were compared with the scale scores. Stouffer found a substantial agreement between judges' rankings and scale scores, suggesting that the relatively more demanding task of assembling and analyzing life histories did not contribute substantially more knowledge about a set of attitudes than did a simple scale score (Stouffer, 1930, as summarized in Faris, 1967: 114-15).[14] From this point the enumerative approach was judged to be the superior mode of attacking most problems: it was more efficient and faster, it permitted ease of handling, and it was as effective in many of the areas previously judged to be "sacred." The use and development of the case method continued, but it no longer occupied the spotlight as it had through the twenties.

The efflorescence of analytic induction came from students of the early students at the University of Chicago, or of pioneers in symbolic-interactionist psychology. Four studies constitute the nucleus of the contribution of analytic induction to modern sociological method. They are Robert Cooley Angell's *The Family Encounters the Depression* (1936); Alfred Lindesmith's dissertation at the University of Chicago, *Opiate Addiction* (1947); Donald Cressey's *Other People's Money* (1953); and Howard S. Becker's "Becoming a Marijuana User" (1953) and "Marijuana Use and Social Control" (1955).[15]

Sociologists have continued to develop their quantitative methodology into increasingly deductive and mathematical approaches, (e.g., Berger, Zelditch, & Anderson, 1966) while the life-history-human-documents approach has become almost exclusively the domain of the anthropologists.[16] Anthropologists have accumulated an almost incredible stock of biographies and autobiographies (see Langness, 1965) with no appreciable advance in the theory of method of analysis.

THE PROCEDURE

Analytic induction does not admit to an easy, pithy definition. It is too much a product of a period in sociology when philosophical issues were central.[17] Znaniecki himself never published a quotable statement, and there are surprisingly few references to "analytic induction" in sociological compendia.[18] *Analytic induction is a nonexperimental qualitative sociological method that employs an exhaustive examination of cases in order to prove universal, causal generalizations.* Rather than accepting evidence suggesting "some S is P," it maximizes exposure to negative instances in order to claim confidently that "all S is P."

Turning now from formal definition to practice, Donald Cressey's description of his own procedure is illuminating.

The complete methodological *procedure*, then, has essentially the following steps. First, a rough definition of the phenomenon to be explained is formulated. Second, an hypothetical explanation of that phenomenon is formulated. Third, one case is studied in light of the hypothesis with the object of determining whether the hypothesis fits the facts in that case. Fourth, if the hypothesis does not fit the facts, either the hypothesis is re-formulated or the phenomenon to be explained is re-defined, so that the case is excluded. This definition must be more precise than the first one. Fifth, practical certainty may be attained after a small number of cases has been examined, but the discovery by the investigator or any other investigator of a single negative case disproves the explanation and requires a re-formulation. Sixth, this procedure of examining cases, re-defining the phenomenon and re-formulating the hypothesis is continued until a universal relationship is established, each negative case calling for a re-definition or a re-formulation. Seventh, for purposes of proof, cases outside the area circumscribed by the definition are examined to determine whether or not the final hypothesis applies to them. This step is in keeping with the observation that scientific generalizations consist of descriptions of conditions which are always present when the phenomenon is present but which are never present when the phenomenon is absent (Cressey, 1953: 16).

In Cressey's statement we discover the core features of the method as practiced: definition, tentative explanation, possible reformulation, and generalization. As he implies, the process may continue until a point of closure is achieved. This point is not defined in a straightforward manner.

Robinson's important review article (1951) summarizes two further characterizations of analytic-induction research: restating the hypothesis to cover negative evidence, or altering the definition of the phenomena to exclude some cases.

The initial continuing problem is one of definition and of developing related tentative hypothesis. The task is not one of "mere semantics"; it marks one of the important distinctions between enumerative and analytic induction. Whereas enumerative induction attempts to capture through correlations and associations a partial generalization true for some members of the class of objects at issue, analytic induction seeks to explain only those phenomena at issue. These phenomena must be precisely defined to eliminate the extraneous or unexplained. For example, if one defines "juvenile deliquent" as a young person taken into custody for a violation of law, there are likely to be a few characteristics shared by members of the class (though many of them may have little to do with the offenders, but more with enforcement procedures), but there are many more that are not shared. If on the other hand one defines deliquents in the Gluecks' (e.g., 1956) terms, then the associations found in the class of deliquents will yield only what the Gluecks' definitions have supplied (cf. Znaniecki, 1928, 1934: 233-34). Relevant features of a class of objects can be best understood and extracted if the objects are defined on the basis of close examination and analysis, not by a preconceived, deductive-type token scheme.

For example, Cressey recast his study of embezzlement as the "criminal violation of financial trust." He redefines the legal term *embezzlement* into a more limited phenomenon of violation of a position of trust taken in good faith. From this definition he is able to trace out the conditions that underlay the act, including: (1) awareness of an unshareable problem; (2) further awareness that this problem may be solved by embezzlement, and (3) the construction of a rationalization that permitted both the criminal act and the maintenance of a self-conception as a law-abiding citizen.

Revision of hypotheses in the light of negative evidence is characteristic of analytic induction. This preference is based on the notion that accumulated evidence alone is inadequate proof; one must look for evidence where clear logical contradiction may be obtained (Lindesmith, 1968: 9-10). Lindesmith's study of opiate addiction, based on interviews with approximately 50 addicts, concluded that addiction existed only when the following process occurred: The person had to take the drug knowingly, recognize the withdrawal distress as a product of the absence of the drug, and define the drug as the source of an alleviation of distress (1947: 8). This was the final form of his hypothesis, however, the product of two previous revisions. Lindesmith discovered negative evidence in a limited number of cases, and this forced a reformulation.

A few cases initially examined may be the basis for a revision of the hypotheses, as in Lindesmith & Angell's work. In Cressey's study another strategy was followed—some of the cases were excluded from further analysis because the criminals he interviewed in prisons had not taken the occupational positions in good faith—they had lied to employers or had aimed initially to exploit their job opportunities (Cressey, 1953: 22).

These investigators were apparently not content with discovering a plausible pattern of results or only a few exceptions to their formulations, as in the case when researchers accept discovery of a generalization that covers 95 percent of the events examined. A search for a complete *causal* statement led Cressey to attempt a comparison between his interviewees at an earlier time (when they were law-abiding citizens without a notion of trust violation as a personal act) to see if the conditions he identified were present prior to the events he argued were unique to the outcome. It was also the impetus for Lindesmith's interviews with nonaddicts to discover if in fact the conditions were present but addiction was not. (This issue is further discussed below.)

Angell's study (1936) was an attempt to predict the responses of families to a rapid decline in income during the Depression. He identified eight types of families, ranging from highly integrated and highly adaptable to unintegrated and unadaptable. (This range of predictions is primarily what makes Angell's study the most promising use of the method.) In the course of working out his analysis Angell feels the scientist should "play around with the relationships and the units of analysis until he hits upon a scheme that is very parsimonious in explanatory power" (Angell, 1954: 476). Angell did just this, as his appendix on method explains:

Glancing back over my work sheets, I see that I became obsessed at this point with the idea of quantification. I tried no less than seven different schemes of giving numerical values to the different degrees of original integration and adaptability and to the different pressures associated with the decrease, hoping that by processes of addition and subtraction a numerical result would be reached which would accurately represent the subsequent situation. Although in the majority of instances the best of these schemes worked out fairly well, there were some cases which refused to be quantified in this way. (Angell, 1936: 293)

One more debt I owe to Znaniecki. This is for his term "analytic induction" which he contrasts with "enumerative induction." I had been following the procedure of analytic induction from the start but had not had a good term for it, nor indeed had I had as clear a concept of what I was doing as I secured from reading his chapter on the subject. (Angell, 1936: 296-97).

. . . the sample of 50 was designed to be only exploratory if it yielded results, I planned to try to secure a much larger number for verification and more detailed analysis. This has not been done. The decision not to go ahead was not made explicitly at any one time. Like so many things in life, I drifted into it. The reasons which now support such a decision. . . (Angell, 1936: 300)

The "quest for universals," as Turner (1953) labels analytic induction, is the search for empirically established causes based on a select number of well-analyzed cases. In the process, as the Angell quote above shows, many of the most problematic features of social research must be bared and realistically faced. The "public" readjustment of definitions, concepts, and hypotheses is in a sense an intrinsic feature of the approach.

AN EXAMPLE OF ANALYTIC INDUCTION: "FIXING WHAT YOU FEARED"

A contemporary example is illustrated by the results of some research on successful abortion seekers on a college campus (Manning, 1971). It was patterned after the inductive approach advocated by Znaniecki. Since it manifests many of the difficulties and weaknesses, as well as some of the strengths, of the approach, it may be of value as a contemporary illustration.

Taking a theme from Cressey, we sought to discover whether a definable sequence or conjunction of events is always present when abortion is present and never present when abortion is absent, and the correlated problem of identifying the antecedent background factors determining the presence or absence of events (paraphrase from Cressey, 1953: 12). These two approaches can be termed the *genetic*—concerned with a pathway of events leading up to a given type of situation—and the *situational*—exploration dealing with the response and behavior of the individual (Cressey, 1953:, 11-12ff; see also Lewin, 1935; Brown, 1963, and Sutherland & Cressey, 1970: chap. 4, for an application of the genetic approach to explanation of crime).

The research began as a result of a student who announced to me that she would not be able to take her final exam because she was having an abortion. I asked her to keep a document of her experience. The following winter I taught a course in human sexuality and asked my class to gather case histories of their acquaintances who had obtained an abortion. I later employed two female students to obtain case histories and one to embark on a simulated abortion search.[19] In this manner, some 15 cases were collected and analyzed. The natural-history approach was initially adopted.[20]

I described it in a preliminary report.

> The notion of a natural history of the construction or production of a social object takes into account the shifting meaning of events as they are temporally patterned. Within each of the posited stages, the objective facts, or constraining features of the social environment, are perceived and defined differentially as the perspectives of those involved shift. Thus, although each stage may have salient *features*, and associated *contingencies*, it essentially comes to pass when the persons involved take these features into account. An explanation of the course of events involved in the search for a campus abortion must take into account "objective social facts" salient at each stage—e.g., raising money, contacting an abortionist, maintaining secrecy with some of one's peers, as well as those matters of definition, perception, and meaning that arise (Manning, 1971: 138-39).

In other words, there are a number of attitudes and values associated or correlated with abortion as an accomplished fact and with the approval or disapproval of it in the abstract. However, the object (an abortion, for example) can never be explained with reference to past events or antecedents, for, strictly speaking, any outcome is a product of innumerable instances, and the relative importance of any given series of facts may vary from case to case. The precise effect of any given one remains undetermined and changing. One must seek to trace back a few facts to their causes and to determine how they act in concert to produce a given result (Znaniecki, 1928: 309-11). The matters of principal interest are the precise combination of those factors defined by the actors involved. The result should be a set of generalizations about the phenomena that include or explain all the cases examined and consequently result in a universal explanation of it. We encountered a problem that paralleled Cressey's. The concept "embezzlement" as a legal category, ". . . did not describe a homogeneous class of criminal behavior" (Cressey, 1953: 19). Cressey decided to redefine the focus of his study as "trust violation," or the use of a position taken in good faith to commit a crime. "Abortion" as a legal category covered a wide range of both legal and illegal acts. On the other hand operations termed "D and C" by hospitals and clinics contain an unknown proportion of dilation and curettage where a fertile ovum was scraped from the walls of the uterus. Legal and medical categories collapse a variety of social pathways to obtaining the physical act, and a number of self-definitions result. Abortion was defined as the self-defined illegal termination of a pregnancy seen as a problem. It was limited to unmarried coeds. This definition excludes legal (therapeutic) abortions, miscarriages that were not self-induced, and pregnancies terminated "under duress" (i.e., demands by parents). What is the medical definition of abortion?

Abortion . . . is the induced termination of pregnancy before the normal fetus has attained viability, or the capacity for life outside the womb. The word applies only to INTENTIONAL termination as opposed to SPONTANEOUS abortion, which occurs when fetal growth is impaired, and, frequently referred to as MISCARRIAGE.

The standard hospital technique of abortion is known as a dilation and curettage, or a "D and C." The patient, anesthetized to eliminate all pain, is protected against infection by antibiotics and rarely kept in the hospital for more than one night.

First, the cervix is dilated or stretched to permit the use of curette . . . a tiny metal instrument shaped like a rake [with which] the surgeon . . . removes the embryo, alternating curette and forceps until the uterus is clean.

If an abortion has to be performed after three months of pregnancy, the standard technique is a hysterotomy, or miniature cesarian, requiring a small, longitudinal incision in the lower abdomen. (Lader, 1966: 18)

The question of abortion is not exclusively medical but is also a moral question. Under what conditions will this operation, and those on whom it is willingly performed by experienced people, be labeled "good" or "evil." An abortion is the consequence of biological processes, aleatory social processes, ecological factors, location in a social structure, and a sequential process of transformation of self and other definitions.

Thus, a whole variety of causes may be identified for premarital intercourse (e.g., Reiss, 1967; Vincent, 1969), particularly in the form of attitudinal or class correlates. Other reasons might include such diverse accounts as the "failure" of consciously utilized birth control devices by either sex, risk-taking or thrill-seeking in the gamble with pregnancy, forgotten birth control pills, "trying it" to see, passions of the moment, attempts by females to "trap a husband" or play on male vulnerability, male aggression or exploitation, the result of regular cohabitation or intercourse among couples in love, mutual indifference, and so on.

The social structure of control on the campus and the consequent rise of a variety of infrastructures to provide demanded "deviant services" is the context within which the search occurs. There was no official policy of providing birth control information and/or services in the midwestern university where the research was conducted. There are no abortions performed on the campus by the University Health Service. There was a fairly well-known "demimonde" of illegal services available in the form of drugs, homosexual contacts, etc. This information is apparently a part of the students' everyday/anyday life.

Once a female discovers she is pregnant, there are a number of logical options available to her: First is the choice between marriage or nonmarriage; given this decision, the child may be aborted, kept, or offered for adoption. If abortion is chosen, it may be obtained legally or illegally, professionally or unprofessionally (if done illegally). These logical options may not be apparent to the women themselves. It was first hypothesized that the search began when the female defined herself as pregnant, eliminated marriage as an option, and saw her problem as "unshareable." Further investigation revealed that eliminating marriage was not as critical as *disinterest* in marriage at the time and little desire for a child.

Once they defined the problem in this way, all the women we talked with embarked on the search (and all were successful). The search itself involved a varying degree of participation by parents, male friends (biological father or not), and some sex peers. Neither the degree of participation by others nor the status characteristics of those with whom the problem was shared had an effect on the outcome. Those who shared the problem, and particularly those who urged the abortion, may have had an effect on the self-concept of the abortee.[21]

The women interviewed had little trouble in obtaining names of abortionists. Other interviews (not in the sample) and informal conversations suggested that in the absence of the information, some left the country for a European abortion, failed in tries at self-induced abortion, or were married.

All of the women interviewed had developed a "rhetoric of motives" or a verbal explanation, for their action (Mills, 1940). Cressey found that trust violators had to develop a self-conception as law-abiding people while making an exception for their own act of embezzlement (Cressey, 1953: 142). They felt it was an essentially *expedient* act.

An abortion takes place when an unmarried woman defines herself as pregnant, is neither willing to marry at that time nor to rear a child, is advised by friends to solve the problem by abortion, neutralizes her self-concept as deviant, and finally is able to locate an abortionist. Exceptions to these generalizations failed to obtain abortions and were either married, were dissuaded by friends, or failed to neutralize it in advance.

Two summary points may be made about this research. First, the factors are cumulative but not necessarily sequential or *time-ordered*. A girl may have been able to rationalize the possibility of pregnancy *before* it occurs and therefore anticipate seeking an abortion as a solution to pregnancy. She may have knowledge of an abortionist from a friend's experience. Second, in this very small sample it appears that without all of the stages the act will not occur.

A CRITICAL EVALUATION OF ANALYTIC INDUCTION

Research by Lindesmith, Cressey, and Angell stimulated two important critical papers, written in the early 1950s, and, since then, scattered commentary (Becker, 1970; Denzin, 1970). Let us now turn to a critical evaluation of the method of analytic induction.

Science attempts to understand, predict, and control events. The social sciences have adopted a model of enumerative induction in concert with a hypothetical deductive theory (Douglas, in Tiryakian, ed., 1971). Although there is no single paradigm or mode of doing sociology, this rough procedural form first established by Durkheim continues to influence the practice of sociology and the evaluation of its methods (Friedrichs, 1970; Gouldner, 1970). Not surprisingly, most discussions of analytic induction are grounded in the statistical model (cf McAuliffe & Gordon, 1974). Others, by Turner (1953) and Denzin (1970), are more sympathetic. We will now address the disadvantages and advantages of analytic induction.

The major *disadvantages* may be summarized as its failure to *predict*, its inability to deal with *matters of degree* or variation, its *inefficiency*, and its failure to produce true *causal* analysis.

Prediction is the regular capacity to anticipate the relationships found in the empirical world either by scientific reasoning, observation, or experience. In sociology there are, roughly speaking, two kinds or modes of prediction—one can attempt to predict either individual behavior or the existence of rates. Individualistic predictions take a form such as, people with x characteristics will tend to do y; rate prediction has to do with the correlations of x with y—e.g., suburban neighborhoods have low rates of delinquency.

Lindesmith's theory of opiate addiction relies on the recognition of the symptoms of withdrawal as critical to the later association between relief of this distress and the reuse of the drug. In Cressey's argument the rationalization stage is the most critical; one must be able to construct a verbal rationale that will insulate the self from a deviant or criminal stigmata.[22] In each case the existence of these events is said to be a part of the causal complex, therefore necessary for the predicted outcome.

Turner (1953) argues that neither of these schemes allows true prediction. They do not permit individualistic prediction—i.e., one cannot identify a priori *which* individuals will become addicted or become trust violators. Nor do they suggest those personal special traits that might be associated with a movement from one to the next stage. For example, are there aspects of self or body awareness (e.g., field versus self orientation) that predispose some people to identify withdrawal distress earlier? Are some people or groups more likely to rationalize their actions verbally? Are these groups not likely to be prisoners who have been caught and must try to resolve the consequence of their criminal action to a researcher?

In Becker's study of marijuana use (1963) another difficulty is encountered. The conditions necessary for the final outcome are only known *retrospectively*, after the investigator identifies them—". . . the alleged preconditions or essential causes of the phenomenon under examination cannot be fully specified apart from the observation of the condition they are supposed to produce" (1953: 606). Becker argued that continued marijuana use for pleasure occurs when a willing person first learns the technique of smoking, then learns to perceive the effects, and finally defines these effects as pleasurable. If these conditions are absent, a person will not continue to use marijuana for pleasure. But is it possible to claim that people have learned the technique of smoking unless they achieve the effects? Can one know a "high" without having it defined by others associating it with smoking? In short, it is difficult, if not impossible, to establish causation when the factors claimed to cause something cannot be independently observed. Although theoretical *prediction* does not seem possible without the retrospective knowledge of the investigator, analytic induction *explains* or accounts for findings based on its emerging premises (Doby, ed., 1967: 50-62).

The second major criticism deals with the *simplicity* with which the variables in the causal complex have been defined. With the possible exception of Angell's study, the variables are seen as dichotomies, or phenomena that are either present or absent. The marijuana smoker either learns the technique or does not; the embezzler either defines the problem as nonshareable or does not; and the opiate addict either associates relief of the withdrawal distress with the drug, or does not. This is an aspect of the search for universals; the procedure attempts to show that all "*s* is *p*," and therefore derives a complete explanation, not a partial one. Partial explanations are logically linked to probablistic inferences and statements about *degrees* of association between variables. Such standard research procedures as scales, indexes, and measures of correlation and association are means of estimating parameters in a population from a sample. In the case of analytic induction the features of a process for the cases examined may be established, but the inference to other populations will remain difficult, at the very least, because most of the aspects of social life of greatest interest are not easily dichotomized.

The issue of causal analysis and that of proof are deeply intertwined because a truly causal analysis will result in proof. W. S. Robinson (1951) suggests that an evaluation of the argument of analytic inductionists may be judged using a simple two-by-two table:

	P	$\overline{P}$
C	X	?
$\overline{C}$	O	X

According to Robinson statisticians would study all four cells, hoping for a pattern shown by the Xs, and would hope in addition for low values in the other two cells. They would not demand a zero value there, however. Analytic inductionists would study only cases in the left column and would insist on zeros in the lower column. They would ignore those cases where the conditions were present and the results were not present (the ? cell). In practice, however, Cressey did argue that his interviewees were a "normal" population prior to defining their problem as unshareable (i.e., they were cases in the right-hand column of the table above). Lindesmith (1947: 14) studied nonaddicts to ascertain whether addiction ever failed to occur when the specified conditions were present.

According to Robinson analytic induction does in practice require a search for exceptions in the same manner that statistical analysis does—i.e., in the upper-right-hand cell as well as in the lower left. Robinson concludes that the difference between enumerative and analytic induction is therefore only one of *degree*: Statisticians accept a small number of exceptions to their thesis, while the analytic inductionists accept none.

How does one evaluate this claim? First, it clearly takes the statistical mode of analysis as the framework for the criticism of analytic induction. It asks a statistical question, relying on probability as the answer to a causal problem. Second, it assumes that the relevant causes and the effects are already known through a deductive theoretical perspective. The first issue does not address the question of whether there are sociological question that need not be addressed by inductive enumeration, relying on random sampling frames, probability statements, and a priori assertions of the nature of social reality. The second issue is an assumption of the viability of a deductive approach to theory when combined with statistical inference (see Camilleri, 1962). However, with these pros and cons we cannot answer the most important practical question—which questions are best answered by one approach and which by the other? (see Turner, 1953). On balance, it does seem that to this point analytic induction does not permit the answer of causal questions.

As we pointed out initially, there are a variety of forms of the analytic-induction argument, ranging from the typological procedure of Angell, to the Lindesmith, Becker, and Cressey explanations of individual behavior, to finally some of the generally inductive approaches used by Sutherland, Thomas and Znaniecki, and Becker. However, all of these procedural variations are more like each other than they are like the present mode of sociological work. The inductive approach has been most effectively used as a part of a larger project—e.g., in the series of studies of Chicago described above or in the classic *Polish Peasant*. It has depended on a search for data, often in depth, involvement in human lives, and "messy" qualitative coding and manipulation—it is thus open to the charge of *inefficiency*.

Research methods are taught in the main as variations on the survey-research theme, with relatively little attention given over to experimental work, unstructured interviewing, participant observation, and other qualitative methods, as well as those approaches that are likely to be "messy," lengthy, or somewhat unconventional. Intensive analysis of single cases, life-history documents, or historical and/or community analyses are also seldom taught. The reward structure of modern sociology emphasizes the single study (Becker introduction to Shaw, 1966: xvi-xvii) designed to independently verify a limited thesis, to produce a bounded set of findings or "results," and to be easily condensed and written up for journal article publication. Whatever the present mode of sociological work, dealing with "human documents" (biographies, autobiographies, case histories of families, persons, institutions, or groups) and qualitative analysis requires greater firsthand immersion in the social world than other methods. This "first-line sociology" does not make time the constant and depth of analysis the variable. The opposite is true. The data-gathering process is often difficult and demanding, less than neat, and generally time-consuming. The records and notes are cumbersome, often running into thousands of pages of notes for a single study. Analytic induction and other qualitative approaches demand patience, time, and tenacity as well as a tolerance for ambiguity.

The human document is not easily coded, interpreted, or made an aspect of systematic theory. Blumer clearly shows this in his critique of *The Polish Peasant*.

This flexibility of a document to interpretation would be of no importance if the document could be used as an effective test of the specific interpretation which is made of it, but it is at this point that difficulty enters. In the case of simple facts, the document may indeed prove or disprove an assertion made about it, but the closer one approaches to abstract interpretation the less satisfactory is the document as a test. Human documents seem to lend themselves readily to diverse interpretations. One can see this in the ease with which they can be analyzed by different theories of motivation. Theories seem to order the data. (Blumer, 1939: 48)

The feature of the method that many take to be its *strength*—the careful analysis of a few cases (Lindesmith, 50-60; Becker, 50; Cressey, 133; Angell, 50) in qualitative terms—are viewed by others as a *weakness*. The decision concerning advantages and disadvantages of the method is best answered with reference to a specific research problem.

Turning now to the *advantages of analytic induction*, they should be distinguished from the general advantages of qualitative analysis or field research. Many of the strengths of qualitative methods characterize analytic induction as well—they both seek to capture the nature of the empirical world firsthand, often through the subject's perspective, and seek to minimize the significance of preconceived stances toward the world in the form of previously sanctioned concepts, models, axiomatic approaches, and hypotheses. [23] These general dimensions are treated in passing, for the strengths of greatest import are those that solely characterize analytic induction and that do not characterize other methods either at all or in significantly lesser degree.[24]

Perhaps the most significant advantages of analytic induction reside in the following features:

1. Its capacity to generate conceptual formulations and hence to provide the basis for theories. If we are to follow Blumer's suggestion (1954) that the basis for theory must initially be sensitizing concepts, this method

best constrains the researcher to attend to concept development (see also Glaser & Strauss, 1967).

2. Its capacity to induce revision in theories, especially through the careful analysis of deviant cases or negative evidence.

3. Its capacity to integrate sampling models.

4. Its potential for creating processual theories.

Most of the literature in sociology dealing with verifying theory deals with the testing of already-formed theory. A small portion deals with theory construction (Stinchcombe, 1968; Dubin, 1978; Glaser & Straus, 1967; Berger, Zelditch, & Anderson, 1966). Lindesmith's study is self-consciously concerned with developing a theory of addiction; in contrast to the usual approach to a problem, Lindesmith did not study the "literature" prior to his research. Quite the contrary.

The literature on drug addiction was at first not consulted for fear that the opinions expressed would introduce an initial and perhaps decisive bias into the investigation.(1947: 7)

Thus, theory-building was begun with an open mind; the author dealt with the significant problems as they arose, seeking thereby to reflect most accurately the empirical world. As he met new dilemmas, then, he attempted to deal with them. He found he could focus best on only the opiates (opium, including derivatives and synthetic analogs)—not on all drugs—and on those people who were *addicted* (who had experienced withdrawal distress in the process of becoming steady users)—not those who were only *habituated*. In the process of limiting his focus, through definition and redefinition, Lindesmith had outlined the stages of addiction by the time he had fully evolved a definition of the phenomenon he sought to explain. It may be that analytic induction is in fact a search for a precise, delimited definition. When an adequate explanation is developed, it will have to cover those facts and no more. Modification of hypotheses or concepts at each stage tends to be terminated when closure is achieved between definition and causes. The claim made for analytic induction as a mode of causal analysis is not substantiated on the basis of past research utilizing the procedure. The strength of the approach is in the precision in definition that it demands and in its sensitivity to variations of concrete reality. In this sense, then, it is critical not in the testing of theories, causal or noncausal, but in the *generation or construction of theory*. Theory construction based on an inductive approach may facilitate the development of propositions, hypotheses, conditions, categories, or types of social objects (Glaser & Strauss, 1967).

It has been said that negative cases signify the growing edge of science (Mead in Reck, ed., 1964). An accumulation of negative cases—those that cannot be rationalized within the accepted paradigm of a science—provide a fulcrum for a change in the paradigm itself (Kuhn, 1962). A deductive science deals with negative cases as a means of insight (cf. Merton, 1957: 390-93). The importance of the negative case is not parallel to the deductive (or statistical enumerative) model, where the aim is simply to reduce the number of aberrant cases to an acceptable low of say, one to five percent. In its quest for universals analytic induction tolerates no outstanding negative cases. They are either excluded, or the hypothesis is recast. This is not the sole advantage of the inductive technique, however; merely eliminating the negative case would lead only to tautologies and make it almost unnecessary to restate a theory in light of negative evidence (Lindesmith, 1952).

In the abortion study (Manning, 1971) it was discovered that not all the females interviewed sought an abortion (only those for whom marriage and/ or childbirth was not a psychological possibility). It was originally expected that women without a close relationship to a male would be abortion seekers. The relationship with the biological father was highly variable. This finding caused the recasting of the formulation to include a network of supporting people who encourage the abortion, rather than the single potential father. In this case a new piece of objective reality was not discovered, but the problem was redefined. As Mead writes, "It is the indefinite variety of problems which accounts for the indefinite variety of facts. . ." (in Reck, 1964: 197).

The "search for the negative" is closely related to the problem of sampling. Sampling in sociology is but one means of accommodating to the fact that sociology is not an *experimental science* built upon a few critical experiments dealing with a few controlled variables in isolation. In many ways the model for sociology has not been the physical sciences, but the natural or biological sciences (cf. Matza, 1969: chap. 1). Sampling in enumerative induction demands a model of the sampling operation requiring that the sociologist sample the world with reference to a theoretical problem, and to seek a sample of the phenomena at issue that *represent* the larger universe or target population. For example, if a study of voting is undertaken, proportions of the sample should roughly represent the distribution of party affiliation among voters in the population at large.[25] It is assumed that in place of (or in concert with) control of the variables at issue in the sampling frame or in the experimental environment, statistical controls can be applied to isolate the effects of variables upon a given problem. Other variables are assumed to vary randomly in the sample. The results of analysis are often assessed with statistical tests of significance to permit an accurate guess as to the probability of the findings occurring not just in the given sample, but in others from the same population.[26]

Analytic induction uses what might be called a "judgment sample" (Camilleri, 1962). The judgment sample is useful when:

1. A large sample cannot be drawn for reasons of the nature of the variables.

2. The population cannot be enumerated—i.e., no one knows how many adulterers, wife-swappers, or child-molesters there are in a given population.

3. Ethics prohibit a sample.

4. There are theoretical reasons for obtaining a saturation sample to explore in depth a single category or type of event (riots precipitated by police or official violence).

Under these conditions, theoretical or judgment sampling increases the opportunity to discover and understand the event at question, whereas a random procedure would fail to provide the necessary data.

Theoretical sampling models are almost imperative in the study of *deviant behavior* for several reasons: The population is generally unknown; ethics or personal risk often prohibit the random interview technique (Polsky, 1969); and the numbers of available cases in a given area may be quite small (large numbers of heroin addicts are clustered almost exclusively in the cities of New York, Chicago, and Los Angeles). Note also that all the published works utilizing analytic induction deal with disorganization, deviant behavior, or criminality. Obviously, for many important problems alternatives to the random sample must be developed.[27] The sampling strategy of analytic induction is to maximize the chances of obtaining negative evidence. Of course, statistically speaking, one runs the risk of a type II error, or rejecting a true hypothesis. But the sociologist is concerned with what *groups*, and for what *theoretical* purposes, cases should be gathered. Glaser & Strauss defend theoretical sampling in their own approach to qualitative research (which differs from analytic induction in important ways, but shares the concern for sampling models other than the random-statistical).

Theoretical sampling is the process of data collection for generating theory whereby the analyst jointly collects, codes, and analyzes his data and decides what data to collect next and where to find them, in order to develop his theory as it emerges. This process of data collection is controlled by the emerging theory, whether substantive or formal. The initial decisions for theoretical collection of data are based only on a general sociological perspective and on a general subject or problem area (such as how confidence men handle prospective marks or how policemen act toward Negroes or what happens to students in medical school that turns them into doctors). The initial decisions are not based on a preconceived theoretical framework. (Glaser & Strauss, 1967)

Although sociology urgently needs a conception of social change and a theory of process, most present-day sociology grapples more with statics than dynamics, more with maintenance than with change, more with structure than with process. The methodology employed does not *intrinsically* support this theoretical conception, but in fact it has. Correlational or structural approaches to social life, which deal with profiles of "typical voters" or "the drug user," or which rely on official statistics to derive a portrait of the world, tend to produce frozen depictions of events. Enumerative induction has been used to explore a single time, slice of life, relationship between variables *acting at that time*. Analytic induction assumes, contrarily, that a set of factors or variables may work temporally to produce an outcome, but that they act in different ways at different times or stages. Becker's analysis of deviant careers (1963), drawing on Lemert's (1951) concepts, illustrates how the same behavior produced at one time by a given set of variables has one meaning and implication for the actor, while the same behavior may be produced at another time by quite a different set of causes and meanings. For example, Becker (1963) shows that at the initial stages of marijuana use many of the "symptoms" of smoking were unpleasant, absent, unrecognized, or frightening. In later stages these same feelings were considered the "high" and were anticipated and enjoyed by the smoker. In the abortion study early signs of what later became known as pregnancy were at first dismissed by many as "tiredness" or a "missed period," whereas in a later period the signs became something to be "fixed." An analysis that addresses only the correlates of check forging, marijuana smoking, or abortion might overlook these temporally changing self-concepts and consequences associated with stages of a deviant career (see Becker, 1963; Lemert, 1951; and Fabrega & Manning, 1972).

SUMMARY

It has long been obvious that the old cliché, the facts don't speak for themselves, is the entering wedge for the scientific methodologist. It is through method that science constructs and reconstructs the world, and guessing about, hypothesizing, testing, and evaluating facts is an inimical part of this world-building. In the purely inductive mode the scientist does what Bertrand Russell once called "more or less methodical guesswork," while in the purely deductive mode scientists effortlessly derives conclusions, each from a proposition of higher order. But these exaggerated depictions are never in fact the case in sociology, and an examination of practice would reveal a composite of induction and deduction.

Analytic induction is not a means of prediction; it does not clearly establish causality; and it probably cannot endure a principled examination of its claims to making universal statements. According to the most demanding ideal standards of the discipline, analytic induction as a distinctive, philosophical, methodological perspective is less powerful than either enumerative induction or axiomatic-mathematical-modeling methods. However, it should be remembered that what is taken to be methodology at a given time is subject to fads, fashions, and foibles. The evaluative dimensions chosen by the critics of analytic induction are drawn from a positivistic, deductive model of the scientific endeavor, a model seizing on a selected group of concerns.

The strengths of analytic induction derive from its somewhat different aims and intentions. As an aspect of qualitative methods—subsuming life and case histories, social and participant observation, unstructured interviewing, and the analysis of of human documents—analytic induction, whether called "qualitative methodology," "analytic description," or "fieldwork," will continue to be a viable source of data and concepts.

There is another function of analytic induction, too. The case study was originally used in medicine and is well suited to a simultaneous examination of the *particulars* of a given event and those things that are *general* and theoretical. For instance, concepts, hypotheses, typologies, developmental processes, and transactions may be extracted from a case. Some of the insights will doubtless be a function of analogous reasoning—how is this case like others within the range of my experience? Certainly, this reasoning process cannot be accomplished deductively, for it must draw on and systematize human experience. Deduction rests on prior principles, not intuition or the present given meanings of interaction. The investigator attempting to build theory in this way will use the self as an instrument and will shift in and out of the scientific role, bringing the residues of the culture we all take for granted into the scientific armamentarium. In an age of existentialism self-construction is as much a part of sociological method as theory construction. In such a way we may bring our sentiments into line with our theories (Gouldner, 1970; Manning, 1973).

NOTES

[1] I am indebted to the very helpful comments made on earlier versions of this paper by Donald Cressey, Norman Denzin, Marcello Truzzi, and Fred Waisanen. I am particularly grateful for Alfred Lindesmith's encouragement and critical appraisal of my previous drafts. I am of course solely responsible for the present analysis.

[2] Mead did not originate an inductive approach to science. Znaniecki (1934) cites Aristotle and Galileo and other practicing scientists, while most sociologists will recognize the influence of John Stuart Mill's "canon of difference" as one of the early systematic statements of induction—e.g., Goode & Hatt (1952: chap. 7).

[3] Denzin's *Research Act* (1970), drawing heavily on Blumer (1969) and Mead, is a systematic elaboration of this proposition.

[4] See also Bolton (1956, 1963) and Blumer, 1969.

[5] Adopted with slight editorial changes from Kinch (1963: 481-82).

[6] Cf. Dubin (1978). Marcello Truzzi informs me that Pierce's concept of

"abduction" is a third, independent form of reasoning. See Truzzi (1973) on Sherlock Holmes' use of abduction.

[7] The variations on the method are not as considerable or dramatic as the variety found among enumerative inductionists, but they are striking. See Robinson (1951) and Turner (1953).

[8] Unfortunately, the authors did not concern themselves with many of the methodological issues we would now raise concerning the reliability, representativeness, sampling error, and internal consistency of the documents. Blumer's classic critique of the *Polish Peasant* (1939), commissioned by the Social Science Research Council, took issue with the methodology applied to the materials. Blumer, although clearly sympathetic, forcefully claimed that the interpretations were not *independently* derived from the documents (inductively gathered), but were a product of the prior conceptualization of Thomas (1939: 43-50). See also Gottschalk *et al* (1945) for a discussion of the general problem of the analysis of human documents.

[9] Becker, perhaps the leading spokesman for qualitative analysis, implies that this kind of sensitive induction is nearly always the case in qualitative work, and may very well be the case in quantitative studies as well. His view of methodology, particularly what is now taken as methodology, is drawn from Mead's "Scientific Method and Individual Thinker" (Reck, ed., 1964: 171-211), and essentially views all methods as rationalizations for procedures and practical actions sanctioned by unexamined occupational folkways. Cf. Becker's articles in *Sociological Work* (1970): "On Methodology," "Field Work Evidence" and "Social Observation and Social Case Studies." With regard to his own work Becker writes in the preface to *Sociological Work*: ". . . I often found myself improving techniques and using ideas I later realized I did not fully understand. Having done things a certain way, I tried to understand what I had done and make the logic clear; having used a certain concept in an uninspected way; I tried to work out what it might mean in some extended theoretical context . . . this differs from approaches that develop 'correct' methods *a priori* and choose concepts by seeing what will 'fit' with already established theory" (vii).

[10] In my opinion Znaniecki's view of sociological method is better explicated in an article written prior to *The Method of Sociology, viz.,* "Social Research in Criminology," *Sociology and Social Research* 12 (April, 1928), 307-22.

[11] The tradition was said to be stimulated in part by W. I. Thomas's fortuitous discovery of letters as a source of sociological data:

In the lore about W. I. Thomas theat grew up among graduate students at the University of Chicago there was a story of how he came upon the use of letters as a crucial research tool. Thomas had already decided to concentrate on the assimilation of the Poles to test his ideas. Like a professional ethnographer he had mastered the language and made extensive contacts within the Polish community in Chicago. He was concerned with direct observation and especially with collecting data by participating in Polish family life. But following the ethnographic approach—which was developed mainly for nonliterate peoples— he had not as yet explored written documents of Polish-American society, and he was not thinking in terms of written documentation.

One morning, while walking down a back alley in the Polish community on the West Side of Chicago, he had to sidestep quickly to avoid some garbage which was being disposed of by the direct means of tossing it out the window. In the garbage which fell at his feet were a number of packets of letters. Since he read Polish, he was attracted to their contents, and he started to read a bundle which was arranged serially. In the sequence presented by the letters he saw a rich and rewarding account and in time he was led to pursue the personal document as a research tool. Ernest Burgess, who was at the time a graduate student in the Department of Sociology, has attested to the accuracy of the account, although it became embellished as it circulated from one generation of graduate students to the next (Janowitz, ed., 1966: xxiii-xxiv).

[12] Students at the University of Chicago wrote a series of monographs detailing life crises (Cavan, 1928; Faris & Dunham, 1939; Mowrer, 1927), the growth of institutions (Wirth, 1928; Hughes, 1928; Zorbaugh, 1929; Cressey, 1932; Reckless, 1933; Hayner, 1936; and Frazier, 1939), occupations (Anderson, 1923; Donovan, 1920, 1929, 1938; and Sutherland, & Locke, 1936), and deviant behavior (Reckless, 1929, 1933; Sutherland, 1937; Shaw, 1930, 1931, 1938; Thrasher, 1927; and Shaw & McKay, 1929 and 1942).

[13] This sketch of the Chicago school traces some of the themes of the social-psychological framework, while the ecological dimension—of equal and continuing importance—is neglected. This neglect is due to space considerations, not to a decision concerning the relative importance of the two frameworks. There was a continuing tension between the two aspects of Chicago sociology; see Alihan, (1938). For a general description of the University at this time see Faris, (1967).

[14] Or, as Denzin argues (1970: 256), ". . . Stouffer demonstrated in 1930 that life history data were at least as valuable and reliable as structured questionnaire data."

[15] Both Becker articles are republished in his *Outsiders* (1963).

[16] Recent developments in sociology are best described as an elaboration of the case history or institutional analyses done at Chicago in the twenties. These include the works of Becker and Goffman and their students. See, for example, Goffman 1959, 1961, 1965 and Becker, 1963, 1970. The students of Becker and Goffman have also contributed to the growth of qualitative method and concept, although not to the refinement of analytic induction; cf. Cavan, 1966; Scott, 1968; Lofland, 1966, 1969, 1971; Redlinger, 1969. See also Becker's summary, "Social Observation and Social Case Studies" in Sills, ed., 1968, reprinted in Becker, 1970: 75-68.

[17] I mean this to be ironic; many of the methodological issues which have been practically resolved in sociology have not been exposed to a careful examination. Ethnomethodology, a recent challenge to many of the canons of sociological work, may resuscitate many "dead issues." Becker touches on this problem in "On Methodology" (1970); and Cicourel (1964) has published a series of challenges to conventional methodology.

[18] It is not discussed in J. Gould and W. Kolb, *Dictionary of the Social Sciences* (1964) or in either edition of the *International Encyclopedia of the Social Sciences*. It is defined in Theodorson & Theodorson (1969: 199-200).

[19] This work is not relevant to the conclusions reported here and is fully reported in Manning (1971). See also Davis, (1972), and this volume. The reader is reminded that abortions were not widely available at that time (1969).

[20] The natural-history approach is analogous to analytic induction with the major difference found in its assumption of stages in the development of a process, institution, or problem. See Fuller & Myers (1940) and the important critique by Lemert (1967: 31-39).

[21] This was also discovered by Lee (1969: 55). That is, an abotion may be seen as less "deviant" than bearing an illegitimate child. the nature of the information flow itself may be *protective*, for by giving the information one admits to herself that not sharing secret knowledge would create even additional "deviant" consequences. The abortion is a lesser evil. The exchange also affirms to the searcher that she is being supported in an expedient journey that may minimize her exposure to further stigmatizing reaction.

[22] The assumption or nonassumption of a deviant view of self is critical to labeling theory; cf. Lemert (1951)and Becker (1963).

[23] Many of these advantages are described in general in such works as Blumer's *Symbolic Interactionism* (1969), Rose's *Human Behavior and Social Processes* (1962), the works of Mead (1934), and collections such as Manis and Meltzer (1978), McCall and Simmons (1969), Filstead (1970), Becker (1970), and Habenstein (1970). Denzin's treatment of the general problem of sociological method is in this tradition (1970).

[24] Denzin (1970: 198) lists the advantages of analytic induction as: the capacity it has to test alternative theories simultaneously; the strength it provides in revision of theory; the power negative case analysis has in facilitating concern with the relationship of fact, concept, and theory; the potential it has for connecting theoretical and statistical sampling models; its ability to move from a substantive to a formal theory and finally to developmental or processual theories. In my opinion these advantages are not restricted to analytic induction, nor are they all actually advantages of the method. The limitation of my discussion is in the interest of parsimony, for in this limited space, only *distinctive* or essential features can be discussed. This decision does not reflect on the merits or demerits of a broader qualitative approach.

[25] Blumer (1948); Turner, (1948, 1953) and Denzin (1970) all point out, following Thomas and Znaniecki (1918, I:39), that these methods deal with statistical fictions, or *agregates*, whereas sociology studies social systems and patterns, *social groups*.

[26] Although there is a continuing debate concerning the use of tests of significance, they are in widespread continued use (see articles by Camilleri & Morrison and Henkel in Morrison & Henkel, eds., 1970).

[28] Howard S. Becker has written the most important paper on this subject. He reviews a number of alternatives to the random sample in the study of deviance and illustrates the effective use of these options. See "Practitioners of Vice and Crime" in R.W. Habenstein (ed.), *Pathways to Data* (Aldine, 1970).

REFERENCES

Alihan, M. *Social ecology*. New York: Columbia University Press, 1938.

Anderson, N. *The hobo: The sociology of the homeless man*. Chicago: University of Chicago Press, 1923.

Angell, R. C. *The family encounters the depression*. New York: Scribner's, 1936.

Angell, R. C. Comment on discussions of the analytic induction method. *American Sociological Review*, 1954, *19* (August): 476-77.

Ball, D. W. The definition of the situation: Some theoretical and methodological consequences of taking W. I. Thomas seriously. *Journal for the Theory of Social Behavior* 1971, *2*, #1: 61-82.

Becker, H. S. Becoming a marijuana user. *American Journal of Sociology*, 1953, *59* (November): 235-42.

Becker, H. S. Marijuana use and social control, *Social Problems*, 1955, *3* (July): 35-44.

Becker, H. S. *Outsiders: Studies in the sociology of deviance.* New York: Free Press, 1963.

Becker, H. S. Introduction to Clifford Shaw, *The jack roller.* Chicago: University of Chicago Press, 1966. (First published, 1930.)

Becker, H. S. *Sociological work.* Chicago: Aldine, 1970.

Berger, J., Zelditch, M., & Anderson, B. *Sociological theories in progress.* Boston: Houghton Mifflin, 1966.

Blumer, H. *An appraisal of Thomas and Znaniecki's "The Polish peasant in Europe and America."* New York: Social Science Research Council, 1939.

Blumer, H. Public opinion and public opinion polling. *American Sociological Review*, 1948, *13* (October): 542-54.

Blumer, H. What is wrong with social theory? *American Sociological Review*, 1954, *19* (February): 3-10.

Blumer, H. Sociological analysis and the variable. *American Sociological Review*, 1956, *21* (December): 683-90.

Blumer, H. *Symbolic interactionism.* Englewood Cliffs, N. J.: Prentice-Hall, 1969.

Bolton, C. D. Behavior, experience, and relationships: A symbolic-interactionist point of view. *American Journal of Sociology*, 1958, *64* (July): 45-58.

Bolton, C. Is sociology a behavioral science? *Pacific Sociological Review*, 1963, *6* (Spring): 3-9.

Brown, R. *Explanation in social science.* Chicago: Aldine, 1963.

Burgess, E. W. Research methods in sociology. In G. Gurvitch and W. E. Moore (Eds.), *Twentieth-century sociology.* New York: Philosophical Library, 1945.

Burgess, E. W., & Cottrell, L. S., Jr. *Predicting success or failure in marriage.* Englewood Cliffs, N. J.: Prentice-Hall, 1939.

Burgess, E. W., & Locke, H. *The family: From institution to companionship.* New York: American Book Co., 1945.

Camilleri, S. F. Theory, probability and induction in social research. *American Sociological Review*, 1962 *27* (April): 170-178. Also in Morrison and Henkel (Eds.), *The significance test controversy.* Chicago: Aldine, 1970.

Cavan, R. S. *Suicide.* Chicago: University of Chicago Press, 1928.

Cavan, S. *Liquor license.* Chicago: Aldine, 1966.

Cicourel, A. *Method and measurement in sociology.* New York: Free Press, 1964.

Cooley, C. H. The roots of social knowledge. *American Journal of Sociology*, 1926, *32* (July): 59-79.

Cressey, P. G. *The taxi dance hall.* Chicago: University of Chicago Press, 1932.

Cressey, D. *Other people's money.* New York: Free Press, 1953.

Davis, N. J. The abortion market: Transactions in a risk commodity. Unpublished Ph.D. dissertation, Michigan State University, 1972.

Denzin, N. K. *The research act.* Chicago: Aldine, 1970 (a).

Denzin, N. K. *Sociological methods.* Chicago: Aldine, 1970 (b).

Doby, J. T. *An introduction to social research* (2nd ed.). New York: Appleton-Century-Crofts, 1967.

Donovan, F. R. *The woman who waits.* Boston: R. G. Badger, 1920.

Donovan, F. R. *The saleslady.* Chicago: University of Chicago Press, 1929.

Donovan, F. R. *School ma'm.* New York: F. A. Stokes, 1968.

Douglas, J. The statistical rhetoric and Durkheim's analysis of suicide. In E. A. Tiryakian (Ed.), *The sociology of sociology.* New York: Appleton-Century-Crofts, 1971.

Dubin, R. *Theory building.* New York: Free Press, 1978.

Faris, R. E. & Dunham, H. W. *Mental disorders in urban areas.* Chicago: University of Chicago Press, 1939.

Faris, R. E., *Chicago sociology: 1920-1932.* San Francisco: Chandler, 1967.

Filstead, W. (Ed.). *Qualitative methodology.* Chicago, Markham, 1970.

Frazier, E. F. *The Negro family in Chicago.* (Rev., abridged Phoenix ed.). Chicago: University of Chicago Press, 1966. (First published, 1939).

Friedrichs, R. *A sociology of sociology.* New York: Free Press, 1970.

Fuller, R., & Myers, R. The natural history of social problems. *American Sociological Review,* 1941, *6* (June): 320-29.

Glaser, B., & Strauss, A., Discovery of substantive theory: A basic strategy underlying qualitative research. *American Behavioral Scientist,* 1965, *8* (February): 5-12.

Fabrega, H., & Manning, P. K. Disease, deviance, and deviant careers. In R. Scott and J. D. Douglas (Eds.), *Theoretical perspectives on deviance.* New York: Basic Books, 1972.

Glaser, B., & Strauss, A. *The discovery of grounded theory.* Chicago: Aldine, 1967.

Glueck, S., & Glueck, E. *Physique and delinquency.* New York: Harper & Row, 1956.

Goffman, E. *The presentation of self in everyday life.* New York: Doubleday Anchor Books, 1959.

Goffman, E. *Asylums.* New York: Doubleday Anchor Books, 1961.

Goffman, E. *Behavior in public places.* New York: Free Press, 1965.

Goode, W. J., & Hatt, P. *Methods of social research.* New York: McGraw-Hill, 1952.

Gottschalk, L., Kluckhohn, C. & Angell, R. C. *The use of personal documents in history, anthropology and sociology.* New York: Social Science Research Council, 1945.

Gould, J., & Kolb, W. (Eds.). *International dictionary of social sciences.* New York: Free Press, 1964.

Gouldner, A. W. *The coming crisis of Western sociology.* New York: Basic Books, 1970.

Habenstein, R. W. (Ed.). *Pathways to data.* Chicago: Aldine, 1970.

Hayner, N. A. *Hotel life.* Chapel Hill: University of North Carolina Press, 1936.

Hirschi, T. *The causes of delinquency.* Berkeley: University of California Press, 1969.

Hughes, E. C. *A study of a secular institution: The Chicago real estate board.* Unpublished Ph.D. dissertation, University of Chicago, 1928.

Janowitz, M. (Ed.). *W. I. Thomas on social life and social personality.* Chicago: University of Chicago Press, 1966.

Junker, B. (Ed.) *Fieldwork*. Chicago: University of Chicago Press, 1960.

Kinch, J. W. A formalized theory of the self-concept. *American Journal of Sociology*, 1963, *68* (January): 481-86.

Kuhn, T. *The structure of scientific revolutions*. Chicago: University of Chicago Press, 1962.

Lader, L. *Abortion*. Indianapolis: Bobbs-Merrill, 1966.

Langness, L. *Life history in anthropological science*. New York: Holt, Rinehart and Winston, 1965.

Lee, N. H. *The search for an abortionist*. Chicago: University of Chicago Press, 1969.

Lemert, E. *Social pathology*. New York: McGraw-Hill, 1951.

Lemert, E. *Human deviance, social problems and social control*. Englewood Cliffs, N. J.: Prentice-Hall, 1967.

Lewin, K. *A dynamic theory of personality*. New York: McGraw-Hill, 1935.

Lindesmith, A. *Opiate addiction*. Bloomington, Indiana: Principia Press, 1947. (Republished, with revisions, as *Addiction and opiates*. Chicago: Aldine, 1968.)

Lindesmith, A. Comment on W. S. Robinson's *The logical structure of analytic induction*. *American Sociological Review*, 1952, *17* (August): 492-93.

Lofland, J. *Doomsday cult* (enl. ed.). New York: Irvington, 1977. (First published, 1966.)

Lofland, J. *Deviance and identity*. Englewood Cliffs, N. J.: Prentice-Hall, 1969.

Lofland, J. *Field research in sociology*. San Francisco: Wadsworth, 1971.

McCall, G., & Simmons, J. L. (Eds.). *Issues in participant observation*. Reading, Mass.: Addison-Wesley, 1969.

McAuliffe, W., & Gordon, R. A. Testing Lindesmith's theory: Euphoria in addicts. *American Journal of Sociology*, 1974, *79* (January): 795-840.

McKinney, J. C. Methodology, procedures and techniques in sociology. In H. P. Becker and A. Boskoff (Eds.), *Modern sociological theory*. New York: Dryden, 1957.

Manis, J., & Meltzer, B. (Eds.). *Symbolic interaction* (3rd ed.). Boston: Allyn and Bacon, 1978.

Manning, P. K. Fixing what you feared: Notes on the campus abortion search. In J. Henslin (Ed.), *The sociology of sex*. New York: Appleton-Century-Crofts, 1971.

Manning, P. K. Existential sociology. *Sociological Quarterly*, 1973, *14* (Spring): 200-25.

Matza, D. *Becoming deviant*. Englewood Cliffs, N. J.: Prentice-Hall, 1969.

Mead, G. H. *Mind, self and society* (ed. by C. W. Morris). Chicago: University of Chicago Press, 1934.

Merton, R. K. *Social theory and social structure*. New York: Free Press, 1957.

Mills, C. W. Situated action and vocabularies of motive. *American Sociological Review*, 1940, *5* (December): 904-13.

Mowrer, E. R. *Family disorganization*. Chicago: University of Chicago Press, 1927.

Park, R. E., & Burgess, E. R. *An introduction to the science of sociology*. Chicago: University of Chicago Press, 1921. (Reissued 1969.)

Reck, A. J. (Ed.). *Selected writings of George Herbert Mead*. Indianapolis: Bobbs-Merrill, 1964.

Reckless, W. C. *Six boys in trouble*. Ann Arbor: University of Michigan Press, 1929.

Redlinger, L. *Dealing in dope: Market mechanisms and distribution patterns of illicit narcotics*. Unpublished Ph.D. Dissertation, Northwestern University, 1969.

Reiss, I. *The social context of premarital permissiveness.* New York: Holt, Rinehart and Winston, 1967.

Robinson, W. S. The logical structure of analytic induction. *American Sociological Review*, 1951, *16* (December): 812-18.

Rose, A. (Ed.). *Human behavior and social processes.* Boston: Houghton Mifflin, 1962.

Scott, M. *The racing game.* Chicago: Aldine, 1968.

Shaw, C. R. *The jack roller: A delinquent boy's own story.* Chicago: University of Chicago Press, 1930 (reissued, 1966).

Shaw, C. R. *The natural history of a delinquent career.* Chicago: University of Chicago Press, 1931.

Shaw, C. R. *Brothers in crime.* Chicago: University of Chicago Press, 1938.

Shaw, C. R., & McKay, H. D. *Delinquency areas.* Chicago: University of Chicago Press, 1929.

Shaw, C. R., & McKay, H. D. *Juvenile delinquency and urban areas.* Chicago: University of Chicago Press, 1942 (reissued, with introduction by James F. Short, Jr., 1969).

Stinchcombe, A. *Constructing social theories.* New York: Harcourt, Brace, 1968.

Stouffer, S. A. *Experimental comparison of statistical and case history methods in attitude research.* Unpublished Ph.D. dissertation, University of Chicago, 1930.

Sutherland, E. H. *The professional thief.* Chicago: University of Chicago Press, 1937.

Sutherland, E. H., & Locke, H. J. *Twenty-thousand homeless men.* Chicago: University of Chicago Press, 1936.

Sutherland, E. H., & Cressey, D. *Principles of criminology* (8th ed.). Philadelphia: J. B. Lippincott, 1970.

Theodorson, T., & Theodorson, A. (Eds.). *A modern dictionary of sociology.* New York: T. Y. Crowell, 1969.

Thomas, W. I. *Source book of social origins.* Chicago: University of Chicago Press, 1909.

Thomas, W. I. *The unadjusted girl.* Boston: Little, Brown, 1923.

Thomas, W. I., & Thomas, D. S. *The child in America.* New York: Alfred Knopf, 1928.

Thomas, W. I., & Znaniecki, F. *The Polish peasant in Europe and America* (5 vols.). Chicago: University of Chicago Press, 1918.

Thomas, W. I., & Znaniecki, F. *The polish peasant in Europe and America* (2 vols.). New York: Alfred Knopf, 1927.

Thrasher, F. *The gang.* Chicago: University of Chicago Press, 1927. (Reissued with Introduction by James F. Short, Jr., 1963).

Truzzi, M. Sherlock Holmes: Applied social psychologist. In M. Truzzi (Ed.), *The humanities as sociology.* Columbus, Ohio: Charles Merrill, 1973.

Znaniecki, F. Social research in criminology. *Sociology and Social Research*, 1928, *12* (April): 307-22.

Znaniecki, F. *The method of sociology.* New York: Farrar and Rinehart, 1934.

Zetterberg, H. L. *On theory and verification in sociology* (3rd enlarged ed.). New Jersey: Bedminster Press, 1965.

Zorbaugh, H. W. *The gold coast and the slum.* Chicago: University of Chicago Press, 1929.

Chapter Twelve
Enumerative induction: quantification in symbolic interaction

ROBERT B. SMITH

A principal goal of this volume is to develop the reader's competence in qualitative methods. This is not an easy task because there
are differences in opinion about standards of competence. This disagreement
is indicated by the Blumer-Lazarsfeld debate that was codified in Volume I.
The controversy is still not completely resolved; it lives on in spite of our
recent attempts and adjudication in terms of social process analysis. It does
so because this debate is not merely about the articulation of qualitative and
quantitative methods. Rather, it is about meta-theoretical orienting propositions, and methods thought to be best suited to the problems they suggest.
Perhaps it is about a basic conception of sociology, which some view as an art
form, others as a science (Nisbet, 1976). Followers of Herbet Blumer, the
symbolic interactionists who hark back to Weber, are concerned with
verstehende, developing a subjective understanding of the definition of the
situation, action, social process, or problem being studied. They believe that
qualitative methods, especially participant observations, are best suited to
their goals. Followers of Samuel Stouffer or Paul F. Lazarsfeld, the
functionalists and structuralists, are concerned, like Durkheim and Marx,
with the development and corroboration of systems of interrelated propositions. They believe that the articulation of qualitative and quantitative
methods is best suited to their goals. Quantitative methods can be used to
elaborate and corroborate insights from qualitative analyses; given that
quantitative studies can be designed as formulations of qualitative studies,
the latter can guide the conceptualization and logic of the former.

A classic debate concerning the relative appropriateness of two methods
of qualitative field research—participant observation and unstructured interviewing—clearly illustrates this divergence in opinion. Howard S. Becker
and Blanche Geer (1957a: 28-32; 1957b: 39-40), followers of Blumer, stressed
the virtues of participant observation over detailed interviews. Martin Trow,
a Columbia-trained sociologist, argued (1957: 33-35) for the articulation of
these and other methods. Figure 1 presents key aspects of the debate. The
topics are similar to those of the earlier Blumer-Lazarsfeld discussion.

Becker and Geer are oriented toward obtaining subjective understanding of some particular group or substantive social problem, rather than
hypothesis testing. They believe that the problem under investigation
properly dictates the methods of investigation, that given their goal of
subjective understanding, participant observation gives them the most
complete information about social events.

303

Figure 1 Participant Observation Versus Articulated Qualitative and
Quantitative Analyses.

Becker & Geer (Participant Observation)	*Trow (Qualitative and Quantitative Analyses)*
I. *Concerned With Exploration* Participant observation is most suited to . . . the problem in which one is more interested in understanding some particular group or substantive social problem rather than in testing hypotheses about the relations between variables derived from a general theory. In the study aimed at understanding substantive problems, the greatest difficulties lie in discovering appropriate problems for sociological analysis and in discovering valid indicators for theoretical variables. Participant observation is particularly useful. in meeting these difficulties.	I. *Concerned With Corroboration* I would argue that there is more than one way to gain knowledge of the richness, subtlety, and infinite variety of social life, and that sufficiently sensitive and intensive analysis of "crude" survey data is one such way . . . Our progress will come as we are increasingly able to develop systems of theoretically related propositions—propositions that are "checked" at more and more points against data collected through a variety of means.
II. *Methods Suited to the Problem* Trow believes us to have said that participant observation is the best method for gathering data for all sociological problems under all circumstances. We did not say this, and in fact we fully subscribe to his view "that different kinds of information about man and society are gathered most fully and economically in different ways, and that the problem under investigation properly dictates the methods of investigation."	II. *Methods Suited to Problem* It is with this assertion, that a given method of collecting data—any method—has an inherent superiority over others by virtue of its special qualities and divorced from the nature of the problem studied, that I take sharp issue . . .

Figure 1 Continued.

Becker & Geer (Participant Observation)	Trow (Qualitative and Quantitative Analyses)
III. *Participant Observations Are Superior* We did say, and now reiterate, that participant observation gives us the most complete information about social events and can thus be used as a yardstick to suggest what kinds of data escape us when we use other methods. This means, simply, that if we see an event occur, see the events preceding and following it, and talk to various participants about it, we have more information than if we only have the description that one or more persons could give us.	III. *Multimethods are Superior* A recent study in the sociology of medicine—the field from which Becker and Geer draw their own illustrations—emphasizes the need for the widest variety of research methods in attacks on comprehensive problems. The index to the volume in which the first reports of this study are published lists, under the heading "Methods of Social Research," the following sources of information used: diaries,; documentary records; intensive interviews; observation; panel techniques; questionnaries; sociometry. Most of the papers in this volume deal with problems that could not have been studied solely through direct observation.

Trow is oriented toward the development of systems of interrelated propositions. He also believes that researchers should utilize methods that are suited to the problem being studied, and that given his goal of substantive theory development, there is a need for the articulation of a variety of research methods in the study of comprehensive problems.

There is little doubt that many present-day social researchers who are oriented toward the development of systems of variables realize that the articulation of quality and quantity is worthwhile. Instructive examples of ways of doing this are presented and discussed in the Introduction to the *Focused Survey Research* volume of this Handbook.

The present debate, and others like it, indicate that it is difficult to persuade symbolic interactionists oriented toward discerning subjective meanings that quantification might benefit their work. Attempts to persuade qualitative symbolic interactionists to quantify will be successful only to the extent that quantification facilitates *verstehende*, the subjective understanding of definitions of situations, interactions, processes, and communications. The subsequent section addresses this problem by reviewing instructive examples of quantitative approaches to symbolic-interactionist problems.

Figure 2   Items from Observation Schedule*

21a. Definition of the situation after arrival of police: [Check the citizens' specification of the problem. If citizens are not present or cannot communicate, check the officers' definition.]

Part I—Usually Felonies
_____01. Assault, aggravated or "serious" (e.g., knifing or shooting)
_____02. Auto theft
_____03. Burglary—breaking or entering, business place
_____04. Burglary—breaking or entering, residence
_____05. Burglary—breaking or entering, unspecified or other
[Writeout:_____]
_____06. Homicide, criminal
_____07. Larceny—theft, auto accessory

. . .

Part II—Other Complaints
_____17. Abandoned auto
_____18. Assault, simple or minor (e.g., assault and battery, threat, etc.)

. . .

Part III—Miscellaneous Incidents and Problems
_____52. Animal trouble—dogbite
_____53. Animal trouble, unspecified or other
[Writeout:_____]

. . .

_____71. Unspecified or other request or incident
[Writeout:_____]
b. If any *criminal* damage or loss of property or money was involved, specify the approximate value of the damage or loss: $_____

22. Did citizen verbally specify a particular service he wanted?
_____1. Yes   _____2. No   _____0. Inapplicable
If "yes"—check or write out:
_____1. transportation to medical setting
_____2. an arrest
_____3. settlement of an argument or dispute
_____4. advice or counseling
_____5. special police surveillance or attention

_____7. other—specify: _____

*This Figure courtesy of Albert J. Reiss, Jr., and Donald Black. All rights reserved.

Figure 2   Items from Observation Schedule

23. Was there anything unusual about how the citizens related to the police? (e.g., with hysteria, like boss to employee, etc.)
    ____1. Yes   ____2. No
    If "yes—specify: _____
    _____
    _____

24. Was there any noteworthy disagreement among the citizens as to the proper definition of the situation?
    ____1. Yes   ____2. No   ____9. Don't know   ____0. Inapplicable
    If "yes"—specify: _____
    _____
    _____

25. What was the general police response to the prevailing definition of the situation?
    ____1. agreed and proceeded to take some kind of action (verbal or otherwise)
    ____2. disagreed but proceeded to take police action—specify the disagreement:
    _____
    _____
    ____3. saw as "unfounded" (without basis)
    ____4. saw as civil matter or "not police business"
    ____7. other—specify: _____
    _____
    _____
    ____9. don't know

EXAMPLES OF ENUMERATIVE INDUCTION

Surprisingly, within the symbolic-interactionist tradition there is a range of good examples of quantification of symbolic-interactionist sensitizing concepts, and the study of their interrelationships in systems of quantified variables. Six approaches are discussed: (1) systematic observation procedures; (2) surveys involving the self-concept; (3) laboratory experiments about defining the situation and sources of self-evaluation; (4) computer simulations of definitions of situations; (5) the development of grounded theory; and (6) typologies and quantification.

Systematic Observation

As indicated by Van Maanen's essay and bibliography in Volume I, the study of the police recently has been a popular focus for participant observations in the symbolic-interactionist tradition. Van Maanen actually enrolled in a police academy in order to gain a subjective understanding of what the police were taught and how this might affect their subsequent definitions of situations. He also wore a police uniform when accompanying policemen so that he would not affect the transactions between police and citizens, which he was studying.

Reiss (1966) and his associates have utilized systematic observation surveys to study police-citizen transactions. This method is a formalization of participant observation. The observer plays a role analogous to that of a survey interviewer. But instead of asking questions of the police or citizens, the observer accompanies the police and observes the police-citizen transaction noting the occurrence of certain events as they happen by answering the questions on an observation schedule.

Observation schedules are developed much like survey questionnaires. First, detailed field observations are gathered. Then, these are analyzed to abstract a set of topics, an accounting scheme, that gives a structure to what will be observed. Each topic in the accounting scheme is covered by a set of questions to the observer. These focus the specific observations.

Figure 2 presents a portion of the police observation study that gauges the definition of the situation after the arrival of the police. The observer assesses the citizens' specification of the problem, and if citizens are not present or cannot communicate, the officers' definition is assessed. Subsequent questions gauge the citizen's behavior: Did he request services? Did he relate to the police in an unusual way? Did he define the situation? Was there disagreement among the citizens as to the proper definition of the situation?

It is perfectly clear that definitions of situations can be studied using systematic observation procedures that produce quantitative data for statistical analyses. For further explication of this procedure see Reiss (1968, 1971, 1975).

Surveys Involving the Self-Concept

In the recent Festschrift for Herbert Blumer (Shibutani, 1970), the first chapter by Bernard N. Meltzer and John W. Petras (1970: 3-17) describes the Chicago and Iowa schools of symbolic interaction. Herbert Blumer is closely identified with the Chicago school, which emphasized the intuitive *verstehende* approach of feeling one's way inside the experience of the actor. The late Manford II. Kuhn led the Iowa school, which stressed that the key ideas of interactionism could be operationalized and successfully utilized in quantitative empirical research. Kuhn rejected as not feasible all attempts to get inside the individual and directly observe subjective plans of action or infer them from overt behavior (Meltzer & Petras, 1970:8). Given this generic orientation, Kuhn then proceeded to develop the Twenty State-ments Test (TST), more commonly known as the "Who Am I?" test, an instrument for eliciting self-attitudes. This measure has been utilized in more than 100 reported quantitative researches, and is the most widely used instrument for the study of self-conceptions.

Other research studies also document the feasibility of studying self concepts using survey techniques. Rosenberg (1965) developed a measure of self-esteem and related the self-image of adolescents to variables of social structure. The Equality of Educational Opportunity survey (Coleman et al, 1966) gauged children's self-concept and related this variable to their educational achievement. Kohn (1969) has studied various linkages between social class and aspects of the self. Wylie (1974) has reviewed and critiqued the numerous psychological measuring instruments of the self-concept; and Wells and Marwell (1976), the measures of self-esteem.

On this basis there is little doubt that symbolic-interactionist concep-tions of the self can be operationalized and studied through quantitative survey analyses.

Experiments

Experiments are also useful. There are at least two theoretical research programs that have developed symbolic-interactionist conceptions utilizing laboratory experiments. The first, by Peter McHugh (1968), is an experi-mental test of concepts fundamental to definitions of situations. The second, by Webster and Sobieszek (1974), probes the sources of self-evaluation.

Defining the situation

McHugh (1968) studied the fundamental components of definitions of situations. He reasoned that when order is present, a situation is defined, and two properties of definitions of situations are salient: (1) *emergence* and (2) *relativity*. Emergence refers to definition and transformations in defini-tion of an event over time; relativity, to that across space. When there is a situation of disorder or anomie, then these aspects of definitions of situations breakdown, and emergence and relativity are attenuated.

To test this theory McHugh created an experimental situation in a laboratory. Subjects were solicited and asked to participate in an experiment on psychotherapy. Each subject thought about a bothersome personal problem, related some background to it, and then asked 10 questions that could be answered either yes or no. Paradoxically, in the orderly experimen-tal condition, the experimenter randomly answered the questions. In the anomie condition, different subjects received different proportions of yes and no answers, ranging from 50-50 splits to all yes or no. These patterns of disruptive answers were designed to lead the subjects to question whether the original definition of the situation, psychotherapy, was actually occurring, thus creating the possibility of anomie.

McHugh analyzed transcripts of the interaction, coding statements as indicative of various components of emergence and relativity. He compared the distributions of responses for the order and anomie conditions. Emergence predominated during orderly interaction; relativity predominated in the anomic. He concluded that emergence and relativity are empirically meaningful ideas for depicting definitions of situations.

Sources of self-evaluations

Webster and Sobieszek (1974) are concerned with specifying the interactionist conception of the self. Their central problem is to assess how others affect the formation of an individual's self-concept. Their work is based on the conceptions of Cooley, Mead, and James, and on Berger's theoretical and empirical expectations state research program. From Cooley they take the generic perspective of the looking-glass self—the idea that one's self-concept directly depends on the opinions and actions of others. From Mead they develop the idea of the generalized other and the self-structure. For instance, a man may play several different roles within several social contexts; his self-conception will not conform perfectly with the image of him held by whomever he happens to be interacting with at the moment. His perception of the other and his own self-assessment affect his interpretation of a given opinion from another with whom he interacts. As did James and Mead, they recognize that not all "significant others" are equally significant in determining the self. Finally, from Berger and his associates they utilize a set of concepts and propositions that can generate empirical predictions for behavior as a function of ability conceptions, and they have a standardized experimental setting to test the theory.

On this basis they go on to specify clearly via a series of interlocked experiments the characteristics that make another significant in determining a given individual's ability self-conception. Their first experiment corroborates the Cooley "looking-glass self" hypothesis. They found that in a simple situation of one evaluator of known ability, opinions of an evaluator of high ability are likely to be accepted by the individuals and to be used by them in forming assessments of their own and others' abilities. Their first elaboration of this basic experiment widened the scope of the theory to include cases in which the ability of the evaluator was unknown, but his status was known. The subjects acted as if these two attributes were highly correlated, they attributed ability conceptions to evaluators in accord with their status: high-status evaluators were treated like high-ability evaluators; low-status evaluators were treated like low-ability evaluators.

The second elaboration developed the ideas of James and Mead by bringing in multiple evaluators who may differ in ability and in their judgments of the individual's ability. In the case of two evaluators who are differentiated by ability, high-ability evaluators are more likely to be accepted than low-ability evaluators. When two high-ability evaluators disagree, an individual's self-image tends to be an "average" of the two assessments.

It is apparent from this brief review that experimental developments of symbolic-interactionist conceptions of definitions of situations and self are both feasible and fruitful.

Regression Analyses and Computer Simulations of Definitions of Situations

David Heise (1977, 1978) has reinterpreted attitudinal responses to simple sentences gauged by semantic differentials as clarifying how people define their immediate situations. His research program first focused on responses to simple sentences; now the research is conceptualized in terms of affect control theory and definitions of situations.

The core of the early research is Heise's (1965) dictionary of semantic differential profiles for 1,000 frequently used English words. These are rated in terms of EAP, that is, their connotations of Evaluation (good or bad), Activity (lively or sluggish), and Potency (powerful or weak). Given these word profiles, Heise (1969, 1970) demonstrated that in simple sentences like

"The father killed the uncle."

original attitudes toward the words "father," "killed" and "uncle" predict how one feels toward the sentence. Sets of regression equations predict attitudes of Evaluation, Activity and Potency in terms of the original attitudes toward the sentences' subjects, verbs, and objects and their interactions. These equations form the basis for the more recent studies in the symbolic interactionist tradition.

Heise (1977) distinguishes between fundamental and transient feelings. The former are relatively entrenched attitudes or habit strengths. These fundamental sentiments are stable components of feelings and have substantial test-retest correlations that can be measured by averaging transient feelings. These are attitudes that are manifest at any particular moment which are tapped by psychometric instruments like the semantic differential. Heise (1977: 164) assumes that the fundamental sentiments serve as reference values for interpreting transient feelings generated by perceived events.

The actor implements actions to bring the transients back in line with fundamentals. Thus, as in cognitive dissonance theory there is a strain toward cognitive consonance.

In terms of symbolic interactionism the theory's basic premise is that people act so as to confirm the fundamental sentiments about self and others that are evoked by definitions of situations. These definitions are essentially semantic differential profiles for words. To illustrate this Heise (1977: 167-172) develops an hypothetical example in which the focus is on interaction between two persons, Robert and Mac. Robert acts as a host and defines Mac as a guest. Mac is not in a good mood and plays the role of killjoy, defining Robert as a chatterbox. The simulation begins by retrieving EAP profiles for each person according to their definition of self and other. Robert's key words are host and guest. Mac's are killjoy and chatterbox. The scale scores that operationally define these profiles are substituted into the various empirically derived regression equations to obtain simulated EAP profiles for Robert's ideal behavior toward Mac, and Mac's ideal behavior toward Robert. On the basis of these simulated scale scores, verbs are found in an act catalog that describe appropriate behaviors for Robert and Mac. These scale scores can be substituted into other regression equations to obtain ratings of Evaluation, Activity and Potency, etc. This system has been programmed for the computer for interactive computer simulation; for further information see Heise (1978).

Grounded Theory

The grounded-theory strategy, which is incorporated in the process of cumulative social science that has informed and guided the development of the volumes that comprise this Handbook, was originally developed by two sociologists; one, Anselm L. Strauss, was trained in the Chicago tradition of symbolic interactionism; the other, Barney G. Glaser, was trained at Columbia University in the tradition of Merton's "middle-range" theory and Lazarsfeld's quantitative methodology. Their book, *The Discovery of Grounded Theory* (1967), which often is thought of as a polemic against the Merton strategy of hypothetico-deductive theorizing and verificational research, can also be viewed as an attempt to resolve the Blumer-Lazarsfeld debate.

Glaser and Strauss are primarily concerned about improving social scientists' capacities for generating theory from their own data. By generating theory they mean the improvisation of categories of analysis and their interrelationships by the inductive analysis of data. They desire to prevent the opportunistic use of analytic categories and typologies that have dubious fit to the empirical reality to which they are applied.

This concern has led them to analyze the linkage between qualitative and quantitative methods and data. They believe that both qualitative and quantitative data can be used to generate and to verify theory and for mutual corroboration (Glaser & Strauss, 1967: 17-18):

> There is no fundamental clash between the purposes and capacities of qualitative and quantitative methods or data. What clash there is concerns the primacy of emphasis on verification or generation of theory—to which heated discussions of qualitative *versus* quantitative data have been linked historically. We believe that *each form of data is useful for both verification and generation of theory,* whatever the primacy of emphasis. Primacy depends only on the circumstances of research, on the interests and training of the researcher, and on the kinds of material he needs for his theory.
>
> *In many instances, both forms of data are necessary*—not quantitative used to test qualitative, but both used as supplements, as mutual verification and, most important for us, as different forms of data on the same subject, which, when compared, will each generate theory.

The Glaser-Strauss resolution of the Blumer-Lazarsfeld debate is appealing because it invites qualitative researchers to quantify, and quantitative researchers to be more exploratory and less hypothetico-deductive and to ground their analyses in qualitative studies. Also, they recommend the joint use of qualitative and quantitative data for corroboration and development of empirically grounded theories. For further discussion of this strategy see Glaser (1978), Turner (1981) and below.

Typologies and Quantification

Typologies are a crucial linkage between qualititative and quantitative analyses. Qualitative analysts and grounded theorists often infer themes or syndromes from their data. Typologies can be derived by first conceptualizing these qualities as dichotomous attributes, and then cross tabulating them. Ideal-types such as Riesman's, *et al.*, (1950) inner-directed, other-directed and autonomous personalities organized a large number of focused interviews and qualitative observations, providing insight about man and contemporary society. Typologies systematize the definitions of such ideal-types, and facilitate quantification. The ideal-types are defined as the intersections of the dimensions that comprise the typology. The preface to this volume presents (p.xix) an example of a typology derived from the cross tabulation of two dimensions of the investigator; whether or not the subjects know the investigator, and whether or not the investigator participates in the setting. The intersections of these dichotomous attributes define the four types of qualitative research presented in this book, namely, participant observation, undisclosed participant observation, interviewing and use of informants, and documentary analysis.

Survey questions and indexes can be used to gauge dimensions of typologies thereby operationally defining the typology for use in survey researches. This process of qualitative analysis of themes, typology construction and quantification is illustrated next, elaborating upon Howard Schuman's (1972) seminal analysis of moral and pragmatic antiwar sentiment, a topic bearing on the symbolic interactionists' interest in understanding collective behavior and social movements. Anti-war Sentiment: Two Themes and a Typology.

Schuman conducted a thematic analysis of open-ended responses from a cross-section sample of Detroit adults who indicated opposition to American intervention in Vietnam. He compared theses data to a small sample of University of Michigan students, finding two key themes of antiwar dissent: *moral* objections to the use of American military power in Vietnam, and a *pragmatic* dissent deriving in part from the failure of U.S. military investments to yield victory. The dissent of college students was largely moral in nature, and that of the general public, largely pragmatic.

The typology of antiwar dissent presented in Figure 3 results from the cross tabulation of the moral and pragmatic dimensions, conceptualized as dichotomous attributes.

Figure 3.   Four Types of Dissent

		Moral dissent	
		YES	NO
		Type I	*Type III*
	Yes	Forceful Antiwar Dissent	Pragmatic Disenchantment with the war
Pragmatic Dissent			
		Type II	*Type IV*
	No	Moral indignation	No dissent: Support for the war

These four types systematize Schuman's insights about the sources of antiwar sentiment, making explicit distinctions that were implicit. These types are next defined and illustrated by passages paraphrased from Schuman:

Type I—*FORCEFUL ANTIWAR DISSENT* was both moral and pragmatic. It was articulate, coming from students and faculty at leading universities (p.517). These dissenters approved of mass demonstrations and protests to end the war. They criticized U.S. involvement in Vietnam as not merely unsuccessful, but also as morally wrong.

Type II—*MORAL INDIGNATION* about the war was primarily moral and not pragmatic. This dissent was prevalent in the early phases of the war, at teach-ins at major universities. It focused on the injustice of U.S. intervention in what was a civil war in support of a corrupt and unpopular government, and the devastation that such intervention would cause in Vietnam (p.514).

Type III—*PRAGMATIC DISENCHANTMENT* with the war was primarily pragmatic and not moral, it characterized the public who has turned against continuation of U.S. involvement because of the lack of success in winning it. American casualties and the economic costs of the war produced this disenchantment (p.519).

Type II—*NO DISSENT*, support for the war, expressed itself in hostility toward antiware protestors, a desire to further escalate the war and a commitment to containment of communism.

These four types of dissent can be quantified by questions from a survey, circa 1970, of students at the University of California, Santa Barbara. In this survey moral dissent was gauged by agreeing that the violence in Vietnam was more morally objectionable than the occasional violence of protestors in the United States—about 41 percent of the undergraduates indicated moral dissent on this measure. Pragmatic dissent was gauged by agreeing that the war in Vietnam was a mistake—about 72 percent indicated pragmatic dissent.

Table 1 presents the quantified typology and the effects of moral and pragmatic dissent on a four-item index of support for forcible protest and on being a Dove—desiring rapid withdrawal of American troops from Vietnam. Coleman effect parameters, a statistical measure explicated in *Quantitative Methods*, are used to quantify effects. In these data all four types of dissent were present. Forty-one percent expressed forceful antiwar dissent, only 5 percent were morally indignant, 36 percent were disenchanted pragmatically, and 28 percent did not dissent, presumably supporting the war.

The two types that include the moral factor had stronger effects on support for forcible protest than did the other two types. Eighty seven percent of those classified as forcible dissenters did in fact support forceful dissent, this was the highest percentage, as did 71 percent of the morally indignant. When the moral factor was absent, support for forcible dissent dropped—only 40 percent of the disenchanted and 33 percent of those classified as supporting the war approved of forcible protest. The average

Table 1. Quantification of Typology

	Forceful Antiwar	Moral Indignation	Pragmatic Disenchant-ment	No Dissent: Support for the war
Percent of total	36%	5%	36%	23%
Number of Cases	(165)	(24)	(162)	(106)
Percent supporting protest	87%	71%	40%	33%
Percent Doves	88%	83%	68%	34%

Coleman Effect Parameters (unweighted)	Protest	Dove
Effect of moral dissent on:	.43	.35
Effect of pragmatic dissent on:	.12	.20
Interaction effect on:	.05	− .15

effect on support of protest of the moral factor is three and one half times that of pragmatic dissent.

The pattern of support for troop withdrawal is similar, but not identical—considerably more of the pragmatically disenchanted were Doves than approved of forcible protest—the difference is 28 percent. This finding is consistent with Schuman's conjecture that disenchantment with the war was related to being a Dove (p.520), but did not imply approval of protests (p.516). Overall, the types including the moral factor had stronger effects. Eight-eight and 83 percent, respectively, of the forceful dissenters and the morally indignant were Doves. This percentage dropped to 68 percent of the disenchanted and 34 percent of the supporters of the war. The average effect on being a Dove of the moral factor was two and one-third that of pragmatic dissent.

This exercise has documented that typologies and quantification of qualitative themes can enhance even exemplary qualitative analyses. The four-fold typology of dissent further systematized passages from Schuman's text, further clarifying his distinctions and definitions. Quantification of this typology corroborated his finding that the moral aspects of this war were particularly salient for college students, and led to new findings. Pragmatic dissent was also a factor, and at the time of this survey very few of the students were merely morally indignant, those morally concerned about the war also indicated pragmatic dissent and supported forcible protest.

IMPLICATIONS

This review of enumerative induction, theorizing and quantitative research in the symbolic-interactionist tradition, indicates that there may be benefits to this perspective if interactionist elaborate and develop their sensitizing concepts through systematic observations, surveys, simulations, and experiments; create grounded theories that combine qualitative and quantitative data; and quantify their syndromes and typologies.

REFERENCES

Becker, Howard S., & Geer, Blanche. Participant observation and interviewing: A comparison. *Human Organization*, 1957, *16*: 28-32. (a)

Becker, Howard S., & Geer, Blanche. Participant observation and interviewing: A rejoinder. *Human Organization*, 1957, *16*: 39-40. (b)

Coleman, James S., Campbell, Ernest Q., Hobson, Carol J., McPartland, James, Mood, Alexander M., Weinfeld, Frederic D., & York, Robert L. *Equality of educational opportunity*. Washington, D.C.: U.S. Govt. Printing Office, 1966.

Glaser, Barney G. *Theoretical sensitivity: Advances in the methodology of grounded theory*. Mill Valley, Ca.: Sociology Press.

Glaser, Barney G., & Strauss, Anselm L. *The discovery of grounded theory*. Chicago: Aldine, 1967.

Kohn, Melvin. *Class and conformity: A study of values*. Homewood, Ill. Dorsey, 1969.

McHugh, Peter. *Defining the situation: The organization of meaning in social interaction*. Indianapolis: Bobbs-Merrill, 1968.

Meltzer, Bernard N., & Petras, John W. The Chicago and Iowa schools of symbolic interactionism. In Tamotsu Shibutani (Ed.), *Human nature and collective behavior*. Englewood Cliffs, N.J.: Prentice-Hall, 1970.

Nisbet, Robert. *Sociology as an art form*. New York: Oxford University Press, 1976.

Reiss, Albert J., Jr. Studies in crime and law enforcement in major metropolitan areas. Field Surveys III, Vol. 1 and 2. Washington, D.C.: President's Commission on Law Enforcement and the Administration of Justice, U.S. Government Printing Office, 1966.

Reiss, Albert J., Jr. Stuff and nonsense about social surveys and observations. In Howard S. Becker et al., (Eds.), *Institutions and the person*. Chicago: Aldine, 1968.

Reiss, Albert J., Jr. Systematic observations of natural social phenomena. In Herbert Costner (Ed.), *Sociological methodology* (1971) San Francisco: Jossey-Bass, 1971.

Reiss, Albert J., Jr. Systematic observation surveys of natural social phenomena. In H. Wallace Sinaiko & Laurie A. Broedling, *Perspectives on attitude assessment: Surveys and their alternatives*. Washington, D.C.: Smithsonian Institution, 1975.

Rosenberg, Morris. *Society and the adolescent self-image*. Princeton, N.J.: Princeton University Press, 1965.

Riesman, David, with Nathan Glazer and Reuel Denney. The lonely crowd. New Haven: Yale University Press, 1973.

Rosenberg, Morris. Conceiving the self. New York: Basic Books, 1979.

Shibutani, Tamotsu. Human nature and collective behavior. Englewood Cliffs, N.J.: Prentice-Hall, 1970.

Schuman, Howard. Two sources of antiwar sentiment in America. American journal of sociology, 1972, 78: 513-536.

Trow, Martin A. Comment on "Participant observation and interviewing: A comparison." Human Organization, 1957, 16: 33-35.

Turner, Barry A. Some practical aspects of qualitative data analysis. Quality and quantity, 1981, 15: 225-247.

Webster, Murray, Jr., & Sobieszek, Barbara. Sources of self-evaluation: A formal theory of significant others and social influence. New York: John Wiley, 1974.

Wells, Edward L., & Marwell, Gerald. Self-esteem: Its conceptualization and measurement. Beverly Hills: Sage Publications, 1976.

Wylie, Ruth C. The self-concept. Lincoln: University of Nebraska Press, 1974.

Contributors

David Arnold is Professor of Sociology at Sonoma State University, Rohnert Park, California. He was formerly on the faculty at University of California, Santa Barbara and has held research positions at UCLA and Brandeis. He received his A.B. degree from the University of Chicago; M.A. from the University of Iowa, and Ph.D. from the University of California, Berkeley. His prior publications include a book on subculture theory, plus articles and book chapters on research methods, drugs, sport and leisure, and violence. Most recently he has been teaching, writing about, and doing visual sociology.

Odis E. Bigus received his Ph.D. in Sociology from the University of California, San Francisco in 1974. He is currently Associate Professor of Sociology at the University of Tulsa. His publications and research interests relate mainly to the evolvement of social relationships and the social aspects of alcoholism.

Bob Blauner teaches sociology at the University of California, Berkeley. He is the author of *Alienation and Freedom, Racial Oppression in America,* and numerous articles. Presently he's working on a book contrasting American racial consciousness in the late 1960s and the present period.

M. Herberg Danzger is Associate Professor of Sociology at Herbert H. Lehman College and at the Graduate Center, City University of New York. Professor Danzger, recently a Fulbright Professor at the Hebrew University in Jerusalem, Israel, is chairman of the Department of Sociology at Lehman College. He has received grants from the National Institute of Mental Health and the National Science Foundation for his research on community conflict and a book on this work is in preparation.

Nanette J. Davis is an Associate Professor at Portland State University. Her research interests center on deviance and social control. She has published *Sociological Constructions of Deviance: Perspectives and Issues in the Field* (Second Edition), and has written with Bo Anderson, *Social Control: The Production of Deviance in the Modern State.* Davis has also written a number of critical papers on the state of deviance and criminology theory, employing a sociology of knowledge approach, as well as other papers on women and deviance. The "archaeology" of abortion, her most recent book venture, examines in detail the breakdown of the reproductive myth and its impact for social relations and institutional orders.

Barney G. Glaser is a Professor at the University of California Medical Center. He is author of several articles and books including *Discovery of Grounded Theory* (with Anselem L. Strauss) and *Theoretical Sensitivity: Advances in the Methodology of Grounded Theory.*

Stuart C. Hadden is an Assistant Professor of Sociology at Northern Arizona University. He received his Ph.D. from Washington State University in 1973. Previous publications have been primarily in the fields of deviance and social problems theory. Most recently, Professor Hadden has authored two papers (with Marilyn Lester) extending grounded theory to ethnomethodological concerns. He is currently involved in an extended project applying the processional notion of Grounded Theory to the Criminal justice system.

Dr. Edward F. Kelly was an undergraduate scholar at Yale University and received his Ph.D. from Harvard University in 1970 in Social Psychology and Psycholinguistics. During his post doctoral year (1970–71) he studied computational linguistics with Dr. Kuno. In 1972 he began to study experimental parapsychology, first at the J. B. Rhine Institute on Parapsychology in Durham, N.C., and then at the Department of Electrical Engineering of Duke University. His current work focuses on possible physiological correlates of Psi performance.

Marianne T. Kleman graduated from The University of Minnesota with a B.A. in Psychology in 1961. From 1961 to 1965 she was a Psychologist, Laboratory of Psychology, National Institute of Mental Health, Bethesda, Maryland and at the Institute of Personality Assessment Research, Berkeley, California working under the direction of Dr. Morris Parloff. She worked as a Research Analyst at the Institute for Research in Social Behavior, Berkeley, California from 1965 to 1975 designing studies and directing data collection and analysis efforts in human population studies.

Barbara Lindemann teaches American History and Women's Studies at Santa Barbara City College. She specializes in social, political, and intellectual history of the revolutionary and early national period.

Dean I. Manheimer is President and Founder of the Institute for Research in Social Behavior, Berkeley, California. He was educated at New York University, where he took B.A. and M.B.A. degrees, and has worked at the Bureau of Applied Social Research, Columbia University, and the California Department of Public Health. He currently serves as Executive Secretary for the Task Force on Comparability in Drug Research. Among his publications are (with R.H. Somers and S.T. Davidson) "The Amotivational

Syndrome and the College Student," *Annals of the New York Academy of Science*, 1976, and (with M.B. Balter, I.H. Cisin, and H.J. Parry) "Psychic Distress, Life Crises and Drug Use: National Drug Survey Data," *Archives of General Psychiatry*, 1977.

Peter K. Manning (Ph.D., Duke, 1966) is a Professor of Sociology and Psychiatry at Michigan State University, where he has taught since 1966. He was a Visiting Research Scholar at the University of London, Goldsmith's College in 1972–73 and a Visiting Fellow at the Department of Justice in 1974–76. A member of several national and international societies in sociology and anthropology, he has presented research papers at international meetings in Canada, Belgium, England, Norway and Brazil. He has done fieldwork on the logic of disease and illness in Mexico and Peru, and on the police in London and the United States, and recently completed a six city study of narcotics enforcement. His publications report research in organizations, occupations, field work methods, socialization and deviance and control. He has edited or written five books and has three in press. His *Police Work*, published in 1977 by Massachusetts Institute of Technology Press, is a comparative study of policing cast in a dramaturgical perspective. His most recent book is *The Narcs' Game: Organizational and Informational Limits Upon Drug Law Enforcement*, also published by Massachusetts Institute of Technology Press.

Glen D. Mellinger is Executive Director, Institute for Research in Social Behavior, Berkely, California. He took his B.A. at Oberlin College and did graduate work in Sociology and Social Psychology at the University of Michigan, where he received both M.A. and Ph.D. degrees. He is currently principal investigator of the study "Changing Life Styles and Values Among University Males." Among his publications are "Use of Licit Drugs and Other Coping Alternatives: Some Personal Observations on the Hazards of Living," in D. J. Lettieri (Ed.) *When Coping Strategies Fail*, Beverly Hills: Sage Publications, 1977, and (with M. B. Balter, H. J. Perry, D. I. Manheimer and I. H. Cisin) "An Overview of Psychotherapeutic Drug Use in the United States," in E. Josephson (Ed.) *Epidemiology of Drug Use*, Washington: Winston, 1974.

Daniel Ogilvie did his undergraduate work at Harvard University and completed his Ph.D. in Social Psychology at Harvard in 1967. He was appointed as Lecturer at Harvard until 1971 when he accepted an appointment at Livingston College, Rutgers University. He is currently Chairman of the Department of Psychology at Livingston College. His current research is on the psychology of experience and on the subjective contexts of human information processing.

Joan M. Reitzel received her Ph.D. from Brown University and has since been associated with the University of California at Santa Barbara. Dr. Reitzel studies the evolution of academic and charitable institutions in France and England.

Paul Rock is Senior Lecturer in Sociology at the London School of Economics. He received his B.Sc. in sociology from the London School of Economics and his D. Phil. from Oxford in 1970. He has written widely on symbolic interactionism and deviance. His most recent books are *The Making of Symbolic Interactionism* and *Deviant Interpretations.*

Robert B. Smith received his training in research at the Bureau of Applied Social Research and at the Department of Social Relations of Johns Hopkins University. After receiving his Ph.D. in sociology from Columbia University, he was a faculty member at the University of California, Santa Barbara and a Senior Social Scientist at Abt Associates Inc. His prior publications have elucidated political and social consequences of war, dynamics of social processes, effects of stratification, and statistical methodology. Currently, he is a Research Affiliate of the Center for Policy Research Inc. and the Center for the Social Sciences of Columbia University, and is Director of Social Structural Research, Inc. During the 1972–73 academic year he was a Fulbright-Hays Lecturer in Structural Sociology at the State University of Ghent, Belgium.

Robert H. Somers obtained his undergraduate education at Antioch College, and his graduate training at Columbia University (Ph.D., 1901). He taught in the Sociology Departments of the University of Michigan (Ann Harbor) and University of California (Berkeley). From 1970–1978 he was engaged in research on illicit drug use at the Institute for Research in Social Behavior (Berkeley) and since 1978 has been with the Corporate Research Division of Pacific Telephone and Telegraph, San Francisco. In addition to many professional publications. Somers developed a commonly used measure of association for ordinal data.

Philip Stone is Professor of Social Relations at Harvard University. He took his undergraduate education at the University of Chicago and his doctorate at Harvard in social psychology. His work in content analysis dates back to 1961, when he and Robert F. Bales were developing methods of analyzing the content of small group interaction. His work in other fields includes participation in a multi-national study of time diaries (cf. Szalai, A., et al (eds.) *The Use of Time*, Mouton, 1972) and the analysis of social coordination processes. In psychology, his work includes research on induction processes, on psychophysiological responses, and on human memory. He has been a

Fellow at the Center for Advanced Study in the Behavioral Sciences and a guest professor at the University of Cologne.

David Wellman is Associate Professor of Sociology at the University of Oregon and Associate Research Sociologist at the Institute for the Study of Social Change, University of California, Berkeley. He is author of *Portraits of White Racism*, Cambridge University Press.

D. Lawrence Wieder is Associate Professor of Sociology and Adjunct Professor of Philosophy at the University of Oklahoma. His recent research on reminiscing in nursing homes and gossiping in prisons extend and elaborate theoretical themes he developed in his *Language and Social Reality*, 1974 and his article with D. H. Zimmerman, "Reglen im Erklarungspruzess," 1976. Through the Center for the Study of Phenomenology at the University of Oklahoma, he is working on the clarification and further development of the foundations of the social sciences, in this connection he is currently doing research on the problems of intersubjectivity and the problem of animal awareness.

Don H. Zimmerman is Professor and Chair of the Department of Sociology, University of California, Santa Barbara. His recent research, with Candace West, deals with the influence of gender on patterns of conversational interaction. He is also exploring the problem of topic introduction in conversations between strangers in collaboration with Douglas Maynard.

Problems

Fieldwork Ethics

1. Read the special issue of *Social Problems* (Vol. 24, No. 3, February 1980) devoted to clarifying ethical problems of fieldwork. In this book read Peter Manning's discussion of ethics in his Introduction, Blauner and Wellman's "The Researcher and the Researched," and Somers', *et al.*, "Structured Interviews: Technical and Ethical Problems." On the basis of these readings and your own sensitivities, formulate a set of ethical guidelines for fieldworkers. These guidelines should cover participant observation, undisclosed observation, interviewing, the care of data, confidentiality, and reporting of results. Compare your guidelines with the requirements of the Federal government for research that it sponsors. (See Department of Health and Human Services, Final Regulations Amending Basic HHS Policy for the Protection of Human Research Subjects. *Federal Register*/Vol. 46., No. 16/Monday, January 26, 1981: 8366–8392.). Are your guidelines more strict or more lenient?

Exploration: Perspective and Method

2. Compare and contrast Paul Rock's exposition of symbolic interaction with that of Herbert Blumer. (See his *Symbolic Interactionism: Perspective and Method*. Englewood Cliffs, N.J.: Prentice-Hall, 1969). Are these expositions similar or different?

3. After reading Peter Manning's Introduction, David Arnold's "Field Methods," and Nanette Davis' "Researching an Abortion Market" choose a setting and observe the participants, using whatever mode of observation that is methodologically and ethically appropriate. Study the field notes appended to Arnold's chapter. Develop your own style of taking field notes. Write a brief report of your findings.

Interviewing

4. The chapters on interviewing introduce three different types: (1) unstructured, (2) focused, and (3) structured. Choose a topic to focus your inquiry, and after reading each chapter conduct some interviews of each type. Move from unstructured to structured, with the latter building upon the former. First, tape record some unstructured interviews and transcribe them. On the basis of these transcriptions and prior theoretical considerations abstract a set of themes that will provide a focus for your focused interviews. Conduct these focused interviews, taking copious notes or tape

recording the conversations. From these qualitative data formulate a list of topics (an accounting scheme) and formulate a structured questionnaire or interview guide for a survey. Pretest this instrument on several respondents and revise it. Then pretest it again and revise it. When it seems satisfactory, administer it to a small sample of respondents. Be sure to follow the ethical guidelines that Somers, *et al.*, suggest.

5. Television researchers often try to assess viewer ratings of the television programs they watch by asking a sample of viewers to keep diaries. Many people asked to be diarists do not agree to do this, and those that do agree may record their viewing patterns not at the time of viewing, but instead later reconstruct these patterns when they mail back their diary. What are called *telephone coincidentals* (interviews) collect data soon after the time of viewing. These interviews are more accurate than diaries, but cost more and the phone calls late at night may disturb the interviewee. A third approach is the *telephone diary* system. The diary-keepers are called at an agreed-upon time of the day and are asked to read back the information they recorded the previous day.

Read Don Zimmerman and Lawrence Wieder's "Diaries and Diary-Interviews," and Somers, et al., "Structured Interviews." Then design a procedure to produce high response rates and accurate results.

6. How did Somers *et al.* earn the cooperation of their respondents? How did they protect the confidentiality of the information on sensitive topics that they obtained? Were their precautions necessary? Were they adequate?

Documents

7. Read *Marienthal* (Chicago: Aldine, 1971) by Marie Jahoda, Paul F. Lazarsfeld, and Hans Zeisel. Focus on how the authors used documentary evidence, and how these data were combined with first-hand observations. Analyze how the authors utilized qualitative and quantitative data, and how measures were improvised to gauge concepts.

8. What do Reitzel and Lindemann mean by internal and external context of an historical study? Are these terms similar to internal and external validity. Did Jahoda, Lazarsfeld and Zeisel establish an internal and an external context for their study? How?

9. Scientific reports are regarded as having a high degree of credibility. What is there about the nature of scientific work and about the organizational structure of science that produces a high degree of credibility. Comparing historians' interpretations to more scientific reports, under what conditions should historians' analyses have high credibility and under what conditions low?

10. On the basis of Danzger's writings, for what types of events are newspapers likely to be most trustworthy, and for what types of events least trustworthy. Compare for example a description of a ball game, a demonstration and a riot. Why the differences? Look at these examples in terms of the clarity of the event itself, the observers, and news policy.

11. Examine the files of any newspaper and compare it with a newspaper on the next broader level of circulation (That is, compare a school newspaper with a small town newspaper, or a small town paper with a regional paper, etc.) Determine which stories published in the lower level media are also published in the broader level. Develop criteria for the kinds of stories that are likely to be published on a given level.

12. Interview public relations officers in colleges, businesses or elsewhere. Try to determine what they attempt to publicize, how they reach the mass media (who are their contacts and what are their techniques, what they attempt to hide, and how successful are they in publicizing or in hiding stories.

13. How might computer-aided content analysis be used to develop social indicators? What types of data might be processed? How could the resulting trends be validated?

Inspection and Patterning

14. Read Barney G. Glaser and Anselm Strauss' *Discovery of Grounded Theory* (Chicago: Aldine, 1967) and compare their strategy for qualitative research with that of Odis Bigus, Stuart Hadden and Barney G. Glaser in their "Basic Social Processes." How are these studies similar and how are they different?

15. Read William N. McPhee's "Introduction" to his *Formal Theories of Mass Behavior* (New York: Free Press, 1963). How does his conception of standard processes compare to Bigus, Hadden and Glaser's idea of basic social processes? Are these ideas similar or different? How do McPhee's simulation modules differ from basic social processes?

16. Compare and contrast Manning's exposition of analytic induction with Paul Lazarsfeld's exposition of reason analysis. For the latter see Paul F. Lazarsfeld and Morris Rosenberg (New York: Free Press, 1955; Section Five: 385–491).

17. Read Robert B. Smith's "A Process Model of Residential Resettlement" (Quality and Quantity, 15, 1981: 31-34). Is this computer simulation model consistent with the basic social process perspective? How does this process model exemplify the process of cumulative social science? How did Smith describe the social processes? How did he combine qualitative and quantitative data? Restate the process description in terms of an analytic

induction statement that accounts for residential mobility in every case. What evidence is there that these processes hold for blacks as well as for whites? How can this model be further used, elaborated and tested?

18. Carefully read Smith's discussion of typologies in his "Enumerative Induction." Also read Allen H. Barton, "The Concept of Property Space in Social Research," pages 40–53, in the Lazarsfeld and Rosenberg reader cited above. Then substruct a property space for a typology in the literature. You might do this for David Riesman, et al., *The Lonely Crowd*, or Michael Macoby's, *The Gamesman* (New York, Bantam: 1978).

19. Read *Lives in Stress: Women and Depression* edited by Deborah Belle (Beverly Hills: Sage, 1982). How does this study compare with *Marienthal* in terms of subject matter, findings and methodology? Analyze how these researchers combined qualitative and quantitative observations.

20. In Smith's concluding chapter study how he quantified the typology of Vietnam dissent as in Table 1. Do you think a student's draft status affected his or her attitude about the Vietnam war? How could you assess the effects of draft status using qualitative methods? How could you assess this using quantitative methods? Design an analysis plan for this proposed research.

21. Now that you have mastered this material, choose a problem and a setting and conduct a field study using the techniques of data gathering and analysis presented in this book. Try to use both qualitative and quantitative data, first hand observations and interviews, documents and records, etc. Write up the results of your inquiry in a readibly study. Summarize your findings in causal diagrams, using appropriate concepts. Think about how you might corroborate and extend your analysis using quantitative methods. Formulate a plan for subsequent studies.

Index

Abortion, 79, 283-284, 292; network, 79; stigma of, 94

Analysis, causal, 282, 328; in history, 176; of qualitative data 67, of quantitative data, 316

Abuses of the sponsor, 22-23

Accessory to a crime, 24

Action by respondents against the researcher, 24

Action by the state to secure research information, 23

Active social science, 21

Adequacy of theory to data versus theoretical relevance, 303-305

Affinity between observation and qualitative methods, 54

Alcoholic beverages, xvii

Analytic induction, 7, 100, 134, 247, 273, 277, 280; advantages of, 290; disadvantages of, 287

Analytic magnification, low level of, 8, 38

Antagonizing prospective participants, 22

Anti-informant position, 23

Anti-police stance, 24

Applied research, 21, 23

Approximation of meaning in content analysis, 232

Arrests, 16

Attitudes, 274, 278

Autobiographies, 279

Basic or discipline research, 21; examples of, 307-317

Basic social processes, 247, 251-252, 267

Biases, 11, 203; in qualitative research, 16

Biographies, 35

Black opinion, 109

Blumer-Lazarsfeld debate, v, 303

Brokers (abortion), 89, 93

Categorizing new information, 70, 87, 109, 306-307

Chicago and Iowa schools of symbolic interaction, 308

Coding, 70, 87, 109, 154

Collective life, fundamental features of, 35

Common-sense knowledge, 3, 40, 258

Community conflict, 197

Completion rates, 146

Complexity and openness of social performances, 36

Computer simulation, 307, 311-312, 327

Concepts as constraints, 130

Conception of the subject as diarist, 123

Conditions that constrain organizations, 82

Confessionals, 29

Conflict model of society, 13, 43, 209

Constructing a pattern, 94

Consumers, 22

Content analysis, 219-220, 243; definition of, 221

Contexts, 39; historical, 185

Continuous redefining of research, 79

Cooperation, 146

Corrective processes, 204

Corroboration of conjectures, xiv, 304

Counter-culture, 134

Creating new evidence, 173

Critical approach, 79

Culture, 132

Cumulative social science, xiv, 79; examples of, 307-317

Data collection, 106

Day dreaming, 59

Decolonization of research, 99, 100-103

Deductive reasoning, 275, 294-295

Defining the situation, 278, 307-309

Democracy, 186-187

Demographic method, 178-179

Description, 130

Deviant behavior, 259-260, 293

Deviant career, 45

Dialectic, the 37

Diary-diary interview method, 115-116; analytic process in, 133; working criteria in, 129

Diary format, 124; dimensions of, 126

Diary interview, 127; effectiveness of, 127; expansion in, 129

Dictionaries, 225, 228, 236

Differences between casual reading and formal content analysis, 220

Disambiguating the meanings, 235-236

Discrete laws of development, 43

Disguised role in field work, xix, 61, 120, 308, 325

Diversity within roles, 117

Division of labour and structural separation of research, 21

Documents, xvii, 115-116, 172-173, 181, 278-279, 290

"Dove" and "Hawk" attitudes, 316

Drug using behavior, 262

WITHDRAWN
UNIV OF MOUNT UNION LIBRARY